GCSE

Business Studies
second edition

ALAIN ANDERTON

Causeway Press

Cover design by Caroline Waring-Collins
Cover illustrations provided by Tony Stone Images
Graphics by Caroline Waring-Collins, Elaine Sumner and Alan Fraser
Cartoons by Alan Fraser
Photography by Andrew Allen, Ian McAnulty and Ian Sager
Page design by Caroline Waring-Collins; Andrew Allen
Edited by Dave Gray

Every effort has been made to locate the copyright owners of material
used in this book.
Any errors and omissions brought to the notice of the
publisher are regretted and will be credited in subsequent printings.

British Library Cataloguing in Publication Data
A catalogue record for this book is available from the British Library.

ISBN 1-873929-84-6

Causeway Press Limited
PO Box 13, Ormskirk, Lancs, L39 5HP
© Alain Anderton
First edition 1995 (reprinted 3 times)
Second edition 1998

Design, page origination and production by Caroline Waring-Collins
and Elaine Sumner (Waring-Collins Partnership)
Printed and bound by Cambus Litho Ltd, East Kilbride.

Acknowledgements
The publishers and the author would like to thank the
following for their help in the production of this book.

ABB; Allied Carpets; Beauford PLC; Belgrade Insulations Limited;
British Airways; British Telecom; Business Link; Cadbury Schweppes;
Capital Radio; Charles Barker plc; Chris Sawyer; Chris Dee; Chloride
Group; Co-operative Union Limited; Coats Viyella; Commercial Union;
Courtaulds; Danka Business Systems plc; De La Rue; DfEE; DJ Quine;
DTI; Emap; Equal Opportunities Commission; Etam; *Express and Star*;
Expro International Group; Fatty Arbuckles; Fiat; *Financial Times*; Ford;
Galliford; Games Workshop; George Wimpey PLC; GKN; Global Group;
Greenalls PLC; Hamley's; Hardy Spicer; HSE; Ian McAnulty; Inchape;
Intelek plc; IPT Group; Isle of Wight Studio Glass; Jacques Vert; Jim
McCall, Cambus Litho Ltd; Jim Russell, Powell & Heilbron; Kate
Haralambos; Kiren Darashah, Ben-Go-Tig; Lancaster City Council;
Ladbroke Group; Lawtec; Lever Brothers; Leyland Trucks; Magnet;
Man Made Sole; Marks & Spencer; Merlin; MGA Developments; Mike
Dixon; Mike Forshaw; Mitsubishi; National Westminster Bank; Nestlé;
Northern Foods; Orange; P&O; Paramount 21 Ltd; Paul Quirk, Quirk's
Records; Peter Downes & Peter Howcroft, Bender Forrest Ltd; Pittards;
Portmerrion Potteries; Prince's Youth Business Trust; Prontaprint; Rank;
Reckitt & Colman; Regalian Properties; Richer Sounds; Rover Group;
Sainsbury's; Scott Ltd; Sea Containers Ltd; Shell LiveWire; Shell; Sky
Television; Snakeboard International; Spirax-Sarco; St.Ivel Ltd; Stannah;
Streamline Holdings; Street Crane; Tesco; Thames Water; The
Advertising Standards Authority Limited; The BOC Group; The Body
Shop; The Boots Company; The Car Group; The Communication
Workers Union; The Guiness Group; The LEGO Group The Original
Propshop; Tomkins PLC; Toyota UK; Unigate; Unilever; United Norwest
Co-operatives Limited; United Utilities; Virgin; Vitec Group;
Volkswagen; Wagon Industrial Holdings; Walker Greenbank; Waterford
Wedgewood; Wood 'u' Learn;

Photographs provided by:
Corel pp 36, 80, 86, 100, 125, 156, 186, 206, 213, 224; **Digital Stock
Corporation** pp 13, 15, 55, 88, 91, 100, 106, 108,114,156, 163, 173,
178,183,192, 196, 200, 216, 217, 218, 219,222, 223, 234; **Huw Evans
Picture Agency** p 186; **Image Bank** p 183; **Northern Picture Library**
p 231; **Rex Features Ltd** pp 9, 13, 14, 23, 63, 87, 95, 140 (twice),
165; **Photodisc Inc. © 1995** pp 5, 38, 101, 139, 145, 197, 208; **Sally
& Richard Greenhill** p 116; **Telegraph Colour Library** pp 97,189;
Topham Picture Point pp 8, 14, 16, 36, 149; **Tony Stone
Images/Hulton Getty** pp 34, 222.

A source is given at the end of each unit. This shows the source of the
information on which the unit is based **or** that a business has approved
the material in the unit relating to its activities. Units that do not contain
a source have been based on real business operations.

PREFACE

GCSE Business Studies (second eddition) has
been designed to be used as the core textbook for
GCSE courses in Business Studies and will also be
useful for candidates being prepared for standard
and higher grade examinations and Intermediate
GNVQ in Business. It has been designed in colour to
give candidates a distinctive and unique resource for
use in the classroom.

The book has a number of key features.

Comprehensive The book covers the content of full
course and half course GCSE Business Studies. It
has also been designed to be used by those taking
optional units in Accounts, Enterprise, Commerce,
Business and Change, Technology and Change or
Information Technology. The IT suggestions give
pupils opportunities to display IT skills. They do not
attempt to cover the IT required for a Business and
Information Systems course.

Unit structure The material has been organised
into two or four page units. Each unit contains text, a
section which outlines some of the key decisions
which businesses have to make, data questions and
case studies, research exercises, short answer
questions and definitions of key terms.

Case study based Each unit uses a business or an
industry to illustrate the text. This case study
approach is followed through with a large number of
other case studies in the unit with questions attached.

I would like thank Dave Gray, who as usual has done
a superb job editing the book. Peter Chapman and
Diane Wallace gave invaluable feedback on the
manuscript. Mike Kidson proof read the work with
great skill. The page origination of the book was
sensitively accomplished by Caroline Waring-Collins
and Elaine Sumner. Not least I would like to thank my
wife for all her help with the project.

The author and Causeway Press would welcome any
comments you have to make about the book, whether
critical or otherwise. We hope it will greatly help you
in your teaching or learning of Business Studies.

CONTENTS

Making decisions

People in business constantly have to make decisions. Businesses produce goods and services to satisfy the needs and wants of consumers. They have to decide:
- what goods and services will be produced;
- what resources, like raw materials and workers, are needed for production.

Do you drink milk delivered by a Unigate milkman? Do you buy Unigate milk from a supermarket? Have you eaten a St.Ivel Shape yogurt? Do you drink St.Ivel Florida squeezed orange juice? Do you spread Country Life English butter or St.Ivel Utterly Butterly on your bread? All these products and more are made by a business called Unigate PLC. So what makes a business?

What is a business?

A BUSINESS is an organisation which produces GOODS or SERVICES. Unigate makes all the PRODUCTS mentioned above. Other businesses make products too. For instance, Coca Cola makes drinks. British Telecom provides telephone services. McDonald's produces fast food. Barnados provides child care services.

Some businesses like Unigate are large. Unigate, although UK based, owns companies in France. It sells its products in other European countries too. Its sales are worth over £2 billion a year. It employs 27 000 workers. Most businesses, however, are small, like the local butcher or hairdresser. Their sales might be measured in thousands of pounds rather than billions. They might employ just a few workers, or the owner of the business might be its only worker.

Unigate is a **private sector** (☞ unit 3) business. This means that it is not owned by government. Charities like Barnados are private sector businesses too. The business organisations owned and run by government, like the National Health Service or the Royal Navy, are in the **public sector** of the economy.

Most private sector businesses, like Unigate, aim to make a **profit** (☞ unit 33). Other businesses, like Barnados or the National Health Service, have other **objectives** (☞ unit 17) as well, such as providing high quality care for people.

Production

To produce anything a business has to use resources. St.Ivel, part of Unigate, makes Shape yogurt from milk and strawberries, which are RAW MATERIALS. St.Ivel buys the packaging for the yogurt from other businesses. Products made by one business and sold to another are called PRODUCER GOODS.

1 What goods and services do each of the businesses shown here produce? Write down as many as you can.

Workers
(LABOUR)

A factory (CAPITAL)

Machinery (CAPITAL)

Raw materials (LAND)

St Ivel

Figure 1.1 *Factors of production used by St.Ivel Limited to make yogurt.*

Services are non-physical products like hairdressing.

Goods are physical products like Country Life butter made by Unigate.

St.Ivel employees (or LABOUR) then produce yogurts in a factory. The factory and the machines (called CAPITAL or CAPITAL GOODS) used are also essential to the production process. Sometimes, these resources are called the FACTORS OF PRODUCTION - raw materials (or LAND), labour and capital.

Selling the product

Simply making Shape yogurt or Country Life butter isn't enough for Unigate. It will only survive as a business if it can find CUSTOMERS for its products. Its customers are other businesses like Sainsbury's or Tesco. They buy yogurt in large quantities and then sell it in small amounts to their own customers, people like you. When you eat yogurt, you are the CONSUMER of the product. CONSUMER GOODS are the products which ultimately get used (or consumed) by people.

Why consume?

Why do people buy yogurt or any of the other products that Unigate makes? Consumers have NEEDS. These are the things people must consume to survive. People need food, drink, shelter, warmth and clothes. Eating a Shape yogurt, drinking Unigate milk or eating Utterly Butterly on a piece of bread could satisfy people's need for food.

Needs are part of people's broader WANTS. Wants are people's desires to consume all goods and services, not just those products needed for basic survival. There seem to be no limits to how much people want to consume. In the rich countries of the world, such as the UK, people are not just buying more but also increasing the quality of what they are buying. Unigate has to cope with this changing demand. For instance, people in Britain are drinking less milk than before but eating more yogurt.

The business environment

Businesses have to operate in a harsh environment. If their products

The snakeboard

Not all skateboards are the same. A Snakeboard is an advanced form of skateboard. The board has rotating footplates which are connected by a moulded bar. The design allows for much greater flexibility of movement than a traditional one piece skateboard.

The product is aimed to appeal to young people aged 12-20 who enjoy 'X-Treme sports' - rollerblading, snowboarding, mountain biking, surfing, rock climbing and, of course, skateboarding. Snakeboard International plc holds the design patents on Snakeboards. It wants Snakeboarding to become as well known as rollerblading or surfing. This would mean that Snakeboarding wouldn't just occur on the streets. There would be televised national and international Snakeboarding competitions just as with surfing or rock climbing. It could then sell its range of Snakeboard clothing and shoes not just to Snakeboarders, but also to those who want to be seen to be associated with the sport.

Source: adapted from the placing of Snakeboard International plc.

1 Who are the likely customers of Snakeboard International?

2 Consumers buy products to satisfy their 'wants'. What 'wants' do you think buying a Snakeboard will satisfy?

3 Snakeboarding is a new sport. Suggest FOUR ways in which Snakeboard International could help the sport grow in popularity.

don't sell, they are likely to go out of business. Even if they have successful products at the moment, their competitors might launch better products onto the market in future. The government might affect businesses too by passing laws which restrict what they can do. For instance, there might be restrictions on the ingredients a food business like Unigate uses in its products.

Successful long term businesses, like Unigate, are businesses which find solutions to these problems. Over a period of time they continue to provide products which appeal to their customers. They adapt how they operate to conform to government regulations and laws. They motivate their workers to produce as high quality goods as possible within cost budgets.

Source: adapted in part from Unigate plc, *Annual Report and Accounts* and information provided by St.Ivel Limited.

You have organised yourself into a mini-company. EITHER answer the following questions for the business idea which you have chosen OR assume you have decided to make washing cars your business activity.

1 Make a list of all the resources your business will have to use to provide this service.

2 Find out how: (a) a local garage; and (b) a local valeting service cleans cars. How do they differ from you in the resources they use?

3 How would you decide whether your business has been a success?

Assume that each member of your class or teaching group could spend up to £20 on one item. It could be a CD, a trip to the bowling alley, or a new pair of jeans, for instance.

1 Survey ten or more people in your class and find out what they would spend the money on.

Database

2 Produce a database from your findings. The diagram will help you. The database should include:
   (a) the name of the product bought;
   (b) the name of the business which produced the product;
   (c) whether it was a good or a service;
   (d) the want which you think the product satisfies (e.g. food, transport, entertainment);
   (e) a business where the product might be bought (e.g. a CD produced by Sony might be bought at Our Price Records. In the case of a service, like a trip to a bowling alley, the business both produces the service and sells it.)

3 Describe your findings, using graphs where appropriate. For instance, were people buying very similar products or were they very different? Were they buying similar products but from different businesses?

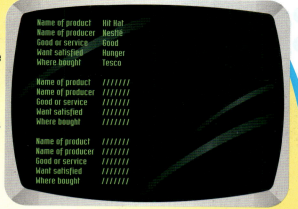

```
Name of product    Hit Hat
Name of producer   Nestlé
Good or service    Good
Want satisfied     Hunger
Where bought       Tesco

Name of product    ////////
Name of producer   ////////
Good or service    ////////
Want satisfied     ////////
Where bought       ////////

Name of product    ////////
Name of producer   ////////
Good or service    ////////
Want satisfied     ////////
Where bought       ////////
```

Figure 1.2

Key terms

Business - an organisation which produces goods and services.

Capital goods - physical goods used to produce other producer and consumer goods and services.

Consumer - the person who ultimately uses (or consumes) a product.

Consumer goods - goods and services which are sold to people (consumers) rather than other businesses.

Customer - any person or organisation which buys or is supplied with a product by a business.

Factors of production - land (natural resources), labour (workers) and capital (defined above in capital goods) used in the production process.

Goods - physical products, like a car or a cabbage.

Needs - the basic products that people need in order to survive: food, drink, shelter, warmth and clothing.

Producer goods - goods which are sold by one business to another and which are then used to produce other goods and services.

Products - goods made or services provided by businesses.

Raw materials - natural resources, like copper or coffee beans, used to make products.

Services - non-physical products, like a haircut or a train journey.

Wants - the desire to consume goods and services. Wants are unlimited because there is no limit to the amount of goods and services people would like to consume.

SEA CONTAINERS LTD

Sea Containers is an international company based in Bermuda. It has a number of different activities, one of which is shown in the photographs.

1 What business activity operated by Sea Containers is shown in the photographs?

2 Who are the customers of this business?

3 What resources are used in the business?

4 Suggest THREE ways in which Sea Containers could make this business more successful.

Checklist ✓

1 What is a business?

2 'British Gas is a private sector business.' What does this mean?

3 What resources do you think are needed to make a McDonald's hamburger?

4 What are the THREE factors of production?

5 What is the difference between a customer and a consumer?

6 Here is a list of products: a tin of baked beans, a shop counter, a washing machine, a pair of jeans, a factory, an industrial sewing machine, a cup and saucer, a fork lift truck. Explain which of these are: (a) consumer goods; and (b) producer goods.

7 What are a person's basic needs?

8 What is the difference between a need and a want?

unit 2

Making decisions

Businesses operate in markets. They have to decide what they are going to sell to their customers and how they are going to organise production. The market then gives its verdict. If the business is providing a product that customers want, it may make sales and, more importantly, make a profit if the price is right. If customers don't buy enough or pay enough, the business will make a loss. Profits and losses are the sign for businesses to expand or cut back production. Businesses which fail to respond to the market and don't provide what their customers want in the long term are likely to go out of business. Businesses have to respond to the market if they are to survive.

The Rank Group Plc is one of the leading leisure and entertainment companies in the world. It is split up into four operating divisions. Film and entertainment services include the Pinewood film studios in the UK and Rank Film Distributors. Hard Rock owns or franchises Hard Rock Cafes around the world. Its holiday division includes Haven and Butlin's. The leisure division includes Mecca and Top Rank Bingo, Odeon Cinemas and Tom Cobleigh pub-restaurants.

Markets

Rank has to operate in the **market place**. When the word MARKET is used, most people think of a street market where there are numerous stalls with traders selling everything from food to clothes to furniture. Consumers wander round the market buying the products. In business studies, the word 'market' is used more widely. It exists in any situation where buyers and sellers exchange goods and services.

1 What is being bought and sold in each of the markets shown in the photographs?
2 Who are the likely buyers and who are the likely sellers in each market?
3 Is the market shown in each photograph a local market, a national market or an international market?

DTP

4 With a small group of friends, you decide to set up a business.
(a) What market could you realistically enter? (e.g. you could sell stationery to other people in your school or college but you couldn't set up as an international car manufacturer).
(b) Design an advertising poster about your business, showing the product that you are selling and who are the potential customers for your product. You could use a desktop publishing package to do this.

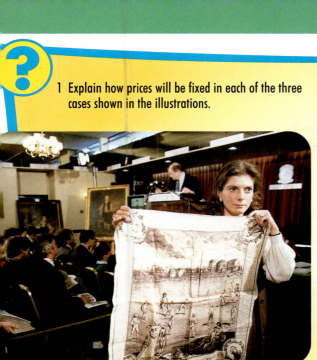

?

1 Explain how prices will be fixed in each of the three cases shown in the illustrations.

MUSIC DIRECT

300 albums to choose from

5 CDs from 99p each + P&P
or 5 cassettes from 49p each

Hobbies

TYPEWRITER Portable manual type, Underwood 315, £25.
MODEL train power controller, Hammond and Morgan Duelle model controls 2 separate trains, as new, top quality, £20.
RUCKSACK 40 litre size, outbounds make, latest design, fully padded, red and black waterproof material, very comfortable, unused, cost £40, bargain £20.
JAPANESE Tin Plate Car, no markings, boxed, mint, £25.
TIN Plate Toys, crawling baby, clockwork, boxed, £10.
PAYA Saloon Car tin plate toy, 1982, mint condition, boxed, very rare piece, £80 ono.
CLOCKWORK tin plate toy, Clown on scooter, 1960s, £15 ono.
TRAIN set, 6 x 4, 3 tracks, part landscaped with new batchments, class 158, regional rail livery 2 car set, £125 ono.
CRAWLING baby tin plate toy, with plastic body, clockwork, boxed, £10 ono.
LETHAMANN Rigger 900 Cable Car, mint condition, boxed with full instructions and cardboard people, £35 ono.

Different types of market

There is a wide variety of markets. The local street market is one. Another is the local market for entertainment, where businesses compete with each other to provide entertainment services. For instance, Rank offers customers a night out at the cinema through its chain of Odeon Cinemas; or a night out playing bingo at its Mecca and Top Rank Bingo clubs; or a meal at a Tom Cobleigh pub-restaurant. There is a national market for holidays where companies, like Butlin's owned by Rank, compete for customers throughout the UK. There are also international markets. The film industry, for instance, is a global industry. Rank competes with businesses across the world to supply video duplication and film processing services.

In some markets, buyers and sellers meet face to face. At a Hard Rock Cafe, for instance, the person buying the meal has to meet the Rank employees selling the meal. But in many markets, buying and selling is done by letter, over the telephone or by fax. A deal to use facilities at Pinewood Studios, owned by Rank, might be negotiated over the phone and confirmed by letter.

Fixing the price

In some markets, buyers and sellers haggle over or negotiate a price. A film company wanting to produce a whole film at Pinewood would negotiate a price with Rank. The eventual price agreed is usually somewhere between the seller's original price and what the buyer first offered.

In other markets, the seller fixes the price. For instance, the price of a game of bingo is fixed at a Mecca Bingo club. The player either accepts the price and buys a card or doesn't play.

In an auction, buyers compete amongst themselves, bidding up the price until one buyer is left. However, the seller is not legally bound to accept the bid if it is less than the reserve price - a minimum price that the seller has decided upon before the auction starts. If the bid price doesn't reach the reserve price, the sale does not go through.

Opportunity cost

Prices provide an easy way for a business like Rank to calculate OPPORTUNITY COST. This is the benefit lost when making a decision about how best to allocate resources. For instance, Rank might decide to build and open a new Odeon cinema in London. The opportunity cost might then be the benefit lost from not being able to open a similarly priced cinema in Manchester.

Businesses are constantly having to make opportunity cost decisions. They have to decide how to allocate their scarce resources between different uses. For the same price, what would have to be given up if a computer was bought, or certain offices were rented, or a particular worker was employed?

Market forces

The market is very powerful. This is because it allocates so many resources in the world today. The market is like a vast voting machine with buyers and sellers being the MARKET FORCES which determine what is bought and what is produced.

Buyers Buyers have money to spend. They choose which products they want to buy from the millions on offer from sellers. For instance, an ordinary family will perhaps buy 500 different items

Rank provides services in local markets (Odeon cinemas), national markets (Butlin's) and international markets (video duplication).

per week. Each time the family buys one of these products, it is casting a spending vote. Each week, the number of spending votes cast by buyers in the UK runs into billions.

Sellers Producers need those votes in order to survive. Rank would go out of business if nobody wanted to go to the cinema, go on holiday or eat out. On the other hand, if cinema admissions at Odeon cinemas went up by 50 per cent, then it would probably get a large reward - a big increase in profits.

Profit is essential to the working of the market system. A business will tend to stop making a product if it can't make a profit. Big profits will encourage more production. Profit is what decides Rank whether or not to close a bingo hall or open another Hard Rock Cafe.

The markets in which Rank competes are **competitive markets**. This is where there is a number of businesses competing for supplies or customers. In the holiday market, for

instance, Rank, through its Haven and Butlin's holiday businesses, competes with thousands of other businesses to attract customers.

Many markets are not so competitive. At the other extreme, some businesses are **monopolists**, the only sellers of a product to a group of customers. In the UK, for instance, households have no choice about where to buy their water. The local water

company, like Thames or Severn Trent, is a monopoly seller. The more a business can control a market, the less power its customers will have. This gives the business more of an opportunity to make profits.

Source: adapted from information provided by Rank and Rank *Review and Final Summary*.

Dodge F1 boots

Paul Dooner was a man with ideas. He was watching a grand prix race in 1994 when he remembered something he had seen when he was in Germany - roofers with boots resoled with old tyres. He thought that grand prix enthusiasts would pay a lot of money to have shoes soled with the tyres used in races by the top Formula 1 drivers.

He produced some samples, got a shoe factory to produce a batch and in 1995 the first shoes went on sale at Harvey Nichols and Selfridges in London as well as Kendals in Edinburgh. They sold well, but the soles had a tendency to come unstuck. The shoes also didn't carry the logos on the product which would have immediately shown that they were racing shoes.

So he went back to the drawing board. He knew that the shoes needed redesigning and then marketing. He contacted a number of large shoe companies many of whom were very interested in the idea. But they wanted to own and control most of the new business that would be created. Luckily, though, he was contacted by a private investor. He was prepared to put £250 000 into the business and leave Paul in control.

The shoes went on sale at £100 a pair. They were high quality and carried logos associated with Formula 1 racing. At the Monza Grand prix in 1996, they were voted the most innovative and original new product in Formula 1. Paul began to prepare the launch of a further range of boots.

Source: adapted from *The Times*, 5 November 1996.

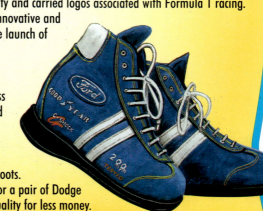

1 'The opportunity cost for Paul Dooner of going into business selling shoes was the wages he could have earned if he had had a full time job.' Explain what this means.
2 Suggest what might have been the opportunity cost :
   (a) to the investor of putting £250 000 into the business;
   (b) to a customer of paying £100 for a pair of Dodge F1 boots.
3 Suggest why some customers were prepared to pay £100 for a pair of Dodge F1 boots when they could buy a similar boot in terms of quality for less money.

Restoring Land Rovers

Peter Hobson runs a business supplying spare parts for Land Rovers. The parts are reconditioned. They are taken from old Land Rovers or stocks of new parts which are being sold off as scrap. These might be from overseas or he might buy ex-Ministry of Defence vehicles and parts. His business then works on the parts and restores them to at least 80 per cent effectiveness. The parts are sold at a fraction of the price of expensive new genuine Land Rover parts. They are also of far higher quality than cheap new parts made by other companies than Land Rover.

The business was set up in 1986 and grew rapidly. By 1993, he employed 21 people. But the business was too successful for many UK Land Rovers dealers selling new parts. They complained that he was taking away their customers. So he did a deal with Land Rover. He agreed not to sell to UK customers. But he could sell anywhere else in the world. The loss of UK customers was quickly filled by expanding existing overseas sales. By 1996, the business employed 32 people and was selling over £1 million worth of parts each year, one third more than in 1993.

Source: adapted from the *Financial Times*, 20 January 1996.

1 (a) Who were Peter Hobson's customers in 1992?
   (b) How had this changed by 1996?
2 Why did UK Land Rover garage dealers object to Peter Hobson's business in 1993?
3 Who does Peter Hobson buy from?
4 Who are Peter Hobson's competitors in the market for Land Rover parts?

Key terms

Market - where buyers and sellers meet to exchange goods and services.
Market forces - the forces of buying (or demand) and selling (or supply) which determine price and quantity bought and sold in a market.
Opportunity cost - the benefit lost from the next best alternative when making a choice.

SUMMARY CASE STUDY

S&A FOODS

Perween Warsi started her business in 1986. She couldn't find any samosas or tandoori chickens worth eating in her local supermarket. She started off cooking in her own kitchen and selling to a local Greek take-away. Then she found a distributor who supplied local pubs and restaurants. In 1987, she approached Asda, the supermarket chain, who agreed to stock her chilled products. Within ten years, the business was selling £20 million worth of food a year both in the UK and in Europe.

Competition in the market is fierce. Supermarket chains can drop suppliers whose products don't sell, perhaps because the price is too expensive or the quality is not right. So Perween is constantly monitoring food production. For instance, she tastes all batches of food made. If the flavour is not quite right, the batch will be destroyed, costing between £200 and £1000 depending upon the ingredients. She or her husband also blend all the spices themselves, to ensure quality and to keep the formulae for each dish secret.

When she is not in the factory overseeing the day to day running of the business, she is out meeting new and existing customers and suppliers, keeping the business growing.

Source: adapted from the *Financial Times*, 27 January 1996.

1 'Perween Warsi started selling in a local market, and now sells in national and international markets.' Explain what this means.
2 What might be the opportunity cost for Perween of spending time blending all the spices used in the preparation of food?
3 Explain whether or not you think S&A Food operates in a competitive market.
4 A large food company has offered to buy S&A Foods but, if Perween sold, she would leave the business. Discuss whether the business would be as successful if Perween left.

Checklist ✓

1 In any market there are two groups. (a) Who are they and (b) what do they do in the market place?
2 The oil market is a market. Give FIVE other examples of markets.
3 Give an example of a business which operates: (a) in your local market selling bread; (b) in the national market selling cars; (c) in the international market buying coffee beans.
4 Who decides what price is fixed: (a) in a supermarket; (b) when a house is bought; (c) at a cattle auction; (d) when a car is serviced; (e) when a car is bought second hand?
5 A business spends £10 000 on Xerox photocopiers. What might be the opportunity cost of this decision for the business? In your answer, give THREE possible examples.
6 How are producers rewarded in a market system when they sell products which consumers want to buy?
7 Explain what happens to businesses which fail to supply goods that consumers want to buy.

TYPES OF ECONOMY

Making decisions

Businesses operate in a particular economy and economic system. These differ from country to country. How the economy is organised will determine how a business behaves and operates. In the UK, for instance, most businesses aim to make a profit. However, businesses which are owned by the government might have different objectives and make different business decisions.

Fiat is an Italian company but it operates worldwide. In 1996, it had nearly 240 000 employees working in 60 different countries. Many of these were in its 220 manufacturing plants. Roughly half of Fiat's sales come from cars. The other half is from sales of trucks and lorries, agricultural and construction vehicles and automotive components. Fiat has a long history of working with enterprises in Eastern Europe and Russia. The Lada car was based on an old Fiat model.

Market economies

Fiat operates mainly in market economies. An **economy** is a system. This system sets the rules which influence what is produced, how it will be produced and who will receive the products. In a market economy, most production and distribution takes place through **markets** (☞ unit 2).

- Producers, like Fiat, buy **factors of production** (☞ unit 1). Fiat hires workers in countries from Italy to Brazil in labour markets. It buys raw materials and components such as steel, electricity and brakes in **product markets**. It buys machinery, factories and offices in **capital markets**.
- Producers then attempt to sell what they have made either to other businesses or to consumers. Fiat, for instance, sells most of its cars to independent car dealers. However, it also owns some

dealerships and so sells some cars direct to consumers or to businesses which buy company cars.

In a market economy, most businesses need to make a **profit** to survive. If they make large enough losses, they will go out of business. Successful businesses like Fiat are the ones which can survive the competition of other firms. This means they have to supply the goods and services that customers want to buy, at the right price.

The role of the state

Markets aren't always the best way to provide goods and services. When this happens, the state (i.e. government) usually steps in. Examples of products typically provided by governments are defence (army, navy and air force), the police, roads and schools (☞ unit 16). The state pays for these by charging taxes which people and businesses like Fiat have to pay.

Free market and mixed economies

There are two main types of market economy. The United States and Japan are examples of FREE

MARKET ECONOMIES. In these economies, up to 40 per cent of consumer goods and services are provided by the state. This is the PUBLIC SECTOR of the economy. 60 per cent or more of goods and services, though, are provided by the PRIVATE SECTOR of the economy. Businesses like Fiat are private businesses because they are not owned by the state.

Italy, France, Germany and the UK are examples of MIXED ECONOMIES. In a mixed economy, between 40 and 60 per cent of consumer goods and services are provided by the state, with the rest being provided by the private sector.

In both free market and mixed economies, businesses like Fiat have the opportunity to sell both to other private sector businesses and consumers, and to governments.

Command economies

A third type of economy is a COMMAND ECONOMY. In this type of economy, businesses are mostly owned by the state. Government planners decide what is going to be produced, how, where and when, and who will receive the products. The role of businesses is to carry out the orders of the state.

For instance, Russia was a command economy from the 1920s to the 1980s. Avtogaz was the country's second largest car business. Like other Russian businesses, it was given annual production targets by government planners. It was told how many raw materials it could use and how many workers to employ to meet its targets. The business had no real competition because there were long waiting lists for new cars.

Today, Russia, like nearly all former command economies, is being turned back to a mixed economy. This is because command economies haven't provided the benefits that mixed economies and free market economies seem to have done. Fiat is helping in this. It has set up a joint venture with Avtogaz to manufacture three models of Fiat cars for sale in Russia. Fiat is providing much of the expertise and some of the equipment. Avtogaz will provide the factory and the workers, and will buy the necessary raw materials. The joint venture will help to modernise this part of the Russian economy.

Source: adapted from information provided by Fiat.

?

1 Which of the goods or services shown here are likely to be provided: (a) through a market; or (b) by the government in the UK?

2 British Steel and British Petroleum (BP) are two large companies. What part do you think that they play in producing the goods and services shown?

SUMMARY CASE STUDY

PRIVATE PRISONS

HM Prison Parc is in Wales. It is a prison built, owned and operated by Securicor, a private sector company. The government pays Securicor a fixed amount per prisoner kept in the prison. It needs this to recoup the running costs and the £80 million it spent building the prison. The prison is very 'hi-tech', with computer systems, swipe cards and personalised voice identification equipment. The inmates are free to move around certain parts of the prison using their swipe cards to unlock doors. They can use communal leisure facilities, including a large TV. There is an 8 000 book library as well as an intensive education and training programme. The inmates earn small amounts of money by doing a variety of jobs in the prison, including low level maintenance work. By using the most up-to-date computer and surveillance equipment, Securicor has cut down the number of staff needed in the prison and has increased security, making it more difficult for prisoners to escape.

Source: adapted from the Financial Times, 27 September 1997.

1 'Most prisons are operated within the public sector.' What does this mean?

2 Securicor sells prison places to the government. The Rover Group sells Land Rovers to the army. Give THREE other examples of goods or services which the private sector sells to the government.

3 Why do you think that the government has signed contracts with Securicor for prison places rather than building and operating its own prisons?

4 Why do you think Securicor has invested money in building and operating prisons?

5 The government is thinking of selling some of its high security prisons to a private business that would then sell places in the prison back to the government. Discuss what should be the minimum standard of service that the company would have to provide.

Checklist ✓

1 What is an economy?

2 'A market economy is one where most consumer goods and services are produced by businesses and are then sold to consumers.' Explain what this means.

3 What is the difference between a free market economy and a mixed economy?

4 What types of services are often provided by government in a mixed economy?

5 What is the role of a business in a command economy?

6 Explain what has happened to the command economies of Eastern Europe in recent years.

Key terms

Command economy - economy where most consumer goods and services are produced by the public sector.
Free market economy - economy (or economic system) where over 60 per cent of consumer goods and services are produced by businesses and sold through markets.
Mixed economy - economy where over 40 per cent of consumer goods and services are produced by the state and not sold through markets.
Private sector - the rest of the economy apart from the public sector, owned and controlled by private individuals and businesses.
Public sector - part of the economy owned and controlled by the state or government.

TYPES OF PRODUCTION

Making decisions

Businesses choose to make a particular range of products. Some businesses are involved in primary production, but most businesses either make manufactured products or supply services. The changing structure of the economy provides businesses with opportunities and threats. The growth in demand for services, for instance, may allow new businesses to set up.

The Global Group is a business with a sales turnover of over £150 million per year. Most of that comes from the food side of the business. The food trading division specialises in buying products such as pork, lamb and beef from abattoirs and selling them to buyers such as supermarkets. Its food processing division manufactures food products including sausage rolls and frozen vegetables and sells mainly to the catering trade. In food retailing, it owns Express Cafes which specialises in catering for outdoor events including Formula 1 races and the Badminton Horse Trials.

A *Diamond mining*

B *Polishing diamonds*

C *Selling jewellery*

1 Describe what is being produced in each of the photographs.
2 What industry (primary, secondary or tertiary) is shown in: (a) photograph A; (b) photograph B; (c) photograph C?
3 How might the following affect businesses in the diamond industry: (a) a rise in the world price of diamonds; (b) an increase in the UK in VAT (a tax) on jewellery; (c) the discovery of large new diamond reserves; (d) an increase in the wages of diamond mining workers in South Africa?

Primary, secondary and tertiary industry

The food bought by The Global Group is first grown or reared on farms. Farming is part of PRIMARY INDUSTRY, where raw materials are extracted, grown or cut down. Fishing, mining and oil extraction are also examples of primary production.

Some of the animals reared by farmers are bought by abattoirs. The Global Group buys its meat from these abattoirs. Some of the meat is processed to make a finished product like a meat pie or a sausage roll. This is an example of production by SECONDARY or MANUFACTURING INDUSTRY. In secondary industry raw materials are turned into manufactured goods.

The Global Group is also part of TERTIARY or SERVICE INDUSTRY. This is where services are provided. It includes retailing (mainly shops), hairdressing, education, health, financial services and hotel accommodation. The Global Group provides services in two ways.

● It trades in food products like

Ingredients **Production of savoury pastries** **Sales to consumers**

Figure 4.1 *A chain of production for a pastry product made by The Global Group.*

meat, acting as an intermediary between abattoirs in secondary industry and retailers like the big supermarkets in tertiary industry.

- Express Cafes provides a service to those attending large outdoor events.

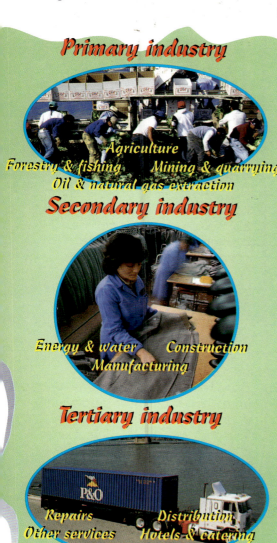

Primary industry
Agriculture
Forestry & fishing *Mining & quarrying*
Oil & natural gas extraction

Secondary industry

Energy & water *Construction*
Manufacturing

Tertiary industry

Repairs *Distribution*
Other services *Hotels & catering*
Transport & communication

Figure 4.2 *Types of production.*

The chain of production

Primary, secondary and tertiary industries are linked together in a CHAIN OF PRODUCTION. Farmers rearing pigs are part of primary industry. They also grow vegetables and wheat and collect milk from cows. These ingredients are bought by the food processing division of the Global Group. It then processes them into a variety of foods, such as sausage rolls, pastry products and frozen foods. This processing is a secondary industry activity. The pastries might then be sold to a catering company which serves them at a buffet for business executives. This service is part of tertiary industry.

Businesses add value at each stage of production, as the ingredients are transformed into a product sold to the final customer, the business paying for the buffet.

Interdependence

The chain of production shows that businesses and their customers are highly INTERDEPENDENT. Farmers are dependent on firms like the Global Group for sales of their products. The Global Group is dependent on firms which transport ingredients for its products. The transport industry is dependent on the oil companies which make

1 Draw and label a chain of production for a woollen top. Start with primary industry and finish with tertiary industry.

petrol to power its trucks. The oil companies are dependent on workers all round the world who are employed in the oil industry. Workers are dependent on farmers for their food.

Specialisation and the division of labour

Interdependence leads to SPECIALISATION. This means that businesses, as well as individuals and whole economies, concentrate on making just a few products. For instance, the Global Group specialises in manufacturing food. Microsoft specialises in producing software for computers. Boeing specialises in manufacturing aeroplanes.

Specialisation explains why businesses today are so efficient and can produce so much.

- It allows knowledge and skills to be built up. The Global Group is expert at producing pastry products, but it doesn't know anything about producing computers. If it wants a computer, it buys it from a specialist manufacturer.

- It means that specialist machinery and equipment can be used for production. For instance, the Global Group has specialist manufacturing equipment for its pastry products and sorting equipment at its vegetable processing plant.
- It permits businesses to employ specialised workers. They can do different jobs, building up their expertise through training and experience. This specialisation of workers is known as the DIVISION OF LABOUR.

Production in the UK

What businesses produce in the UK changes over time. Figure 4.3 shows production since 1960 has gone up. Businesses are now producing more than before. However, there has been a faster growth in the provision of services than in the production of manufactured goods. Service businesses, like the food trading division of the Global Group, have prospered. The output of primary industry has only increased because of North Sea oil. In 1960, the UK produced almost no oil.

This relative growth of tertiary

businesses has occurred for three reasons.

- Wages are going up over time. Consumers are spending much of the extra money they earn on services rather than on goods. This has attracted new businesses to service industry.
- Many of the manufactured goods we buy are imported from abroad. 30 years ago, they would have been made in Britain. UK businesses which export have had to fight hard to survive and many have gone out of business. However, UK businesses are now selling more services abroad.
- The prices of services have gone up much faster on average than the prices of manufactured goods. It costs more today to buy the same amount of services than the same amount of goods. Manufacturing businesses have had to cut costs to survive the competition from low cost imports from abroad.

The labour force

Changes in what is being produced in the economy are bound to lead to changes in where and how people work. There has been a growth in jobs in service industries and a fall in those in primary and manufacturing industries.

What is more, the rate of decline of jobs in manufacturing has been even greater than the relative fall in manufacturing output. One reason for this is new technology. Manufacturing industry has been revolutionised over the past thirty years. Machines have replaced workers. New, ever more productive, machines have been replacing older ones. A few factories today employ almost no labour at all. In

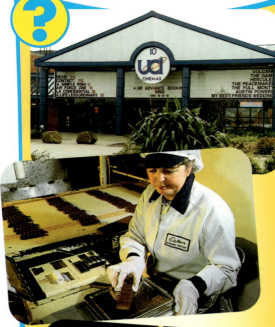

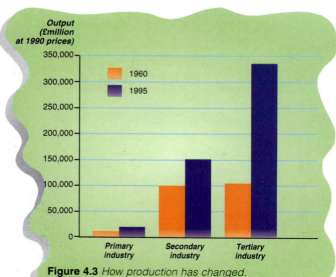

1 Explain what each business shown in the photographs specialises in producing.
2 How are the three businesses shown in the photographs interdependent?

fifty years time, it could be usual for factories to employ no workers and just a few supervisors.

Service industry doesn't have the same scope for **automation** (☞ unit 49). In some service industries, like restaurants, better service means more workers such as waiters rather than less. In others, such as banking and finance, automation only began affecting them in the 1980s. The 1990s have seen large redundancies in some sectors of service industries.

Source: adapted from The Global Group, *Annual Report and Accounts*.

Output (£million at 1990 prices)

Figure 4.3 *How production has changed.*

Table 4.1 shows changes in how consumers (people) spent their money between 1990 and 1996. For instance, the first column shows spending on food such as baked beans, beef and Bovril. Catering includes spending in restaurants and take-aways as well as people hiring caterers for wedding receptions etc.

Table 4.1 *Changing consumer spending in the UK.*

	Food	Alcohol & tobacco	Clothing & footwear	£ billion[1] Catering[2]
1990	41.8	30.0	20.9	29.8
1991	41.9	29.0	20.8	27.6
1992	42.4	27.7	21.5	27.7
1993	42.8	27.2	22.7	28.3
1994	43.4	27.6	23.9	28.3
1995	43.6	27.5	24.8	29.4
1996	44.7	27.5	26.2	30.5

1 at constant 1990 prices
2 eating out, such as at McDonald's

Source: adapted from ONS, *Monthly Digest of Statistics.*

DTP/Graphics

You work for a food manufacturing company. It produces beverages such as instant coffee, canned foods such as baked beans and chilled and frozen foods. You have been asked to produce a report on trends in spending in the economy. In particular, the company is thinking of expanding into new markets. It thinks there might be opportunities in expanding into the alcoholic drinks market, or into clothing or catering.

Your report should include the following terms: 'manufacturing industry', 'service industry', 'chain of production', 'specialisation'. The report could be produced using a desktop publishing package. It should be structured as follows.

1 An introduction explaining the purpose of the report.
2 A section on trends in consumer spending in the four industries shown in Table 4.1. Give a detailed account of how spending has changed. This should include a line graph constructed from the figures in the table. Put years across the bottom of the graph and £ million on the vertical axis. There should be four lines on the one graph corresponding to the four types of spending.
3 A concluding section which explains which of the three markets looks most promising for the company. You will need to consider which markets have grown the fastest. You should also think about whether the company has any expertise it could offer in the production or sale of alcoholic drinks, clothing or catering services.

Key terms

Chain of production - the various production stages through which a product passes before being sold to a consumer.

Division of labour - specialisation of workers.

Interdependence - where economies, businesses, consumers and workers are linked together and where they are reliant upon each other for their welfare.

Primary industry - activities which mine, grow, collect or cut down raw materials, such as in mining or in agriculture.

Secondary or manufacturing industry - activities which transform primary products into manufactured goods.

Specialisation - system of production where economies, regions, businesses or people concentrate on producing certain products.

Tertiary or service industry - activities which provide services.

Checklist ✓

1 Explain the difference between primary, secondary and tertiary industry.
2 Are the following workers part of primary, secondary or tertiary industry? (a) A coal miner; (b) a car production worker; (c) a shop assistant; (d) a hairdresser; (e) a teacher; (f) a secretary in an engineering company; (g) a farmworker; (h) a North Sea oil diver; (i) an estate agent; (j) a furniture maker; (k) a banker.
3 What is the chain of production?
4 Construct a chain of production for: (a) a bed; (b) a lesson in a school or college; (c) a packet of oven chips.
5 Why does the chain of production lead to interdependence in the economy?
6 Why does specialisation mean that more can be produced?
7 Specialisation by workers is given a special name. What is it?
8 What has happened in the UK since 1960 to: (a) the volume of total production; and (b) the monetary value of the output of the service sector compared to the manufacturing sector?
9 Why has automation led to a loss of jobs in the economy?

THE CAR GROUP

SUMMARY CASE STUDY

The Car Group is a company which specialises in selling used cars which are 0-5 years old. In 1997, it sold 23 000 cars, worth £161 million, from two sites in Cannock in the West Midlands and a large site in Northampton. It carries a stock of 2 500 cars, including all the major makes such as Vauxhall or Ford. Its success lies in selling large volumes of cars very quickly. In so doing it can sell the cars at a cheaper price than the typical second hand car dealer. By the year 2000, it hoped to have extended the formula throughout the UK by opening 10 new sites.

Source: adapted from *An Introduction to the Car Group*, The Car Group plc.

1 General Motors, owner of Vauxhall in the UK, is the world's largest manufacturer of cars. In which industry does it operate?
2 Explain in which industry The Car Group operates.
3 In what ways are General Motors and The Car Group interdependent?
4 Discuss THREE factors which will affect whether The Car Group is successful in its expansion.

BUSINESS IN THE LOCAL ENVIRONMENT

Making decisions

A business has to operate in a local environment. The business will affect that environment. It will have to decide how many local people to employ and whether to sell its products locally. It may also have to consider its impact on the local landscape. In turn, the business will be affected by the local environment. It will have to respond to changes in orders from local businesses. The availability of local labour may affect its ability to recruit new workers. The quality of the local roads, railways and airports may affect its costs.

Thames Water is the UK's largest water company. It provides water services to 11.7 million customers in London and the Thames Valley. In 1996, its sales were £1.3 billion. Although most of its business comes from the local area it serves in the UK, it also operates internationally.

Producing for the local community

Many businesses, like Thames Water, operate at a local level. Their **market** (☞ unit 2) is a local community. For instance, Thames Water supplies water to towns and villages in the Thames Valley and London areas. It also provides sewage and waste disposal services. Thames Water doesn't just supply water to 7.4 million households. It supplies to over 300 000 businesses. These include everything from restaurants to power plants to schools.

Equally, Thames Water buys from businesses in its local area. It uses local building contractors to maintain its buildings. Local business consultants have been involved in training Thames Water employees. Pipes and other equipment have been bought from local firms.

Creating jobs in the community

Businesses provide jobs for local people. Thames Water employs thousands of people in its main business. Even more workers, such as those employed by businesses supplying goods and services to Thames Water, are dependent for jobs on the success of Thames Water.

So Thames Water is directly and indirectly responsible for the creation of thousands of jobs. It is also responsible for training workers. It gives them skills which they can use for the company or for other businesses if they choose to change jobs. More skills tend to lead to higher pay. Training creates

Thames Water serves local households and has over 300 000 commercial customers.

Your teacher will give you a map of your local area.
1 Mark on it TEN businesses located in the area. Each business should produce a different product or service.
2 On a separate sheet of paper or in your books, write down what each business produces for the local community.

prosperity in the local community.

Thames Water is a **utility,** providing an essential product and service to households. Households and businesses will always want water. However, some industries suffer declines because demand for their product falls. For instance, demand for shipbuilding, steel and coal have fallen in the UK over the past 40 years. Some areas of the country, like the North East and Scotland, were heavily dependent for jobs on these industries. When businesses shrink or close, unemployment rises. Job creation goes into reverse and the local area becomes less prosperous.

Demography

DEMOGRAPHY is the study of population. Business is affected by the size of the population in a local area and how it is changing.

Equally, changes in the business environment could well affect the size of the population. Thames Water is the largest water company in the UK. This is because London and the Thames Valley is a densely populated area of the UK. The population of London since 1980 has hardly changed. However, the Thames Valley has seen growth. Thames Water therefore needs to install new supplies of water to areas of new housing in the Thames Valley.

The water business is a relatively mature business. In London and the Thames Valley, Thames Water is unlikely to find large numbers of new customers. To expand its business activities, it has developed an international division which specialises in water projects worldwide. For instance, in co-operation with Bovis, another UK business, it is operating a water treatment plant which will serve 2 million people in Shanghai. Growing world population gives Thames Water the opportunity to expand overseas.

Not all industries are mature or are expanding. The contraction of the steel, coal and shipbuilding industries had very damaging effects on some areas of the UK. Some people responded to very high unemployment in a local area by moving out. This then creates a downward spiral in the area. If people move out, they stop spending money on local services, like shops and restaurants. Some of these firms will then go out of business creating more unemployment.

Industrial tradition

Particular local areas tend to attract certain types of business. For instance, London is a major centre for financial businesses, attracted by the concentration of other similar businesses in the City of London. Stoke-on-Trent has a heavy concentration of pottery companies like Wedgwood. This happens

because pottery companies gain by being close together. There is a long history of pottery businesses in Stoke. The local workforce is trained in the skills required for the industry. Individuals also have specialised knowledge to allow them to set up new businesses in the industry. Finally, there are many local firms which supply the pottery industry and so it is easy to get raw materials and components locally.

Businesses also tend to be sited in particular areas in a town. Thames Water sewage treatment plants are not located in town centres. Sewage treatment avoids residential areas. Land prices are too high and land is scarce. Locating downstream from a town allows waste water to flow under gravity, avoiding pumping costs. Businesses that need to be in town centres and can afford the rents tend to be shops and financial services like banks. Near the town

centre are likely to be office blocks for a wide variety of workers, from local authority employees to headquarters staff for a construction company. Out on the main roads from the town will be shops like Toys 'R' Us or motor repair centres like Kwikfit where rents are cheaper and parking is easy.

Manufacturing industry is often found on industrial sites separate from local housing. Land prices are lower than in the town centre. Also, keeping industry separate from housing means that there are fewer social costs of production.

Infrastructure

Thames Water provides part of the local INFRASTRUCTURE because it builds and maintains water pipes, pumping stations, reservoirs and water treatment works. Infrastructure is the built environment of an area. Other examples of infrastructure are roads, bridges, buildings, schools, houses, telephone networks,

A static market

What do you do when the number of people buying your product is unlikely to change very much? What if the amount they buy is fairly constant too? This is the problem faced by British brewers. The number of drinkers in the population is fairly static and they are not buying more drink in pubs. Banks's Brewery, a local West Midlands brewer, faces this problem. In 1996, for instance, sales from its traditional pubs hardly changed.

The brewers have found three solutions, though. Instead of selling customers drinks, they are increasingly selling them food. Pubs are becoming restaurants. Refurbishment of pubs usually now starts with the kitchens.

Traditional drinking pubs are also becoming 'themed'. By changing the decor, the music and the range of games in a pub, customers can be attracted in from other pubs. Well sited pubs in town centres can become highly successful with the right level of investment.

The third solution is to buy more pubs. Each pub comes with a loyal clientele and a location. By buying more pubs, Banks's has managed to increase sales of drinks by the company.

Source: adapted from the *Express and Star*, 3 February 1997.

1 Why is a static population a problem for a brewing company?
2 How has Banks's brewery got around this problem?
3 In some industrial areas, where there is little housing, factories near to a pub have closed down.
  (a) What effect do you think this has had on trade for the pub? (b) Explain whether you think serving more food or changing the decor of the pub would help to increase sales.

electricity lines and gas pipes.

The size and quality of the local infrastructure is important to businesses. For instance, a restaurant would find it difficult to operate if its water supplies were polluted, or it were without water for part of the day. Thames Water would find it difficult to operate if the electricity supply wasn't reliable. Thames Water also relies on local schools and universities to provide it with skilled workers. It needs local hospitals to treat its workers when they fall ill and get them back to work quickly. A supermarket store would find it more difficult to get supplies in and attract customers if local roads were severely congested.

The environment

Thames Water has a major impact on the local environment. When it makes decisions about how to operate, it looks at its PRIVATE COSTS and PRIVATE BENEFITS. These are the costs and benefits to the company. For instance, when it

bids for a contract to supply or treat water in the Far East, it estimates its costs and the revenues likely to be received. It will bid if it thinks that the revenues will be larger than the costs, so that it can make a **profit**.

But the activities of Thames Water don't just affect the company. For instance, Thames Water is continually working with local groups on habitat enhancement schemes. It uses the land and water areas it owns to improve the local environment. Its work on the ThamesClean litter reduction project and efforts to reduce waste received the Queen Mother's Birthday Award. It has won an award for the last four years in the Mars and Berkshire Environment Award.

Improvements which bring no private benefits to the company are known as EXTERNALITIES. The private benefits to Thames Water added to the positive externalities to the community equal the SOCIAL BENEFITS of the activity. The social benefits are all the benefits to society of an economic activity.

Positive externalities. Thames water in partnership with The Wildlife and Wetlands Trust is creating a new wildlife centre at Barn Elms.

Businesses can sometimes impose costs on society which are not included in their own private costs. Any pollution that results from business activity is an example of an externality. The private costs added to the negative externalities equal the SOCIAL COSTS of business activity. The social costs are all the costs to society of an activity.

A company like Thames Water is very environmentally conscious. It knows that it is being judged on its environmental record. So, it attempts to eliminate environmental costs and works towards increasing social benefits.

Local government

Government affects a business like Thames Water in many ways. At a local level, Thames Water has to work with local authorities to get planning permission for new works. These local authorities provide the roads which Thames Water vehicles travel along. The local police and fire service protect Thames Water property. Local schools provide schooling for future employees of the company. The local authority is responsible for enforcing consumer protection laws, some of which cover water supply. The European Union (☞ unit 8) also imposes regulations which affect Thames Water's construction plans, such as the building of sewage treatment works.

Source: adapted from information provided by Thames Water.

Litter and discos

Wolverhampton has become the nightlife centre of the West Midlands. Tens of thousands of young people come into the town on Friday and Saturday evening to go to the hundreds of pubs, clubs, restaurants and discos in the town centre.

This has been good news for those businesses catering for the party goers. Existing businesses have seen their takings go up whilst many new businesses have come to the town. The new trade has created many jobs, although these have tended to be part time and low paid. The expansion has also made Wolverhampton a safer place to be at night. You are far less likely to be mugged in a town centre where there are another 20 000 people than in one which is virtually deserted.

There are some problems though. One is litter. Local fast food outlets are doing booming business, but packaging taken away from the outlet is too often dropped in the street rather than put into a bin. The situation is made worse by the fact that street cleaning takes place between 6 a.m. and 4 p.m. Bins become half full by the time commuters have gone home at 6 p.m. and there is already some litter on the street. This discourages the young people who come into town later on to respect the local environment by dropping their litter into bins.

Source: adapted from the *Express & Star*, 11 October 1997.

1 What have been the private benefits to local business of the rapid expansion of Wolverhampton's night life?
2 Suggest ONE example of a positive externality, one which has benefited the local community, of this expansion.
3 Explain why litter would be a negative externality for a Wolverhampton fast food outlet.
4 It has been suggested that Wolverhampton Borough Council should install more and bigger rubbish bins in the town centre and increase cleaning hours from 4 in the afternoon to 8 o'clock at night. Discuss who should pay for this if the proposals were implemented.

Boost for Wolverhampton

In 1996, Wolverhampton announced that it had won a £18.75 million regeneration grant from the government. The town has traditionally been a major centre for manufacturing industry, particularly metal engineering. However, the shrinkage of manufacturing over the past 30 years has hit the town hard. Many factories have closed down and others have shed labour as machines have replaced workers. Large areas of land became derelict. At times, as many jobs were being lost as were being created.

The 1990s have seen an upturn in the local economy. There are now far more service sector jobs. The £18.75 million grant will be used to lure new investment into the town. It is expected that private sector companies will invest £100 million, as a result creating 7 000 new jobs and making sure that a further 4 000 jobs are not lost because firms move away from the area.

The local council hopes that most of the jobs created will be in manufacturing industry. However, they are prepared to be flexible and work with service sector firms too.

Source: adapted from the *Express and Star*, 16 December 1996.

1 How did government help the local Wolverhampton economy in 1996?
2 Why did Wolverhampton need this help?
3 What effect do you think the grant might have on: (a) local businesses; (b) local jobs; and (c) the local environment?
4 A local firm making car parts is considering relocating to another site from an old factory in Wolverhampton which is now too large for its needs.
Suggest: (a) THREE costs of moving; and (b) what help it might receive from the regeneration grant which would persuade it to stay in Wolverhampton.

key terms

Demography - the study of population.

Externalities - the cost or benefit of an activity which is not paid for or received by the individual, business or government engaged in that activity.

Infrastructure - the built environment, like roads, factories, schools and hospitals.

Private costs and benefits - the costs and benefits to individuals, businesses or governments of an economic or business activity.

Social costs and benefits - the costs and benefits to society as a whole of the activities of individuals, businesses and governments. Social costs and benefits = private costs and benefits plus externalities.

SUMMARY CASE STUDY

TOURISM IN LIVERPOOL

Fifty years ago, Liverpool was a centre for manufacturing. Its docks were busy with exports to the USA and to Britain's colonies. In the 1970s and 1980s, the city fell on hard times. Many of the manufacturing jobs disappeared as firms went out of business or shrank their activities. Production was shifted abroad or to other areas of the country which were more competitive. The docks suffered too as the focus of trade shifted to Europe and ports on the south coast. The result was a sharp rise in unemployment.

Today, the economy is recovering and tourism is playing an unlikely part in that recovery. By the late 1990s, it had come from nowhere to being the city's 9th largest employer. Much of the former dockland has been transformed into hotels, museums, shops and restaurants.

The single most important Liverpool attraction is the Beatles. In a 1995 survey, one third of all visitors who spent a night in Liverpool said they had come because of the pop group. Local businesses are cashing in on the interest. The area round The Cavern Club, where the Beatles played, is now full of restaurants, boutiques and discos. Cavern City Tours, set up in 1983, organises a Magical Mystery Tour round the Liverpool of the Beatles, including trips to Penny Lane and Strawberry Fields. The company now employs 79 people. Down at the docks, the Beatles Story, an exhibition charting the history of the group, attracts 5 million visitors a year.

Source: adapted from the *Financial Times*, 11 January 1997.

1 What effect do you think the decline in manufacturing in the 1970s and 1980s had on: (a) the local Liverpool economy; and (b) the local environment?
2 What impact might the opening of a new restaurant near to The Cavern Club have on the city?
3 Two Beatles fans want to set up in business in Liverpool. They want their business to have something to do with the Beatles.
(a) Outline TWO different ideas for businesses they could run.
(b) Explain the opportunities they could exploit and the difficulties they might face in making their business successful.

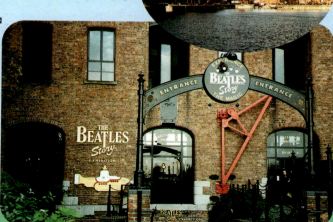

Checklist ✓

1 A building society is opening a new branch in the near future. At the moment, work is being done on the building before the opening. What jobs are going to be created in the local community: (a) in the short term; and (b) in the longer term?
2 Give FOUR social costs created by a local coal mine.
3 Give FOUR social benefits created by a local hairdressing salon.
4 Give THREE examples of industries where negative externalities might be quite large.
5 There is a large increase in the number of old people aged 80 and over in your local area. What effect might this have on local businesses?
6 A tyre manufacturer, the largest employer in an area, closes down. What effect will this have on: (a) workers; and (b) other businesses in the area?
7 (a) Stoke-on-Trent is famous for what industry? (b) Why do firms in that industry concentrate together in the same locality?
8 Give FIVE examples of the infrastructure in your local area.
9 Why is infrastructure important to a local business?
10 How can local government affect a business?

BUSINESS IN THE NATIONAL ENVIRONMENT

Making decisions

Businesses operate in a difficult national environment. Although the UK economy is growing slowly over time, it keeps on moving from boom to recession. Businesses need to decide how to cope with these changes in demand for their products. They also need to know how best to cope with changing patterns of demand coming from increased consumer incomes or changing population patterns. Inflation too can cause difficulties for businesses. Alongside this, businesses must meet government rules and regulations which set out how they can operate.

George Wimpey PLC is the UK's largest private house building group. In 1996, the Group sold over 12 000 homes in the UK and had an operating profit of £51.7 million. It builds homes under two main brand names in the UK - Wimpey Homes and McLean Homes. McLean Homes builds mainly 4 bedroomed detached houses. Wimpey Homes builds mainly two and three bedroomed terraced and semi-detached homes. Both brands are committed to building high quality homes which represent excellent value for customers.

Growth, boom and recession

Economies tend to grow in size over time. Over the past forty years, for instance, production in the UK has more than doubled. So people can buy and consume more.

Some businesses have benefited more than others from this growth. Many service industries, such as health or catering, have grown faster than the average for the rest of the economy. The construction industry, which includes George Wimpey PLC, grew at roughly the same rate as the rest of the economy until 1990. Other industries have grown less quickly. Jam makers, for instance, have suffered. Consumers have bought less jam as their incomes have risen. They have switched to convenience foods like crisps or to healthier food like fresh fruit.

This overall growth in the economy is uneven. When the economy is in BOOM, it is growing very fast. Spending is high and unemployment falls. Businesses

Wagon Industrial Holdings plc is a UK based engineering company. Although it sells throughout the world, two thirds of sales are within the UK.

1 Look at Table 6.1. Give the output of the whole economy in: (a) 1989; (b) 1992; and (c) 1996.

2 'Between 1990 and 1992, the economy went into recession.' (a) What does this mean? (b) Explain what effect this might have had on the output of the engineering industry and the output of Wagon Industrial.

3 From 1993, the economy staged a recovery. How might this explain the change in sales of Wagon Industrial?

4 In 1997, the economy was expanding. What factors do you think might influence how much Wagon Industrial invests in new machinery?

DTP/Graphics

These questions could be answered in the form of a report. Use a DTP, spreadsheet and/or graphics package to show what happened to output in the economy, of the engineering industry and of Wagon Industrial.

A six jaw chuck manufactured by a part of the company.

Table 6.1

at 1990 prices

	Output of the whole economy £bn	Output of engineering industry £bn	Output of Wagon Industrial Holdings plc £m
1989	476	61.0	212
1990	479	61.0	270
1991	469	56.8	242
1992	466	55.7	207
1993	477	56.4	216
1994	496	60.2	240
1995	509	61.8	304
1996	520	63.4	335

1 i.e. adjusted for inflation

Source: adapted from ONS, *Monthly Digest of Statistics*; Wagon Industrial Holdings PLC, *Annual Report and Accounts*.

In his July 1997 Budget, the Chancellor announced a number of tax measures. These included: a cut in corporation tax, the tax on company profits; rises in taxes on petrol, cigarettes and alcoholic drink; a cut in VAT from 8 to 5 per cent on gas and electricity to homes; a windfall tax on the profits of the water, gas, electricity and telephone companies; and a rise in the amount that homeowners have to pay on their mortgage because of a cut in the tax subsidy given by the government.

1 Explain which of the tax measures will have benefited businesses.
2 Drinks companies, electricity companies and house building companies may have been particularly affected by this budget. Explain why.

Wordprocessing

3 You work in the public relations department of a large petrol company. Write a letter (preferably wordprocessed) to the Chancellor complaining about the latest rise in tax on petrol and explaining why it may be bad for customers and businesses in the UK.

tend to do well in a boom because it is easier to sell products. In the boom of 1986-88, output of the construction industry increased by one quarter. This was over twice the average increase in output in the rest of the economy.

In a RECESSION, the economy doesn't grow or even shrinks, as was the case between 1990 and 1992 in the UK. Less is spent and produced than before and unemployment rises. Businesses tend to do badly because consumers are buying fewer of their products. The construction industry was very badly affected by the recession of 1990-92. Output fell by 10 per cent. Even worse, when the rest of the economy began to recover from 1993, construction industry output barely changed. By 1997, construction output was little more than it had been in 1990.

Inflation

INFLATION is a general rise in prices in the economy. Businesses lose and gain from inflation. They lose because their costs go up. For instance, a construction company will lose out because it will have to pay more for building materials like bricks and wood. It will also lose out because it will probably have to pay its workers more. They will want higher wages to pay the higher prices in the shops.

Businesses can also gain. If prices are rising, a construction company is likely to be able to put up its prices to its customers. Higher prices should mean less sales. But if all businesses are putting up their prices, and workers are getting higher wages, then sales for a business should stay the same.

Taxes and government spending

Decisions that government makes about its spending and taxes (called **fiscal policy**) affect all businesses.

For instance, the government might lower taxes on people's income (income tax or National Insurance contributions). As a result, people will have more money left in their wage packet to spend. They might spend more at the supermarket, or on holidays, benefiting supermarket and tourist companies. Equally, they might decide that they can now afford a larger home, for instance, built by George Wimpey PLC.

The government might also change tax rates on goods and services. Value added tax (VAT) has to be paid on most products at 17.5 per cent. New homes, though, are exempt. An increase in VAT would hit sales of products like televisions or clothes.

George Wimpey PLC would be affected if the government raised corporation tax, the tax on company profits. In 1996, for instance, it had to pay £9.3 million in UK corporation tax.

A general increase in government spending will mean more spending in the whole economy. This should benefit a construction business because some of that extra spending will be on new homes. Increases in government spending on particular programmes can also benefit businesses. For instance, a significant increase in government spending on housing for rent might give George Wimpey PLC a business opportunity to expand its operations in future. A decrease in defence spending, in contrast, might hit manufacturers of

Figure 6.1 *Booms and slumps. Businesses are producing more and more over time. However, sometimes in a boom, growth in business is particularly fast. At other times, in a recession, output can sometimes fall.*

weapons like GEC.

Interest rates

Most businesses borrow money (☞ unit 31). George Wimpey PLC, for instance, in 1996 had £114 million in borrowings which were due to be paid after 2001. Rises in interest rates usually add to the costs of a business because it will have to pay more in interest on its loans. A fall in interest rates, on the other hand, means lower interest payments.

Rising interest rates also affect the customers of a business. The mortgage rate is the rate of interest on money borrowed to buy a home. If it goes up, then repayments on the loan to buy a house will increase. This will discourage people from buying new houses. Construction companies could be faced with falling sales. A fall in interest rates

will have the opposite effect. It will make the repayments on buying a new car, some new furniture or a new home fall. So car and furniture manufactures and construction companies should benefit.

Population

The population of the UK is fairly stable. This might seem bad news for a business like George Wimpey PLC. But people are buying new homes. One reason for this is that the structure of the population is changing. There are more old people than before living on their own. The number of single parent families has increased. Increased divorce rates have split up families. So the number of households has increased as the numbers in each household has tended to fall. Each household needs a home. So George Wimpey PLC could sell new homes.

Changes in the structure of the population can have effects on other businesses. In the 1980s, for instance, a fall in the number of school aged children meant that many schools closed. Rising numbers of those over 75, on the other hand, increased the business opportunities for retirement homes.

George Wimpey PLC may also benefit from changes in where people live. For instance, over the past 20 years, the numbers living in the South East of England have gone up, but the population of the Merseyside area has fallen. More homes therefore need to be built in the South East.

Government regulations

The government imposes many constraints on businesses. For instance, health and safety laws (☞ unit 62) have to be complied

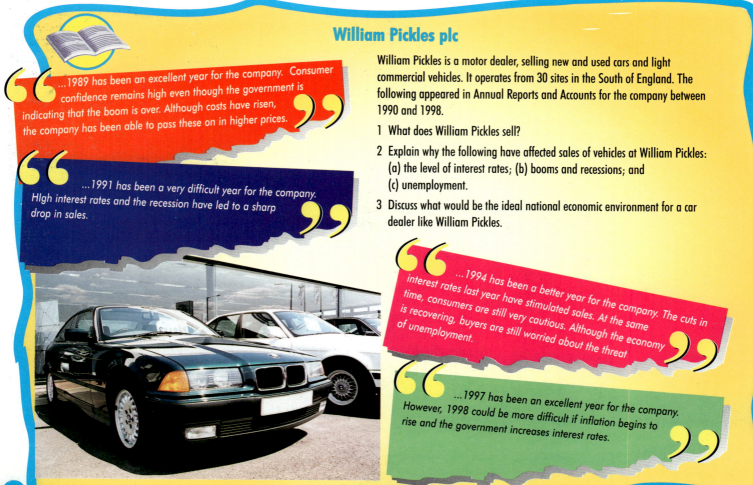

William Pickles plc

...1989 has been an excellent year for the company. Consumer confidence remains high even though the government is indicating that the boom is over. Although costs have risen, the company has been able to pass these on in higher prices.

...1991 has been a very difficult year for the company. HIgh interest rates and the recession have led to a sharp drop in sales.

...1994 has been a better year for the company. The cuts in interest rates last year have stimulated sales. At the same time, consumers are still very cautious. Although the economy is recovering, buyers are still worried about the threat of unemployment.

...1997 has been an excellent year for the company. However, 1998 could be more difficult if inflation begins to rise and the government increases interest rates.

William Pickles is a motor dealer, selling new and used cars and light commercial vehicles. It operates from 30 sites in the South of England. The following appeared in Annual Reports and Accounts for the company between 1990 and 1998.

1 What does William Pickles sell?

2 Explain why the following have affected sales of vehicles at William Pickles:
(a) the level of interest rates; (b) booms and recessions; and
(c) unemployment.

3 Discuss what would be the ideal national economic environment for a car dealer like William Pickles.

with on George Wimpey PLC building sites. George Wimpey PLC has to obtain planning permission from the local authority to build any new homes. Consumer protection laws determine how George Wimpey PLC can market its homes. Other laws fix how the purchase of a home should be completed.

Source: adapted in part from George Wimpey PLC, *Annual Report and Accounts.*

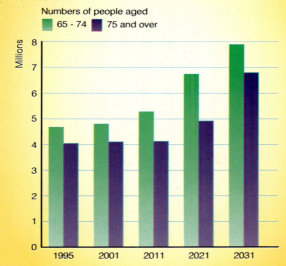

1 What is projected will happen to the number of people aged: (a) 65-74; and (b) 75 and over in the population to the year 2031?

2 What opportunities will this create for businesses in terms of selling products aimed at this age range of people?

3 Discuss TWO problems for businesses that may result from these trends.

Source: adapted from ONS, *Social Trends*, 1997.

Figure 6.2 *Projected changes in the population aged 65+ in the UK.*

key terms

Boom - period of time when the economy is growing particularly fast.

Inflation - a general rise in prices.

Recession - period of time when the economy is slowing down or output is even falling.

Checklist ✓

1 What is the difference between a boom and a recession?

2 What is the likely effect of a recession on a business?

3 What happens to unemployment in a recession and how might this affect businesses?

4 How does inflation affect a business?

5 Explain how the following tax changes might benefit or harm businesses: (a) a rise in income tax; (b) a fall in VAT; (c) a fall in corporation tax.

6 Which businesses might benefit most from an increase in spending on road building?

7 'Rocketing interest rates have hit my costs and my orders.' Explain why this could be true for a business.

8 Explain which businesses might be affected by a rise in the number of births in the population: (a) now; (b) in 20 years time; (c) in 75 years time.

9 Find and list FIVE examples of government regulations which affect businesses.

THE HUMPTY DUMPTY PLAYGROUP

The Humpty Dumpty playgroup operates on a large new estate of owner-occupied houses in a Sussex town. The estate is yet to be finished, with another 300 houses planned. It has attracted mainly families, many with children, or young couples hoping to have children. New houses are currently selling very fast because the local economy is booming.

Sarah Milford set up the playgroup from scratch. The initial advertising, purchase of equipment and the first year's loss came to around £3 000 which she borrowed from the bank. The playgroup's current running costs are about £30 000 per year. That includes hire of a hall, staff costs including a wage for herself, and materials. She charges £4 a session (morning, afternoon or after school) and last year the fees came to £31 000.

All playgroups today are strictly regulated. They have to conform to the requirements of the Childrens Act, which, for instance, lays down how many staff there have to be per child.

1 The Humpty Dumpty playgroup is a success. Explain why: (a) population changes in the local area; and (b) the state of the economy are helping it to be successful.

2 At the moment, interest rates are low. Why is this an advantage to Sarah?

3 How do government regulations affect Sarah's business?

4 Discuss THREE factors which in the future could cause the playgroup to turn from being in profit to suffering losses.

THE INTERNATIONAL DIMENSION

Making decisions

All businesses are likely to be affected by the world economy. Some businesses decide to export their goods and services abroad. They have to make decisions about which foreign customers to sell to and where to focus their export efforts. Even if businesses don't export products, they are likely to buy products from abroad. They have to decide whether to buy British products or foreign products.

British Airways is a multi-billion pound business. In 1996-7, its total sales were £8.4 billion and it carried 38.2 million passengers. It operates services around the globe and aims to be the undisputed leader in world travel. The future of British Airways lies in carrying more passengers, both British and foreign, and in increasing its share of the world airline market.

Exports

BA is a favourite airline of many British passengers. But it also relies on sales to foreign passengers. Goods (sometimes called **visibles**) and services (sometimes called **invisibles**) which are sold to foreigners are called EXPORTS.

BA sells a **service** to foreigners. This could be a flight for which passengers pay. BA, a British company, receives the money from the sale of the ticket. So the flight is an exported service because it is a service sold to foreigners.

Imports

BA is always looking to get the best value for money. When it buys supplies from other businesses, it wants to buy at the lowest price. It also wants **goods** of the 'right' quality, which can be delivered on time and which, if necessary, offer an after sales service. Sometimes, a British company can offer this package. But equally, the best value might be offered by a foreign company. For instance, British Airways buys many of its new aeroplanes from Boeing, a US company.

When BA takes delivery of a new Boeing aeroplane, it has to pay Boeing, a foreign company. This becomes an IMPORT for the UK. It is an imported good because a

Mitsubishi

Mitsubishi is a large Japanese company producing a range of goods, including nuclear power plant equipment, laser processing machines, microchips and consumer products like televisions and VCRs.

1 Mitsubishi has manufacturing plants all around the world. For instance, it sells microchips made in Japan to UK manufacturers. For Japan, these are exports. What are they for the UK?
2 Mitsubishi has to bring its products to Europe by ship or aeroplane. If it uses a UK shipping company, why would this be an export of a service for the UK?
3 If Mitsubishi used the banking services of a British bank, what would this be classified as for the UK?
4 Suggest THREE ways in which Mitsubishi could increase the amount it sells into its UK markets.

Figure 7.1 *UK exports and imports.*

IMPORTS

EXPORTS

Goods such as fruit

Goods such as woollen clothes

Services such as insurance

Services such as transport

Foreign passengers flying on Concorde pay money to BA. This is an example of an export of a service for the UK.

British company is buying a physical product from a foreign company.

Threats and opportunities

Working in an international environment leads to both threats and opportunities for British businesses. One threat is that competition from foreign businesses may take away sales from UK businesses.

BA, for instance, is in direct competition with other airlines like Delta, TWA or Air France. BA needs to provide a high quality service, to the right airports in the world and at a competitive price to keep its share of the market.

On the other hand, without its foreign customers, 60 per cent of whom originated from overseas in 1998, BA would be a much smaller business. It also has the chance to take away sales from its foreign competitors. Providing greater comfort in its Business Class seating, or offering cheaper fares on various flights at different times of the year, could increase the numbers travelling with BA.

Being able to buy from abroad also means that BA can get the most competitive supplies for its operations rather than just having to rely on British suppliers.

Exchange rates

A British traveller is likely to pay for a BA service in pounds sterling. A USA tourist, however, is likely to pay in dollars. But the price of

dollars for pounds, the EXCHANGE RATE, is constantly changing. These changes can have an important effect on BA.

Assume that the exchange rate is $1.50=£1. This means that $1.50 can be exchanged for £1. A £1 000 BA holiday to London will therefore cost an American $1 500 (£1 000 x $1.50).

What if the exchange rate changed? The value of the pound might fall so that there is now $1=£1. BA has to decide whether to change its prices. If it chooses to keep the price at £1 000, the price in dollars will fall. The price of the same holiday in dollars will now be $1 000 (£1 000 x $1). This new lower price should encourage Americans to use BA's services more. In general, a fall in the value of the pound means that foreigners can buy British goods more cheaply and should buy more.

If instead the value of the pound rises, so that $2=£1, then the holiday would be more expensive for Americans. It would cost $2 000 (£1 000 x $2) and Americans should buy fewer BA services. A rise in the value of the pound will tend to make British goods and services more expensive to foreigners and they should buy less.

The opposite will be true for imports of goods and services into the UK. A fall in the value of the pound will make imports more expensive to British buyers. A fall from £1=$1.50 to £1=$1 could increase the price of a $1 000 American holiday to a British holidaymaker from £667 ($1 000 ÷ $1.50) to £1 000 ($1 000 ÷ $1). So imports should fall.

A rise in the value of the pound from £1=$1.50 to £1=$2 makes imports cheaper to the British. The price of a $1 000 American holiday could fall from £667 to £500 ($1 000 ÷ $2). Imports should rise as a result.

The government helping business

A government can help businesses

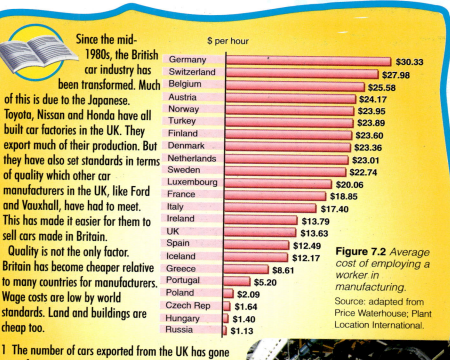

Since the mid-1980s, the British car industry has been transformed. Much of this is due to the Japanese. Toyota, Nissan and Honda have all built car factories in the UK. They export much of their production. But they have also set standards in terms of quality which other car manufacturers in the UK, like Ford and Vauxhall, have had to meet. This has made it easier for them to sell cars made in Britain.

Quality is not the only factor. Britain has become cheaper relative to many countries for manufacturers. Wage costs are low by world standards. Land and buildings are cheap too.

$ per hour

Country	$ per hour
Germany	$30.33
Switzerland	$27.98
Belgium	$25.58
Austria	$24.17
Norway	$23.95
Turkey	$23.89
Finland	$23.60
Denmark	$23.36
Netherlands	$23.01
Sweden	$22.74
Luxembourg	$20.06
France	$18.85
Italy	$17.40
Ireland	$13.79
UK	$13.63
Spain	$12.49
Iceland	$12.17
Greece	$8.61
Portugal	$5.20
Poland	$2.09
Czech Rep	$1.64
Hungary	$1.40
Russia	$1.13

Figure 7.2 *Average cost of employing a worker in manufacturing.*

Source: adapted from Price Waterhouse; Plant Location International.

1 The number of cars exported from the UK has gone up four times since 1985. Explain TWO reasons why this has occurred.
2 A Japanese car producer is looking for another manufacturing base in Europe but not in the UK. Much of the production from this factory will be exported. Giving reasons, suggest where in Europe it might locate.

27

deal with foreign competitors. For instance, it could:

- subsidise exports - this means giving a grant for each export sold, allowing businesses to charge lower prices and win more orders;
- impose tariffs on imports - tariffs (sometimes called **customs duties**) are a tax on imported goods, making them more expensive;
- impose quotas on imports - a quota is a limit on the number of goods coming into the country over a year;
- try to push down the value of the pound which will make the price of imports more expensive and the price of exports to foreigners cheaper.

However, the British government is limited in what it can do. The UK is a member of the European Union which doesn't allow tariffs and quotas on trade between European countries. The UK is also a member of the World Trade Organisation which limits tariffs and quotas.

Many British companies don't want restrictions on trade. If the UK keeps out foreign goods through tariffs and quotas, there is more chance that other countries will do the same to UK exports.

The government and managing the economy

The UK has to pay its way in the world. Exports have roughly to equal imports over time. If imports were greater than exports, the difference would have to be borrowed from foreigners. To repay it, exports would have to be greater than imports.

The values of UK exports and imports are shown on the BALANCE OF PAYMENTS. The balance of payments is a record of all the money coming into and going out of the UK. Sometimes, on the news, you may hear about the BALANCE OF TRADE. This is the difference between values of exports and imports of goods only. The difference between the value of exports and imports of both goods and services is called the CURRENT BALANCE. .

What if there is a current account deficit (i.e. where imports are greater than exports)? The government may try to correct this.

- It could try to force down the value of the pound, making it easier for UK businesses to export and making imports more expensive.
- It could push up interest rates. This should lead to a fall in spending in the UK and so lead to a fall in imports. However, a fall in spending could lead to a recession in the economy which would be bad for UK businesses.
- It could increase tariffs and quotas, although this would be difficult because of membership of the European Union.

Source: adapted in part from information provided by British Airways.

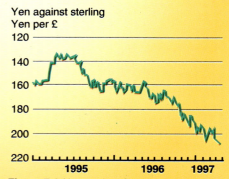

Japanese tourists

In 1996, the number of Japanese tourists coming to Britain dropped as the value of the yen dropped against the pound.

* At its high point in 1995, the Japanese could get £1 for 135 yen.
* By the end of 1996, they had to pay 200 yen to get the same £1.

This made a big difference in prices for the Japanese. In 1995, with 135 000 yen to spend, they could buy £1 000 worth of goods in London. By the end of 1996, the same 135 000 yen could only buy £675 worth of goods (135 000 ÷ 200). A trip to Harrods, or to see a West End musical, was over 30 per cent more expensive.

Not surprisingly, the Japanese reacted in two ways. Many decided to go to Paris or Rome rather than come to London. Those that did come to London spent less in pounds sterling than they had before.

Source: adapted from the *Financial Times*, 4 March 1997.

1   Look at Figure 7.4. What happened to the value of the yen against the pound in 1995 and 1996?
2   A Japanese tourist plans to take 100 000 yen of spending money on a package tour to London.
   (a) What value of UK goods would she have been able to buy at the end of 1996?
   (b) What value of UK goods would she have been able to buy in mid-1995 when the pound was worth 135 yen?
   (c) How does this help explain why there were fewer Japanese tourists in London in 1996 than in 1995?
3   A hotel in central London relies heavily on Japanese tourists for business. Suggest ways in which it could have attracted more tourists in 1997.

Japanese visitors to the UK
% change 1996 v 1995

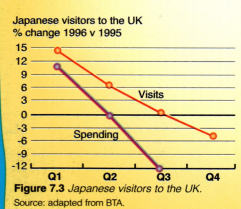

Figure 7.3 *Japanese visitors to the UK.*
Source: adapted from BTA.

Yen against sterling
Yen per £

Figure 7.4 *Yen against Sterling.*
Source: adapted from Datastream.

A low value of the pound, 1992-95

In September 1992, the UK was forced out of the Exchange Rate Mechanism (ERM) of the European Monetary Union. The value of the pound in the ERM was very high. Immediately after leaving, the pound dropped in value against other currencies by 10 per cent. It then carried on dropping. By 1995, it had fallen 25 per cent in value against the German deutschmark, 20 per cent against the US dollar and 35 per cent against the Japanese yen.

The government allowed the value of the pound to find its own market level. However, its low interest rate policy at the time helped keep the pound at a very low price in terms of other currencies.

Exporters were delighted by the changes. Before, in the early 1990s, they had found it very difficult to compete in export markets.

1 Explain carefully why low exchange rates helped British exporters.
2 A UK company exported high quality shirts to Germany, the USA and Japan in 1991. By 1995, it had cut its prices in all three markets, but its Japanese prices had fallen the most. Explain why this might have been so.
3 Newspapers are suggesting that the Bank of England will shortly raise interest rates. As the Managing Director of a business manufacturing car components, some for export, write a letter to the Governor of the Bank of the England explaining why a rise in interest rates would be bad for your company.

Key terms

Exchange rate - the price or rate at which one currency is changed for another.
Export - good or service sold to a foreign buyer.
Import - good or service bought from a foreign seller.
The balance of payments - a record of the money coming into and leaving a country in exchange for goods and services over a period of time, such as a year.
The balance of trade - visible exports minus visible imports.
The current account balance - exports (both visible and invisible) minus imports (both visible and invisible).

Checklist ✓

1 What is the difference between an export and an import?
2 Explain whether each of the following is an export of a good, an export of a service, an import of a good or an import of a service: (a) a car sold by Rover to Germany; (b) a Japanese made personal stereo bought by an British consumer; (c) medicines made in the UK and sold to France; (d) a British tourist taking a holiday in Austria; (e) a Japanese company insuring its company with a British insurer; ((f) a French company buying steel from the UK.
3 What are the advantages of being able to export for a UK business?
4 What are: (a) the disadvantages; and (b) the advantages of being able to import for a UK business?
5 What is an exchange rate?
6 Explain whether a fall in the value of the pound would be good for: (a) a UK business exporting cars to France; (b) a French business exporting clothes to the UK; (c) a UK engineering business buying steel from Germany.
7 Why do fluctuating exchange rates pose a problem for businesses?
8 How can government help UK businesses to export and compete against imports?
9 (a) What is the current account on the balance of payments? (b) How might government measures to correct a deficit on the current account affect UK businesses?

SUMMARY CASE STUDY

CHIEF

Chief is a London based manufacturer of chef's hats. Of its £12 million sales per year, around 60 per cent are exported. Making hats at Chief is a hi-tech business. They are made with the latest automated equipment, using the newest British made materials on the market. They certainly aren't the cheapest hats around, but they are keenly priced given the high quality of the product.

In 1996, the company became increasingly worried about the rising pound. By the end of the year, it was 20 per cent up on average against other currencies compared to the start of the year. In early 1997 it was having to raise its prices, with a likely fall in demand resulting and possible future losses.

Source: adapted from the *Financial Times*, 21 January 1997.

1 Suggest why businesses buy hats from Chief rather than other manufacturers.
2 What impact does Chief have: (a) on exports; and (b) on the balance of payments of the UK?
3 Explain why a rise in the value of the pound is bad for Chief.
4 Discuss TWO ways in which Chief could respond to the situation in which it found itself at the start of 1997. Remember that you need to talk about advantages and disadvantages of each proposal in this 'discuss' question.

unit 8

THE EUROPEAN UNION

Making decisions

The European Union (EU) is increasingly important for businesses in Europe. Today European businesses have to comply with EU regulations. More importantly, though, the Single European Market is opening up Europe to competition, making it easier for UK firms to sell products in Europe and for Continental firms to sell into the UK. European businesses have to face up to these challenges and make decisions about how to meet the competition.

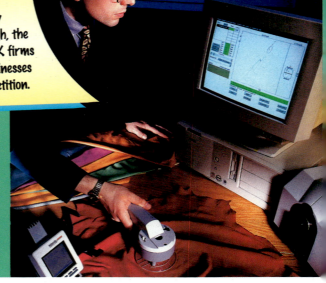

Pittards plc develops and produces technically advanced leathers for many of the world's leading brands of gloves, shoes, and sports and leisure goods. Its leathers can be found, for instance, in Clarks shoes, Foot-Joy and Nike gloves, and Puma King soccer boots. It exports most of its output from its factories in the UK. The existence of the EU poses both opportunities and potential threats for a company like Pittards.

A common market

The European Union (EU) is a common market. This means that trade between member countries should be as easy as trade within a country. Pittards, for instance, doesn't have to send its glove leather through customs control or pay taxes when it sends them from its factory in Leeds in England to a customer in Scotland. Similarly, there are now no taxes (taxes on imported goods are called **tariffs**) or customs controls on trade between EU countries.

When Britain joined the EU in 1973, this was a great opportunity for British companies. Before 1973, some countries had imposed tariffs on products made in the UK. After Britain joined, UK businesses could compete on the same terms as other European companies and win orders throughout the EU. In 1996, around 20 per cent of Pittards' sales were to Europe. Sales of dress glove leather to France and Germany increased from 1995 to 1996. It also maintained its sales of military glove leather in Europe.

On the other hand, European businesses could also compete with British businesses on the same terms in the UK. **Competition** within the UK increased.

European Monetary Union

There are still barriers to trade between EU countries. One is the fact that there are different currencies. The pound goes up and down in value every minute of the day against the French franc and the German deutschmark. 60 per cent of Pittards' output is exported. So Pittards may not know exactly how much it will receive in pounds for its leather sold abroad if sold in foreign currency. Equally, it might

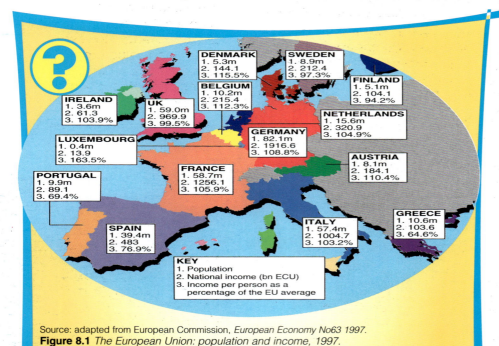

DENMARK
1. 5.3m
2. 144.1
3. 115.5%

SWEDEN
1. 8.9m
2. 212.4
3. 97.3%

FINLAND
1. 5.1m
2. 104.1
3. 94.2%

BELGIUM
1. 10.2m
2. 215.4
3. 112.3%

IRELAND
1. 3.6m
2. 61.3
3. 103.9%

UK
1. 59.0m
2. 969.9
3. 99.5%

NETHERLANDS
1. 15.6m
2. 320.9
3. 104.9%

GERMANY
1. 82.1m
2. 1916.6
3. 108.8%

LUXEMBOURG
1. 0.4m
2. 13.9
3. 163.5%

AUSTRIA
1. 8.1m
2. 184.1
3. 110.4%

PORTUGAL
1. 9.9m
2. 89.1
3. 69.4%

FRANCE
1. 58.7m
2. 1256.1
3. 105.9%

GREECE
1. 10.6m
2. 103.6
3. 64.6%

SPAIN
1. 39.4m
2. 483
3. 76.9%

ITALY
1. 57.4m
2. 1004.7
3. 103.2%

KEY
1. Population
2. National income (bn ECU)
3. Income per person as a percentage of the EU average

Source: adapted from European Commission, *European Economy No63 1997*.
Figure 8.1 *The European Union: population and income, 1997.*

1 How many member countries of the European Union were there in 1997?
2 Which country had the largest population and which had the smallest?
3 Which country had the highest income and which had the smallest?
4 What are the (i) opportunities and (ii) threats, if any, of the UK's membership of the EU for: (a) Rover, the manufacturer of Rover cars and Land Rover vehicles; (b) a supermarket chain like Sainsbury's or Tesco; (c) a local hairdresser in Bristol?

not know how much in pounds it will pay for the hides that it imports if contracts are signed in foreign currencies.

What is more, Pittards has to pay banks a commission to exchange foreign currency. Even if this is only 0.1 per cent, it still means a cost of £10 000 on a £1 million order.

There are ways in which businesses can minimise the risk of large changes in the value of the currency. For instance, it can agree a price at which to buy or sell currency for delivery in three months time. This is known as **hedging**. However, it costs money to do this.

To try and get round these problems, the EU has proposed that there should be a monetary union. There will be a single currency. This would mean that the money used in the UK would be the same as the money used in Germany, just as £1 in Scotland is the same as £1 in Wales. France, Germany and some other EU countries will be creating a monetary union probably by the year 2000. The UK might join at a later date. This might put British

companies at a competitive disadvantage. This is because French and German firms won't have the costs of changing their currencies when they trade with each other.

Regulations

Membership of the EU affects UK businesses in other ways. The EU has its own laws and regulations to which British businesses and British courts have to conform. For instance, Pittards has to comply with EU health and safety regulations. Its workers have rights under European law on issues such as **equal opportunities** (☞ unit 62). Its production is affected by EU directives on the environment and pollution, such as the environmental management standard BS EN ISO 14001. It also has to comply with product standards and **copyright** and **patent** (☞ unit 50) laws of the EU.

Barriers to trade

Barriers to trade between European

countries still exist though.

Language could be a problem. Selling to Germany means that Pittards has to communicate in German with its customers or its customers have to speak English. Language barriers are coming down as more people speak two languages. For instance, Pittards employs language graduates as sales executives. However, continental companies are more likely to have English speakers than British companies to have, say, French or German speakers. This can put British companies at a competitive disadvantage.

There are **different market characteristics**. Pittards sells a product which has appeal in many countries. However, china manufacturers like Wedgewood find it hard to sell into many European countries because they have their own long established and well known china manufacturers.

Distance may also be a problem. Communicating with businesses in different time zones can be difficult. Transporting goods can also be very costly for low value high bulk products like cement or bricks. Pittards, however, has a high value product and therefore it can be competitive throughout Europe.

Source: adapted in part from Pittards plc, *Annual Report and Accounts*, 1996.

PORTMEIRION POTTERIES

Summary Case Study

Portmeirion Potteries is based in Stoke-on-Trent. It is a manufacturer of tableware, giftware and cookware. For instance, it sells plates, cups, bowls, vases and dishes. It has an international reputation for the quality of its designs. Some of its oven-to-table and kitchen accessory pieces are decorated with patterns taken from Victorian cookbooks.

Over half its sales are to the United States with most of the rest being sold in the UK market. Sales to Europe are growing. The company faces stiff competition, though, in Europe from long established companies which have well known brand names in their markets. In the United States market, British companies like Portmeirion have a reputation for quality, but face similar competition from US manufacturers.

Source: adapted from Portmeirion Potteries (Holdings) PLC, *Report and Accounts*.

1 Explain why Portmeirion is: (a) a manufacturing company; and (b) an exporter.
2 Portmeirion exports products both to the USA and to France. (a) In what ways might exporting to France be easier for the company than exporting to the United States? (b) In what ways is it easier for the company to export to the USA than to France?
3 To what extent would the UK joining the European Monetary Union help Portmeirion?

Checklist ✓

1 Explain THREE reasons why Pittards found it easier to export to Europe after 1973.
2 Why was Britain joining the EU both a threat and an opportunity for UK businesses?
3 (a) Why might you find several languages on the wrapping of a food packet? (b) Why do you think businesses don't simply use different wrapping for each country?
4 How would European Monetary Union help a business like Pittards?

BUSINESS ETHICS

Making decisions

Businesses have to make decisions which involve issues about what is right and what is wrong. These ethical decisions occur, for instance, when a business decides what to produce, who to sell to, who to buy from, how to treat its workers, how to care for the local environment and whether or not to get involved in the local community. The law provides some guidelines on ethical issues, but many believe that businesses should often do more than the legal minimum.

The Body Shop was started by Anita Roddick in 1976 from a shop in Brighton. In August 1997 there were 1 530 shops in 47 countries. By 1997 the company had worldwide retail sales of £622.5 million. The Body Shop prides itself on its ethical approach to business. Unlike many other businesses, making a profit is only one of the company's goals.

The ethical business

Businesses, like people, have to make ETHICAL choices. They have to decide whether an activity is morally correct or not. The Body Shop is a business that has taken a very strong ethical position on key business issues.

Customers Businesses must decide what products it is 'right' for it to sell. The Body Shop won't sell products which contain ingredients which have been tested on animals. Businesses must also decide what they are prepared to say about their products. The Body Shop refuses to make exaggerated claims about its cosmetics. Unlike other cosmetic companies, it doesn't promise to make skin younger. Finally, businesses have to consider who they will sell to. The Co-operative Bank, for instance, won't accept as a customer any business which sells guns.

Suppliers Businesses buy supplies from other businesses around the world. In the UK, businesses have tended not to think they have any responsibility for where they get supplies. The important thing is that the supplier provides high quality goods, at the best price and on time. Some argue, however, that businesses should think about who they buy from. They shouldn't buy, for instance, from businesses which exploit workers or damage the environment. The Body Shop screens all its manufacturers and suppliers. To ensure The Body Shop's values are not compromised by the conditions and working practices of these manufacturers and suppliers, they must agree to follow The Body Shop line on animal testing, environmental policy

The package tour industry

In 1997, the Monopolies and Mergers Commission (MMC) issued a report on the package tour industry. The MMC is responsible for investigating abuses of power by companies which enjoy large shares of their market. The package tour industry is dominated by a few large companies. Thomas Cook and Thomson, the two largest tour operators, for instance, sell four holidays in every ten.

The MMC found that customers were being pressurised into buying travel insurance. Typically, customers would be offered a discount on a holiday, but only on condition that they bought travel insurance at the same time. The travel insurance was usually more expensive than if it had been bought separately from a travel insurance company. So much of the discount on the holiday was lost because the customer had to pay higher insurance at the same time. Most customers didn't realise they were paying higher prices for the insurance because they didn't shop around. The MMC recommended that the government should ban travel agents from being allowed to link insurance with discounts.

Source: adapted from the *Financial Times*, 31 December 1997.

1 What is the MMC?
2 (a) Why do you think travel agents charged higher prices for travel insurance? (b) Would it have been better for customers if they had been allowed to shop around for their travel insurance? (c) Explain whether you think the MMC was right to recommend a ban on the link between insurance and discounts.

Anita Roddick in Ghana.

and human rights. The Body Shop Purchasing Rule states that it will not buy any ingredient tested on animals for cosmetic purposes since at least 31 December 1990. The Body Shop also has a Fair Trade department, which works towards building trading relationships with communities in need, especially in the developing world.

Competitors Businesses have to decide how far they can go in trying to win customers from their competitors. Is giving a bribe acceptable? Should businesses use private detectives to find out what other businesses are planning? Should they drive another business out of the market by pushing down their prices so low for a period of time that the other business loses all its customers?

Workers Businesses have to consider their workers. Are they only interested in reducing costs to a minimum? The Body Shop has a well developed policy towards its workers and the workers of the **franchisees** (☞ unit 14) who own and run the shops worldwide. It is committed to training the staff well and to giving them opportunities to work in the local community in company time.

The environment All businesses have an impact on the environment. Some, like coal mines or waste disposal companies, can damage the environment. Businesses have to decide whether to carry on producing despite this. The Body Shop makes it a policy to use recycled materials wherever possible. It offers a refill service for its liquid products so that bottles aren't needlessly thrown away, and can be returned to the shop for recycling.

The local community Many businesses have little or nothing to do with their local communities apart from providing jobs and perhaps selling goods. Some argue, however, that businesses should do more than this. The Body Shop, for instance, gets involved with local community projects. It is involved with education by taking pupils or students on work experience programmes.

Can businesses be ethical?

Some argue that businesses exist purely to make a profit. So long as an activity is legal, then the business has no further responsibilities.

Others, like The Body Shop, say that businesses have much wider obligations. Aiming always to gain the most profit can lead to businesses making unethical decisions. Some also say that doing what is right, and not just what is most profitable, is likely to lead to higher profits in the long run anyway. The Body Shop, for instance, has been very successful because everyone knows that it tries to do what is right. It also has very loyal and hard working staff because it treats them well. It can attract customers and new workers in the locality because it is involved with the local community.

Source: adapted from information provided by The Body Shop International plc.

key terms

Business ethics - ideas about what is morally correct or not, applied in a business situation.

SUMMARY CASE STUDY

PEPSI AND BURMA

In 1997, PepsiCo, the US manufacturer, announced that it would no longer be selling Pepsi-Cola in Burma. The country has a long history of human rights abuses. It is run by a military dictatorship which refuses to hold democratic elections. Opponents of the government are subject to arrest and torture.

PepsiCo is virtually the last large US company to pull out of Burma. For instance, Apple the computer group, Walt Disney and Kodak had already stopped selling products to Burma and buying supplies from Burmese businesses.

PepsiCo's decision is an extension of a 1996 decision when it announced that it would be selling its stake in the Burmese company which bottles and distributes Pepsi. Its 1997 decision goes further, with all supplies of Pepsi being cut off from May 31.

PepsiCo's decision was in part influenced by a boycott by US university students of products made by companies which had dealings with Burma. This included Pepsi as well as food produced by Kentucky Fried Chicken, Pizza Hut and Taco Bell, all businesses owned by PepsiCo. The boycott was successful enough, for instance, to force some Kentucky Fried Chicken and Pizza Hut outlets on university sites to close.

The only major US company left in Burma is Unocal, an oil company, which is building a pipeline to transport natural gas from the Adaman Sea to Thailand.

Source: adapted from the *Financial Times*, 28 January 1997.

1 What does PepsiCo produce?
2 Explain why the boycott of PepsiCo products was harming the company.
3 Discuss whether a company should be selling to or buying from a country with a record of human rights abuses. In your answer, discuss the advantages and disadvantages of trading to: (a) the owners of the company; (b) businesses and ordinary people in the country concerned; and (c) the government of the country.

Checklist ✓

1 Explain whether you think a business should make and sell: (a) products which have first been tested on animals; (b) toy guns; (c) cigarettes; (d) landmines.
2 Is the Body Shop right deliberately to attempt to buy supplies from the Third World?
3 Give THREE examples of unfair competitive practices.
4 Why might treating workers well benefit a business even though it might seem more costly?
5 Explain what responsibility a business might have to the local environment in which it operates.

SOLE PROPRIETORSHIPS

Making decisions

A person wanting to set up in business has to decide what legal form the business organisation should take. This will depend on many factors.

- How many people are going to own the business?
- Can the owner take the risk of having unlimited liability?
- What will be the tax position of the business?
- Does the owner want to be in complete control of the business?
- Does the owner want all the profits from the business?
- Does the owner want complete privacy in the affairs of the business?
- What will happen to the business in case of the owner's illness or death?

Serena Johnson found herself in a difficult position. She had just lost her highly paid job. She had two children to support as well as having to pay a large mortgage on an eight acre property that she had bought in Sussex. After moving to the new house, she had paid for a barn to be dismantled on a nearby farm. At first, she planned to put it back up again on her property as a garage. But, when she lost her job, she began selling off materials from the dismantled barn. A business idea was born.

Sole traders

Serena set up a SOLE PROPRIETORSHIP, a business which she alone owned. She became a SOLE TRADER or SOLE PROPRIETOR. Her business was buying old buildings, dismantling them and then selling off the bricks, timbers, chimneys, fire places and everything else that could be salvaged.

To set herself up properly in business, she needed money. She borrowed £25 000 from the bank. This paid for turning part of the 8 acre plot into a building yard. She bought a Land Rover and a trailer. She also needed money to buy buildings to demolish. In her first year, she sold £28 000 worth of materials and made a profit of £9 000. Any profits made by sole traders are kept by themselves.

One of the main disadvantages of being a sole trader is that the owner has UNLIMITED LIABILITY. This means that the owner has to pay for any losses made by the business. If Serena had made a £9 000 loss instead of a £9 000 profit, she would

have had to find that £9 000 from somewhere. She might have been forced to sell the Land Rover or perhaps even her house.

For a sole trader, there is no difference in law between the profits and debts of the business and the finances of the individual owning the business. Legally, they are one and the same.

The advantages of being a sole trader

As Figure 10.1 shows, many businesses in the UK are sole proprietorships. There must therefore be some important

Inwood

Brian Inwood is a furniture maker. He worked on his own as a sole proprietor, making high quality pieces like tables in oak. In the first few years of trading he did well. By showing at big exhibitions in the UK and the USA, he received a number of commissions. In his first year, he managed to make a £9 000 profit on sales of £30 000. His best year was his third when he sold £60 000 worth of furniture and made £25 000 in profit. However, orders began to dry up. The economy went into recession and people could no longer afford to buy expensive handcrafted furniture. Sales slumped and in his fifth year he made a loss of £10 000. He was forced to sell his stock of wood and move out of his rented premises. He was afraid that he would run up more debts and risk losing his house. So he got a job working for a furniture making company.

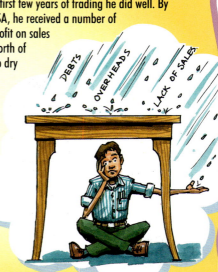

1. 'Brian Inwood is a sole proprietor.' What does this mean?
2. What did the business sell?
3. Who received the profit from the business in its first year?
4. Explain, using the idea of 'unlimited liability', why Brian Inwood closed his business.
5. Suggest TWO ways in which Brian Inwood might have saved his business from closing.

Woollen cot mattresses

Hanna Jacobs didn't want her newly born child to sleep on a foam mattress. She was scared of the research evidence linking foam mattresses with infant cot deaths. She had a friend who ran an organic farm and who suggested that she make a wool mattress from her sheep. The mattress was made. Then a friend of Hanna's asked her if she could make a wool mattress for her. From that point, a business was born.

Hanna had a lot of problems on the way. She had to find the money to buy the looms to spin the organic wool as well as rent premises. She had to work long hours to build up the business. However, she got a great deal of satisfaction making a product with which mothers felt safe. She enjoyed working with the two part time workers she took on. The finance side of the business was always a worry. But she had always made a profit and she felt she could cut costs very quickly if new orders ever failed to come through. She was proud of the fact that she was her own boss and enjoyed dealing with the problems that any business faces in day to day trading. What's more, the business was flexible enough to give her the time to bring up her children.

DTP

1 Hanna has been interviewed by a reporter from a local newspaper. The reporter is running a feature on the advantages of being a sole trader. Write a short article based on the facts in the case study. If possible, produce the article as it might appear in a newspaper using a desktop publishing package.

2 Hanna is thinking of expanding her product range by making other wool products, like cot mattresses for ordinary sized beds.
(a) What might be: (i) the advantages; and (ii) the disadvantages of this for her?
(b) Do you think she should do this and why?

---

advantages to setting up this type of business.

Easy to set up One important advantage is that it is easy to set up. A sole trader can set up in business immediately. There are few, if any, complicated forms to fill in or procedures needed to set up. However, Serena had to fill in an income tax return for the Inland Revenue, which collects income tax, recording the profits of the business. She had to register with Customs and Excise which is responsible for collecting Value Added Tax, a tax on the sale of products. She also had to get the approval of her local council to change part of her land into a building yard.

Easy to run Any business is difficult to operate successfully, but a sole proprietorship is easier to run than other types of business. The owner is in sole charge and doesn't need to get the agreement of other owners to make changes to the business. Lawyers and accountants don't have to be employed. To start with, for instance, Serena kept her own books.

Tax advantages A sole trader is taxed in a different way to other types of business. National Insurance contributions (NICs) are a tax on a worker's earning. Serena saved herself hundreds of pounds in NICs on her profit of £9 000 by being a sole trader instead of setting up a **limited company** (☞ unit 12) and having to become an employee of the company.

Control The owner is in sole charge and so can make whatever changes are necessary as the business operates over time. Serena didn't have to call **shareholders'** meetings (☞ unit 12), or get the agreement of other directors or managers to make changes.

Capital A business nearly always needs some capital to start trading. Serena needed to convert part of her land, buy a Land Rover and get stocks of building materials to sell. However, the amount of money needed to set up a sole proprietorship is often small and can be just a few hundred pounds.

Profits All the profits of the business are kept by the sole trader. They don't have to be split up amongst several or perhaps even millions of other owners or shareholders. This means that there is a link between effort, success and money earned. The harder a sole trader works, and the more successful the business, the more can be earned.

Privacy Only the Inland Revenue and Customs and Excise need to know how well a sole trader is doing financially. The business doesn't have to publish any information which could be seen by the general public or other businesses.

Labour relations The larger a work organisation, the bigger the scope for misunderstanding and problems. Many sole traders work on their own. Serena didn't employ anyone to start with. Other sole traders employ one or perhaps several workers. However, because the team of workers is so small, relations between the workers and the employer are likely to be good.

Flexibility Many sole traders have some choice about when they work. Serena, for instance, can organise

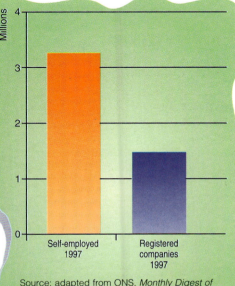

Source: adapted from ONS, *Monthly Digest of Statistics; Business Monitor PA P003.*

Figure 10.1 *Most self-employed people are sole traders, the rest being partners in partnerships. The number of self-employed people outweighs the number of companies in the UK.*

Sole traders usually work long hours, especially when they first set up in business.

to be a purchaser, a sales person, a truck driver, a building labourer, an accountant, a receptionist and a secretary amongst other jobs. A larger business, however, could afford to buy in specialist workers. A supermarket employs shelf stackers, accountants and lawyers. So, Serena might find that her costs are higher than those of larger businesses because she can't gain the advantages of the **division of labour** (☞ unit 4).

Limited economies of scale

Serena hires lorries by the day. A large construction company would own its lorries because this is cheaper if they are kept in use all the time. But Serena only needs lorries some of the time. This is an example of **economies of scale** (☞ unit 18). In general, the larger the business, the more scope there is to reduce costs per unit produced. Sole proprietorships are nearly always small businesses. So they often don't have the cost advantages that large businesses enjoy because of large scale production.

her working week so that she can have a few hours off to go to the dentist. She could also take a whole day off to visit her elderly mother who lives a couple of hours drive away.

The disadvantages of being a sole trader

Being a sole trader also has disadvantages.

Unlimited liability Serena could have lost the £25 000 she put into the business at the start. If things had gone badly wrong, she could have lost her house and any other high value items she owned.

Lack of continuity Because Serena **is** the business, there is no guarantee that it will survive when she no longer wants to carry on running it. She might be able to sell it to someone else. She might, for instance, pass the business on to her children, especially if they had worked and help run the business. However, the business could simply stop trading and all its **assets** (everything of value that could be sold, ☞ unit 26) sold off.

Illness If Serena were to have a long illness, she might be forced to shut the business. Her income and profits would then stop.

Long hours Many sole traders work very long hours to keep their business afloat. Serena works six days a week, ten hours a day. When there was a slump in the construction business in the early

1990s, she considered opening on Sunday as well to increase trade, but decided against it. She didn't want to work a 70 hour week.

Difficulty of raising capital Serena was lucky to own a house against which she could borrow her initial £25 000 to put into the business. Some people have the money already to start up a business. They might have some redundancy money, for instance. Most small businesses, though, find it difficult to get suitable start up capital. They also find it difficult to get money to expand their business (☞ units 30-32).

Limited specialisation Serena has

Shona Mackie wants to set up in business. She has asked a friend who knows about business for advice. One of the things her friend talked about was tax and fees for setting up and running a company rather than being a sole trader. This advice is summarised in Table 10.1. Shona hopes to earn £10 000 from the business in the first year.

1 Look at Table 10.1. Would she be better off from a tax and fee viewpoint becoming a sole trader or setting up a limited company?

Table 10.1

	Sole trader	Limited company
Legal fee to set up in business	None	At least £100
Annual accounts fees for audit	None	At least £700
Income tax	Payable twice yearly	Payable monthly, immediately after the money has been earned
National Insurance contributions	Class 2 contributions £319.80 per year **plus** Class 4 contributions 6% on income earned between £7 010 and £24 180 a year (i.e. £2 990 for Shona)	Class 1 contributions Employees' contributions of 2% on earnings up to £62 a week and 10% on earnings between £62 and £465 a week **plus** Employers' contributions 7% of income up to £10 919

The difficulties of boatbuilding

Kim Chang trained as a boatbuilder three years ago. Before that, he had spent four years as a boat repairer in Bristol. However, his dream had always been to make traditional small wooden boats.

When he completed his training, he spent £1 000 on a single mahogany log and started his boat building business. This one log built his first boat. However, despite it being much admired at boat exhibitions, he couldn't sell it at the asking price of £10 000. He built a second boat in marine ply, but this too failed to sell despite again getting a lot of positive comments in the boat press and at exhibitions. His start up capital was now almost exhausted as a result of the cost of going to exhibitions and the materials bought. But for the income that his wife was bringing in from her job, he couldn't have survived.

In the end, he was forced to take a £12 000 contract to repair a motor cruiser. This was not the work he wanted to be doing. But at least it was in the boat trade and it was earning him money. He was working long hours to complete the contract on time. He was very afraid of what would happen if he fell ill because there was a penalty clause on the contract which fined him if he didn't complete on time.

The good news came one month before the end of the repair contract deadline. He managed to sell his second marine ply boat for the asking price, £4 000.

1 What does Kim Chang's business produce?
2 Kim Chang is seriously considering giving up the business and taking a job. Suggest reasons why.
3 What advice would you give to Kim to persuade him that he should carry on with the business?
4 Why might a larger boat builder be able to make boats more cheaply than Kim?

key terms

Sole proprietorship - a business owned by a single person who has unlimited liability.
Sole trader or sole proprietor - the owner of a sole proprietorship business.
Unlimited liability - a legal obligation on the owners of a business to settle (pay off) all debts of the business. In law, there is no distinction between the assets and debts of the business and the personal assets and debts of the owner.

Checklist ✓

1 Who owns a sole proprietorship?
2 Who keeps the profits of a sole proprietorship?
3 'Sui Chan had unlimited liability.' What does this mean?
4 What tax advantages do sole traders have?
5 Why are sole proprietorships easy to: (a) set up; and (b) run?
6 What happens to a sole proprietorship if the owner falls ill or dies?
7 Why do sole traders often find it difficult to raise the money to start a business?
8 'A lack of specialisation can often hinder the success of a sole proprietorship.' Explain why.

SUMMARY CASE STUDY

SMALL BUILDINGS

Chris Davenport was made redundant from his job eight years ago. He used his redundancy payment to set up in business making wooden outdoor buildings. These are more substantial than just garden sheds. They are properly insulated, permanent structures which can be used for anything from an office to a classroom. They are built to be an attractive feature in, say, a garden. Because they are well designed, using high quality materials, they are more expensive than a typical prefabricated temporary building.

Chris has built up his business over time. In the first year, he sold £53 000 worth of products. Today, sales turnover is averaging £300 000 per year. This has not been without its problems. Three years ago, with the economy in recession, orders seemed to dry up and the business made a loss for the year of £20 000. Without a sympathetic bank manager, who increased the overdraft by £15 000, the business would have been in serious trouble.

However, Chris has never thought of giving up. He enjoys running his own business and being his own boss, even if he does have to work long hours. His 6 workers are highly valued. Without them, he would not be able to deliver the quality product that he guarantees to deliver to customers.

One problem facing the business is Chris's age. As he gets older he knows that he might have a period of long illness or even die. None of his family work in the business.

1 (a) Explain FOUR advantages for Chris of being a sole trader. Use evidence from the passage to support your answer.
(b) Explain FOUR disadvantages for Chris of being a sole trader, again supporting your answer with evidence from the passage.
2 During the recession, Chris considered cutting his prices by reducing the quality of his structures. Discuss whether this would have been a good strategy for Chris to adopt.
3 (a) Suggest how Chris can deal with the potential problem for his business of illness or even death.
   (b) Are there any potential disadvantages to your suggestions?

PARTNERSHIPS

Making decisions

A person setting up a business has to decide whether to run it alone or with others. This to some extent will depend upon:

- how much control they want over the business;
- whether they are prepared to share the profits;
- whether they can get the necessary money to start up the business.

The person also needs to decide whether he or she is prepared to accept the risk of unlimited liability.

Anne O'Henry and Marie Dixon are two sisters who run a family partnership called Tiny Tots in Newcastle. They have a shop where they sell toys and children's clothes. They also have a mail order business. The business sells high quality products. Many of the toys, for instance, are made of wood rather than plastic. They employ two part time workers and take on temporary workers in the important sales period in the run up to Christmas. A year ago, Ruth, Anne's daughter, joined the business.

Partnerships

The law says that in an ORDINARY PARTNERSHIP there can be between 2 and 20 partners. PARTNERS are the joint owners of a business. The business has three partners - Anne and Marie, and Anne's daughter, Ruth. The partners have unlimited liability (☞ unit 10). This means that they have to pay any debts of the business, even if they have to sell their house and other valuable personal possessions. In a partnership, all the partners are liable for the debts even if the debts have been caused by another partner. For instance, if Anne ordered a large amount of new stock on credit, all the partners would be liable to pay off the debt even if she hadn't got their permission to order the stock.

Deed of partnership

The three partners have been very sensible. They have gone to a solicitor and drawn up a DEED OF PARTNERSHIP. This is a legal contract which sets out:

- who are the partners;
- how much money (or capital) each partner has put into the partnership;
- how profits should be shared out;
- how many votes each partner has in any partnership meeting;
- what happens if any of the partners want to

withdraw from the business or if new partners are brought in.

If there is no deed of partnership, the law says that every partner is equal. Each partner then gets an equal share of the profit and has the same voting power as any other partner. In the deed of partnership for Tiny

James Appleton and David Harris became involved in the oyster business in the 1980s. James had inherited some land by the sea and decided to grow oysters. David provided some financial capital and ran the sales side of the business. The two partners knew that the first few years would see almost no income coming into the business as their oyster park became established. However, James began to build up a trade in shellfish, buying from local fishermen and selling on to restaurants.

In 1989, they borrowed money from the bank and bought some buildings to convert into a restaurant specialising in sea food. The move was almost disastrous for the business because the economy went into a deep recession between 1990 and 1992. Sales in the restaurant were only 50 per cent of what had been forecast. Between 1990 and 1992, the restaurant lost £50 000. Fortunately, the oyster side of the business was beginning to take off. Even so, the partners lost money from the business in those years.

Since then, though, the business had become very successful. By 1998, a second restaurant had been opened, sales of oysters exceeded £600 000 and the partners were looking for further opportunities for expansion.

1 In 1998, what products and services did the partnership make?
2 Who owns the business?
3 (a) Explain why the business had difficulties between 1990 and 1992.
    (b) The business lost money during this period. How were the two partners affected financially by this?
4 Discuss ways in which the business could now expand profitably.

Sandwiches with a difference

Mad Max runs a sandwich bar in Birmingham but it's a sandwich bar with a difference. Where else would you find a 'Mad Max Madras Express' - a roast beef sandwich, topped with a cabbage and peppers salad, and dressed with curried mayonnaise?   His sandwich bar has been a roaring success, offering a number of different types of exotic and delicious tasting sandwiches and other snacks. In two years, he has doubled sales.

Now he wants to expand by opening another sandwich bar. He hasn't got the money to buy or even rent a second bar, and so he has found another person who is willing to enter a partnership with him. Mad Max would help the new person set up the new sandwich bar and provide all the recipes.

1   What would be the advantages to Mad Max of getting a partner?

2   Mad Max has approached you as a solicitor to draw up a deed of partnership.

(a) What are the essential points which must be covered in the deed of partnership?

(b) What terms would you advise Mad Max to offer his new partner in the partnership agreement? (For instance, how should the profits be distributed? What should happen if Mad Max finds that the new partner is not offering a good service at the new sandwich bar?)

Wordprocessing

(c) Draw up a simple partnership agreement. You could use a wordprocessing package to present the agreement.

Partnerships can have advantages over sole proprietorships. Forming a partnership is one way for a sole proprietor to get extra capital for the business. Two people can normally raise more money to start or expand a business than one.

Getting extra partners willing to invest money in the business is a way of financing expansion. Equally, new partners might be able to add expertise to the business. One reason why Anne and Marie were keen for Ruth to join the business was that Ruth had studied Economics at university and was very clear in her thinking about business decisions.

Some partnerships have **sleeping partners**. These are partners who, whilst owning part of the business, play little or no part in its day to day working. When joining the partnership, these partners provide vitally needed money to help set up or expand the business.

The advantages of a partnership

Partnerships have many of the advantages of a sole proprietorship. They are very easy to set up. They don't have to employ solicitors or accountants to help run the business. (In practice, most do use these professional services because their businesses are larger and more complicated than sole proprietorships.) Profits belong to the partners, who usually work in the business. The affairs of the partnership can be kept private because only the tax authorities need to be told how much the partners are earning and what is the profit of the business. Partnerships tend to be small, so that there are often good relations between partners and any workers employed.

The disadvantages of a partnership

Partnerships mean that people have to work together. However, sometimes people disagree. When partners in a business disagree, it can be very bad for the business.

For instance, Anne and Marie want to encourage Ruth to be involved. This is the reason why they have given her a share of the profits of the business. Equally, they are afraid that she might lose interest in working for it and want to pull out. Hence, the deed of partnership says that Ruth isn't entitled to anything in the business if she pulls out.

Also, Anne and Marie want to keep control of the business in

Tots, the two sisters, Anne and Marie put up all the starting capital for the business. They have an equal say in how the business should be run. Ruth has no vote in the business. However, she is entitled to receive 20 per cent of the profits. Anne and Marie each receive 40 per cent of the profits. If Ruth pulls out of the business, she loses the right to receive any profit. Anne and Marie both have to give consent for either to sell their part of the business or bring in a new partner.

An extract from the deed of partnership of Tiny Tots.

IS DEED OF PARTNERSHIP is made, the 1st day of
nuary – 1998

TWEEN

ANNE O'HENRY of 125 Gateshead Road, Newcastle (Mrs O'Henry); and

MARIE DIXON of 10 School Lane, Newcastle (Ms Dixon); and

RUTH O'HENRY of 2 Wayland Drive, Bedlington (Ms O'Henry); and

HEREAS

Mrs O'Henry, Ms Dixon and Ms O'Henry have agreed to enter o partnership together to practise as a children's toy d clothing retailer and mail order service.

case Ruth wants to organise the business in a different way. They have arranged for Ruth not to have any voting rights in the business.

In the long term, though, they hope that Ruth will take charge of the day to day running of the business. They can see a time when they are retired and have become sleeping partners. The deed of partnership would then be rewritten giving Ruth full voting rights and a greater share of the business. Eventually, they hope Ruth will inherit the business and perhaps some of her children will become partners. This will solve a problem that many small businesses face: who will carry on the business when those who set it up retire?

Anne and Marie have sorted out some of the problems that might arise in the future through the deed of partnership. However, some partnerships don't have a deed of partnership. This can lead to great problems if they break up. Even with a deed of partnership, there can be problems if there are disagreements amongst the partners. For instance, what would happen if Anne and Marie fell out over how to develop the business? What would then happen to the business?

Partnerships in business

Most partnerships are relatively small businesses. Shops, farms and catering businesses account for half of all partnerships in the UK. Many of these partnerships, particularly in farming, are family partnerships like Tiny Tots.

In some professions, like medicine, accountancy, the law and architecture, it is standard for businesses to be partnerships. Doctors, dentists, accountants and other professionals like to keep their business affairs private. However, they need to offer the range of services their customers expect.

waring collins *partnership*

Partnerships are often found in professions such as design businesses, accountants and estate agents.

You need to do this exercise as a group with 2 or 3 others. You are about to set up a business in your school or college. You may be going to run a real mini-company and already have decided on a business idea. If you haven't, assume that you are going to sell stationery - pens, pencils, paper, note pads, plastic wallets, etc.

If you are running a real mini-company, you need to make the decisions below. If this is a role play, share out the roles shown with the photographs between the members of your group.

You have decided to organise your business as a partnership. Draw up a deed of partnership. As a group, you need to decide on matters such as:
- who will own the business?
- who will get profits from the business and in what proportion?
- who is going to put up the capital (the money) to buy stock for the business to sell and how much capital is needed?
- what happens if one of the group doesn't do anything in helping to run the business?

Remember, these are just some of the issues you need to take into account when drawing up your deed of partnership.

Faisal - hardworking, a natural leader, has two part time jobs, willing to put £20 into the business to start it off.

Susan - meticulous, likes everything organised properly, always on time and well prepared, doesn't like people who don't pull their weight, has £300 in the building society.

Claire - not very reliable, gets excited about work to start with, often stands up for 'her rights', never had a job, thinks her mum will put some money in.

Wayne - not very interested, only in the group because he's got to be, sometimes doesn't get on with others in the group.

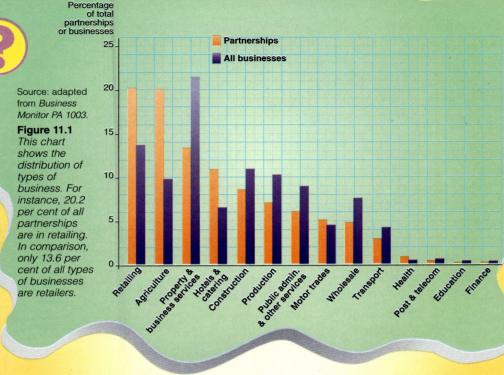

Percentage of total partnerships or businesses

■ Partnerships
■ All businesses

Source: adapted from Business Monitor PA 1003.

Figure 11.1
This chart shows the distribution of types of business. For instance, 20.2 per cent of all partnerships are in retailing. In comparison, only 13.6 per cent of all types of businesses are retailers.

(Chart categories: Retailing, Agriculture, Property & business services, Hotels & catering, Construction, Production, Public admin. & other services, Motor trades, Wholesale, Transport, Health, Post & telecom, Education, Finance)

key terms

Deed of partnership - the legal contract which governs how a partnership will be owned and organised.
Ordinary partnership - a business organisation which has between 2 and 20 owners, all of whom have unlimited liability.
Partners - the owners of a partnership.

Checklist ✓

1 Who owns a partnership?
2 'Partners have unlimited liability.' What does this mean?
3 If there is no partnership agreement, how are profits distributed in a partnership?
4 What might be written in a deed of partnership?
5 What advantages do partnerships share with sole proprietorships?
6 Why might a partnership be a better form of organisation than a sole proprietorship?
7 What are the disadvantages of partnerships?
8 Why is disagreement between partners a problem in a partnership?

Figure 11.1 shows what proportion of partnerships are found in different types of industry. It also compares this with the proportion of all types of business (sole proprietorships, partnerships, limited companies, etc.) by industry.
1 11 per cent (11 out of every 100) of all partnerships are in what industry?
2 In which industry are partnerships most common?
3 (a) What percentage of partnerships is found in the construction industry? (b) How does this compare with figures for all types of business?
4 (a) Are partnerships more common or less common than the average of all types of business in retailing? (b) Suggest reasons why this is so.
5 (a) Are partnerships more common or less common than the average of all types of business in production (mainly manufacturing)? (b) Suggest reasons why this is so.

JUGGLING WITH FINANCE

SUMMARY CASE STUDY

Sophie and Bill Waites run a juggling business. For ten years, they ran juggling parties for children where they would do some funny sketches and tell some jokes with juggling as part of the act. This was done in their spare time whilst both had full time jobs in a manufacturing company.

Then they decided to put the skills they had acquired in their full time jobs to set up a business manufacturing juggling equipment. They knew that they would need help on the marketing side to sell the equipment to wholesalers who in turn would sell it to shops. A friend introduced them to Pat Irvine, a marketing consultant. Impressed with the proposal, he agreed to come in as a partner. Sophie, Bill and Pat each put up £10 000 start up capital for the partnership.

The business was a success. In its first year, it sold £80 000 worth of equipment and a £20 000 profit was made. But Sophie and Bill found Pat almost impossible to work with. Although he had been successful in gaining orders, he didn't seem to be putting very much time into the business. They felt that he was now losing interest and allowing other business opportunities to occupy his energies. They were afraid that orders would start to fall off.

Pat was very angry when they confronted him with this. He said that he was mainly responsible for the success of the business. When Sophie and Bill offered to buy him out, he said the partnership was now worth £100 000. Unfortunately, no deed of partnership had been drawn up.

1 What is a partnership?
2 What skills did each partner bring to the business?
3 Suggest why Sophie and Bill now face problems because there is no deed of partnership for the business.
4 Discuss: (a) why the partnership might have a value of £100 000; and (b) what problems this would give Sophie and Bill.

unit 12

LIMITED COMPANIES

The Original Propshop is a company which designs and builds props, exhibition stands and conference sets. These can be anything from props for an Arabian evening in a hotel, to marbling display areas in Selfridges department store in London's Oxford Street, to floats for the Lord Mayor's Show in London. Sales turnover in 1997 was over £2.5 million. Approximately one third of this was sales of props to Mothercare stores, part of the Storehouse group.

Limited liability

The Original Propshop is a **limited company**. It is owned by the two people who founded the business, Christopher Dann and Martin Blake. The owners of a company are called the SHAREHOLDERS. They have LIMITED LIABILITY.

Limited liability is important for Chris and Martin, the shareholders, if the company goes out of business leaving debts (i.e. the company becomes **insolvent**). They will only lose the money that they have put into the company (the value of their shares). But they won't be forced to sell off their own personal possessions, like a house, to pay off the company's debts. This is because a limited company has a separate identity in law from its shareholders. To show that it has a separate legal identity, a limited liability business is normally called a COMPANY.

The Original Propshop has made a healthy profit in recent years. However, this doesn't take away the risk of a loss. With sales turnover of over £2.5 million, the company could make a loss in any one year in future. Owners of a business prefer to have limited liability if it has large debts.

The Registrar General

The Registrar General (or Registrar of Companies) keeps records on all UK limited companies. Two documents have to be sent to the Registrar of Companies to set up a limited company.

- The MEMORANDUM OF ASSOCIATION gives details

Mining problems

The Strongfellow Mining Company Ltd was founded four years ago by five miners made redundant from a local coal pit. The mine they bought with their redundancy money for £100 000 was an old stone mine, producing high quality stone which sold at a premium price. The mine was in a reasonable state of repair. During the first year, they were able to run it without having to invest in any new equipment. Having paid themselves £12 000 each in wages, the mine made a small profit of £8 000 in that year.

Encouraged by this, they decided that the company could be more profitable if it could sell another type of stone. They found a disused sandstone quarry about ten miles away. The owners of the quarry didn't want to sell but were prepared to accept a mixture of rent for the site and a royalty on sales. This suited Strongfellow Mining because they then wouldn't have to find the capital to buy the site.

However, it took 18 months to get planning permission. Buying equipment cost a lot more than expected and the quarry proved more difficult to work than planned. The quarry wasn't fully operational even one year after opening. The time and effort put into the quarry meant that output of stone from the mine fell sharply. So sales revenue for the company went down just when they needed more cash to repay the rent and overdraft on their loan. Four years after they first set up, the company was forced into liquidation (i.e. it was forced out of business). It owed £150 000 to the bank and to a variety of suppliers. After sale of assets, £50 000 was still owing.

1 What does it mean to say that The Strongfellow Mining Company was a 'limited company'?
2 Why did the company get into financial difficulties?
3 (a) How much did the company owe to its bank and suppliers when it went into liquidation?
   (b) Suggest what assets of the company could be sold to pay its debts.
4 What did the five shareholders lose because the company went into liquidation?
5 Who gained and who lost out because The Strongfellow Mining Company was a limited liability rather than an unlimited liability business?

TECHEX LIMITED

SCOTT LIMITED

about the names of the company, the address of its registered office, a statement that the shareholders will have limited liability, the type and amount of share capital and a description of the business activities of the company (in the Original Propshop's case, the provision of props).

- The ARTICLES OF ASSOCIATION give details about the voting rights of the

You have decided with a friend to set up a company. You may already have a business idea. If you don't have an idea, assume that you have decided to set up a company selling costume jewellery in your school or college.

1 Draw up a Memorandum of Association for the company as follows.

The Companies Act 1985

Company Limited by Shares

Memorandum of Association of _____ (name of your company)

The Company's name is _____.

The Company's registered office is _____ (unless you have decided otherwise, put the home address of one of the shareholders).

The Company's objectives are _____ (description of your trading activity).

The liability of the Members is limited.

The Share Capital of the Company is £ _____ (figure for your starting share capital) divided into _____ shares of £1 each.

2 Now draw up the Articles of Association. Use the following heading.

The Companies Act 1985

Company Limited by Shares

Articles of Association of _____ (name of your company)

Write one sentence about each of the following under your heading: (a) which of the shareholders has a vote and how many votes each shareholder has; (b) what proportion of the profit will go to each shareholder; (c) the duties of the company directors (e.g. they have the right to authorise the company to borrow money); (d) who will act as chairperson for the AGM and where it will be held.

shareholders, how the profits will be distributed, what are the duties of the directors of the company and what procedures will be followed at the annual general meeting (the AGM). The Registrar of Companies has to issue a **certificate of incorporation** before a company can start trading, i.e. start up in business. Every year, a limited company has to send audited accounts and various other documents to the Registrar of Companies at Companies House. These can be seen by anyone who asks to see them. The affairs of the business, therefore, can't be kept private like a sole proprietorship or a partnership. Anybody can know what the sales of the company were and what profit was made according to the last set of accounts sent to Companies House.

Ltd and plc

There are two types of limited company - PRIVATE LIMITED COMPANIES and PUBLIC LIMITED COMPANIES. Private limited companies add Ltd after their names as in The Original Propshop Ltd. Public limited companies add plc after their name as in Storehouse plc.

Differences between private and public limited companies

There are important differences between private limited companies and public limited companies.

Sales of shares The shares of a plc must be tradable on a stock

exchange. Storehouse plc, for example, is **listed** on the London Stock Exchange. New smaller plcs in the UK tend to get a listing on AIM (the Alternative Investment Market). A listing means that the stock exchange is prepared to allow the shares of the company to be bought and sold through the stock exchange. There is no open market for the shares of private companies like The Original Propshop. This might be a problem for them if they want to raise a large amount of finance ( unit 30).

Share capital A plc by law must have at least £50 000 in share capital to start up. A private company can start up with just £2 in share capital. In practice, new plcs today have to have a market value of millions of pounds in order to get a listing on a stock exchange.

Size and number of shareholders The number of shareholders is likely to be far greater in a plc than in a private limited company. The Original Propshop has just two shareholders. In 1997 Storehouse had 40 020 shareholders. Plcs tend to have more shareholders because they are bigger companies. There is no open market for shares in private limited companies. Anybody wanting to sell shares in a private limited company has to have the permission of the majority of shareholders. This can make it difficult to sell shares to people outside the business. Anyway, the major shareholders in a private

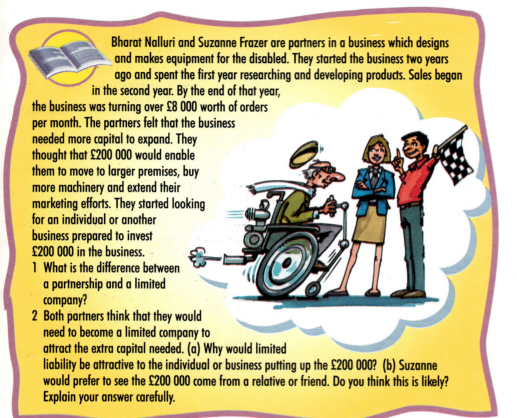

Bharat Nalluri and Suzanne Frazer are partners in a business which designs and makes equipment for the disabled. They started the business two years ago and spent the first year researching and developing products. Sales began in the second year. By the end of that year, the business was turning over £8 000 worth of orders per month. The partners felt that the business needed more capital to expand. They thought that £200 000 would enable them to move to larger premises, buy more machinery and extend their marketing efforts. They started looking for an individual or another business prepared to invest £200 000 in the business.

1 What is the difference between a partnership and a limited company?

2 Both partners think that they would need to become a limited company to attract the extra capital needed. (a) Why would limited liability be attractive to the individual or business putting up the £200 000? (b) Suzanne would prefer to see the £200 000 come from a relative or friend. Do you think this is likely? Explain your answer carefully.

limited company are likely to work in the business and wouldn't want to sell. Chris and Martin, for instance, are unlikely to want to sell shares in The Original Propshop to outsiders.

Control In theory, shareholders control a limited company. Each year, at the annual general meeting, they elect DIRECTORS to represent the interests of shareholders. The board of directors will appoint MANAGERS to run the company as shown in Figure 12.1. The most important manager, the managing director, is also automatically a director of the company as well. Some of the other managers will also sit on the board of directors.

The shareholders, the directors and the managers in a private limited company are often the same people because the company is small. However, in a plc, the directors and the managers are likely to own only a small fraction of the shares of the company. This means that the people who are responsible for the day to day running of the company

(the managers), and the long term direction of the company (the directors), are different from the shareholders.

In theory, the directors are elected by the shareholders at the annual general meeting of company to defend the shareholders' interests. In practice, what the shareholders want and what the directors want and what the managers decide to do might be different. This is known as the **divorce of ownership and control**. This might affect the **goals** of the company (☞ unit 17).

The advantages and disadvantages of becoming a limited company

The great advantage of being a limited company is that it is easier to attract extra shareholders to invest money in the business because of limited liability. This means that the business can grow and become large.

One disadvantage is that information about the company

has to be given to the general public. More information has to be given if the company is a plc than if it is a private limited company. Giving information is also costly. It costs at least £700 a year to prepare a report and accounts for a private limited company. The minimum cost for a plc is over £100 000. The published report and accounts of a plc alone costs tens of thousands of pounds to prepare, print and distribute.

Another disadvantage of being a plc is the cost of complying with stock exchange rules. The London Stock Exchange imposes a variety of rules on companies seeking a listing. These are meant to protect future shareholders by giving them more information about the business. The advantage of getting a listing on the Alternative Investment Market (AIM) is that regulations are less strict and so it is cheaper for a company to get a listing. On the other hand, the shares are seen as higher risk and it might be more difficult to raise money through new share issues.

It is also sometimes claimed that shareholders in a plc are only interested in making short term profits. They are not interested in taking the long term view. So the company is discouraged from investing money in projects which will be profitable in the long term but not in the short term.

Source: adapted from information provided by The Original Propshop.

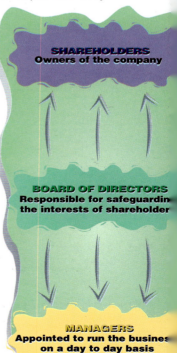

SHAREHOLDERS
Owners of the company

BOARD OF DIRECTORS
Responsible for safeguarding the interests of shareholders

MANAGERS
Appointed to run the business on a day to day basis

Figure 12.1 *Control of a limited company.*

Table 12.1 gives details about the share prices of retailers which are public limited companies.

On the 27 October 1997, what was the price in pounds and pence of one share of:
(a) Dixons; (b) Harvey Nichols;
(c) Storehouse?

What had been the highest price that each of the shares in question 1 reached in 1997?

The market capitalisation of the company shows how much the company is worth according to its share price. What was the total value in millions of pounds on 27 October 1997 of the following: (a) Allied Carpets; (b) Body Shop; (c) Marks & Spencer.

The number of shares issued times the share price is equal to the market capitalisation of a company. Use a calculator to find out how many shares there were in October 1997 in: (a) Etam; (b) Laura Ashley; (c) MFI Furniture; (d) Marks & Spencer.

Table 12.1 *Share prices of companies in general retailing, 27 October 1997.*

	TODAY'S PRICE pence	1997 PRICE HIGH pence	1997 PRICE LOW pence	MARKET CAPITALISATION £m
Allied Carpets	225.5	320	200.5	203.9
Ashley (Laura)	52.5	208	49	125.3
Body Shop	167.5	224.5	148.5	324.8
Dixons	690	715	462	2 946
Etam	131.5	160.5	102.5	86.5
Harvey Nichols	268.5	353.5	227.5	147.7
Marks & Spencer	603	672.5	458.5	17 197
MFI Furniture	121	201.5	121	719.6
Storehouse	229	305.5	184	966.2

Source: adapted from the *Financial Times*, 28 October 1997.

SUMMARY CASE STUDY

GREENALLS PLC

The Greenalls Group is a leading retailer of food, drink, accommodation and leisure. It owns pubs, leisure venues, quality hotels and specialist off-licences, and manufactures white spirits including gin and vodka. Look at Table 12.2.

1 How many shareholders did the company have?
2 How many shareholders owned:
   (a) between 1 and 1 000 shares;
   (b) more than 1 000 shares?
3 How many shares in total did:
   (a) small shareholders owning 1-1 000 shares hold; (b) large shareholders each owning more than 500 000 shares hold?
4 'Although Greenalls is owned by over 20 000 shareholders, it is mainly owned by a fraction of that number.' Do you agree with this statement? Give evidence from the table.
5 The directors of the company own nearly 50 million shares. Three of these directors are members of the family which founded Greenalls Group. These three directors own 49.9 million of these 50 million shares.
(a) What proportion of the total number of shares in the company is owned by the directors? (b) To what extent do you think there might be a 'divorce of ownership from control' in this company?

Table 12.2 *Greenalls plc - number of shareholders at 27 September 1996.*

Number of shares owned	Number of shareholders	% of shareholders	Number of shares (millions)	% of shares
1-1 000	11 186	55	5	2
1 001-5 000	6 841	34	15	5
5 000-499 999	2 178	10	92	31
500 000 and over	115	1	183	62
Total	20 320	100	295	100

Note: figures for the last three columns have been rounded.
Source: The Greenalls Group plc, *Annual Report and Accounts*.

Checklist ✓

1 What does 'limited' mean if it refers to a company?
2 A company goes out of business leaving debts of £100 million. How much will the shareholders of the company have to pay as a result?
3 Who owns a company?
4 What documents does a company have to give to the Registrar of Companies before it can begin trading?
5 What document does the Registrar of Companies issue which allows a company to start trading?
6 How can a company check to see whether another company has made a profit or a loss recently?
7 What is the role of (i.e. what is the job of): (a) a director; (b) a manager of a company?
8 If a company has 'Ltd' after its name, what does this mean?
9 What are the differences between a private limited company and a public limited company?
10 Why is it easier to attract new shareholders to a plc than a Ltd company?
11 What is meant by the 'divorce of ownership from control'?

unit 13

CO-OPERATIVES

Making decisions

Most businesses are set up to make a profit for the owners. However, not every business today has this as its main goal. Some businesses prefer instead to concentrate on benefiting customers, or workers, or perhaps on caring for the environment. These businesses might consider setting up as a Co-operative.

United Norwest Co-operatives Limited is one of the North West's largest businesses, with sales of £700 million in 1998. Its main division is the food division which runs superstores, supermarkets and convenience stores. But United Norwest also runs pharmacies, a funeral business, travel agents and a car dealership.

The Co-operative movement

United Norwest Co-operatives is part of the UK Co-operative Movement. It is made up of:

- Co-operative retail societies, known as CONSUMER or RETAIL CO-OPERATIVES because they sell goods and services to consumers;
- The Co-operative Wholesale Society, which is owned by the retail societies and provides them with products, including 60 per cent of 'Co-op own brand' goods;
- a variety of other Co-operative operations, such as insurance, banking and travel.

Figure 13.1 shows details about the UK Co-operative Movement.

The first societies

The first retail Co-operative society was formed in Rochdale, Lancashire, in 1844. A group of workers joined together to buy food and other goods collectively. These were then sold to working families. Profit from the shop, the dividend, was distributed back to the workers according to how much each had spent. By the end of the nineteenth century, there were

1 400 Co-operative societies in existence, with goods provided by the Co-operative Wholesale Society.

Co-ops compared to plcs

Co-operative societies are in some ways similar to public limited companies like Sainsbury's or Tesco. Co-operatives and plcs have limited liability. Both are separate legal entities, able to own property, be sued, etc. However, there are also important

differences.

Public limited companies tend to be run to make a profit for their shareholders. Each shareholder receives a share of the profit and has a vote at the AGM of the company in accordance with the number of shares they own. Plcs want satisfied customers because they can create profit for the owners of the company.

Co-operatives were originally founded to serve the needs of consumers. Profit was to be given back to customers who were

1 What, according to the extract, were the advantages of shopping at the Rochdale Society?
2 (a) How did the dividend system work?
   (b) Why did it encourage people to join the society and shop there?

The Rochdale Equitable Pioneers Society original store, today a museum.

On the night when our store was opened, the 'doffers' came out strong in Toad Lane inspecting the scanty arrangements of butter and oatmeal.

Since that time two generations of 'doffers' have bought their butter and oatmeal at the shop, and many a wholesome meal, and many a warm jacket, have they had from that store, which articles would never have reached their stomachs or their shoulders, had it not been for the co-operative weavers.

Mr. Charles Howarth proposed the plan of dividing profits among the members in proportion to their purchases. At the end of the first quarter the Rochdale Society did pay a dividend of 3d in the pound. In 1844 the number of members was 28, amount of capital £28...In 1857 the number of members was 1,850, the amount of capital £15,142.

Note: a 'doffer' was a young boy who worked in the mills.

George Holyoake, The History of Co-operation in Rochdale, 1878.

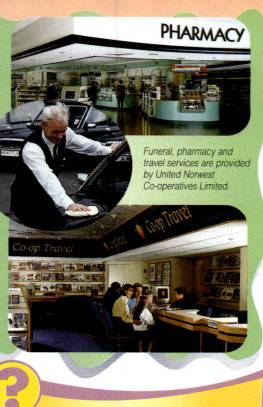

PHARMACY

Funeral, pharmacy and travel services are provided by United Norwest Co-operatives Limited.

?

Tesco	United Norwest Co-operatives Limited
155 600 Shareholders	**967 765 Members**
↓ ↓ ↓	↓ ↓ ↓
Elect with one share one vote	Elect with one member one vote
	Regional Boards
	↓ ↓ ↓
	Elect
↓ ↓ ↓	↓ ↓ ↓
Board of directors 14 directors (including executive, non-executive and departmental)	**Board of directors** 18 directors
↓ ↓ ↓	↓ ↓ ↓
Appoint managers, some of whom are directors	Appoint officials, 3 of whom are directors
↓ ↓ ↓	↓ ↓ ↓
Managers	**Management**
↓ ↓ ↓	↓ ↓ ↓
Run the company to make a profit, part of which is distributed as a dividend per share owned to	Run the Co-op to serve the needs of its customers. The surplus (= profit) is, in part, distributed as fixed interest per share to members
↓ ↓ ↓	↓ ↓ ↓
155 600 Shareholders	**Customers** **967,765 members**

Source: adapted from *Annual Report and Accounts*, 1997 of Tesco plc and United Norwest Co-operatives Limited.

1 What are the differences shown in the diagram between Tesco plc and United Norwest Co-operatives Limited?

members of the society as a dividend. It was paid out in proportion to how much they had spent at the Society. Profit was less important than providing a high quality service. Each member has only one vote at the AGM of the Society however many shares they might own. Co-operatives are democratically owned.

The Co-op today

Where they compete against similar organised businesses, Co-operative societies have done well over the past 50 years. For instance, the Co-operative societies have remained the largest firm of undertakers in the UK. The travel agency businesses of the societies are very successful. The travel division of United Norwest, the Co-operative society based in the North West of England, is the seventh largest tour operator in the UK. The Co-operative Wholesale Society is the largest wholesaler and farmer in the UK. The Co-operative Insurance Society and the Co-operative Bank are both very successful.

The grocery business, however, has been less successful. The Co-operative societies taken together are still the largest grocery retailers in the UK. However, they have seen their **market share** (☞ unit 18) slowly fall since 1945. The problem has been the growing competition from supermarket chains like Sainsbury's and Tesco.

- The supermarket chains have grown so large that they can buy in bulk and sell at prices equal to if not cheaper than the Co-operatives. The Co-operatives have been caught with too many small local grocery shops which are expensive to run, unless they trade extended hours.
- As chains like Sainsbury's and Tesco opened bigger and bigger stores, the Co-operative

UK CO-OPERATIVE MOVEMENT FACTS AND FIGURES	
CO-OPERATIVE RETAIL SOCIETIES	
Turnover	£8 Billion
Trading surplus	£138 Million
Staff	69,000
Number of societies	49
Member's benefits/dividend	£28 Million
Number of shops	4,600 (77 Superstores)
Number of members	9,132,000
THE CO-OPERATIVE WHOLESALE SOCIETY	
Turnover	£3.0 Billion
Staff	35,000
Farms	50,000 acres
Distribution centres	9
Co-op Brand lines	4,500
Number of CWS food shops	641
THE CO-OPERATIVE BANK GROUP	
Assets	£4.5 Billion
Staff	3,928
Outlets	158
Handybanks	249
Customer accounts	2 Million
Link cash machines	11,800
THE CO-OPERATIVE INSURANCE SOCIETY	
Total Income (Premium Income + Investment Income)	£2.0 Billion
Assets (held on behalf of policyholders)	£14.2 Billion (market value)
Number of families insured	3.5 Million
Staff	11,800
Regional, Claims and District Offices	196
Surplus profits (1996) for benefits of life assurance and pension policyholders	£627 Million
Premium discounts to household and motor policyholders for the current year.	£14 Million
CO-OPERATIVE TRAVEL (all societies inc. 250 CWS)	480 Branches
SHOE FAYRE	324 Branches
CO-OPERATIVE OPTICIANS	72 Practices (57 CWS)
NATIONAL CO-OPERATIVE CHEMISTS	238 Branches
WORKER CO-OPERATIVES (UK)	1,500 (ICOM Directory)

Figure 13.1 *The UK Co-operative Movement - facts and figures.*

societies found it hard to open enough superstores to compete. They couldn't raise large amounts of money through issuing new shares on the stock market to pay for new stores.
- They also didn't want to close their local small shops because they felt that they were providing a service to local people. The service was particularly useful to poor and old people, or people such as parents with young children who didn't want to travel to large superstores. Such people didn't own cars and so couldn't get to and from the new supermarkets easily.
- The dividend, which kept customers loyal to Co-operatives in the past, became less and less important as shoppers could see lower prices at the nearest KwikSave or Tesco. Hence, retail Co-operatives today need to find a new role for themselves. Recently many Co-operative societies have revised their

business strategy. They have moved away from opening large superstores and hypermarkets. Instead, they have reemphasised their community roots by developing medium sized supermarkets and small convenience stores serving clearly defined local communities. In the North West of England, for example, the Co-op runs the largest chain of convenience stores, with over 150 branches opening from 7 am to at least 11 pm.

Worker co-operatives

Worker co-operatives are different from retail co-operatives. A WORKER CO-OPERATIVE is a business which is owned by its workers, the **producers** in the business.

Edinburgh Bicycle is a worker co-operative which designs bicycles, has them manufactured under contract, and then sells them from its store in Edinburgh. It had 20 owner/workers in the business in 1998. There were under 1 500 worker co-operatives in the UK in 1997. These tended to be relatively small businesses.

The workers are also the owners of the business, and so they have to make decisions about how it should be run. Normally there are more meetings in a worker co-operative compared to a limited company because of this. In many worker co-operatives, each worker is entitled to one vote when it comes to making a decision, even if workers own different numbers of shares in the business. In others, like in a limited company, the number of shares owned determines how many votes a worker is entitled to use. At Edinburgh Bicycle, each worker only owns one share and so only has one vote. The workers/ shareholders enjoy limited liability.

The advantages and disadvantages of worker co-operatives

Worker co-operatives have several advantages, all linked to the fact that the workers own the business.

- There is less likely to be a conflict of interest between owners and workers because the profits made by the business go to the workers or are invested back in the business to ensure its long term success. For instance, the £60 000 profit that Edinburgh Bicycles made in 1997 was split between bonuses paid to workers and the retained profit fund.

- The business is likely to be conscious of its place in the community. For instance, Edinburgh Bicycles offers evening classes in bicycle maintenance to its customers. Other Co-operatives may give a proportion of their profits to charity.

However, there can be problems with worker co-operatives.

- It is usually difficult to persuade other workers to establish a worker co-operative because it is much easier to set up a partnership.
- New workers usually have to become owners of the business, but they might find it difficult to raise the money to buy a share

Halliwell C. Ltd

Halliwell C. Ltd is a small worker co-operative with 12 members. The Co-operative also employs a further 4 workers who are not members. It manufactures industrial fastenings, including bolts and nuts.

Geoff is the manager. He is responsible for the day to day running of the factory. Bob is responsible for sales. This isn't a full time job, so he can also often be found on the shop floor working alongside the other members. Carol is the secretary. She is not a member of the Co-operative, but she is married to Bob who is a member.

All the members, apart from Geoff and Bob, are paid what they would earn in a normal company. The rules of the Co-operative state that no worker member should be paid more than twice the wage of the lowest paid worker member. Geoff admits that he could earn more if he got a job in a normal company. Bob too is probably underpaid compared to a full time sales executive and he has to share the only car owned by the company with other members when he is not using it for business purposes.

Each month there is a members' meeting when important policy issues are discussed. Most meetings are fairly uncontroversial. However, there is usually a fair amount of disagreement when each year the Co-operative has to decide what to do with its profits. Geoff tends to want to put all of it back into the business to finance investment. Some of the members, though, press for it to be distributed to members.

1 Explain: (a) who owns Halliwell C. Ltd; and (b) how decisions are made in the business.
2 Geoff is seen looking at adverts for managers in the local newspaper. (a) Why might he be tempted to move job? (b) Why might he want to stay with the Co-operative?
3 Bob wants Carol, his wife, to become a member of the Co-operative. Carol is currently paid less than any of the shop floor workers and her wage is only one third that of Geoff's. Under the rules of the Co-operative, she would have to pay £3 000, the amount each of the other members paid, to buy in. Any worker leaving the Co-operative would only get what they put in to become a member, i.e. £3 000. Last year, the Co-operative paid each member £1 500 as a bonus out of the profits made. The company, if sold, is currently valued at £200 000. The rules of the Co-operative state that it could be sold if three quarters of the members agree. The proceeds of the sale would be distributed equally to each member. Carol's membership is to be discussed at the next meeting. What arguments do you think might be put forward by members: (a) in support of Carol's application; and (b) against it?

in the business. At Edinburgh Bicycles, this is not a problem because no worker is allowed to buy more than one £1 share in the business. Any worker who has worked for the Co-operative for more than two years is entitled to become a member of the Co-operative.

- Very successful worker co-operatives often end up being sold to other limited companies, with the worker/owners only too happy to pocket the money gained from selling their shares.

- If the worker co-operative needs extra money to expand the business, it can't look to new shareholders to finance that expansion. This means that worker co-operatives often find it difficult to grow. At Edinburgh Bicycles, the Co-operative relies on **overdrafts** and **bank loans**

(☞ unit 31) as well as **retained profit** (☞ unit 30) for finance.

- Worker co-operatives often set limits on the amount that top workers can be paid. The workers who founded the Co-operatives often believe that all workers should be paid roughly the same for the same amount of work. At Edinburgh Bicycles, for instance, the top paid worker is only paid 3.8 times the amount of the lowest paid worker. It can then be difficult to recruit workers like managers who would otherwise be able to get a higher salary working for a business that is not a Co-operative. This can pose problems for the worker co-operative because it many not be able to get the best worker for the job.

Source: information provided by United Norwest Co-operatives Limited; Co-operative Union Limited; the *Financial Times*, 24 February 1998.

KEY TERMS

Consumer (or retail) co-operative - a business organisation owned by customer shareholders and which aims to maximise benefits for its customers.
Worker co-operative - a business organisation owned by its workers who run the business and share the profits among themselves.

Checklist ✓

1 Explain why the first Co-operatives in the UK were organised.
2 What are the differences between a consumer or retail co-operative and a public limited company?
3 Why have consumer or retail co-operatives found it hard to compete against large supermarket chains like Sainsbury's?
4 What other Co-operatives are there apart from those in retailing?
5 Who owns a worker co-operative?
6 How are decisions made in a worker co-operative?
7 What are the advantages of worker co-operatives?
8 What are the problems of worker co-operatives as a form of business organisation?

THE WAY FORWARD

SUMMARY CASE STUDY

The Co-ops are still big business in the UK. The 51 Co-operative societies sell billions of pounds worth of products each year. They sell 7 per cent of all food purchased in the UK. 15 per cent of holidays are booked through Co-op travel agents. They bury one in four people. The problem is that the Co-ops are in decline. In the 1950s, before Sainsbury's and Tesco were household names, they sold 11 per cent of all food bought. The Co-operative empire was enormous, with Co-ops producing and selling a much wider range of products and services than today.

In the 1990s, they have begun to address this decline seriously. The retail co-operatives have been prepared to close down unprofitable shops, even when this means loss of service to a local community. Investment in refurbishing stores and opening hypermarkets has increased. They have listened to their customers by converting small stores into convenience stores which open late and on Sundays. This is despite worries that workers should not be expected to work unsocial hours. The Co-operative Wholesale Society (CWS) sold off its unprofitable manufacturing and packaging businesses in 1994. It now runs, with 16 other societies, a purchasing alliance which aims to get the best deals from manufacturers. In general, the retail co-operative societies are more committed to earning profits which they can use to invest in their businesses.

But Co-ops have to ask themselves how they differ from any other profit making business. Some argue that it is pointless trying to be better than a Sainsbury's or Tesco at giving low prices or better products. 150 years ago, when Co-ops first started, consumers were regularly cheated by the shops they used. They paid high prices for poor quality food. Today, supermarket chains are highly efficient at what they do. Co-ops must be as good as them to survive but they are unlikely to be able to offer a much

better service.

Instead, they might look at the success of the Co-operative Bank and Body Shop. These businesses have grown successful through being ethical. They take account of issues such as animal welfare rights, the arms trade and the poor in the Third World when making decisions. This would make the Co-ops different from ordinary businesses. It would accord with Co-operative principles of improving the world in which we live. It would attract customers who wanted to know that their purchase of coffee or trainers was not causing pollution or ill health to other workers.

Sources: adapted from *The Sunday Times*, 16 February 1997; the *Financial Times* 25 April 1997.

1 Why were Co-ops first started?
2 Suggest what problems the Co-ops have faced over the past thirty years.
3 'Co-ops must be as good at offering low prices and high quality food as the major supermarket chains to survive.' Explain whether or not you agree with this statement.
4 Discuss whether customers would be attracted to shop at Co-ops if they adopted ethical principles.

unit 14

FRANCHISING

Making decisions

You want to go into business. Do you:
- want to reduce the chance of failure considerably?
- want help to set up and run your business?
- find yourself short of money to put into the business to start it up?
- want to be part of a regional or national chain of businesses?

Are you not too bothered if:
- you don't have full control of your business?
- you have to pay a fee or a share of the profits to another business?

If your answer is yes to all these questions, then you may want to consider buying into a franchise.

Prontaprint was established in 1971 as a print concept. It provided a same day printing service based on quality, speed and value for money. These values are true today, but Prontaprint now offers a complete design and print service. This includes short run, on demand printing in black and white and colour, as well as a disk-to-print service, creative design work, and presentation and copying services. Prontaprint Limited has a turnover of £56 million and nearly 250 owner-operated centres in the UK and Ireland.

?

1 These businesses operate franchises. What is meant by a 'franchise'?

2 The largest number of franchises are found in food outlets, property care, home care services, walk-in retailers and motorist services. Are any of the businesses shown here in these industries? If so, which?

3 You are considering becoming a franchisee. (a) Which of the franchises shown in the photographs would most appeal to you? Explain carefully why. (b) What sort of person might you need to be to be a successful franchisee? For instance, would you need to be hard working or independent? Would you need business experience and an ability to deal with people? Think of as many characteristics as possible and explain why they are important.

Franchisors and franchisees

Prontaprint is an example of a FRANCHISE. Prontaprint is the FRANCHISOR. This means that it earns revenue by giving other businesses, the FRANCHISEES, the right to sell goods or services using its name. These other businesses, which sign a franchisee agreement, could be large or small. In Prontaprint's case, its 250 owner-operators are either sole traders, partnerships or private limited companies.

There are many examples of franchise operations, such as Body Shop, Benetton, McDonald's, Pierre Victoire, Snappy Snaps and Dyno-Rod. The franchisor is likely to be a national or even an international company. It has developed a good or service that it wants to sell. Rather than selling it directly

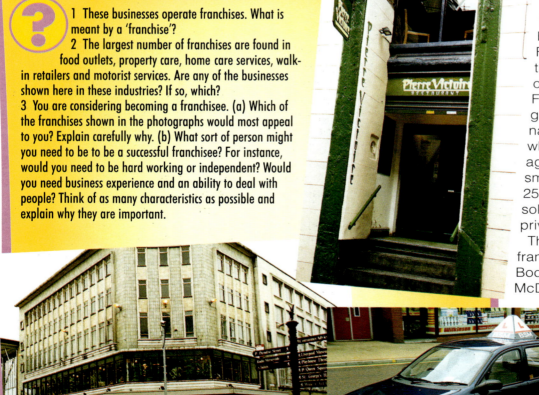

At Prontaprint, staff are given training to start the business, as well as ongoing training.

?

1 What service does this franchise offer to customers?
2 What benefits does the franchisor give to the franchisee?

What are the costs to the franchisee of buying and operating the franchise?

---

me of Franchise: 1ST CALL

scription: One stop shop - 24 hour - Emergency
air & property maintenance business for
mercial and domestic customers

ur company established: 1986

. of franchised outlets: 35

. of franchises planned: 100 plus

st of franchise - Total: £15-£30,000

yalties/Fees payable: 12% max

reakdown of package: Stationery - Telephone
e - Business plan - Sales & marketing - Van -
omputer - Working capital

rojections turnover: 1st year £60-£80k
nd year: £60-£120k

inancial assistance available: All high street
anks

Training provided: 1 week at Head Office -
Ongoing in-field or with existing franchisees

Support services: 24hr National control centre -
Hotline - Business development sales & marketing -
Technical support - Centralised billing

Source: adapted from *The United Kingdom Franchise Directory*.

---

to customers, it chooses to use other businesses to do the selling.

What the franchisor provides

There are certain benefits to a business of becoming a franchisee. These may include:

- training to start the business. At Prontaprint there is a four week induction course, followed by post-completion training, with ongoing training after the business has been launched. Staff training is also comprehensive. Courses cover all the skills which the team will need, including in-store and external sales techniques, art and design skills, and print room management;

- equipment, such as shop fittings or a van. Prontaprint-approved architects help to refit premises and a technical team advises on new equipment;

- materials to use in the production of a good or service. Prontaprint has central purchasing and uses nominated suppliers. This gives the group great buying power, enabling dramatic cuts in costs. There is also an estate

management team to help in property matters;

- finding customers. Prontaprint provides ongoing advertising and sales promotion to support each franchisee's business. For example, 12 weeks after a franchisee opens, a high profile sales promotion and an extensive local PR campaign is launched;

- a whole range of back up services, like advice, loans and insurance cover. Prontaprint support teams are on hand in the first three months to help the franchisee settle into the day-to-day running of their business. Once established, a business development manager visits regularly to help and advise on planning, developing and promoting the business;

- a brand name which is backed by national advertising. Prontaprint is known nationally because of its size and advertising. Branding can be crucial to the success of the franchisee;

- an exclusive area in which to sell products;

- goods or services to sell. Prontaprint constantly develops new products and services for its franchisees to offer to customers.

The cost to the franchisee

The franchisor doesn't provide all its services for nothing. Franchisors tend to charge a fixed sum at the start of the franchise agreement to cover the costs of starting up a new branch. Then they charge either a **fee** (a proportion of the value of everything sold) or they charge higher prices for the products they sell to the franchisee than they would if bought in an open market.

In the case of Prontaprint, franchisees pay an initial amount of £10,000 at the start for the right to trade as Prontaprint in a particular area. After this, franchisees pay an ongoing fee of

Only a few per cent of franchisees fail in their business compared to an ordinary business failure rate of 50 per cent.

On the other hand, the franchisee doesn't have the freedom to operate that an ordinary business would have because of the franchise agreement. In particular, the franchisee can't sell the business without the franchisor's permission. In some franchises, the franchisor can end the franchise without reason and without having to give any compensation. The franchisee is also tied to making payments to the franchisor. Successful franchisees often feel that they are being overcharged by the franchisor.

Advantages for the franchisor

For the franchisor, there are two main advantages.

- The franchisee puts up money at the start and during the running of the business. This means that the franchisor doesn't 10 per cent of sales of the business.

Advantages and disadvantages for the franchisee

For the franchisee, franchising is a relatively safe way to start a business. Only 6-7 per cent of franchisees fail. In other types of business, the failure rate is about 50 per cent within the first two years. The difference in failure rate comes about because:

- the franchisor carefully selects people from those who want to buy a franchise; this tends to eliminate people who are unsuitable for the business;
- the franchisor sets out at the start how much money the franchisee needs to put into the business; many new businesses fail because the owners badly underestimate the amount of money they will need to survive in business.
- the franchise formula has already been tried out and tested and has been successful; the franchisee only has to repeat the success of other franchisees.
- the franchisor provides on-going support and can help the franchisee sort out any problems such as quality control or tax problems.

ServiceMaster

ServiceMaster is a successful US franchise which came to Britain in 1959. There are 360 franchise outlets in the UK. ServiceMaster offers three distinct franchises. On Location provides carpet and upholstery cleaning services. Merry Maids is the market leader in domestic cleaning services. Furnishing Services specialises in furniture repair including remedial repair, leather restoration and French polishing. The cost of a franchise is between £11 000 and £20 500. A royalty of between 4 and 10 per cent of sales turnover is payable by the franchisee. The franchisor offers initial training. It offers comprehensive ongoing support including marketing and sales support.

Source: adapted from *Franchise World*, January/February 1998 and *The United Kingdom Franchise Directory*.

Jim and Dot Truepenny are looking to operate a franchise. Jim is 50 and has just been made redundant from his job as a skilled machinist in a factory. Dot works as a till operator at her local superstore. Jim has been given an early retirement package from his company which includes a £10 000 cash payment as well as regular pension payments.

1 What advantages would Jim and Dot get from buying a ServiceMaster franchise?
2 What would be the cost to them of buying and running the franchise?
3 Which of the three franchises being offered by ServiceMaster would most suit Jim and Dot? Explain your reasons carefully.

have to find that money to run its business. It can therefore expand at a faster rate than it might otherwise.

- The franchisee is as keen and motivated to make a success of the business as the franchisor. This might make the whole business more successful than if the franchisor simply employed staff to run branches of the business.

Does a franchise work?

Not all franchises work. The franchisor might have a poor business idea and mislead people into buying a franchise. Both the franchisor and the franchisees might then go out of business.

Equally, franchisees might not provide a good product or service because they run the business badly. In a well run franchise, the franchisor monitors quality and could tell the franchisee to improve or risk losing the franchise. However, in a badly run franchise, poor quality could be a major problem, dragging down both the business of the local franchisee and the national business of the franchisor.

Source: adapted from information privided by Prontaprint and Charles Barker plc.

Key terms

Franchise - the right given by one business to another to sell goods or services using its name.
Franchisee - a business which agrees to manufacture, distribute or provide a branded product.
Franchisor - the business which gives franchisees the right to sell its product, in return for a fixed sum of money or a royalty payment.

Checklist ✓

1 What is the difference between a franchisor and a franchisee?
2 What may the franchisor provide for the franchisee?
3 How does the franchisor make a profit?
4 What are the advantages of a franchise for the franchisee?
5 Why might a person decide not to become a franchisee but set up his or her own business in competition with a franchise?
6 Why are businesses willing to franchise their valuable business ideas to other businesses?
7 Why might franchising be a problem for; (a) the franchisee; and (b) the franchisor?

French Connection

French Connection, the women's fashion retailer, is moving into franchising. It will open three UK franchise outlets this year following a trial in York. This will be in addition to eight new shops in the UK and the USA, its main markets, which will increase retail space by 30 per cent.

The chairman of French Connection said franchising would enable the company to expand its brands and distribution quickly and at minimum cost. 'If we compare our chain to competitors', we see how many areas we're not in. There is tremendous scope for broadening.'

The expansion will include development of new products like underwear and a wider range of accessories.

Source: adapted from the *Financial Times*, 11 April 1997.

1 What does French Connection sell?
2 (a) Why do you think French Connection wants to expand its business? (b) How is it planning to do this?
3 (a) What are the advantages to French Connection of using franchising to expand? (b) What might be the long term disadvantages?

FATTY ARBUCKLES

1 What does Fatty Arbuckles sell?
2 Fatty Arbuckles is a franchise operation. Using information from the advertisement, explain THREE features of a franchise.
3 Rosie Fletcher is 46 and has just left her job as manager of a shoe shop. She didn't like working for other people because she felt they often made the wrong decisions. She's got £5 000 saved in the bank for a rainy day. Her friend has set up a successful franchise operation and Rosie thinks she would make an ideal franchisee. Rosie visits the National Franchise Exhibition and has arrived at your Fatty Arbuckles stand. Would you, as a representative of Fatty Arbuckles, want to encourage Rosie to become a Fatty Arbuckles franchisee? Explain your reasons carefully.

Fatty Arbuckles American Diners, Laser House, Waterfront Quay, Salford Quays, Manchester M5 2XW. Tel. 0161 877 0881. Fax. 0161 877 0882.

Fatty Arbuckles American diners are a chain of themed table service restaurants that specialise in providing very generous portions of quality American style food at an affordable price for any age group or occasion. The relaxed atmosphere is in keeping with the keynote that a Fatty Arbuckles is "Where eating out is fun". Prospective franchisees do not require restaurant experience as full training is provided, and have the added advantage of on-going operational support from a professional franchise team; extensive national and local marketing; and negotiated discounts from nominated suppliers. Total investment, which includes the £10,000 franchise fee, ranges from £200,000 to £360,000.

Making decisions

As businesses grow in size, they might find that their national markets are too small for them. They may begin to export their products. Later they might find it to their advantage to switch some production to foreign countries. At this point they can be called multinational companies. These companies must decide how to operate successfully across several countries, faced with a variety of different local legal, tax and social situations. They must decide on the most profitable location to produce and where it is profitable to sell.

The BOC Group (British Oxygen Company until 10 April 1975) is a British company with worldwide sales in 1997 of nearly £4 billion. Most of this comes from sale of gases, like oxygen and nitrogen. It also has three other businesses - health care, vacuum technology and distribution services - which account for about one quarter of sales.

Multinational companies

The BOC Group is a MULTINATIONAL COMPANY. This means that it operates not just in the UK but in other countries around the world. It owns companies, factories and sites everywhere from the United States to South Korea to Kenya and Australia. It sells its products to businesses and governments worldwide.

A UK multinational will almost certainly be a **plc** (☞ unit 12). All major industrialised countries have their own multinational companies, owned by shareholders in their own countries, but operating internationally. Some multinationals have major shareholders in several other countries as well.

Company structure

Multinational companies often have complicated structures. There is likely to be a PARENT COMPANY. The BOC Group plc is a parent company. This is a company with shareholders which owns other companies. These other companies are called SUBSIDIARY COMPANIES. In 1997, The BOC Group owned all of 195 other companies worldwide. It also owned part of another 264 companies. In Japan, for instance, The BOC Group plc wholly owned BOC Japan and owned 50 per cent of Osaka Sanso Kogyo Ltd.

One reason why a UK multinational may have subsidiaries in other countries is because tax may be lower in these countries. Also, each subsidiary company will have **limited liability** (☞ unit 12).

Benefits of larger size

Companies often become multinationals because size can help them compete against other businesses. Size can lead to lower

Revenues per Region 1996

25%

18%

57%

Employees per Region 1996

20%

15%

65%

- ■ Europe
- ■ The Americas
- ■ Asia/Australasia/Africa

 ABB is one of the world's largest companies. In 1996, its sales were $36 billion (equivalent roughly to £22 billion). It is a manufacturer of industrial equipment, from trains to power plants to process control equipment for oil rigs and paper mills. In 1996, it employed 215 000 workers in five continents.

Source: ABB Asea Brown Boveri, *Annual Report and Accounts.*

1 What makes ABB a 'multinational company'?

2 ABB has been formed by the merger of a large number of companies. Originally the companies were European. What evidence is there from the pie charts that ABB is a European multinational?

3 The 1996 company report and accounts stated that: 'ABB is the only company in its markets that can meet the full range of its customers' engineering needs ... they need only deal with a single supplier. This means fewer contracts to co-ordinate, simplified purchasing and streamlined scheduling of project deadlines. Another advantage is the improved performance that results from matched components and technology from a single supplier ... ABB with its broad range of products, global economies of scale in supply and production, and its local presence in all parts of the world is uniquely positioned to tap the growing demand for cost-effective and eco-efficient full-system energy solutions.' How does this explain why the size of the company helps it to win orders?

costs of production, perhaps because of **economies of scale** (☞ unit 18). The company may also be able to locate production more cost effectively (☞ unit 52). Of more importance to The BOC Group is that size can lead to better products. Not many businesses have the expertise to manufacture and distribute industrial gases. BOC is also in the forefront of technology. In 1996, for instance, the group filed 152 **patents** (☞ unit 50) worldwide to protect new inventions and discoveries.

Problems facing multinationals

A multinational needs to develop strategies to cope with a number of different problems.

Size The BOC Group employed 41 374 people in September 1997. Only 15 008 of these work in Europe and even fewer in the UK. This is not surprising since only 31 per cent of its 1997 sales were in Europe. With some 260 subsidiary companies and thousands of sites worldwide, The BOC Group needs to find ways of making everyone work together to achieve the goals of the company. The sheer size of the company and its geographic spread means that good **communication** is essential (☞ unit 59).

Law and politics The BOC Group owns businesses in 52 countries and sells products in many more. This means that it needs to understand at least 52 different legal systems. It is also constantly dealing with government, both at a local level and a national level. It needs permission to operate factories and open offices. It might need government approval to employ workers. It must pay tax to the local government. Permission might also have to be obtained to import and export its products, as well as pay bills and send profits from one country to another. The BOC Group is also subject to a wide variety of environmental regulations because its manufacturing processes affect the local environment.

Exchange rate fluctuations

Multinationals may sell products and earn profits in a large number of different currencies (☞ units 7 and 8). However, the values of currencies are constantly changing against each other. If the value of the pound against other currencies changes, this can have an important effect on profits and the values of overseas sales of a multinational. For instance, in 1997, in local currencies, BOC sales worldwide increased by 6 per cent and profits went up 7 per cent. But the value of the pound was also increasing sharply at the same time. This meant that the 7 per cent profit increase in local currencies generated hardly any increase in profits when measured in pounds.

Source: adapted in part from the BOC Group, *Annual Report and Accounts*, 1997.

SUMMARY CASE STUDY

OIL COMPANIES

Multinational oil companies are never far from controversy. In 1996 British Petroleum (BP) was criticised for its oil operations in Casanare, Columbia. Critics argued that it had given little in economic benefits to the local economy in this very poor part of Columbia. Local people had seen polluted rivers with dead fish and there had been reports of oil spills and chemical overflows. It was argued that too little had been spent by BP on improving local roads, housing, hospitals and schools. There had also been conflict between local people and migrants moving to the area to find jobs. What's more, BP was accused of helping the army in its fight against local guerrillas opposed to the Colombian government.

In the UK in 1995, Greenpeace was one of the organisations which put pressure on Shell to back down over its plans to sink the Brent Spar oil platform in the North Atlantic. Greenpeace said that dumping it in this way would pollute the North Atlantic.

In 1997 Total, the French oil company, was involved in a dispute with the United States. Total planned to develop natural gas fields in Iran. The US governement threatened to impose sanctions on Total. It felt that investment in Iran's oil and gas industries might allow the country to acquire 'weapons of destruction'.

Source: adapted from the *Independent*, 22 June 1995; the *Financial Times*, 8 November 1996; and the *Guardian*, 1 October 1997.

1 Why might oil companies like BP and Shell be called 'multinational companies'?
2 Oil companies are sometimes criticised for their activities. Explain THREE different criticisms made in the passage.
3 Suggest why companies like BP or Shell operate in a large number of different countries worldwide.

Wordprocessing
4 An oil company has been criticised for its environmental record in a newspaper. Write a letter in response to the newspaper pointing out the advantages that a multinational oil company can bring to a local economy.

Oil companies must be careful to avoid pollution when disposing of oil platforms.

key terms

Multinational company - a business which operates in at least two countries, usually both selling products and producing them in these countries.
Parent company - a company which owns and controls other companies (called subsidiary companies).

Checklist ✓

1 Name FOUR multinational companies.
2 What is the difference between a parent company and a subsidiary company?
3 Why might companies become multinational companies?
4 (a) What problems do multinational companies face and (b) how can they overcome these?

ORGANISATIONS AND THE PUBLIC SECTOR

Making decisions

Government must decide what is to be provided in the public sector of the economy and what is to be produced in the private sector. If it is provided by the public sector, should it be produced by private sector businesses or by state owned businesses? What should be privatised and what should be kept in the public sector?

The Post Office is a large business organisation in the UK. In 1996-7, the Post Office Group had sales of £6 370 million, made £577 million profit and employed 194 000 people. The largest part of the business is the Royal Mail, which handles letter deliveries. However, the Post Office also handles parcels through its Parcelforce division and runs 19 000 post offices through its Post Office Counters division.

The public sector

The Post Office is part of the **public sector** of the economy (☞ unit 3). The public sector is run and owned by the **state**. The two most important parts of the state are **central government** and **local government**.

Central government is controlled from London. The Prime Minister is in overall charge of central government. Citizens elect MPs (Members of Parliament) to supervise central government. Local government is the government of counties, districts, parishes and boroughs throughout the UK.

Producer, provider and buyer

The public sector is a provider, producer and buyer.

Provider The public sector in the UK provides a large range of services, illustrated in Figure 16.1, from health and education to defence and the police. Part is provided free of charge to consumers, like secondary school education. Prices are charged for the rest, like stamps for letters.

Producer The public sector produces some of the goods and services it provides, like defence, education and health care. Because the Post Office is owned by the public sector, it also therefore produces postal services.

Buyer The public sector buys the rest of what it provides from private sector businesses, including tanks, new roads and places in old people's homes.

Public corporations

The Post Office is a PUBLIC CORPORATION. This is a type of business organisation recognised in law, like a **public limited company** (☞ unit 12) or a **co-operative** (☞ unit 13). A public corporation is owned by central government, i.e. the government is the only shareholder. Like a public limited company, it has a **board of directors** (☞ unit 12) which oversees the running of the corporation.

The government sets **goals** (☞ unit 17) for public corporations

? 1 Look at Figure 16.1. Who provides: (a) the army; (b) dustbin collection; (c) unemployme benefit; (d) primary schools; (e) NHS hospita operations; (f) social workers; (g) higher educatio

2 Williams Holdings is a private sector UK company which makes fire and safety equipment and building equipment, including Yale locks and Cuprinol wood preservative. What business opportunities are there for the company of selling to the public sector?

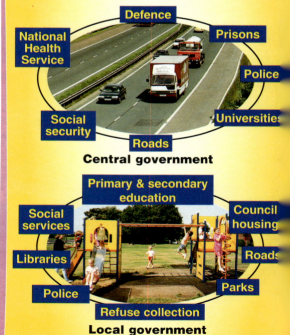

Figure 16.1

to achieve. These are likely to be different from a private company. This is because the government itself has far more objectives than a private company which is most likely to want to maximise returns to the owners of the business.

In the 1979, the list of public corporations was much longer than it is today. It included the gas industry, the electricity industry, the railways, British Telecom, Rover cars, British Aerospace, Rolls Royce, British Airways and British Steel.

Privatisation

During the 1980s, most public corporations were PRIVATISED. This means they were sold off by the government to private buyers. So they are now **private sector companies** owned by private shareholders. The opposite of privatisation is NATIONALISATION. This occurs when the state buys a company from its private sector

shareholders. Many of the companies privatised in the 1980s and 1990s, such as British Steel and British Rail, were nationalised between 1945 and 1951.

The Post Office is the only large public corporation apart from the BBC (the British Broadcasting Corporation) to stay in the public sector. Should the Post Office be sold off to the private sector? There is a number of issues which are important in deciding this.

Costs Most private sector companies aim to make profits. More profit is better than less profit. One way they can make more profit is by keeping their costs as low as possible. Public corporations, on the other hand, have had little incentive to keep costs as low as possible because profits have only been one of many goals set by governments. In practice, the companies and industries which have been privatised, like gas and electricity,

have seen falls in costs. This means they are more **efficient** as producers. So, if the Post Office were privatised, it could be that its costs would fall too.

Prices If costs fall after privatisation, this gives companies the opportunity also to cut their prices to customers. Some industries and companies which have been privatised have operated in **competitive markets** (☞ unit 2). Competition between businesses often forces businesses to set low prices. This is because, otherwise, they would lose customers and sales to other businesses. Telephone charges in the UK have fallen since privatisation, for instance, because British Telecom has been forced to compete with other businesses like Mercury and Orange. Where there is no competition, as in the water industry, the government set up **regulatory bodies**. These are:

- OFWAT for the water industry;
- OFGAS for the gas industry;
- OFFER for the electricity industry;
- ORR for the rail industry;
- OFTEL for the telephone industry.

These regulatory bodies lay down rules for how businesses in the industry can compete. They also tend to fix maximum prices that firms can charge so that the consumer is not charged too much.

If the Post Office were privatised it would be likely to keep its **monopoly** (☞ unit 2) of the postal service. At the moment, businesses cannot by law collect and deliver letters unless they charge at least £1 for each letter. No business can therefore compete with the Royal Mail which charges only one quarter of that price. So, if it were privatised, the government would have to set up a regulatory body for postal services. This would impose maximum prices on the Post Office. If the Post Office could cut costs, the regulatory body would be likely to force the Post Office to cut its prices. This would benefit customers.

The product Public corporations

Competition and the Post Office

The Post Office in the UK is a monopoly. No company apart from the Post Office is allowed to deliver letters or packets for less than £1. This means that no company can compete with the Post Office's letter service. However, the Post Office faces strong competition in its parcels business, where the cost of sending the parcel is more than £1. It faces strong competition from other forms of communication. Instead of sending a letter, you can pick up the telephone or send an E-mail. Fax machines allow instant delivery of messages and documents. It also has to prepare for the liberalisation of postal services in Europe. This will mean that any Post Office, such as the French Post Office, could set up a service in the UK. Equally, the UK Post Office could set up in France and take business away from the French Post Office.

Some directors of the Post Office would like to see the Post Office privatised. At the moment, the Post Office has to give a large share of its profits to the government, which owns it. This limits the amount that the Post Office can keep back to invest in the business. It is not allowed to borrow money for investment. The government also sets it a target for reducing its overall costs to make it more efficient.

It would also like to 'adjust letter prices within a cap formula for letter monopoly services and at competitive rates for non-monopoly services'.

Source: adapted from information on The Post Office Website.

1 What is meant by: (a) privatisation; (b) monopoly; and (c) competition?

2 What competition does the Post Office face?

3 Explain why privatising the Post Office might make it able to compete better against its rivals.

4 It costs far more to collect and deliver letters to rural areas than urban areas. Do you think that the Post Office should be allowed to adjust letter prices to reflect these differences in costs? Explain your answer carefully putting down advantages and disadvantages to those involved.

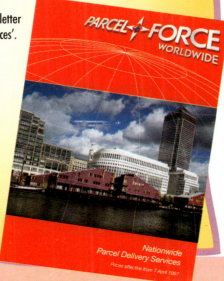

PARCEL✦FORCE WORLDWIDE

Nationwide
Parcel Delivery Services
Prices effective from 7 April 1997

were usually monopolists. Without any competition, they didn't have a particularly strong incentive to provide goods and services that customers wanted. Privatisation can change this. If the company is still a monopolist, one way of earning more profit is to sell more. This means finding out what the customer wants to buy and providing it. So it could be argued that a privatised Post Office would provide a better service than it now does. On the other hand, it might try to increase its profit by cutting out some services. Letters delivered to rural areas make a loss. Many village post offices are also unprofitable. The fear is that a privatised Post Office would cut services in rural areas. Would this be in the best interests of customers?

Other public sector enterprises

Public corporations, like the Post Office, are only one of many examples of PUBLIC SECTOR ENTERPRISES, businesses which are owned by the state.

Public corporations are owned by central government. However, local authorities also own many public sector enterprises, such as local leisure centres, cemeteries, crematoria, airports and market halls.

There is also a growing number of public sector enterprises which are not owned either by central or local government, like Trust hospitals or Grant Maintained Schools. If your school is a Grant Maintained School, then it is a public sector enterprise. It can own property, be sued, is an employer in its own right and can sell its services.

Opportunities for businesses

Privatisation has created new businesses. The electricity industry, for instance, was split up into over ten different companies. Some privatised businesses were then **taken over** (☞ unit 19) by existing private sector businesses. Rover, for

instance, is now part of the German BMW company. However, there are many other ways in which changes made by the government can affect businesses.

Deregulation Government makes a large number of rules about how businesses can operate. Laws like the **Health and Safety Acts** (☞ unit 62) protect workers from unsafe working conditions. Laws like the **Trade Descriptions Act** (☞ unit 45) protect consumers from poor quality goods and services. **Deregulation** occurs when the

government removes some of these rules. In the 1980s, for instance, the government changed the rules about buses. Before, bus companies, mainly owned by local authorities, were given local monopolies. No other bus company could set up in competition. Today, any bus company can provide local or national services. This has greatly increased competition in the bus industry. It provided a business opportunity for companies like Stagecoach to set up in business and expand. It also posed a threat to existing bus

Lower gas prices

The gas industry was privatised in 1986, but it was privatised as a monopoly. One company, British Gas, sold nearly all the gas to both businesses (industrial users) and households in the UK. A regulatory body, OFGAS, was set up which put downward pressure on gas prices. However, it was the introduction of competition into gas supply which transformed the market. In 1992, British Gas lost its monopoly powers to sell gas to businesses. Any company can now set itself up to sell gas to industrial users. The result was almost a halving in price of gas to the industrial customer over the next 5 years.

In 1998, all households were also given the freedom to choose their gas supplier. This competition too is pushing down gas prices for consumers. Not all customers are happy though. Some of the companies which now supply gas have a record of giving poor service. Complaints about wrong bills, for instance, have risen since the introduction of competition. Also, many gas companies avoid signing on low income customers. So Centrica, the company which used to be British Gas, ends up supplying gas to these customers. Centrica has responded by extending the use of pre-payment meters. These are installed in these low income households where there is a record of late or no payment of bills. Customers have to put money into the meter before gas is supplied, but the price charged per unit of gas is higher than that for ordinary customers. Centrica says that it helps customers with their budgeting. It also points out that pre-payment customers only buy 5 per cent of Centrica's gas but account for 20 per cent of costs. Centrica's profits go up because it has fewer unpaid bills. But the gas bills for poor households also go up because they have to pay higher gas tariffs.

Source: adapted from the *Financial Times*, 12 November 1997.

1 What is meant by: (a) privatisation; and (b) monopoly?

2 (a) Suggest why competition in the gas market led to low prices. (b) Is this competition always good for customers?

Wordprocessing

3 Write a letter as an executive of Centrica to the gas regulator. In your letter, explain why it is unfair that other gas companies are not signing on households on low incomes. Suggest that all gas companies should pay a surcharge based on the number of ordinary customers a company has. This money would then be distributed to gas companies according to how many customers each has with pre-payment meters. Explain why this would benefit customers.

Adjusted by GDP deflator
Index (1990=100)

Figure 16.2 *Industrial gas prices.*
Source: adapted from DTI, *Energy Trends*.

companies. The bus companies owned by local authorities tended to lose customers.

Contracting out Many services are now paid for by government but provided by private sector services. For instance, many local authorities put out refuse collection to **tender**. The company putting in the lowest bid - the cheapest price - to provide the service gets the contract. This gives businesses the opportunity to win new orders. Everything from places in old people's homes to catering in hospitals has been put out to tender.

Sheffield supertram

In 1994, four local authorities, through a subsidiary, the South Yorkshire Passenger Transport Executive, began to build a £240 million supertram line in Sheffield. Finished in 1995, it has proved to be a commercial failure. It has attracted too few passengers and it made a loss in each year of its operation. The tram system was built on the existing road system in Sheffield. Failure has been blamed on fierce competition from buses along the route. Trams also do not have priority on routes shared with cars and buses so that they get stuck in traffic jams too. Finally, new housing developments along the route have been postponed.

In 1998, the four local authorities signed a deal with Stagecoach giving it the right to operate the supertram system. The system would continue to be owned by the local authorities. Stagecoach is a private sector company which has grown enormously over the past ten years. It now runs many bus companies throughout the UK and abroad and also runs several train companies including South West Trains.

Source: adapted from the *Financial Times*, 2 December 1997.

1 (a) Who owns the Sheffield supertram system?
  (b) Who now operates the system?
2 Why do you think the four local authorities decided to stop running the system directly and get a private company to do it for them?
3 Explain TWO ways in which Stagecoach might make the supertram more successful.

key terms

Nationalisation - the purchase by the state of a private sector business.
Privatisation - the sale of state owned businesses to the private sector.
Public corporation - a public sector enterprise owned by central government.
Public sector enterprise - a business owned by the state which sells what it produces to the private sector.

Checklist ✓

1 What is the public sector?
2 What is the difference between central and local government?
3 Give FIVE examples of goods and services produced by the public sector.
4 Give TWO examples of services bought by the public sector from the private sector.
5 (a) What public sector enterprises might a local authority run? (b) Are there any examples of these in your area?
6 What is a Grant Maintained School?
7 What is the difference between nationalisation and privatisation?
8 What is a regulatory authority in a privatised industry?
9 What is the difference between deregulation and contracting out?

SUMMARY CASE STUDY

PENSIONS

The Welfare State is in crisis. Spending on benefits, like state pensions and disability benefit, has been rising as a proportion of total government spending over time. There are no easy solutions to the problem because no one wants to see their benefits cut. However, part of the solution might be to involve the private sector more. If people could be persuaded to provide for themselves with private companies, rather than rely on the state, then savings could be made.

With pensions, for instance, one proposal is that the government should force everyone to take out a non-state pension. Many workers are already in pension schemes operated by their employer. Some pay into their private pension schemes. However, many more make no pension provision at all. They rely solely on getting the state old age pension. By forcing these workers to save for their pension, the government could cut back in future years on benefits for the retired.

This proposal would give business opportunities to the companies which organise pensions in the private sector. These are mainly the big insurance companies like the Prudential, the Commercial Union and Scottish Widows. They would be responsible for running these compulsory pension schemes. Individual workers would have the choice of which insurance company to choose. The companies would have to compete on price - the administrative charge they levied - and their long term investment performance.

Source: adapted from the *Financial Times*, 1997.

1 What is the problem facing the Welfare State?
2 What business opportunities might pension reforms of the Welfare State give to private companies?
3 Suggest why it might be better for private companies to run these pension schemes rather than the government setting up its own pensions company to operate the scheme.

THE OBJECTIVES OF BUSINESS

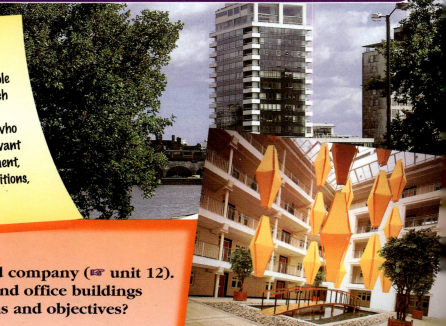

Making decisions

A business needs to decide what are its objectives. Is it just to survive? Does it want to make the largest possible profit? Perhaps it has set itself a number of targets, such as sales growth or increasing market share. To find out what are these objectives, it is important to understand who controls a business. If it is the owners, they are likely to want to see profits maximised. If it is the workers and management, they may be more interested in good pay and working conditions, and the survival of the business.

Regalian Properties is a public limited company (☞ unit 12). It builds or renovates houses, flats and office buildings throughout the UK. What are its aims and objectives? Why is it in business?

Survival

One important objective of most businesses is survival. To survive, the business has at least to break even (☞ unit 24) over time. This means that it makes neither a profit nor a loss. If it continually makes a loss, it will almost certainly go out of business. After all, who is going to pay for the loss that it keeps on making?

In 1992-93, the objective of Regalian Properties was survival.

Due to a sharp fall in the prices of property, it made losses of £27 million in 1992 and £84 million in 1993. Regalian had to find a way of staying in business despite losing over £100 million in two years.

Profit maximisation

Regalian Properties, however, wanted to do more than survive. In its 1993 Annual Report and Accounts, the directors of the company stated that 'the prime objective of the Company is to maximise profit'. By 1994 the company had returned to profit. In 1997 it made £4 million profit.

PROFIT MAXIMISATION should benefit the shareholders, the owners, because they will then receive a large **dividend** (a share of the profits, ☞ unit 30) at the end of the year. For instance, in 1992 and 1993, when Regalian Properties made a loss, the shareholders received no dividend. The company didn't start paying a dividend till 1996, three years after returning to

Jacques Vert Plc

In 1996, Jacques Vert Plc announced that it had made an operating loss of £4.6 million during its financial year 1995-96. The company is a designer, manufacturer, wholesaler and retailer of women's clothing. It has a number of different ranges of clothes, including Jacques Vert and the Grace Collection. Its clothes are of high quality and sell through up-market independent stores and department stores.

The new chairman of the company, appointed in 1996, announced that 'there is a determination among the Directors and employees of Jacques Vert to achieve the recovery which we are seeking'. He said the main reason for the loss had been that the company had failed to get clothes into shops both on time and in the right quantities. For instance, many of the items for the 1995 Autumn Collection had arrived late from the manufacturing plants. Many women had by then already bought their winter outfits. As a result, Jacques Vert was left with a lot of unsold stock in the spring of 1996.

Source: adapted from Jacques Vert, *Annual Report and Accounts*, 1996.

1 Jacques Vert made a loss (a negative profit) in 1995-96. How much was it?
2 Why did Jacques Vert have a problem?
3 What did Jacques Vert have to do financially if it was to survive in business?
4 (a) Explain what you think the objective of the business was likely to have been in 1996. (b) Suggest ways in which it could have achieved that objective.

The Guinness Group strategy

'The Guinness Group strategy is to invest in the world-wide development of our unrivalled portfolio of alcoholic drinks brands, by consistently increasing levels of well-targeted marketing support, and by concentrating our energy on being close to our customers and consumers.

Shareholder value will be enhanced through consistent growth in volumes, revenue and market share, leading to growth in profits and cash flow. We are committed to releasing cash to shareholders when it is not required for reinvestment in the business.'

Source: *Annual Report and Accounts,* 1996, Guinness PLC.

1 What does Guinness PLC produce?
2 List the objectives of the company stated in the 1996 Report.
3 Which objective do you think is the most important for Guinness? Give evidence from the Report to justify your answer.

profitability. Increasing profits should also lead to the share price going up. This is because increasing dividends will attract share buyers to the company.

For a sole trader, profit is the amount earned from the business. A sole trader would obviously prefer to earn £20 000 rather than £10 000 a year for the same amount of work.

Sales objectives

One objective of Regalian Properties was to maximise its profits. Are there any other objectives that businesses set themselves? Many set a number of objectives, each of which is an indicator of how well the business is performing.

Growth in profits Paltran Ram owns a carpet business. He has set himself a target of 5 per cent growth in profits. He thinks that this is a reasonable objective given the current booming economy.

Growth in sales turnover
Perseverance Corporation Limited is a gold mining company. It says that its objective 'is to become a medium size gold producer'. It wants to produce more gold per year from its mines and so raise sales. This should lead to higher profits.

Increase in market share Karen Squires is sales manager for a leading brand of soap powder. She has been given the target of increasing the market share of the brand from 7 per cent to 10 per cent. The **market share** (☞ unit 18) is usually defined as the proportion of sales made in relation to all sales in the market. For instance, at the moment the brand sells at a rate of £7 million per month when the total soap powder market is £100 million: ([7 million÷100 million]x100 = 7%). Her target is to increase this to £10 million per month: ([10 million÷100 million]x100 = 10%). Increased market share could lead to higher profits.

Expansion of the product range
Selling a wider variety of products into more markets could be an indicator of a successful company. In the 1990s, Richard Branson has considerably expanded the Virgin brand name from its base in records and then airlines to cola drinks, train services, and bank accounts.

Selling into more areas of the country or the world   Regalian, for instance, opened offices in Hong Kong and Singapore in 1996. These have increased Regalian's profits.

Sales objectives might be more important than profit objectives. A business usually has to make enough profit to survive. However, once it has done that, it may decide that growth of the business itself is its most important objective. It may prefer to be a large growing company, making reasonable profits, to a smaller company making more profit. To understand why, we need to look at the motives of the people in a business.

Objectives of large businesses

In a large business, like a plc, the shareholders, directors, managers and workers are likely to be different people, all with different objectives.

- Shareholders are likely to want the greatest gain from their shares in the company. This is most likely to happen if the company maximises its profit.
- Workers, managers and directors are interested in how much they earn, their conditions of work, etc. Better pay and conditions of work mean increased costs for the company. This could lead to a lowering of profit.
- Consumers want better quality products at lower prices.
- Environmental groups will want businesses to stop any activity which is likely to harm the environment.

So there could be a conflict of objectives between different groups in the company and outside it. The final outcome might be a mixture of different objectives. For instance, the plc might **profit satisfice**. This means that it makes enough profit to keep shareholders happy, but doesn't aim to maximise profit. It might then give all the directors far more expensive company cars than is necessary to keep them happy. It might also pay higher wages than is usual in the industry to keep the workers happy.

Cheese making

Michelle Kenna makes goats' cheese. Her business started off from small beginnings. She and her family had just moved to a house with a very large overgrown garden. Being the daughter of a farmer, she suggested that they buy a pair of goats to control the problem. Before long, she had a small herd and was selling goats' milk to locals.

Milk, though, was never going to make a substantial profit. She needed to add value to it and for this she turned to cheese making. She converted part of the house into a cheese making 'parlour' at a cost of £15 000 and bought £10 000 worth of equipment. One of the advantages of cheese making from home was that she was able to combine a job with bringing up her children.

Since the first cheeses were produced ten years ago, the business has grown slowly. Today, she sells £12 000 worth per month on average and employs four part-time staff. She really enjoys working with her team whom she regards more as personal friends than employees. Her range of cheeses gives her immense satisfaction. These vary from smoked cheeses, to soft goats' cheese covered in walnuts, to varying strengths of plain goats' cheese.

Despite the growth, the business barely makes any profit after she has paid herself a wage of £10 000 a year. But she doesn't complain. The most satisfying thing for her is when customers come to her dairy saying that they don't like goats' cheese or only eat French cheeses and end up walking out having bought an armful of her cheeses.

1 What is the product range of the business?
2 What do you think is the aim/s of the business? Give evidence for your answer from the article.

Wordprocessing

3 A local businessman visits the shop and is extremely enthusiastic about the cheeses. He offers to buy up the business for £30 000 if he is allowed to carry on using the premises rent free for the next thirty years. He will keep Michelle on to run the business and pay her a salary of £13 000 per year. He will also put an extra £20 000 into buying some new equipment.
(a) Write a letter from Mr Pritchard, the American, to Michelle offering to buy the business. In the letter, explain the advantages of the purchase. Wordprocess your letter if possible.
(b) Write a reply to Mr Pritchard from Michelle refusing the offer. Give reasons for your refusal.

All businesses have to balance the objectives of different groups with a stakeholding. The owners of the business, consumers, workers and others have a 'stake' in the business because the business affects them. They are '**stakeholders**'. Regalian Properties, for instance, says that 'the prime objective of the Company is to maximise profit'. But it also says that 'recognition of the social responsibility of the developer and the ability to reconcile this with the obligation to its shareholders, customers and employees have been fundamental in shaping Company policy'. So customers and workers as well as the shareholders are important to Regalian.

Objectives of small business

In a small business, like a sole proprietorship or a partnership, the owners, managers and workers are likely to be the same people. Many small businesses aim to maximise their profits. However, they may be happy with making some profit and then pursuing other objectives, like sales growth.

Many people own businesses because of the flexibility it gives them in terms of working. They may be prepared to accept lower profits if, for instance, they can take time off when they feel like it. In practice, owners of small businesses tend to work much longer hours than if they were an employee working for someone else. However, they often have more choice about when they work.

A few businesses value their independence very highly. For instance, a worker co-operative set up to promote environmental products might not want to take an order to supply scientific instruments to the nuclear industry.

Objectives of public sector enterprises

Public sector enterprises, like the Post Office or a local council leisure centre, are unlikely to be aiming to maximise profit. Their owners, central or local government for instance, might expect them to make a certain level of profit, or at least cover their costs. However, they are likely to have other objectives as well, such as providing a high quality service.

Public sector enterprises often don't make as high a profit as a private sector business. One reason for this is because they produce a range of goods or services, some of which are sold at a loss in the public interest. For instance, the Post Office makes a loss on letters collected from and delivered to rural areas. It wouldn't want to charge more for delivery to, say, a village in Wales than to Westminster in London because this would be seen as unfair by most people.

Source: adapted from Regalian Properties PLC, Annual Report and Accounts.

'Inchcape represents many of the world's best known companies. It specialises in the international distribution of motor vehicles, soft drinks, consumer and industrial products and office equipment. Its shipping services business is the largest independent shipping network in the world.'

Source: Inchape plc, Annual Report and Accounts, 1996.

1 'Inchcape is part of the service industry.' Explain, giving examples, what this means.

2 Explain all the different objectives of the company given in its Annual Report.

3 What do you think should be the most important objective of the company? Explain your reasoning carefully.

Inchcape vision
Together we deliver the brands the world demands

Inchcape mission
To be the recognised leader in delivering the brands the world demands, we will add value to our **Partners'** products and services by:

World-beating expertise in marketing, sales and distribution;

Anticipating and satisfying **Customers'** needs;

Bringing to our **Partners** our local knowledge, innovation, and an ability to create growth in value through our international network;

Providing a working environment that encourages teamwork, motivates **Employees** and provides continuous development of our people's skills and performance;

Creating consistent and sustainable value for **Shareholders**;

Earning respect from all sectors of the local **Communities** in which we operate.

Inchcape values
Service, Teamwork, Innovation, Respect, Results

Checklist ✓

1 Most businesses must aim at least to break even. Why is this true?
2 Why might the aim of a business be to maximise its profits?
3 (a) What is meant by 'sales maximisation'?
(b) Why might a business want to maximise its sales?
4 What conflict of objectives might there be between different groups in a large company?
5 What is the difference between profit maximisation and profit satisficing?
6 What might be the objectives of a small business?
7 How might the objectives of a plc differ from those of a public sector enterprise?

SUMMARY CASE STUDY

CLIMBING TO SUCCESS

Prakash Raj and Jenny Baker feel that they have the best of both worlds. On the one hand, for six months of the year they are out climbing in the Himalayas. On the other hand, they earned £80 000 between them for the privilege of doing so.

They climbed their way into their business ten years ago when an old university friend of Jenny's offered to pay all the expenses of a climbing trip to Nepal for the three of them. From that experience, Prakash and Jenny thought that others might offer to pay them if they could join their climbing expeditions. They advertised in a specialist climbing magazine and ten people went on their first expedition each paying £2 000.

Ten years on, sales are £1 million with 600 people booked in over the year for a variety of trips. The business now employs 18 trek leaders.

For Jenny, money is not very important even though she earns £40 000 a year, has the latest Land Rover and owns half a business which she believes could be sold for £300 000. For her, what's important is that she can carry on climbing. Prakash is more interested in the business side. 'I enjoy working with the office team in Kendal and seeing the company grow.' At the same time, like Jenny, he spends six months of the year leading expeditions. 'It might make more business sense for me to spend all my time in the office, but where would the fun be then?'

1 Prakash and Jenny's business was recently called a 'package tour company' by a friend. Do you think this is a fair description of their business?

2 Compare the business objectives of Prakash and Jenny. Give evidence from the article to support your answer.

3 One of the trek leaders employed by the company has recently inherited a large sum of money. He thinks the company has great growth potential if it were better managed. He has offered to buy one third of the shares in the company from Prakash and Jenny for £100 000. Should they accept? In your answer, put down the advantages and disadvantages for Prakash and Jenny.

unit 18

BUSINESS SIZE

Making decisions

Businesses range in size from the very small to the very large. Is there any best size for a business if it is to survive in a competitive world? To decide this, businesses have to consider:

- what is the size of their market;
- how much equipment will be needed to produce goods or services;
- what happens to costs per unit of production as more is produced;
- how flexible the business is prepared to be in the face of a changing environment, such as increased competition, changes in government policy and new technology.

Reckitt & Colman plc is a multinational company. It sells leading household and pharmaceutical products in 120 countries around the world. Its UK brands include Haze air freshener, Mr Sheen furniture spray, Harpic lavatory cleanser, Dettol antiseptic/disinfectant, Lemsip cold and flu remedy and Immac wax. It is a large company. What does large mean?

The size of the business

There is a number of ways in which the **size** of a business can be measured.

Value of the business A business worth hundreds of millions of pounds could be described as a large business. How much a business is worth can be measured by its sale price to another business. The sale price of a business depends on how much the owners are prepared to sell it for and how much the buyers are prepared to pay. If the company is quoted on a stock exchange, then an indication of the likely price is given by the **market capitalisation** of the business. This is the current price of each share times the number of shares issued.

Or it could be measured by the value of the **capital employed** (☞ unit 26) in the business. How much would it cost to set up the business from scratch? A measure of this might be the value of total assets (☞ unit 26) of the business, like the value of the machines, offices, factories and stocks of materials and any money it owns. If a business has borrowed money, this would need to be taken away from its total assets to get a value for the capital employed. At 4 January 1997, the capital employed by Reckitt & Colman according to its 1996 Annual Report and Accounts was £1.6 billion.

Sales turnover The value of what the business sells can be used to measure size. Reckitt & Colman, in the 12 months to 4 January 1997, had a **sales revenue** or **turnover** (☞ unit 23) of £2.3 billion. This meant that it sold £2.3 billion worth of its products to its customers over the year.

Market share The MARKET SHARE of a business is usually measured as the sales by one business in a market compared to total sales in

Table 18.1 *Business size in manufacturing.*

	1-199 workers	200-2 999 workers	3 000 or more workers
No. of businesses as a percentage of the total	96	3	1
Percentage of total workers employed	45	44	11
Percentage of total value of goods produced	32	53	15

Source: adapted from *Business Monitor*, PA 1002.

? Wordprocessing and graphics

If possible, use a wordprocessor with a graphics package to present your answer to the following questions.

1 Draw a block graph from the data in Table 18.1. Draw three blocks together for each of the three sizes of business. Use three colours or types of shading for each category. Remember to put a key on the graph.

2 What percentage of businesses in manufacturing are small, employing less than 200 workers?

3 What size of business in manufacturing: (a) employs the most workers; and (b) produces the greatest value of goods?

4 Suggest TWO reasons why most businesses in manufacturing are small businesses.

* Halma is a group of manufacturing companies specialising in niche product areas such as fire detection and security, environmental control and safety products.
* Reg Vardy is a company which owns a chain of car dealerships. It buys cars from manufacturers and sells them to customers. It also provides car service and repairs from its dealerships.
* KwikSave is a national chain of discount food stores.
* Yorkshire Water is a water company which serves part of the Yorkshire area. It also operates an environmental business which deals with waste and environmental analysis.
* Greene King is a regional brewer in the South of England. It owns breweries and over 450 pubs.

Table 18.2 *Company size.*[1]

	Halma	Reg Vardy	KwikSave	Yorkshire Water	Greene King
Value of the business (£m)[2]	78	87	327	1414	255
Sales turnover (£m)	173	677	3254	623	253
Number of employees	2 384	2 347	26 081	3 700	6 426

1 1996/7.
2 Capital employed.

Source: adapted from *Annual Report and Accounts* of the five companies.

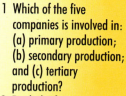

1 Which of the five companies is involved in:
(a) primary production;
(b) secondary production;
and (c) tertiary production?
2 Rank the five companies in order of size. Give reasons why you have chosen the rank order.

the market. This is then put as a percentage. For Reckitt & Colman, this would mean:

Sales by Reckitt & Colman
-------------------------------------- x 100
Total sales in the market

Reckitt & Colman sells products into a large number of different markets. For instance, in 1996 its Air Wick, Haze and Wizard brands had 25 per cent of the total European market for air freshener products. In the USA, 53 per cent of all liquid lavatory cleaners sold are made by Reckitt & Colman.

Number of employees Another commonly used measure of size is the number of employees in a business. In 1996, Reckitt & Colman employed an average of 17 425 workers worldwide.

None of these four measures should be used on its own. For instance, a large car company like Ford or BMW is likely to have a high capital employed and a high sales turnover, but few employees relative to the capital employed. This is because cars today are made mainly by machines rather than workers (i.e. the industry is highly **capital intensive**). A large restaurant chain, on the other hand, may have many employees in

relation to the amount of capital employed. Workers are more important in the production of steak and chips than in a motor car.

There are also other ways of measuring size in specific industries. In retailing (☞ unit 43), size is often measured by the number of outlets or shops owned by a business. It could also be measured by how many square metres of shop floor space a business owns.

It should be remembered that businesses are changing in size all the time. A fast growing, small company could double its size in three years. A large business could become much smaller by selling off its subsidiary companies.

Reasons for the size of businesses

Reckitt & Colman, with a sales turnover of £2.3 billion in 1996, is a large company. Does it need to be a large company in order to survive in its markets?

Economies of scale Some businesses can be very small and remain cost competitive. For instance, a company like Reckitt & Colman hires taxis around the world to take key employees to meetings or to airports. Taxi businesses are typically small businesses. This is

because large taxi businesses have very similar costs per journey made to those of small taxi services. However, Reckitt & Colman can achieve lower costs on many of the products it manufactures than can much smaller manufacturers. For instance, it buys £30 million worth of fragrances each year to put in everything from Harpic to Haze to Mr Sheen. It buys this from just five suppliers worldwide. By buying in such large bulk, it is likely to get lower prices than a manufacturer which is buying, say, just £50 000 worth of fragrances. Another way in which it can cut costs is by manufacturing in large quantities. It can often use factory space and machinery more efficiently than a smaller manufacturer. Falls in **average costs** of production when production increases are known as ECONOMIES OF SCALE. Reckitt & Colman can exploit economies of scale because its business is so large and spread across five continents. A detailed breakdown of types of economy of scale can be found in the case study on grocery retailing on page 66.

Capital employed There are plenty of small companies worldwide making the sort of products made by Reckitt & Colman. But, even so, these 'small' companies are not sole traders working from a shed in the bottom of the garden. Making a product which competes with Dettol needs machinery and factory space costing at least hundreds of thousands of pounds. Setting up a global network of production and distribution facilities for a range of products costs millions of pounds. The danger for a small company competing directly with a giant like Reckitt & Colman is that it won't survive. Reckitt & Colman products

In 1996, Air Wick, Haze and Wizard brands had 25 per cent of the total European market for air freshener products.

Grocery retailing

The local corner grocery store has had a hard time over the past twenty years. As the large supermarket chains have expanded, local corner shops have closed. One of the main reasons why supermarkets have won the grocery battle is because of price. They can sell groceries at lower prices than the corner shop due to economies of scale.

- They enjoy substantial purchasing and marketing economies. Purchasing economies mean that the supermarkets can buy in large quantities and so get bulk purchase low prices. Marketing economies mean that the average cost of promotion is very low when supermarket chains are selling such large volumes.
- They are able to gain managerial economies. The cost of managing a large supermarket per item sold can be very low. Supermarket chains can afford to employ specialist workers, such as checkout assistants, store managers, accountants and lawyers. Small corner shop owners may do these tasks themselves, or perhaps hire expensive expertise to do those they cannot.
- Financial economies are important. A large supermarket chain can borrow very cheaply from the banks. It can also get up to three months' free credit from its suppliers. The local corner shop will have to pay much higher interest rates on borrowed money. It also often has to pay immediately for its supplies.
- Supermarkets can obtain technical economies of scale. They can buy equipment, like a meat slicer, which is used all the time and not just some of the time as in a small grocers shop. Large supermarkets also have a much larger rate of turnover than a small shop. This means they sell goods much faster, cutting back on the time they have to hold expensive stock.

1 What has happened to the number of small grocery shops in recent years?
2 Explain why large supermarkets can sell products at lower prices than the small corner shop.

DTP

3 A new supermarket opens half a mile from your corner grocery store. Design a poster to put in the window of your shop telling your customers why they should still shop with you. You could use a desktop publishing package for this.

will sell so well that the small company won't be able to sell enough even to **break even** (☞ unit 24).

Size of the market Reckitt & Colman sells products which appeal to consumers in London, New York, Cape Town and Rio de Janiero. Its market is global. So Reckitt & Colman can be a large company. The size of the cricket ball market, on the other hand, is very small. Cricket is played in only a few countries round the world. So the manufacturers of cricket balls don't need to be multi-billion pound companies. A very small business with a good product can compete successfully in the cricket ball market.

Flexibility Some small businesses are formed when employees of a large company leave the business and set up on their own. Often they see a 'gap' in the market which the larger company is not satisfying. Or they may see that the larger company is not providing a good enough service in an area of the business. Large businesses can sometimes be slow to spot and react to changes in the market place. Smaller businesses can often be more flexible, moving faster to create new markets and new customers.

Reckitt & Colman is well aware of the dangers of being large. To solve this, it has a structure where every country in which it sells has a director whose task is to stay in touch with and listen to the needs of customers. In South Africa, for instance, it was found that small shops were reluctant to buy Preen, a stain remover, in cases of 24. They had limited space in their shops and couldn't sell 24 very quickly. So Reckitt & Colman repackaged Preen in cases of 12. The result was a 27 per cent increase in 1996 in sales to these shops.

Production methods
Manufacturing furniture polish or household cleaning products is suited to large scale production. So it makes sense for a manufacturer of these products to be large. However, there are some industries where the method of production dictates small scale production. For instance, a high class restaurant can only serve a small number of customers if it is to maintain a high quality of food and service. Any craft business is likely to be small because of the individual nature of the work done.

Entrepreneurship An ENTREPRENEUR is a business person who runs and owns a business. There are many people who would like to own and run their own business. They can often see gaps in the market and can respond more flexibly to this than large businesses. Entrepreneurs are also often prepared to work for longer hours and less money per hour than if they were someone else's employee. This helps reduce their costs and means that they can compete successfully against large businesses.

Reckitt & Colman is a successful, large company because there are large economies of scale that it can gain from its wider international business and the cost for new competitors of setting up is large. Examples of other markets dominated by large firms include banking, car and steel manufacturing and water provision. However, in markets like taxi services, farming, specialist furniture manufacture, restaurants or cricket ball manufacturing small firms dominate the market. This could be because they serve small, usually local, markets or the cost of setting up in the industry might be low. Alternatively many people might be attracted to become entrepreneurs in these markets.

Source: adapted from Reckitt & Colman, *Annual Report and Accounts*, 1996.

Making a success of frozen food

Hillsdown Holdings is a large food manufacturing and processing company. It bought a family business owned by the Hannafords in 1988 and within five months had closed down its factory in Buckfastleigh, Devon. Ali Hannaford, at 27, was made redundant. She fought back though. She got £80 000 worth of funding from her bank and the local council to lease part of the former factory and re-establish the frozen seafood business, Paramount 21 Ltd.

Nine years on, the company is selling £2.5 million worth of products per year. It has specialised in preparing and supplying frozen meals, mainly based on seafood, to hotel and restaurant chains. It also prepares frozen meals for another two companies to sell under their own brand labels.

It doesn't attempt to compete with large firms in the industry which produce high volumes of standard products. Instead, it produces small quantities of a wide range of products. The food has to look and taste special, as if it had just been prepared by a good chef.

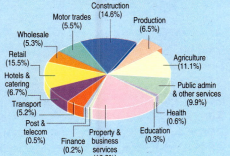

Source: adapted from the *Financial Times*, 18 October 1997.

1 What does Paramount 21 Ltd make?
2 Explain THREE reasons why Paramount 21 has been successful as a small business.
3 An opportunity arises for Ali Hannaford to buy another frozen food manufacturer with sales of £10 million per year. Should she buy it? In your answer, you need to consider: (a) what are the advantages of being a larger business; and (b) what information she would need to have to come to a final decision.

key terms

Economies of scale - the fall in cost of production per unit as output increases.
Entrepreneurs - people who run and own their own businesses.
Market share - the proportion of sales by one business in a market compared to the total size of the market.
Sales revenue or turnover - the money value of the sales of products by a business.

Checklist ✓

1 Explain FOUR different ways of measuring the size of a business.
2 Business A has 60 per cent market share whilst business B has 15 per cent market share of the same market. Explain the difference between the two businesses.
3 A supermarket chain is likely to have a high turnover and a large number of workers compared to a manufacturing company with the same amount of capital employed. Why do you think this is so?
4 Suggest THREE reasons why it can be as cheap to run a single hotel as the same sized hotel which is part of a large chain.
5 Explain FIVE reasons why a small business might be able to survive even though there are larger businesses in its market.
6 There are large economies of scale in the manufacture of motor cars. Suggest THREE reasons why building 10 cars a year is likely to be far more expensive per car than building 10 million cars a year of the same design.
7 Suggest THREE reasons why McDonald's, the hamburger chain, has been successful as a large company, and why there are not more small business hamburger outlets.
8 What can an entrepreneur give to a business which might be missing from a larger business run by managers?

Summary case study

1 Look at Figure 18.1. One-fifth of partnerships are in the agricultural industry, yet only 1.8 per cent of limited companies are in agriculture. Give FOUR other major differences in types of business to be found in particular industries.
2 You are thinking of setting up in business on your own as a sole proprietor. The business will build houses. Up till now you have worked for a building company, first doing a variety of site jobs including bricklaying, and then as site supervisor.

(a) Does Figure 18.1 suggest that you might make a success of this?
(b) Why do you think your business might be able to compete against large national building firms like Wimpey?

All businesses
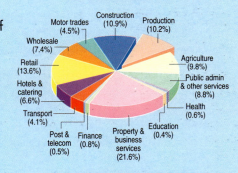

Construction (10.9%)
Production (10.2%)
Agriculture (9.8%)
Public admin & other services (8.8%)
Health (0.6%)
Education (0.4%)
Property & business services (21.6%)
Finance (0.8%)
Post & telecom (0.5%)
Transport (4.1%)
Hotels & catering (6.6%)
Retail (13.6%)
Wholesale (7.4%)
Motor trades (4.5%)

Sole proprietors
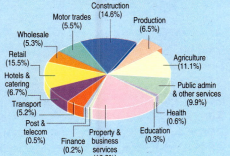

Construction (14.6%)
Production (6.5%)
Agriculture (11.1%)
Public admin & other services (9.9%)
Health (0.6%)
Education (0.3%)
Property & business services (18.2%)
Finance (0.2%)
Post & telecom (0.5%)
Transport (5.2%)
Hotels & catering (6.7%)
Retail (15.5%)
Wholesale (5.3%)
Motor trades (5.5%)

Partnerships
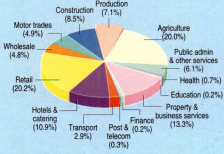

Construction (8.5%)
Production (7.1%)
Agriculture (20.0%)
Public admin & other services (6.1%)
Health (0.7%)
Education (0.2%)
Property & business services (13.3%)
Finance (0.2%)
Post & telecom (0.3%)
Transport 2.9%
Hotels & catering (10.9%)
Retail (20.2%)
Wholesale (4.8%)
Motor trades (4.9%)

Companies and public corporations
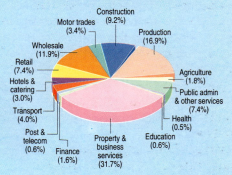

Construction (9.2%)
Production (16.9%)
Agriculture (1.8%)
Public admin & other services (7.4%)
Health (0.5%)
Education (0.6%)
Property & business services (31.7%)
Finance (1.6%)
Post & telecom (0.6%)
Transport (4.0%)
Hotels & catering (3.0%)
Retail (7.4%)
Wholesale (11.9%)
Motor trades (3.4%)

Figure 18.1 *The distribution of types of business in different industries.*
Source: adapted from *Business Monitor*, PA 1003.

THE GROWTH OF BUSINESS

Making decisions

What size might a business want to be? Those who control a business need to decide whether its present size is the best one, or whether the business should be expanded or perhaps reduced in size. Expansion often takes place in order to increase profits and sales. A business must decide whether growth will be profitable.

Tomkins PLC is an international group of companies which manufactures a range of products, including plumbing fittings, power transmission belts and industrial disk brakes. In the United States, its products include windows and doors as well as bicycles. It has two food 'sectors'. The Milling and Baking sector includes the production of flour and the baking of well known bread brands such as Hovis, Mothers Pride and Nimble. The food products sector makes Mr Kipling Cakes, Bisto, Paxo and Sharwood's sauces. Total sales in 1996/7 were £4.6 billion. The group is a conglomerate, so called because it makes such different products.

Stagecoach

Stagecoach plc is a transport company. It owns over 20 bus companies in the UK and overseas as well as operating the South West Trains franchise and running Porterhouse, a company which leases trains.

The UK bus market

'We have been able to increase passenger volumes for the fourth year running.'

'A further 770 vehicles (were) purchased. 1996/7 saw the introduction of more low floor, kneeling buses with tipping seat facilities, improving access and comfort for the elderly and disabled as well as parents with pushchairs.'

'The acquisitions of Burnley & Pendle and Hyndburn Transport were completed in the year and these businesses are being integrated with Stagecoach Ribble.'

Overseas bus market

'Stagecoach purchased Swebus, the largest Scandinavian bus operator, on 2 October 1996.'

'In New Zealand, the Wellington and Hutt Valley operations showed continuing strong organic growth of 4% and 5% respectively over the previous year. This is attributed primarily to increases in service frequencies and the introduction of new vehicles.'

South West Trains

'Turnover was £283.4 million compared to £262.5 million for the equivalent 12 month period, an increase of 8%. The year's results were strengthened by buoyant revenues, particularly on the inner suburban routes as a result of increased London employment, the general improvement in economic conditions and greater focus on the collection of fares. Volumes showed a 6.5% increase in passenger journeys on the equivalent period and 8.1% in passenger miles.'

Source: adapted from Stagecoach, *Annual Report and Accounts*, 1997.

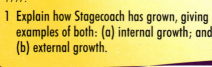

1 Explain how Stagecoach has grown, giving examples of both: (a) internal growth; and (b) external growth.

Ways in which businesses grow

Most businesses increase in size through INTERNAL GROWTH. This means that they produce more. As a result, they may take on more workers, buy more equipment and perhaps move to larger premises. Tomkins has grown internally since it first came to the London Stock Market in 1952. In 1996/7, for instance, sales of its food products sector increased from £1 058 million in the previous year to £1 115 million. In 1997, it planned to build a new £30 million factory for its R F Brookes company which makes pies, pizzas and recipe dishes for Marks & Spencer.

However, businesses can also grow in size through EXTERNAL GROWTH. This is where two businesses join together to form a larger business. This can occur in a number of ways.

Mergers When two businesses agree to join together, it is usually called a MERGER. Mergers tend to be of similar sized businesses.

Takeovers When one business

buys another business, it is usually called a TAKEOVER. The takeover may be an **agreed takeover**, where the business being bought is happy with the terms of the offer. For instance, Tomkins bought Gates, a US manufacturer of power-transmission belts and hose and connectors, in 1996 for £745 million. However, the takeover may be **contested**. This occurs when the business being taken over doesn't want to be bought out or there is another bidder. Takeovers tend to be of smaller businesses by larger businesses because they can afford to buy smaller businesses.

Acquisitions Some acquisitions are takeovers. However, others occur when one business buys a part of another business. For instance, in 1996, Tomkins bought the hose business of Nationwide Rubber Enterprises Pty Limited for £0.8 million. A business can also sell part of its operations. In the same year, Tomkins sold (**divested** itself of) Ferrari Piston Service Limited, a distribution company.

Businesses sell some of their assets because they can get a good price for them or because they feel that these assets are not producing enough profit.

Joint ventures A business may join with other businesses to sell a product together. They might, for instance, set up a **subsidiary company** (☞ unit 15) in which each owns a proportion of the shares.

Types of integration

In 1992, Tomkins bought Rank Hovis McDougall. This company included Rank Hovis, a leading flour milling firm. Some of this flour is used to make Mr Kipling cakes. This is an example of BACKWARD VERTICAL INTEGRATION. It is vertical integration because it is buying a business which is at a different stage of the same **chain of production** (☞ unit 4) as itself. It is backward integration because it is buying a business which is further up the chain of production.

In 1995, Tomkins bought Lyons Cakes. This is an example of HORIZONTAL INTEGRATION because Tomkins already owned Manor Bakeries, makers of Mr Kipling cakes. Horizontal integration is where two businesses making broadly the same products join together or integrate.

FORWARD VERTICAL INTEGRATION occurs when a business buys another business which is further forward in its chain of production. Tomkins buying a supermarket chain selling its range of foods would be an example.

A CONGLOMERATE MERGER occurs when two business merge which have no common interests. Tomkins was originally an engineering company. Buying food companies like Rank Hovis McDougall, might therefore be an example of a conglomerate merger.

In 1996/7 sales of the Tomkins food division increased from £1 058 million in the previous year to £1 115 million. This is an example of internal growth.

In 1996 Tomkins bought Gates, a US manufacturer of power-transmission belts. This is an example of external growth.

Why do businesses grow?

Tomkins started as a small business. By 1984, it had sales of £26 million and the value of the company as measured by shareholders' funds was £8 million. In the financial year 1996/7, sales had grown to £4.6 billion, whilst shareholders' funds were £1.4 billion. What might make a business like Tomkins want to grow in size?

Larger returns for the owners Making money is an important incentive for the owners of businesses. The larger the business, the more likely it is that owners will earn larger profits and own more assets. The same is true when the shareholders are not the founders of the business. Shareholders want to see the company grow even more if that means extra profits and a higher price for their shares. One of the business **objectives** (☞ unit 17) of Tomkins is to give ever increasing dividends to shareholders.

More rewards for the directors and managers In a large company, the shareholders are likely to be different people from the managers and directors. At Tomkins, the directors of the company owned 1 per cent of the shares in 1997. This is high by UK standards. This means that the people who run the company are different from the owners of the company (☞ unit 17). Senior

1 Explain what type of integration is taking place in each of these mergers or takeovers.

CI, the chemicals manufacturer, takes over the speciality chemicals business of Unilever for £4.9bn in 1997.

ilk Marque, the farmer co-operative which collects and sells nearly 60 per cent of e raw milk produced in England and Wales, buys Aeron Valley Cheese, a Welsh aker of farmhouse and mature cheddar in October 1997 for £10 million.

Nomura, a Japanese financial company, buys Phoenix Inns, a chain of 1 800 pubs in the UK in 1995. It then buys Intrepreneur and Spring Inns, two chains of 4 300 pubs in the UK, in September 1997.

m, the UK women's wear retailer is bought in November 1997 by Etam velopment, the French clothes retailer, a completely separate company although h companies had been founded by the same person.

managers and directors have an interest in seeing the business grow. The larger the company, the larger may be the fees and salaries paid to directors and senior managers.

Survival Growth of the business may also be the only way to ensure its survival. Small businesses may be at a competitive disadvantage to larger businesses because they can't exploit **economies of scale** (☞ unit 18). If their costs per unit are too high because they don't produce enough, a solution to the problem is to increase production, i.e. grow in size. Equally, some small companies may be at risk from being bought by larger companies. Growing in size may reduce this risk.

Investment opportunities A business may see that there is a good investment opportunity if it expanded. Tomkins saw buying Gates, the manufacturer of transmission belts, as a way of increasing its profits and returns to shareholders.

Spreading risk A risk of markets collapsing can also be an incentive for businesses to **diversify**. Tomkins operates in a number of different markets. If trade in the engineering industry suffers, perhaps because the economy goes into **recession** (☞ unit 6), profits might still go up because of the company's food operations.

Staying small Not all businesses want to grow. For a sole trader or a partnership, a larger business could mean more work and more responsibility. Some sole traders, for instance, want to work on their own.

A bigger business might mean taking on workers which the sole trader doesn't want to be bothered with. Some owners don't want to lose control of the business they have created and so won't sell out or merge with another business. Some owners are very happy to sell their

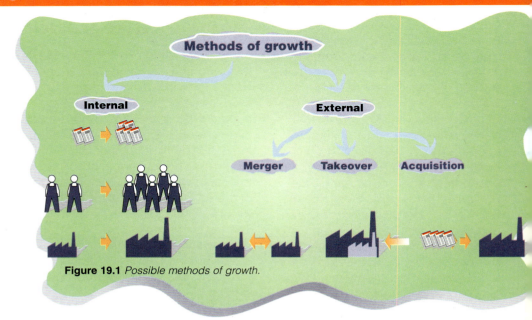

Figure 19.1 *Possible methods of growth.*

businesses and retire once it has reached a certain size. Playing golf or going on holiday may be more important to them than working and running a business.

Source: adapted in part from Tomkins PLC, *Annual Report and Accounts.*

British Telecom

In 1996, it was announced that British Telecom and MCI Communications would merge. MCI is one of the United States' largest telephone companies. British Telecom bought 20 per cent of the shares of MCI and signed an agreement detailing how the merger would take place in the future.

British Telecom wanted to become a 'global player' (a business which operates throughout the world) in the telecommunications market. Access to the United States market was vital because the United States is the world's biggest telecommunications market. By combining with MCI, it could gain new markets immediately. In the longer term, the two companies joined together would find it easier to break into other European, Latin American and particularly Asian markets. They could use their profits to finance investment in these growing areas of the world.

The merger would also give it the economies of scale needed to cope with competition. Many analysts felt that the economies of scale gained would be small because BT operated mainly in the UK whilst MCI was mainly a US company. However, BT argued that there would be significant cost savings on international calls.

What's more, many argued that British Telecom was paying too high a price for its merger with MCI. They argued that British Telecom shareholders were getting a bad deal because their dividends would fall. British Telecom argued that the deal would give good shareholder value because of the possibilities of growth into new markets.

Source: adapted from the *Financial Times*, 11 November 1997.

1 What is a 'telecommunications market'?
2 British Telecom and MCI operated in different markets. What were they?
3 What arguments were put forward in favour of the merger?
4 In 1997, MCI was subject to a takeover bid from WorldCom, another US telecommunications company. The bid was successful and BT sold its 20% stake in MCI.
   (a) Suggest ONE reason why WorldCom might have wanted to buy MCI.
   (b) Discuss how BT could still become a global company in the future.

SUMMARY CASE STUDY

GO-GETTER PLC

Go-Getter is a manufacturer of sports shoes, trainers and sports equipment. Its famous brand makes it one of the top trainer manufacturers worldwide. The last year has proved difficult for the company. It has decided that it needs to grow through acquisition if it is to improve its performance considerably.

Go-Getter plc, recent financial statistics

	1994	1995	1996	1997	1998
Sales turnover (£m)	66	84	120	129	106
Profits (£m)	7	6	8	9	(8)
Net assets (£m)	19	21	22	25	26
Share price (average, pence)	83	84	96	109	70
Number of issued shares (m)	35	35	35	35	46

Figures in brackets are minus figures
Net assets = a measure of the value of the company

HAMES PLC

A shoe retailer with over 400 shops throughout the UK. It concentrates on providing value for money shoes. The group has recently been through difficult times. It has suffered intense competition from new chains of budget range shoes. Customers also seem to be more willing to pay higher prices for fashion shoes from more up-market shoe chains than before. Hames hopes that its trading performance will improve. However, shareholders have not been happy with the decline in the share price of the company.

Hames plc, recent financial statistics

	1994	1995	1996	1997	1998
Sales turnover (£m)	91	92	98	85	82
Profits (£m)	7	4	3	(8)	(11)
Net assets (£m)	47	44	42	42	22
Share price (average, pence)	188	160	140	87	66
Number of issued shares (m)	25	25	25	25	25

Figures in brackets are minus figures
Net assets = a measure of the value of the company

GRAIL HIP PLC

A manufacturer of sports shoes and trainers with a well known brand name in the UK. The group also manufactures leisure and sports clothes under license from a number of well known international groups which wish to extend their market presence into the UK. The group has fought off two takeover bids in the last 5 years.

Grail Hip plc, recent financial statistics

	1994	1995	1996	1997	1998
Sales turnover (£m)	47	54	60	70	64
Profits (£m)	3	1	4	4	(1)
Net assets (£m)	7	7	9	16	11
Share price (average, pence)	26	25	35	46	41
Number of issued shares (m)	32	32	32	32	32

Figures in brackets are minus figures
Net assets = a measure of the value of the company

PRINT PLC

The company specialises in providing special photographic images, linking with cameras, photocopiers, video discs and related technologies. Its fastest growing business is identification systems - printing imaged identity cards for instance. It is rumoured that the group would like to find a larger partner which would finance considerable investment in its technologies.

OMEGA DATA SERVICES Ω
ANNE WILSON RECEPTION

Print plc, recent financial statistics

	1994	1995	1996	1997	1998
Sales turnover (£m)	50	49	54	58	67
Profits (£m)	8	8	9	8	9
Net assets (£m)	26	25	23	24	29
Share price (average, pence)	28	26	24	31	32
Number of issued shares (m)	60	60	60	60	60

Net assets = a measure of the value of the company

Go-Getter wants to take over another company.

1 Which of the three companies described do you think it should take over? In your answer consider carefully: (a) which company would fit best with the business interests of Go-Getter plc; (b) which company has the best financial prospects judged from the recent financial statistics.

2 Suggest a maximum price Go-Getter should pay for this company. Explain your reasoning carefully.

KEY TERMS

Backward vertical integration - where one business further forward in the chain of production buys another business which is further back in the chain, e.g. a newspaper company buying a print company.

Conglomerate merger - where two businesses merge which have no common business interests.

External growth - an increase in size of a business achieved through the purchase of other businesses.

Forward vertical integration - when one business further back in the chain of production buys another business which is further forward in the chain, e.g. a newspaper company buying a newsagents.

Horizontal integration - when two businesses join together through merger or takeover which make the same products at the same stage in the chain of production, e.g. a textile company with another textile company.

Internal growth - an increase in size of a business which is not achieved through taking over other businesses but through the existing business increasing profits, sales and employment.

Merger - when two or more businesses join together to form a larger business.

Takeover - when one business buys another business and takes it over.

Checklist ✓

1 What is the difference between internal and external growth?
2 'Harrisway and Jones agreed a merger.' What does this mean?
3 What happens when one company takes over another company?
4 What is a 'joint venture'?
5 What type of integration would the following be: (a) J Sainsbury buying a breakfast cereal manufacturer; (b) British Telecom buying a bank; (c) Ford Motor company buying a steel works; (d) the merger of Lloyds Bank with Barclays Bank; (e) a bakery buying a bread shop.
6 Explain FIVE reasons why a business might grow in size.
7 Why do some businesses choose to stay small in size?

THE INTERNAL ORGANISATION OF A BUSINESS

Making decisions

Every business has to decide how to organise itself. In a large business, there might be hundreds of thousands of workers to be organised. The business must decide:
- how workers will be put into groups to work together;
- who is going to be in a position of authority, giving orders;
- how many workers will be supervising the work of others and how many will be producing the output of the business;
- how messages will be passed through the business so that employees are kept informed.

Bender Forrest is a specialist manufacturer of stainless steel piping, vessels and fabrications. Based at Heywood in Lancashire, it is a subsidiary company of Bender Machine Service Limited. It not only manufactures stainless steel products, it also designs products using state-of-the-art computerised systems to customer specification.

Organisation

At Bender Forrest, workers **specialise** (☞ unit 4), each taking on a ROLE, a given job of work. Some workers are inspectors, some are clerical workers, some are skilled craftsmen, whilst others are managers. Workers need to know:
- what jobs they are supposed to do;
- who is in charge of them;
- who they are in charge of;
- how they relate to the wider ORGANISATION.

This can be shown on an ORGANISATION CHART.

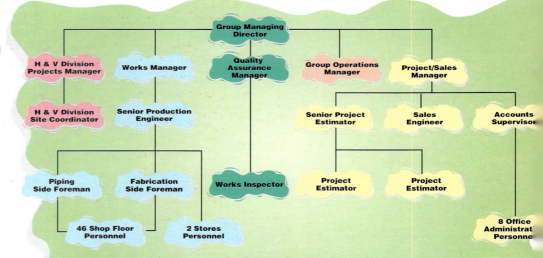

Figure 20.1 *An organisation chart for Bender Forrest.*

Organisation charts

Figure 20.1 shows a simplified organisation chart for Bender Forrest. At the top of this HIERARCHY, the series of layers in the organisation, is the Group Managing Director. Next in the hierarchy are five managers, including the Project/Sales Manager and the Works Manager. At the bottom of the hierarchy are the shop floor workers. Each worker, apart from the Group Managing Director, has a LINE MANAGER. This is someone immediately above the worker, to whom he or she reports.

The business is organised by FUNCTION. This means that Bender Forrest is organised according to what people in the organisation do. So, the department responsible for the

Draw an organisation chart for your school or college. You will need to find out how the school or college is organised. The organisation chart is likely to be complicated because there is a number of different functions being fulfilled by different workers in the hierarchy. You might find that the same teacher or lecturer needs to be put into two separate places on the chart - as a subject teacher and as a tutor for instance.

Tasks delegated to employees will be more likely to motivate them.

production of goods is led by the the Works Manager, whilst the Project/Sales Manager leads a team of workers responsible for the office administration of the company as well as the sales team.

Because there tend to be more people the lower down you go in the organisation, a hierarchy is often said to be a **pyramid**.

The chain of command

The person at the top of the organisational pyramid is in a position of AUTHORITY over workers lower down the pyramid. So the Group Managing Director is

in authority over the managers. He can give orders to workers lower down the hierarchy, his SUBORDINATES. For instance, he could tell the Works Manager to increase production this week. In the organisational pyramid, there is therefore a CHAIN OF COMMAND from the top to the bottom.

The length of the chain of command

The **length** of the chain of command at Bender Forrest is typical of manufacturing companies. For instance, Figure 20.2 shows that there are five layers in the hierarchy from the Group Managing Director through to the shop floor personnel or administration staff.

The longer the chain of command, the more difficulties a business can face.

- Messages can get lost or distorted as they go up and down the chain of command, rather as in a game of Chinese whispers.
- Managing change can be another problem. In a sole proprietorship (☞ unit 10), change is simple. The sole trader decides to change and acts on that decision. In a large organisation, the chairperson might decide on change but it might be resisted further down the hierarchy. The longer the chain of command, the more groups there are to resist that change.

Delayering

Some large businesses try to resolve the problems of a long chain of command by flattening it. This is called DELAYERING. They cut out large numbers of middle managers, pushing responsibility and decision making down the line. In a factory, for instance, supervisors and quality control inspectors can be eliminated if workers are organised into groups and made responsible for their own work in terms of output and quality.

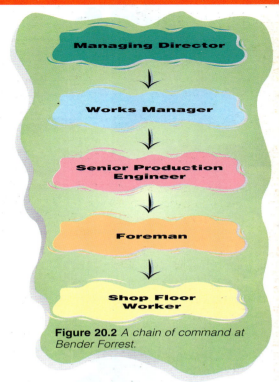

Figure 20.2 *A chain of command at Bender Forrest.*

This EMPOWERMENT of workers can **motivate** (☞ unit 54) them more. However, it usually means that workers have to be better trained to cope with the extra responsibilities. Workers might have to be paid more because they are doing a more responsible job. Delayering should lead to workers becoming more **productive**. Fewer workers are needed to do the same amount of work. Businesses can then DOWNSIZE, making workers redundant whilst producing as much as before.

Span of control

The Project/Sales Manager at Bender Forrest cannot be expected to organise or supervise every single sales and accounts worker. This job would be too large. Instead, he only controls the work of his three immediate subordinates, the senior project estimator, the sales engineer and the accounts supervisor as shown in Figure 20.1.

The number of people that a worker directly controls is called a SPAN OF CONTROL. The span of control of the Project/Sales Manager is therefore three

Workers at Bender Forrest specialise.

employees, whilst for the Accounts Supervisor it is the eight office and administration personnel.

The span of control: how big?

The span of control varies depending upon circumstances.

- The more complex the supervision task, the smaller the span of control. The supervision task can be complex if checking work is difficult and time consuming. It can also be more complex if the workers which need supervising are not particularly good at their job.
- The span of control has to be small if communication with subordinates is time consuming. The Group Managing Director at Bender Forrest can supervise managers more effectively because they are based in Heywood in Lancashire than he could if his subordinates were scattered across the world.
- The better the supervisor, the more people he or she can supervise.
- The more the supervisor DELEGATES his or her work, the greater can be the span of control. Delegation means passing down responsibility to **subordinates** to complete tasks. Delegation frees up a supervisor's time to supervise the work of more workers. It also **empowers** subordinates. Workers further down the chain of command are likely to be more motivated. This is because they are being shown trust and can use their own talents and skills more.

Formal groups

Employees of Bender Forrest are organised into departments and sections, examples of FORMAL GROUPS. These are groups set up by the organisation to carry out tasks.

There are many advantages to organising work through formal groups.

- Each group and possibly even each worker within a group can specialise, leading to higher output and lower costs.
- The group has a clear position within the organisational structure of the business. This means that other groups know which group to turn to when they need help. For instance, finance matters can be referred to the Project/Sales Manager. Knowing who is doing what in an organisation saves time and therefore ensures lower costs.
- Communication in the organisation is helped, again because there is a clear structure.

- Workers can act as a team, receive support from others in the group and also have their work supervised.

Informal groups

An INFORMAL GROUP is a group which is not set up by the organisation but comes into existence by itself. A group of friends at Bender Forrest who play squash together would be an example.

Informal groups can be good for business. People who form a group tend to get on well together and may work better as a result. Informal groups can sometimes lead to information getting though which otherwise would get clogged up in an inefficient chain of command.

Informal groups can also be bad for the business. Most medium to large businesses have groups of people who spend their time together moaning about other workers and bad decision making by their bosses. The group may set out to prevent needed change in the business because the

Buckingham foods

Buckingham Foods produces 1 million snacks a year. Mrs Sharon Roy is a line supervisor. 18 supervisors in the plant are responsible for nearly 500 workers. Sharon is responsible for a production line which makes sandwiches.

Two years ago, Sharon used to think of herself as a line leader who made sandwiches. Everyday she would pick up a sheet which said how many sandwiches had to be produced and what variety. 'I had no influence on the number of staff required on a line, any input into how long processes should take, or any direct control over the machinery.' If anything went wrong, she simply reported it to her superior and left her to sort it out.

Now her role has been changed. She says 'I'd describe myself as a middle manager. I make my own decisions about how I achieve the production targets and I am responsible for quality control. If the line breaks down now, I don't just report it to my superior. Rather, I have the authority to get hold of the engineer to get the work done. I have production targets and I want to meet them.' Before, 'I never thought about profit.' Now she does.

Changing what a supervisor can and can't do has helped empower supervisors at Buckingham Foods. It has also helped the company save £800 000 a year as productivity has increased.

Source: adapted from the *Financial Times*.

1 What is a 'line supervisor'?
2 Draw a simple diagram showing part of the chain of command at Buckingham Foods. It should show Mrs Roy, the people who work under her and Mrs Roy's immediate superior.
3 How large is Mrs Roy's span of control?
4 How has Mrs Roy's job changed according to the article?
5 Why do you think the change has led to an increase in; (a) job satisfaction for Mrs Roy; and (b) productivity for Buckingham Foods?

members of the group don't want that change.

Whether good or bad for the business, the one thing that the business can not do is prevent informal groups being formed. The business therefore has to take these groups into account when managing change and making decisions.

Source: adapted from information provided by Bender Forrest.

Figure 20.3 shows the chain of command at Kwik Save, the national chain of discount grocery shops.

1 Who is: (a) at the top; and (b) at the bottom of the chain of command at Kwik Save?

2 A store manager issues orders. Who would he or she issue orders to?

3 Who would be subordinate to a supervisor?

4 Kwik Save decides that it wishes to reduce the chain of command in the organisation by cutting out one of the layers of management. It decides to abolish the post of assistant store manager. (a) Explain what might be the advantages of this for Kwik Save. (b) What might be the disadvantages?

Figure 20.3 *The chain of command at Kwik Save.*

Board of directors → Directors → Regional manager → Area manager → Store manager → Assistant manager → Supervisor → Staff

LEC

In 1996, Lec Refrigeration was undergoing a transformation. The company had been set up in 1942 by Charles Purley. He ran the company in an autocratic style. He told his subordinates what to do and wouldn't tolerate argument with his decisions.

Shortly after his death, Lec was taken over by a Malaysian company, Sime Darby. It wanted to transform Lec into a major European producer. It spent £30 million investing in a new factory for the company next to the old factory. It also wanted to transform working practices.

It hired Sid Joynson to shake up the way in which people worked. Three quarters of Lec's 1 000 staff work on the shop floor making and assembling refrigerators. Working with small groups, Joynson has encouraged them to rethink the way that they work. It has meant that the traditional chain of command can get overturned. For instance, supervisors have had to adapt to a new role of coaching employees to make suggestions about how work should be reorganised rather than issuing instructions. Vernon Jones, a charge hand who supervises about 30 people, said: 'I used to be like a headless chicken chasing people around telling them what to do. Now I've slowed down, trying to guide people to see where problems are and the job's easier'.

One example of this new approach was the solution to a tooling problem. A worker was having problems and asked a toolmaker to change a mould he was using. Before, he would have had to go to a more senior engineer to get this done.

Source: adapted from the Financial Times, 28 May 1996.

1 What does Lec manufacturer?

2 Who would have been the subordinates of: (a) Charles Purley; (b) Vernon Jones?

3 How did the changes in organisation brought about by Sid Joynson affect: (a) the chain of command; (b) the role of workers; and (c) the empowerment of workers?

4 What do you think might be: (a) the advantages; and (b) the disadvantages of these changes to the company?

Checklist ✓

1 Draw an organisational chart for a company with 32 workers, a board of directors, a managing director, four managers each of whom have two assistant managers. Each assistant manager controls the same number of workers.

2 Explain the term 'middle management'.

3 'The chain of command is very long.' What does this mean?

4 What are the problems of having a long chain of command?

5 In a plc, who has authority over: (a) the managing director; (b) a manager; (c) shop floor workers?

6 'The span of control of the managing director is very small.' What does this mean?

7 What factors determine the best number for a span of control of a manager?

8 What are the advantages of organising work through formal groups?

9 Why can informal groups be; (a) an advantage; and (b) a disadvantage for a business?

METHODS OF ORGANISATION

Making decisions

A business has to decide how it will organise itself internally. Most businesses are organised by function. However, a business has to decide whether it would not be better to organise itself on a regional basis, a product basis or a market basis. In a very large company, it might be most efficient for the business to be organised in two or more of these ways.

Intelek plc is a technology company which specialises in the world markets for electronics and aerospace. Any business with more than a few workers needs to have an organisation. Intelek plc, with companies in the UK and in the USA employing over 500 workers, needs to adopt organisational structures which will best suit its objectives. Its organisational structure will be much more complicated than that of a small business employing just a few workers.

Product based organisation

One way in which Intelek plc is organised is on a **product basis**. Intelek is organised into two product divisions, electronics and aerospace. Both divisions are organised into **subsidiary companies** (☞ unit 15), each specialising in a range of products. Labtech Ltd, for instance, in the electronics division, manufactures microwave circuit boards.

Organising on a product basis allows Intelek subsidiaries to **specialise**. Each company has expertise in manufacturing a specific range of products.

This type of organisation also increases accountability. Each subsidiary has to account for how it is performing. It gives the management and workers an incentive to perform better. It also helps the directors of Intelek to identify those parts of the business which are doing well and those doing less well. It can then make decisions based on this information.

Functional organisation

A typical Intelek subsidiary is organised by **function**, i.e. into a number of departments such as production, marketing and personnel (☞ unit 20).

This type of organisation has two important advantages.
- It allows **specialisation**.
- The structure of the organisation is **clear**. Workers know who to turn to when they need a job done.

However, there are drawbacks which can lead to DISECONOMIES OF SCALE. This is where average costs of production rise as business size increases.
- The organisation may become too large to manage effectively. Management may find it difficult to influence what is happening lower down the organisation.
- Individual departments may

Chloride Group PLC

Chloride is an international electronics group operating in three distinct but complementary sectors - Uninterruptible Power Supplies (UPS), Safety Systems and Power Conversion. It also has a security operation which is part of its safety systems sector. 'Towards the end of the year, additional resources were invested to increase our international sales. In particular, our management in the Far East was reorganised and strengthened and new sales offices were opened in Singapore and Argentina. This investment will enable us to accelerate our business development in the increasingly important markets of the Far East and South America.'

Source: Chloride Group PLC, Annual Report and Accounts, 1997.

1 How is Chloride organised?

2 Suggest what might be the disadvantages for Chloride if: (a) it were organised in just one product division; and (b) all important decisions were made at Chloride's headquarters in the UK.

CHLORIDE GROUP PLC

UPS	Safety Systems	Security	Power Conversion
Australia	United Kingdom	United Kingdom	United Kingdom
Far East	USA		USA
Singapore			
Thailand			
France			
Italy			
Portugal			
South America			
Argentina			
Spain			
United Kingdom			
USA			

Figure 21.2 Chloride Group PLC organisation chart.

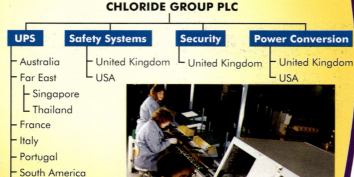

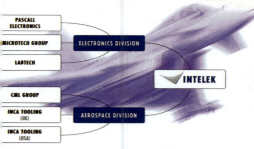

become more interested in promoting their own interests rather than those of the business. They may not want to work together on new projects.

- The whole organisation may become too **bureaucratic**, with departments expecting outsiders to fill in forms and reports if they need help instead of just giving them help.

Intelek has avoided these problems by organising itself into a number of subsidiary companies, each with its own functional structure, rather than being run as one single organisation, with one single functional structure for 500 workers.

Geographical organisation

Some large companies are organised on a **regional** basis. For instance, all the businesses in North America might be organised into a North American division. Companies which organise themselves on a geographical basis may sell a fairly narrow range of products. It then makes sense for operations in a

region to co-operate with each other. They can, for instance, share their knowledge about the market in the region, its economic environment and government regulations.

Intelek has chosen to separate its Inca Tooling operation, which specialises in manufacturing tools for the casting of gas turbine blades and aircraft structural components, into two subsidiary companies. One, based in the UK, supplies all markets. The other, based in the USA, supplies only the American market. This allows the US company to specialise in selling into the US market.

Market based organisation

Some businesses are organised on a market basis. For instance, a publisher might have a number of divisions, such as education and technical. Books will be produced by one division. However, the same book might be included in sales catalogues of other divisions. It might even be sold under a different title by another division if it thinks this will improve sales.

Centralisation

Intelek, in part, is a CENTRALISED organisation. This means that many decisions about the company are made at head office in Swindon.

Deciding on objectives for the whole company and working out strategies to achieve them is done from head office. Common systems and procedures are laid down so that economies of scale can be maximised. The problem with centralised organisations is that they can be slow to make decisions and respond to the needs of the market.

So Intelek is also in part a DECENTRALISED organisation. The power to make decisions is devolved or given to smaller parts of the organisation. For instance, decisions about pricing of gas turbine blades in the USA would be left to the US subsidiary, Inca Tooling Inc. Decentralisation encourages workers to change more quickly as the business environment changes. It gives power to those who are closest to customers, suppliers and the market. A business like Intelek needs to achieve the right balance between centralisation and decentralisation.

Source: adapted from Intelek plc, *Annual Report and Accounts*, 1997.

Checklist ✓

1 What are the advantages and disadvantages of functional organisation?
2 What is the difference between functional and market based organisational structures?
3 Explain how a business could have both a functional and a geographical organisation.
4 What does 'bureaucratic' mean?
5 What is the difference between a centralised and a decentralised organisation?
6 What are: (a) the advantages; and (b) the disadvantages of a decentralised organisation?

SUMMARY CASE STUDY

McDONALD'S TO RESTRUCTURE

McDonald's, the US fast food chain, has decided to restructure its business in the USA. It has recently faced problems because sales have been flagging at a time when competitors, like Burger King and Wendy's International, have been increasing their share of the market. The business is to be reorganised into five geographical divisions, ranging in number of restaurants from 2 210 to 2 820. Each division will operate independently. Divisional presidents will have the authority to innovate to meet business objectives, but they would have maintain a uniform commitment to basic McDonald's principles. The move is intended to bring decision making and accountability closer to customers, restaurants and franchisees. Jack Greenburg, chair of McDonald's, said: 'It should be emphasised that cutting costs is not an objective of this reorganisation. Improved performance is'.

Source: adapted from the *Financial Times*, 10 July 1997.

1 (a) How is the business structure of McDonald's in the USA going to change? (b) Why is this an example of decentralisation?
2 Explain why McDonald's is changing its structure.
3 A couple who own a McDonald's franchise in Florida read about the change in business structure. Discuss TWO measures which its new division could introduce which would help them increase sales.

Key terms

Centralisation - a type of business organisation where decisions are made at the centre or core of the organisation and then passed down the chain of command.

Decentralisation - a type of business organisation where decision making is pushed down the hierarchy and away from the centre of the organisation.

Diseconomies of scale - the rise in average costs as the scale of production increases.

THE BUSINESS PLAN

Making decisions

Many new businesses fail soon after they begin trading. Much of this failure comes about because of lack of planning. Any new business should therefore spend time preparing a good business plan. The business plan needs to show:

- what will be produced;
- how and where it will be produced;
- how the product will be marketed;
- how finance will be obtained to start the business;
- who will work in the business;
- the likely sales, costs, and profit of the business.

Dave Evans and Kari Taylor had been in groups for many years. They noticed how many bands were now duos. Often they would sing or play along with backing tracks. Bands needed tape and disc players, computers, samplers, mixing desks and PA systems to play the tracks. Dave and Kari decided to set up a shop selling this equipment. Finance was going to be tight. They hoped to put in some of their own money and obtain some from a bank. They also hoped to get training and funds as part of a Business Start Up scheme run by a Training and Enterprise Council (TEC). This would involve drawing up a business plan.

The purpose of the business plan

Dave and Kari needed to borrow money from the bank to start their business. The bank manager was interested in the equipment that they were going to sell. But he was also concerned about customers, costs, cash flow and collateral. The manager wanted to see a BUSINESS PLAN. This is a document which puts together all the information showing how a business might survive in a competitive world.

The plan had two main functions. First, drawing up the plan forced Dave and Kari to think about all aspects of their business and not just get carried away with all the great equipment they were going to stock. They may have considered, for example, whether they had enough finance, if they had the skills needed to run the business and what stock they would need. It may also have saved them from making costly mistakes about matters like insurance and tax which they might not have thought about.

Second, it assisted their bank manager and others who helped them set up the business to see whether the business stood a chance of being successful. After all, bank managers will only lend money to a business if they feel that it will be able to repay the loan with interest. If the business fails, the bank could lose the money it has loaned.

The business plan

The bank manager gave Dave and Kari a booklet about what should be included in a business plan. It included details about:

- the name of the business, a brief history, its location, its legal structure (whether it is a partnership for instance) and who would be the owners;
- the key personnel in the

Tieco

Amanda (managing director), Miguel (production manager), Sarah (secretary) and Ruth (sales manager) have decided to make leather and satin women's ties. Ten £5 shares in the company have been issued, one each to the four members of the board of the company and the remaining six to parents. Sample ties have been made. Julie took 40 minutes to make a satin tie and 50 minutes to make a leather tie. It is now early October and the company plans to sell its ties in school during 7 weeks in November and December.

The company has been able to borrow equipment such as scissors and tapes as well as premises for a fixed charge of £20. The raw material costs are £8.00 for a metre of satin. Six ties can be made from a metre of material. Leather is bought in pieces. It costs about £2.00 to buy the leather to make one tie. Presentation boxes can be bought for 50p each.

1. Using the example shown in Figure 22.1 and the description in the text EITHER draw up a business plan for your own mini-company OR draw up a business plan for Tieco.
2. What problems did you have in drawing up the business plan and what extra information would you have liked to have had?

business including their position and salary;

- the product, whether it had been test marketed and what market research had been carried out (☞ unit 36);
- what equipment would be needed and its cost;
- what premises would be needed;
- who would be the suppliers to the business;
- what production methods (☞ unit 47) would be used (which would apply if the business was manufacturing a product);
- what the total costs (☞ unit 23) of the business would be;
- what revenues (☞ unit 23) the business expected to receive;
- the break-even point (☞ unit 24), cash flow forecast for the first 12 months (☞ unit 28) and the anticipated profit of the business;
- what financing the business would need and what assets it could use as security. Dave and Kari then drew up their business plan. Part of this is shown in Figure 22.1.

key terms

Business plan - a plan for the development of a business giving forecasts of items such as sales, costs and cash flow.

The business

a. Name **The Bandbox**

b. Address **6 Headley High Street, London**

c. Limited Company/Partnership/Sole Trader **Partnership**

d. What does your business do?
Sells tape and disc players, computer equipment, samples, mixing and PA equipment to the general public through a retail store.

e. Date you started trading **Hope to start Spring 1998**
(date you will start if you have a new business)

f. Aims **To sell high quality equipment for amateur, semi-professional and professional musicians at a profit.**

- Partnerships and Sole Traders

Name	Amount of capital	% of total
Dave Evans	£1 000	50
Kari Taylor	£1 000	50

Figure 22.1 *Part of Dave and Kari's business plan.*

NatWest

Checklist ✓

1. Why would a bank want to see a business plan before it lent money to a new business?
2. Summarise what should be included in a business plan.
3. A business plan is a forecast. (a) What is being forecast in a business plan? (b) Why do you think it might be sensible to draw up a range of possible forecasts for a business?

BOARD GAMES

SUMMARY CASE STUDY

Fiona Clarke and Andie Hitchman are board game fanatics. Brought up on everything from Monopoly to Scrabble, they decided to set up a company making board games when they left university. Devising their first game took longer than expected because they spent so much time researching the market, securing finance and establishing links with potential suppliers and retailers. They found out that the market was dominated by just a few large US companies, such as Mattel, Milton-Bradley and Hasbro, the company that makes Monopoly. Key to any success was persuading shops to stock games. This meant talking to chain stores like WH Smith, department stores like Harrods and hundreds of individual toy shops up and down the country.

The market was going to be seasonal, with most games bought in the run up to Christmas. This would affect cash flow. Advertising costs would be high. Most customers know what they are going to buy before they go into the shop. Partly this could be because they have already played a game with a friend. Partly, though, it could be because a game has looked exciting when advertised.

The games would need to be manufactured. They identified a number of possible suppliers for the cards, plastic tokens, boards and boxes which would be needed. Getting the finance was crucially affected by having a detailed business plan. They persuaded two venture capitalists to buy £80 000 worth of shares whilst they themselves put in £20 000. To cover their expected costs in their first year, they estimated that they would need to sell 20 000 games, selling at £19.99 in the shops.

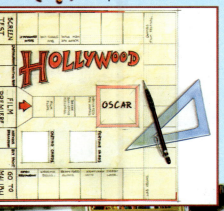

1. Fiona and Andie drew up a business plan based on their research. Explain what would be included in their business plan.
2. In their business plan, Fiona and Andie estimated that they would make a profit of £5 000 in their first year. Instead, they made a loss of £10 000. Suggest TWO reasons why they may have made a loss instead of a profit.
3. At the end of the first year, they have drawn up another business plan. Discuss TWO strategies that they might have planned to bring their business back into profit.

REVENUES AND COSTS

Making decisions

The costs and revenue of a business will determine the profit it makes. If the business wants to maximise profits, it needs to earn the highest possible revenue and to reduce cost to a minimum. To do this, it must know where its revenues are coming from and what are its costs.

The Codsall Cricket Bat Company is a small private limited company which manufactures cricket bats. It has three shareholders, Frank Hudson, John Wilkinson and Pete Burns, all of whom work full time in the business. They also employ 2 part-time workers. Frank and John had worked for the previous owner but low sales had forced the business into liquidation. Together with Pete, they bought the business from the receiver.

Profit

The three owners of the company want their business to grow and make profits. Their PROFIT is the difference between the value of what the company sells, its SALES REVENUE or TURNOVER, and its costs of production. This is calculated over a period of time, like six months or a year.

Profit = Sales revenue - costs

In practice, there are many ways of expressing **profit**, such as gross profit, net profit, profit before tax and profit after tax (☞ unit 25), each of which has a very precise definition. All of them, however, are a measure of some type of revenue minus some type of cost.

Sales revenue or sales turnover

The three owners of the business are very interested in the **sales revenue** or **sales turnover** of the company. This is the value of the sales of the business. Low sales had been one of the main reasons why the previous owner of the business had made losses. Since the three had bought the company, sales revenue had grown. This was a sign that the company was doing better.

The company charges on average £60 for a cricket bat. If it sells 100 cricket bats in a week, its weekly sales turnover would be

Table 23.1 *Stakis plc, turnover and costs for each year to 29 September.*

					£ million
	1992	1993	1994	1995	1996
Sales turnover	154.1	139.0	145.9	173.4	205.6
Costs	202.7	129.6	125.7	147.6	176.4

?

1 Calculate the profit for Stakis plc for each year between 1992 and 1996.
2 Calculate the costs for Thistle Hotels for each year between 1992 and 1996.
3 Which company do you think performed best over the period 1992 to 1996 and why?
4 In 1992, the economy was still in a deep recession. There was a slump in spending in the economy. From 1993, the economy began to recover and by 1996 was in boom. How can this explain the changes in the figures shown in the two tables?

Table 23.2 *Thistle Hotels plc, turnover and profit for each year to 29 December.*

					£ million
	1992	1993	1994	1995	1996
Sales turnover	217.3	214.1	241.2	267.5	290.3
Profit[1]	1.0	7.4	23.2	34.8	(27.7)

Note Brackets around a number in accounts means that it is a minus number. So profit of (27.7) million means that the company has made a loss of £27.7 million.
1 Profit on ordinary activities before taxation.

£60 x 100, which is equal to £6 000. If it sells 4 000 bats a year, its yearly sales turnover would be £60 x 4 000 which is £240 000.

The company makes a range of cricket bats. The most expensive cost £120, but it also makes some at £40, £60 and £80. The cheap cricket bats tend not to sell in large quantities because of competition from larger manufacturers who have greater **economies of scale** (☞ unit 18). They only sell 500 of these bats a year. The sales turnover of cheap £40 bats is therefore £40 x 500 which is equal to £20 000.

This shows that there are at least two ways of calculating sales turnover.

- Sales turnover is equal to the **average price** of the products **times** the number (or **volume**) sold. At an average price of £60, selling 4 000 bats, turnover would be £240 000.
- Sales turnover is equal to the **sum of the sales turnover** of each different product sold. For the Codsall Cricket Bat Company it is £240 000, equal to the sales turnover of £40 bats, plus £60 bats, plus £80 bats plus £120 bats.

One use that the company makes of average price is to calculate possible future revenues. If it could sell 5 000 bats rather than 4 000 bats a year at an average price of £60, it could increase its sales turnover from £240 000 to £300 000. Alternatively, if it could increase sales of the £120 bats by 500 and stop production of the cheapest £40 bats, then total sales would be the same but the average price would go up. If the new average price were £80, sales revenue on 4 000 bats would increase to £320 000.

Fixed and variable costs

The Codsall Cricket Bat Company has to pay a number of different costs. It has to pay for the willow to make the bats. The three owners are paid a wage, as are the two part-time workers. There is the rent to pay on the factory premises as well as costs like the telephone and electricity. John travels 30 000 miles a year visiting sports shops to sell the bats made by the company and so the company car is a major cost too. Codsall Cricket Bat Company sponsors 10 players each season who agree to put the company logo on their cricket bats. The company's overdraft at the bank also costs them interest.

Some of the costs stay the same however much is produced. For instance, it costs the same in rent whether 100 cricket bats a week are produced or just 20. Costs which don't vary with output are called FIXED COSTS.

One very important fact to be realised about fixed costs is that they have to be paid even if nothing is produced. If the company closed down for six weeks over the Christmas period due to lack of orders, it would still have to pay all its fixed costs during this period. The fixed cost line for the Codsall Cricket Bat Company is shown in Figure 23.1. It shows that the business has to pay out £120 000 each year however much is produced.

Some costs vary directly with the amount produced. For instance, the total cost of wood used goes up if more bats are made. Costs which vary with output are called VARIABLE COSTS. The variable cost curve for the business is shown in Figure 23.2. It shows, for instance, that the variable cost of 4 000 bats is £80 000. So the **average variable cost** (the total variable cost divided by the number produced) is £20 (£80 000 ÷ 4 000 bats).

TOTAL COSTS are the sum of these different types of cost. It is usual to assume that all costs are fixed or variable. So:

Total costs = fixed costs + variable costs

A total cost line is shown in Figure 23.3. It is drawn by adding together

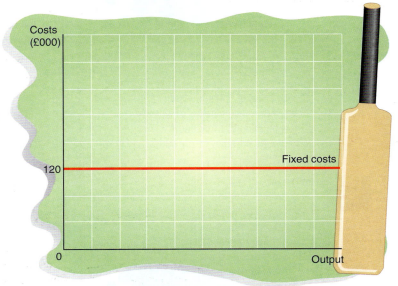

Figure 23.1 *The Codsall Cricket Bat Company's fixed costs. Whatever the level of output, fixed costs stay the same. This is why the fixed cost line is horizontal on the diagram.*

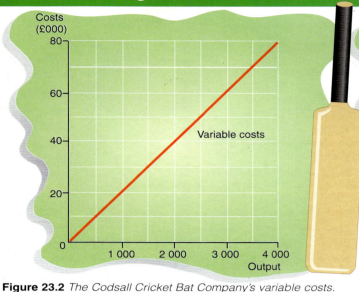

Figure 23.2 *The Codsall Cricket Bat Company's variable costs. Variable costs rise as the quantity produced goes up.*

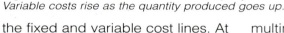

Figure 23.3 *The Codsall Cricket Bat Company's total costs.*

the fixed and variable cost lines. At an output of 4 000 bats:

Total costs = £120 000 + (£20 x 4 000)

So:

Total costs = £200 000

Direct and indirect costs

Some fixed costs are called **overhead costs** or **indirect costs**. Variable costs are then called **direct costs**. For a small business, fixed and overhead costs are likely to be the same. However, strictly speaking, in a large business like a public company or a multinational, fixed costs and overhead costs have different meanings. Direct costs are the costs of production like wood in bats. Indirect costs are all other costs like office costs or advertising.

The Codsall Cricket Bat Company keeps a constant watch on costs. If costs rise when sales revenue stays the same, its profits will be squeezed. Reducing costs, on the other hand, with revenues constant, will lead to a rise in profits.

The company uses costs when pricing products. It knows that, in the long run, it needs to set prices which will covers its total costs. The former owner of the company was prepared to take on orders for bats at less than the total cost price. When business was poor, he was prepared to sell at a price which at least covered the variable cost, but didn't include all of the fixed costs of production. He reasoned that any order which helped pay off at least some of the fixed cost was worth taking if the alternative was that his workers would be idle for some of the time. This is known as **contribution cost pricing** (☞ unit 39).

The CakeMake Company

You are finance director of the CakeMake Company. Your mini-company idea has been to make cakes and sell them to adults at various school functions, such as school concerts, jumble sales and open evenings.

You are making some financial projections about revenues for a future school fete.

1 How much revenue would you make if you sold:
(a) 60 fairy cakes at 5p each?
(b) 20 large chocolate gateaux at £2 each?
(c) 30 sponge cakes at £1.00 each?
(d) 50 chocolate brownies at 20p each?
(e) all of (a) to (d)?

Spreadsheet

2 You know that your task as finance director, projecting revenues, costs and profits, would be simpler if you used a spreadsheet package. Enter the data for price and sales of each type of cake on a spreadsheet in order to calculate total revenue. Calculate what would happen to total revenues if prices changed to: (a) fairy cakes 10p, chocolate gateaux £3, sponge cakes £1.50 and chocolate brownies 30p; (b) fairy cakes 3p, chocolate gateaux £1.50, sponge cakes 75p and chocolate brownies 15p.

3 If the cost of making a fairy cake was 2.5p, a chocolate gateaux £1.25, a sponge cake 60p and a chocolate brownie 12p, what would be the total cost of making the batch of cakes for the fete?

4 What would be the profit at each of the three levels of prices?

5 Assuming that you could sell all the cakes, which level of prices would you choose to charge and why?

? Many businesses offer leisure facilities to customers. Sometimes cinemas, theatres and concert halls are only open for part of the day. Look at the photographs.

1 Explain what you think the fixed costs of these businesses might be.

2 Explain what might be their variable costs.

3 How do these businesses earn revenue?

4 (a) Suggest TWO ways in which the businesses could increase their revenue.

(b) What are the likely effects of these suggestions on: (i) fixed costs; and (ii) variable costs?

Checklist ✓

1 How is profit calculated?

2 A business increases its profit but costs too have increased. What must have happened?

3 A business sells dresses at an average price of £10. What is the sales turnover of the business if its weekly sales are: (a) 10 dresses; (b) 100 dresses; (c) 898 dresses?

4 The monthly turnover of a company is £2 million. The turnover of its tractor division was £1/2 million. What was the monthly turnover of the rest of the company?

5 What is the difference between a fixed cost and a variable cost?

6 List: (a) TWO fixed costs; and (b) TWO variable costs which a music shop is likely to face.

7 Which of the following are likely to be (i) fixed costs and (ii) variable costs for a garden centre:
(a) fertilizer; (b) a new car park; (c) ice creams; (d) plant pots; (e) the manager's salary;
(f) a new potting shed; (g) new tables and chairs for the restaurant?

Key terms

Fixed costs - costs which remain the same whatever the level of output of the business.

Profit - the difference between sales revenue and costs.

Sales revenue or turnover - the money value of the sale of products by a business.

Total costs - all the costs incurred by a business over a period of time. It is equal to fixed cost plus variable cost.

Variable costs - costs which vary directly with the output of the business.

SUMMARY CASE STUDY

WEDDINGS GALORE

Victoria Skeldon runs a business making and selling one off creations - mostly wedding dresses. She started the business four years ago with the help of a large redundancy package. Having sold her house as well, she was able to move into a large Georgian property which could double up as business premises and a home. Even so, she had to borrow to convert part of the property and give her the working capital she needed to start.

Every month she has to make repayments on the loan. Then there are the electricity, gas and telephone bills to pay. She advertises in national magazines. An accountant does her books and sorts out her tax affairs. She also runs a car for the business to pick up materials and deliver work to her outworkers. Other costs include repairs to the building, buying new fixtures and fittings and exhibiting at shows.

Every dress she makes is a one off creation designed according to the requirements of the customer. When she set up, she equipped the shop with samples of material. However, she carries virtually no material in stock. Material for a particular dress is specially ordered. Equally, she has no permanent staff on her pay roll. All the sewing and cutting work is done by out workers who are paid by the job.

The average outfit is priced at £1 500. This year, she sold 100 outfits. The cost of the materials and paying her outworkers came to £60 000. Her other costs came to £70 000.

1 Make a list of Victoria Skeldon's: (a) fixed costs; and (b) variable costs in running her business.

2 (a) How many outfits did she sell this year? (b) What was the average price paid by customers for each outfit? (c) What was her total sales revenue for the year?

3 (a) State the value of her total variable costs. (b) Calculate the average variable cost of making each dress.

4 State the value of her total fixed costs.

5 Calculate the value of her total costs - her total variable costs plus her total fixed costs.

6 How much profit did she make by selling 100 outfits?

7 Would she have made a profit if she had only sold 50 outfits during the year? Explain your answer.

8 A friend suggests that she ought to employ at least one of her outworkers on a permanent basis as a full time employee. What might be the advantages and disadvantages for Victoria Skeldon of doing this?

unit 24

BREAKING EVEN

Making decisions

Businesses have to decide how much to produce. Nearly all businesses need at least to break even in order to survive. One way in which businesses can plan is to draw up budgets. Once a draft budget is drawn up, the business must decide whether or not it is going to change its plans because of what the budget shows. Another way is for businesses to calculate the break-even point of production. Will sales levels be high enough for the business to cover its costs and make a profit?

Claire Peakman is planning her spending. Her dad, Roger, is doing the same. He is setting up an business importing lamps and estimating whether or not it will make a profit. They are doing this on Budget day, the day when the Chancellor of the Exchequer, the person responsible for the government's finances, is announcing the government's tax and spending plans for the year. They are all calculating a budget.

Budgets

A BUDGET is a **forecast** of what might happen. Table 24.1 shows Claire Peakman's budget. She gets £50 a month from her parents and earns £50 a month from a part time job. Her monthly income is therefore £100. She plans to spend it on clothes, food and going out. She hopes to have £10 left over to save.

The budget shown in Table 24.2 for Peakman Lighting is more complex. Roger Peakman fell in love with a particular lamp design he found when on holiday in Russia. He thought it was unusual enough to stand out in the UK market, but at the same time the design would fit into a typical UK home. Roger forecasts that he will be will able to sell 5 000 lamps in his first year. At £15 each, this will give his business total sales turnover of £75 000 (£15 x 5 000).

Out of that, he has various costs to pay. The Russian firm supplying the lamps is charging £10 per lamp including transport to the UK. So the charge for the lamps is £10 x 5 000 = £50 000. Roger plans to pay himself £10 000 working full time on the business. Initially, he will spend much of his time visiting lighting and furniture shops selling the lamps to them. Hence, he needs a car and travel expenses. The cost of this he estimates will be £4 000. He plans to spend £2 000 on advertising. He will start with specialist trade journals for the lighting industry. Stocks of lamps need to be stored. Roger didn't want to keep the stocks in a cheap lock up garage because the insurance costs were so high. He also didn't want his business to have no stock to sell if it was stolen. But the cost of arranging secure warehousing including insurance was £1 000. Roger also needed to borrow money from the bank to finance various start up costs of the business, such as buying a second hand estate car. He kept these costs to a minimum but the repayments on the loan were £1 000 a year. Other costs included telephone charges, stationery and some secretarial assistance. These he estimated would come to £2 000.

The budget shows that the estimated profit for the year is £5 000.

Uncertainty

A budget is only a forecast. Many things can happen which could make the actual outturn different

Table 24.1 *Claire Peakman's monthly budget.*

Income (£)		Spending (£)	
Allowance	50	Clothes	45
Job	50	Food	10
		Going out	35
		Saving	10
	100		100

Table 24.2 *12 month budget for Peakman Lighting.*

Revenue (£)		Costs (£)	
Sales	75 000	Lamps	50 000
		Wages	10 000
		Travel costs	4 000
		Advertising	2 000
		Warehousing	1 000
		Loan repayments	1 000
		Other costs	2 000
	75 000		70 000
		Profit	5 000
			75 000

Roger Peakman felt very frustrated at the end of his first year. His lamp had been very well received and had even got into a national paper weekend supplement on design. But his Russian suppliers were unpredictable. They never delivered on time. Out of the order for 5 000 lamps, only 2 000 had been delivered by July. In August, he had received a firm promise from the suppliers that 3 000 would be delivered on 30 September. He had spent a frantic two months in September and October travelling and placing orders in anticipation of Christmas buying. The Russian suppliers put back the date to mid October and then in late October only sent 1 000. So he only sold 3 000 over the whole year. These problems led to increases in some of his costs that he had not predicted.

1 Table 24.3 shows what actually happened to Peakman Lighting in its first year of operation. Compare it with the projected budget in Table 24.2.
   (a) What is the difference between what Roger Peakman budgeted for and what actually happened?
   (b) Suggest why the outturn was different from the forecast.
2 Is Peakman Lighting in difficulties? You need to consider: (a) his finances; (b) the relationship with his suppliers; (c) the relationship with his customers.
3 Roger Peakman has drawn up a budget for the next 12 months. Write down this budget assuming that:
   (a) he finds a new supplier in England who will copy the design and supply 6 000 lamps, but at an increased cost of £11 each;
   (b) he sells all he buys;
   (c) he pays himself £10 000 plus the balance of what he had hoped to pay himself in his first year;
   (d) he cuts his advertising to £1 000;
   (e) all other costs remain the same as in the outturn for his first year.
4 (a) According to this second year budget, will Peakman Lighting be in financial difficulty? Explain your answer.
   (b) Suggest TWO ways in which Roger Peakman could improve his financial position.

Table 24.3 *12 month outturn for Peakman Lighting.*

Revenue (£)		Costs (£)	
Sales	45 000	Lamps	30 000
		Wages	5 000
		Travel costs	6 000
		Advertising	4 500
		Warehousing	1 000
		Loan repayments	1 000
		Other costs	1 500
	45 000		49 000

Spreadsheet

5 Use a spreadsheet package to draw up a range of budget forecasts for the second year based upon the first year outturn in Table 24.3. Place output in the first row and revenue, costs and profit or loss in the first column.
   (a) Get a printout showing the budgets for sales of 2 000, 3 000, 4 000, 5 000, 6 000, 7 000 and 8 000 lamps. Assume that the price to customers is £15, the cost of the lamp is £10 and all other costs are the same as in Table 24.3. Calculate the loss or profit at each of the different output levels.
   (b) Produce three new spreadsheets showing the budgets for sales of 2 000, 3 000, 4 000, 5 000, 6 000, 7 000 and 8 000 lamps at prices to customers of: (i) £16; (ii) £17; and (iii) £18. Assume that the cost of the lamp is £10 and all other costs are the same as in Table 24.3. Calculate the loss or profit at each of the different output levels. Identify the outputs between which the business would break even for each spreadsheet.

from what was budgeted. For instance, Roger may find that he doesn't sell 5 000 lamps a year. His Russian supplier may put up the price so costs increase. The Chancellor of the Exchequer may put up the tax on petrol making his motoring expenses higher than forecast. Roger may decide half way through the year not to spend so much on advertising. The **exchange rate** (☞ unit 7) of the pound against the rouble (the Russian currency) may rise, making the price in pounds sterling of the lamps cheaper.

However, budgets are vital for a business because they help it to plan its finances. If Roger Peakman had produced a budget which showed that he would make a £10 000 loss instead of a £5 000 profit, he would have had to consider whether to go ahead with starting up the business. Would the loss have been just for the first year? The budget would help him decide whether there was any chance of making a profit in the long term.

Break-even

Roger Peakman had forecast a profit of £5 000 in his first year. However, the actual profit may be less than this if he sells fewer lamps or his costs are higher. He wants to know at what point he would just BREAK EVEN. The break-even point is the one where he would neither make a

Budgeting at High Valley School

The economics and business studies department at High Valley School has been given £3 000 to spend on books and other resources by the headteacher. The department would like to buy the following textbooks: 100 copies of **GCSE Business Studies** by Alain Anderton at £13 each; 100 copies of **Economics for GCSE** by Alain Anderton at £13 each; 10 copies of **Business Studies** by Hall, Jones, Raffo and Chambers at £16 each; 20 copies of **Economics** by Alain Anderton at £18 each. These prices include any discount given. The department needs to spend £500 on paper and exercise books. It would like to buy £300 worth of computer accessories including disks. It needs to set aside £500 for photocopying over the year. It would also like to have £300 for buying single books and resource packs. The head of department is grateful that her £3 000 budget doesn't have to cover her new GNVQ courses for which there is a separate budget.

1 Draw up a draft budget for the department. Set it out as in Tables 24.1 and 24.2.
2 The department can't overspend its £3 000 allowance given by the headteacher. Explain whether the budget shows there is a problem for the department.
3 How could the head of department resolve any problem?

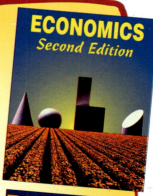

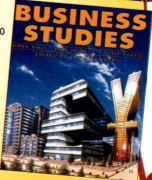

profit or a loss. He is going to use the figures in his draft budget in Table 24.2 as a basis for his projections.

The simplest break-even calculation involves total revenue, total fixed costs and total variable costs (☞ unit 23).

Total revenue Total revenue can be calculated by multiplying average revenue and the quantity sold. The average revenue in this case is the price of the lamp - £15. Table 24.4 shows how total revenue rises as the number of lamps sold rises. At 2 000 sales, it is £30 000. At 3 000 sales, it is £45 000. At 4 000 sales, it is £60 000.

Total variable cost The only variable cost for Peakman Lighting is the cost of buying the lamps from the Russian suppliers. This is £10 per lamp. So if he sells 2 000 lamps, the total variable cost would be 2 000 x £10 or £20 000. Selling 3 000 lamps would give a variable cost of 3 000 x £10 or £30 000.

Total fixed cost All his other costs are fixed costs. They do not vary whether he sells 20 000 or 60 000 lamps. So the total fixed costs are £20 000.

Table 24.4 shows that the **break-even point,** where total costs equal total revenue, is at 4 000 sales per year. If sales are more than this, he will make a profit. If they are below this level, he will make a loss.

Break-even charts

The information in Table 24.4 can be shown on a graph, called a BREAK-EVEN CHART. In Figure 24.1, the total revenue line starts at 0 because with no sales, there is no revenue. It rises as every extra sale brings in an extra £15 of revenue.

The total cost line does not start at 0. This is because, whatever the number of sales, there will always be fixed costs of £20 000. The total fixed cost line is therefore a straight horizontal line across the chart. However, total variable cost does increase as sales increase. It is equal to the distance between the total cost line and the total fixed cost line. In this case, it is equal to total cost minus £20 000. The total cost line (equal to the sum of total fixed cost and total variable cost) starts therefore at £20 000 and then rises.

The BREAK-EVEN POINT is where the total cost and total revenue lines cross. This is at a sales level of 4 000 and at a total cost and revenue level of £60 000.

Table 24.4 *Break-even analysis for Peakman Lighting.*

					£ per year
Sales	Total revenue (average price, £15, x quantity sold)	Total fixed cost	Total variable cost (£10 x quantity sold)	Total cost (fixed cost plus variable cost)	Profit/loss (total revenue minus total cost)[1]
2 000	30 000	20 000	20 000	40 000	(10 000)
3 000	45 000	20 000	30 000	50 000	(5 000)
4 000	60 000	20 000	40 000	60 000	0
5 000	75 000	20 000	50 000	70 000	5 000
6 000	90 000	20 000	60 000	80 000	10 000

1 Losses are shown by putting bracket around the number.

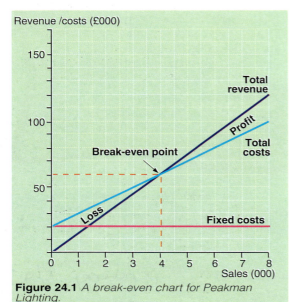

Figure 24.1 *A break-even chart for Peakman Lighting.*

The Lakeland Hotel

Mr and Mrs Singh run the Lakeland Hotel. They have 15 rooms and can accommodate up to 25 visitors. The average guest pays £50 per night for bed and breakfast. In addition, they spend £10 on an evening meal. Most costs are the same whether the hotel is full or half empty; these are the wages of staff, business rates, repairs, etc., which come to £750 per day. Some bills, however, vary according to the number of rooms occupied, such as heating and lighting and laundry bills. These variable costs on average come to £6 per guest. The food cost for the hotel of an evening meal comes to £4 per meal.

Table 24.5

				£ per night
Number of guests	Total revenue	Total fixed cost	Total variable cost	Total cost
5				
10				
15				
20				
25				

1 Complete Table 24.5, showing revenues and costs changing as the number of guests per night change.
2 Draw a break-even chart from your calculations in Table 24.5. Remember to put quantity (i.e. the number of guests per night) along the horizontal axis and costs and revenues on the vertical axis.
   You must have a total revenue line, a total fixed cost line and a total cost line on the graph.
3 Mark the break-even point on the chart.
4 It is June. The average number of guests staying per night so far this year has been 10.
   (a) Explain whether or not you think the Singhs have a problem.
   (b) How could the Singhs reduce their break-even point do you think?

To the right of the point, Peakman Lighting will make a profit whilst to the left it will make a loss.

The number of actual sales above the break-even point is known as the MARGIN OF SAFETY. It is the range of output over which a profit can be made.

Using break-even charts

Break-even charts can be constructed to show the break-even point on past production. This gives a guide to what the current break-even point might be. However, Roger Peakman was using break-even analysis to forecast profit. Any forecast is more than likely to be wrong because the figures on which the forecast is based will change in reality.

For Roger Peakman, the forecast was very important. It allowed him to see what risk he was taking in setting up the business. As the first year went by, he had a good understanding of how he was doing and whether or not he was heading for a profit or a loss. The bank manager who gave him the loan also wanted to see Roger's business plan (☞ unit 22). This included the break-even forecast. The bank manager used it to discuss whether he would be likely to meet the sales targets needed to break even.

(☞ unit 22)

SUMMARY CASE STUDY

STAYFRESH BAKERIES

Stayfresh Bakeries bakes bread and sells it to wholesalers. On average, each loaf is sold for 50p. Figure 24.2 shows production in millions of loaves of bread.

1 What is the break-even point of sales?
2 What is the current margin of safety (in quantity of loaves) if production is 1.2 million loaves?
3 How much profit is the business currently making?

Draw the axes for a break-even chart running from 0 to 1.5 million loaves on the horizontal axis and 0 to £750 000 on the vertical axis. (You will find this easier if you use graph paper.)

4 Stayfresh Bakeries gives staff a pay rise and buys new machinery. This increases fixed costs by £50 000 a year. Plot the new fixed cost line on your diagram.

5 The cost of flour goes up. This increases the variable cost of a loaf of bread by 8 per cent, from 25p per loaf to 27p. Plot the new total cost line on your diagram.

6 Stayfresh Bakeries increases its prices by 4 per cent, from 50p per loaf to 52p per loaf to cover these increases in costs. Plot the new revenue line on your diagram.

7 What has happened: (a) to the break-even point; and (b) profit on sales of 1.2 million loaves?

8 The aim of the company is to make £50 000 profit per year. Suggest how the business could do this.

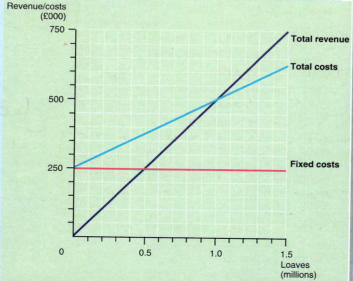

Figure 24.2 *A break-even chart for Stayfresh Bakeries.*

Revenue/costs (£000)

Total revenue
Total costs
Fixed costs

Loaves (millions)

---

key terms

Break-even - where revenues equal costs.
Break-even chart - a graph which shows total costs and total revenues and the break-even point where total revenue equals total cost.
Budget - a forecast of income and expenditure over a period of time, like a week or a year.
Margin of safety - the quantity sold above the break-even point where the business makes a profit.

Checklist ✓

1 'A budget is a forecast.' What does this mean?

2 Each November, the Chancellor of the Exchequer announces his budget. What is in the budget?

3 A business draws up a budget which shows that its costs over the next month will be £1 000 whilst its revenues will be £900. It wants to make a profit during the month. How can this information help in its planning?

4 Why might an actual business' finances be different from what it planned in its budget for the period?

5 Three lines are normally drawn on a break-even chart. What are they?

6 Why is the fixed cost line on a break-even chart horizontal?

7 How much profit does a business make at its break-even point?

8 A business is currently producing 1 000 units per week and it is making a profit. Its break-even point is 600 units per week. (a) What is its margin of safety? (b) How would its margin of safety change if the break-even point: (i) rose to 800 units; (ii) dropped to 300 units?

9 Why do businesses calculate their break-even points?

THE PROFIT AND LOSS ACCOUNT

Making decisions

How does a business and its competitors assess whether it is trading successfully? How does an individual or a pension fund manager know which companies to invest in on the Stock Exchange? How do the tax authorities know how much tax to charge a company on its profits? One way is for them to look at the profit and loss account of a business. The business itself can also use its profit and loss account to help it make decisions now, and to plan for the future.

Coats Viyella is the UK's largest textile business. It sells a wide variety of products such as thread, both to other textile manufacturers and directly to consumers, as well as clothes and home furnishings. It also has a precision engineering division. Each year, by company law, it has to produce a set of accounts. One account is the profit and loss account.

Use of profit and loss accounts

The PROFIT AND LOSS ACCOUNT is a record of revenues and costs of the business over a period such as a year. It shows how much profit the business has made over the past year and what has happened to the profit.

The profit and loss account is a record of **past** costs and revenues. However, it can still help people in the business to make decisions about the future because the account says something about where the business has been in the recent past. On the whole though, other financial data, such as cash flow forecasts (☞ unit 28) are far more useful than the profit and loss account in helping businesses make these decisions.

More importantly, the profit and loss account is a summary of recent business events for the owners of the business and anyone who might want to invest in the business. Shareholders in limited companies, for instance, are particularly interested in trends in profits because they determine, in part, how valuable is their share of the business. Profit and loss accounts are also used by the tax authorities to assess a company's tax. Other businesses may also look at a company's profit and loss account for the previous year to judge whether it is safe to give it credit (☞ unit 31).

The profit and loss account of Coats Viyella is shown in Table 25.1.

The profit and loss account can be split into **three** parts:
- the trading account;
- the profit and loss account;
- the appropriation account.

Table 25.1 *Profit and loss account for Coats Viyella, 1996.[1]*

	£million
Sales turnover	2 455.1
Cost of sales	(1 739.7)
Gross profit	715.4
Operating costs	(603.8)
Other	(17.2)
Net profit[2]	94.4
Taxation	(34.1)
Dividends	(72.9)
Retained profit	(12.6)

1 Brackets around a number mean that it is a minus figure.
2 Profit on ordinary activities before taxation.

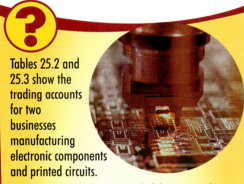

Tables 25.2 and 25.3 show the trading accounts for two businesses manufacturing electronic components and printed circuits.

1 Calculate the gross profit of: (a) M&P Products; and (b) Techmark.

2 Which business, in your opinion, has performed best between 1993 and 1997? Explain your answer carefully.

Table 25.2 *M&P Products, trading account, 1993-199*

					£ million
	1993	1994	1995	1996	1997
Turnover	60	100	200	210	210
Cost of sales	40	80	150	160	170

Table 25.3 *Techmark, trading account, 1993-1997*

					£ milli
	1993	1994	1995	1996	199
Turnover	100	90	100	110	12
Cost of sales	70	65	70	75	8

Gross profit

The **first** part of the profit and loss account is the TRADING ACCOUNT shown in Table 25.5. The trading account is a record of sales turnover and the cost of sales.

- **Sales turnover** is the value of the sales of the business (☞ unit 23). In 1996, Coats Viyella sold just over £2 455 million worth of products.
- COST OF SALES was nearly £1 740 million for Coats Viyella in 1996. This is the cost of production. For Coats Viyella, this included buying in raw materials as well as employing workers to manufacture products such as clothes.

The trading account shows the GROSS PROFIT of the business. This is the profit made before the overheads of the business are taken into account. Gross profit is defined as sales turnover (one measure of revenue) minus cost of sales (one measure of costs):

*Gross profit =
Sales turnover - cost of sales*

In 1996, Coats Viyella had a gross profit of over £715 million.

Table 25.5 *Trading account for Coats Viyella, 1996.[1]*

	£million
Sales turnover	2 455.1
Cost of sales	(1 739.7)
Gross profit	715.4

Note: brackets around a number mean that it is a minus number.

Table 25.6 *Calculating net profit for Coats Viyella, 1996.[1]*

	£million
Gross profit	715.4
Distribution costs	(412.7)
Administrative expenses	(191.1)
Interest received	17.0
Interest paid	(53.3)
Profit on sale of fixed assets	11.6
Other	7.5
Net profit[2]	94.4

1 Brackets around a number mean that it is a minus figure.
2 Profit on ordinary activities before taxation.

Table 25.4 *Trading and profit and loss account Lo-Cost Bakeries Ltd for year ending 31 March.*

	1995	1996	1997
	£000	£000	£000
Sales turnover	2 038	2 372	2 216
less Cost of sales	1 689	1 903	1 854
Gross profit	?	?	?
less Operating expenses			
Wages	195	224	?
Van expenses	70	94	60
Depreciation	12	17	14
Other	?	84	159
Net profit	32	?	(108)

Note: brackets around a number mean that it is a minus figure.

Lo-Cost Bakeries

1 Copy out the profit and loss accounts for 1995-97 and fill in the missing figures.
2 What has happened to:
   (a) sales turnover;
   (b) cost of sales; (c) gross profit; (d) net profit over the three years?
3 Do you think the company is doing well or badly? Give reasons for your answer.

Net profit

The **second** part is the actual profit and loss account. This involves calculating net profit. This is show in Table 25.6. NET PROFIT is the profit made by a business after all its costs have been taken into account. So it is revenue minus both the cost of sales and all the other costs of the business, the overheads.

Not all the revenue of a business is sales revenue. Table 25.6 shows that Coats Viyella, for instance, received interest on money which it had deposited in the bank and elsewhere. It also received cash from the sale of assets, like factories and land. Other income may be profits of **subsidiary companies** (☞ unit 15), for example. These non-sales revenues need to be added to sales revenue in order to be able to calculate net profit.

Equally, not all costs are costs of sales. **Operating expenses** or **overheads** are the costs which are not directly related to production. Table 25.6 shows two different operating costs for Coats Viyella.

Distribution costs These include the costs of **marketing** (☞ unit 34) and selling products. For instance, Coats Viyella owns the Dorma label in bed linen. It spends money on advertising Dorma products in magazines.

Administration expenses These include the costs of employees not directly employed in production. For instance, the salaries of the directors of the company would be an administration expense. It also includes all the other costs of administering the company, such as the cost of running the headquarters of the company in London.

Table 25.7 *Appropriation account for Coats Viyella, 1996.[1]*

	£miilion
Net profit[2]	94.4
Taxation	(34.1)
Dividends	(72.9)
Retained profit	(12.6)

1 Brackets around a number mean that it is a minus figure.
2 Profit on ordinary activities before taxation.

Net profit can be calculated either as:

gross profit + non-sales revenue - operating cost

or, using the definition for gross profit:

sales revenue + non-sales revenue - cost of sales - operating cost

In 1996, Coats Viyella had a net profit before taxation of £94.4 million.

The appropriation account

If the business is a company, then the profit and loss account will end with figures which show where the net profit has gone. This is the **third** part of the profit and loss account, called the APPROPRIATION ACCOUNT.

Net profit can be distributed in three ways. First, part of it has to be paid to the government in taxes, mainly corporation tax, a tax on company profits. Second, the company may distribute part of the profits to its shareholders in dividends. Third, the company can retain (keep back) some of the profit to pay for new investment in the company. This **retained profit** is the main way in which businesses tend to pay for new investment in the UK.

Table 25.7 shows the appropriation account for Coats Viyella for 1996. It paid £34.1 million in taxes on profits and distributed £72.9 million to its various shareholders. It paid out more in taxes and dividends than it earned in profit. So instead of retaining profit, it took some of the money that had been retained in previous years and used this to pay for part of the taxes and dividends.

Depreciation

Coats Viyella owns buildings, machines, cars and office equipment. These wear out over time and, as a result, fall in value. This fall in value is called DEPRECIATION. It is counted as a cost because the fall in value is what it is costing the business to own and operate these assets. Some businesses include depreciation in costs of sales in the trading account. Sometimes it is included as an overhead cost.

There are different ways of calculating depreciation. One way, called the **reducing balance method**, is simply to take off a percentage of the value of the value of any asset, like a machine. Coats Viyella uses this method. For instance, it takes between 5 and 25 per cent of the value of its machinery each year depending upon how long it is expected to last. A machine costing £100 000 and depreciated at 10 per cent per year would suffer depreciation of £10 000 (£100 000 x 10%) in its first year. Its value would therefore then be £90 000.

Another method is called the **straight line method**. Say a machine was bought for £110 000 and would be sold for an estimated £10 000 in five years time. The business would therefore use up £100 000 worth of the machine over 5 years. On this method, it would depreciate the car at a fixed £20 000 each year for 5 years.

Company car depreciation

Billingstone Group is a business which manufactures soap. It employs two sales representatives who travel the country trying to win orders. This year, it bought the senior rep a £16 000 company car and the junior rep a £12 000 car. It is company policy to keep cars for three years and then sell them second hand.

1 The finance director estimates that the senior rep's car will be worth £4 000 and the junior rep's car worth £3 000 at the end of the three years. Calculate (i) the depreciation and (ii) the value of each car at the end of each year and record your answer in Table 25.8. Use the straight line method of depreciation.

2 Now use the reducing balance method to depreciate the cars instead of the straight line method. The company depreciates its reps' cars at a rate of 35 per cent each year. Record your answers using Table 25.8 again. You will find this much easier if you use a calculator.

3 What is the difference between the values of the cars using each method at the end of each year?

Spreadsheet

4 Use a spreadsheet package to show the different amounts of depreciation and book values of a £20 000 car assuming a reducing balance method of depreciation is used. Calculate your answer for yearly rates of depreciation of 10 per cent, 11 per cent, and every whole per cent up to 40 per cent.

Table 25.8

	Senior rep's car		Junior rep's car	
	Depreciation over the year	Value at end of year	Depreciation over the year	Value at end of year
First year				
Second year				
Third year				

£

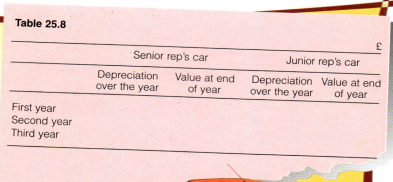

Cost of production and stock

The cost of production used in a profit and loss account includes not just purchases made by the business but also CHANGES IN STOCK.

Stocks are raw materials and finished products like thread or clothes which the company has in store. The raw materials are waiting to be made into products. The products are waiting to be sold to customers. Coats Viyella started its financial year in 1995 with £512.7 million of stocks. It ended its financial year in 1996 with closing stock of £474.4 million. So its stock levels had fallen by £38.3 million.

Since stocks have fallen, some of what was sold in 1996 was made using materials bought in previous years. Hence, the cost of sales must be increased by the amount of the fall in stocks (opening stock minus closing stock) to calculate cost of sales. Alternatively, if stocks had risen the cost of sales would have be reduced by the amount of the fall in stock to calculate cost of sales. As a formula:

Cost of sales = cost of purchases + opening stock - closing stock

Source: adapted from Coats Viyella plc, *Annual Report and Accounts*, 1996.

Canadian Pizza

Canadian Pizza plc is a company which makes and supplies pizza crusts and topped pizzas to the pizza market worldwide. It also manufactures cooking sauces, fruit spread and a variety of ingredients for the retail and health-food sectors through its Meridian Foods subsidiary bought in mid-1996.

Source: adapted from Canadian Pizza plc, *Annual Report and Accounts*, 1996.

Table 25.9 *Appropriation account for Canadian Pizza plc.1*

	£ millions	
	1995	1996
Net profit (profit on ordinary activities before taxation)	1 410	2 125
Taxation on profit	431	639
Dividends	782	875

1 Accounts for the year ended 31 December.

1 A company distributes its net profit in three ways. What are they?
2 Calculate the retained profit for Canadian pizza plc for 1995 and 1996.
3 Suggest why over the period 1995 to 1996: (a) taxes on profits rose; (b) the company chose ti increase its dividends to shareholders; (c) the company retained part of the profit instead of distributing to shareholders.

Checklist ✓

1 Who might look at a profit and loss account of a company and why?
2 What is included in the trading account?
3 What costs are taken into account when calculating net profit?
4 Explain TWO ways of calculating depreciation.
5 Describe THREE types of operating cost.
6 Why would an increase in non-sales revenue increase net profit but not gross profit, assuming all other costs and revenues stayed the same?
7 Explain how a company uses its net profit.
8 How do changes in stocks affect: (a) cost of sales; and (b) gross profit?

key terms

Appropriation account - the part of the profit and loss account which shows what has happened to net profit.
Change in stock - closing stock minus the opening stock.
Cost of sales - costs of production such as raw materials costs, direct wage costs and changes in stock.
Depreciation - the fall in value of fixed equipment and buildings over time as they wear out.
Gross profit - sales turnover minus cost of sales.
Net profit - the profit made after all costs and revenues have been taken into account. It is gross profit plus non-sales revenue minus operating costs.
Profit and loss account - a record of the revenues and costs of a business over a period such as six months or a year.
Trading account - part of the profit and loss account which shows sales turnover, costs of sales and changes in stocks.

SUMMARY CASE STUDY

J SIMMONS JOINERY

Table 25.10 *Profit and loss account J Simmons Joinery for year ending 31 June.*

	1994 £000	1995 £000	1996 £000	1997 £000
Sales turnover	196	193	196	316
less Cost of sales	100	119	?	175
Gross profit	?	?	90	?
less Operating expenses				
Directors' wages	18	18	18	34
Equipment and vehicle hire	18	14	?	19
Motor expenses	8	5	8	13
Other	42	?	35	47
Net profit	?	11	11	?
Corporation tax	0	0	0	3
Dividends	2	3	3	15
Retained profit	?	?	?	?

1 Copy out the profit and loss account for the company and fill in the missing figures.
2 What has happened to the company's: (a) sales; (b) costs; and (c) net profit between 1994 and 1997?
3 How has the company distributed its net profit?
4 How well did the company perform in 1997 compared to 1994?

BALANCE SHEETS

Making decisions

A limited company must, by law, produce a balance sheet showing the assets and liabilities of the company on the last day of its accounting year. The balance sheet is often said to reflect the value of a business. It can be used by other businesses and individuals to judge, for instance, whether a business is safe enough to lend money to, to invest in or to buy out. A business itself can also use it to decide whether it can meet its current debts and to make decisions about the future.

Beauford PLC is a group of companies making ceramic goods. These include ceramic parts for the computer industry, ceramic powders for sale to other manufacturers and ceramic logs used as imitation logs on gas fires. The company also makes a wide range of ceramic ware including whisky flagons, pub ware, figurines and other collectors items, and door and bathroom furniture. In 1996, the company's sales turnover from selling ceramics was £27.5 million and it made a net profit of £1 million.

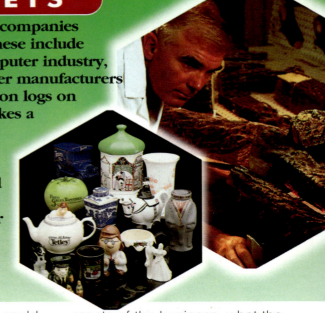

The balance sheet

To operate as a business, Beauford has to have ASSETS. These are what the business **owns**, such as buildings, offices, machinery, stocks and cash.

Without assets, a business could not produce anything. To buy these assets, a business will need to raise funds from different **sources**. For example, Beauford might have borrowed money, or it might owe money to other businesses for materials that it has received but not yet paid for. Money **owed** to others is called the LIABILITIES of a business.

The BALANCE SHEET is a record of the assets and liabilities of a business at a particular point in time. It **must** balance. The

assets of the business, what the business owns, must equal its liabilities, what it owes. Included in what it owes are the monies owed to the owners of the business, such as profit.

By law a limited company has to produce a balance sheet for its shareholders. This shows its assets and liabilities on the last day of its accounting year. For Beauford, this is 31 December each year. Companies can, though, choose any date on which to end their financial year. A company could,

Table 26.1 *Beauford PLC, balance sheet at 31 December 1996.*

	£000
Fixed assets	
Tangible assets	10 254
Investments	3
	10 257
Current assets	
Stocks	3 351
Debtors	6 241
Cash at bank	71
	9 663
Current liabilities	
Creditors: amounts falling due within one year	(6 800)
Net current assets	2 863
Total assets less current liabilities	13 120
Long term liabilities	
Creditors: amounts falling due after more than one year	(4 947)
Provisions for liabilities and charges	(98)
Net assets	8 075
Capital and reserves	
Share capital	10 737
Retained profit and reserves	(2 718)
	8 075

Lane's hardware and electrical shop was always busy. However, Mr Lane wanted to retire and so he put the shop up for sale for £50 000. Fixed assets were valued at £15 000 and the value of stock was £20 000. The goodwill, equal to 1½ times net profit, was £15 000.

1 Make a list of the fixed assets that such a shop might have.
2 The new owner paid £15 000 for the goodwill of the business. Do you think you would have paid the same if you had bought the business? To answer this, make a list of the costs of attracting customers if you had to set up a new business in the area. Estimate or try to find out figures for those costs.

Table 26.2 *Tesco plc, current assets, 22 February 1996 and 1997.*

	1996 £m	1997 £m
Stocks	559	550
Debtors	80	78
Cash at bank and in hand	38	65
Other	54	80
Current assets	731	773

1 Short term investments in the London money markets.
Source: adapted from Tesco plc, *Annual Report and Accounts,* 1997.

for instance, choose a financial year which runs from 1 February to 31 January.

Fixed assets

The balance sheet starts with a record of the FIXED ASSETS of the business. These assets include land as well as buildings such as factories, offices and fixed plant. Fixed assets also include all the machinery and equipment owned by the business, such as machine tools, computers, furniture, cars and trucks. Table 26.1 shows that the value of these TANGIBLE ASSETS was nearly £10.3 million at 31 December 1996. Not all assets are tangible, i.e. assets that you could physically touch. One example of an **intangible asset** is **investments**. These are investments (normally shareholdings) in other companies. They could also be loans to the government (called bonds) which earn interest for the company. Or they could be other types of long term financial investment by the company. Table 26.1 shows that Beauford had £3 000 of

investments. These were in private UK investments.

Some businesses also include other types of intangible assets. The most common is GOODWILL. This is usually the value of the customer contacts of the business. For instance, if the business had to be set up from scratch, it might have to spend money on advertising to build up its customer base. So one way of measuring goodwill is to estimate how much it would cost to set up the business with its customers.

Current assets

CURRENT ASSETS are the assets of the business which can easily be turned into cash or are cash, i.e. they are the LIQUID ASSETS of the business. Table 26.1 shows that there are three main types of current asset.

Stocks Stocks are the raw materials and goods waiting to be processed, and finished goods awaiting sale. Beauford, for instance, would carry stocks of clay and paints to make ceramic products. It would also carry

stocks of finished goods such as logs waiting for delivery to the customer. Stocks at Beauford at 31 December 1996 were valued at nearly £3.4 million.

Debtors DEBTORS are the people and businesses who owe the company money. In business, it is usual to deliver goods to other businesses and then give them a minimum of 30 days to pay. For most businesses, including Beauford, nearly all debtors are other businesses. Beauford was owed about £6.2 million by its debtors on 31 December 1996.

Cash The most liquid asset is cash itself. Beauford had £71 000 in cash held in bank accounts at 31 December 1996.

Current liabilities

CURRENT LIABILITIES are what the business owes and will have to pay within the next 12 months. For most businesses, the most important current liability is the money it owes to its CREDITORS.

Just as a business has to give credit to other businesses, so it can get credit from other businesses. When Beauford buys paint, for instance, it doesn't have to pay for it until at least 30 days after it is delivered. Beauford owed about £2.6 million to its **trade creditors** on 31 December 1996.

Many businesses have also borrowed money from the bank on **overdraft** (☞ unit 31). In theory, the bank can demand that the money be repaid immediately. So overdrafts are a current liability. Beauford had an overdraft of £348 000 on 31 December 1996.

Another important current liability is tax owed to the **government**. The company may have earned profit in the past on which it will have to pay corporation tax and advanced corporation tax in the future. Beauford owed £470 000 in profits tax on 31 December 1996.

In total, Beauford owed £6.8 million to creditors which was repayable within one year from 31 December 1996.

Net current assets or working capital

Current assets minus current liabilities is called NET CURRENT ASSETS. Another name for this is **working capital**. The working capital of the business is very important as will be explained in unit 29. Beauford had net current assets of about £2.9 million at 31 December 1996.

Long term liabilities

The LONG TERM LIABILITIES are what the business owes and which has to be paid back in more than 12 months time. This includes long term loans which, for instance, might be repaid over 5 years. It could include **mortgages** (☞ unit 31). These are loans taken out where land or buildings are given as SECURITY. This means that if the firm goes out of business, the lender (usually a bank) can sell the security, in this case the land or building, and hopefully get its money back. For smaller companies, there might be **hire purchase agreements** (☞ unit 31), basically another form of borrowing. Other liabilities might be taxation owed (or deferred) from previous years. Beauford had about £3.4 million of bank loans and £0.3 million of hire purchase obligations amongst its £4.9 million of long term credit.

Capital and reserves

The final type of liability of a business is the money owed to its owners. Beauford is a plc, and so its owners are its shareholders. The shareholders put money into the business when the shares were first sold. Hence, the business owes this money to its shareholders. At 31 December 1996, the value of Beauford's **share capital** was about £10.7 million.

Note that this value has nothing to do with the current value of the shares on a stock market. The value of the share capital in a company reflects their value when they were first issued. The current value of the shares reflects what the business is currently worth.

Most businesses are also likely to have kept back some of their **profits** from previous years. This is money which is owed to the owners of the business. It is therefore a liability for the business. Instead of distributing (giving) it to the owners, the business has decided to set it aside to finance future investment, or to cover possible problems.

As Table 26.1 shows, Beauford had negative **reserves** on 31 December 1996 (figures in brackets are minus figures). This is unusual for a company. It shows that shareholders paid more in total for their shares in the past than the net assets of the business on 31 December 1996. It has come about because Beauford has bought other companies in the past and paid more for them than their net assets, i.e. it has paid for 'goodwill' (see above). Rather than putting goodwill as an asset, it has decided to show negative reserves on its balance sheet.

The balance sheet of a sole proprietorship or partnership is different from that of a limited company. The **main** difference is that there would be no share capital because there are no shareholders. So the value of the money put into the business by the sole trader or the partners would be shown where the shareholders' capital is shown in Table 26.1.

Source: adapted from Beauford PLC, *Annual Report and Accounts*, 1996.

De La Rue plc

De La Rue is a large UK company which in the financial year 1996/7 had sales of £768 million. Its business is manufacturing banknotes, travellers cheques, passports, credit and identity cards, and cash handling machines for sorting and counting money. Its major customers include banks, building societies and governments.

1 Copy out Table 26.3, filling in the missing numbers shown by '?'.
2 Who might be the trade creditors of the company?
3 (a) What is a 'dividend'? (b) Why do you think that dividends appear as a current liability for De La Rue?
4 Write a short report highlighting THREE important changes in De La Rue's current assets and liabilities between 1994 and 1997.

Table 26.3 *Current assets and liabilities, De La Rue plc at 31 March.*

				£ million
	1994	1995	1996	1997
Current assets	568.8	533.0	?	?
Bank loans and overdraft	63.6	166.6	85.1	62.6
Trade creditors	33.4	41.2	49.4	?
Tax on profits owed	34.1	47.4	47.1	39.0
Proposed dividend	27.0	35.7	37.0	37.1
Other creditors	152.1	202.3	180.2	147.4
Current liabilities	?	?	?	337.2
Net current assets	?	?	14.3	16.3

Source: adapted from De La Rue plc, *Annual Report and Accounts*, 1995 and 1997.

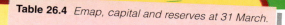

Emap plc

Emap is a media group publishing a wide range of magazines and owning radio stations.

Table 26.4	Emap, capital and reserves at 31 March.			
				£ million
	1994	**1995**	**1996**	**1997**
Share capital	123.3	201.4	242.6	242.4
Retained profit and reserves	67.4	63.5	73.7	116.8

Source: adapted from Emap, *Annual Report and Accounts*, 1995 and 1997.

1 Calculate the capital and reserves for Emap between 1994 and 1997.
2 In 1995, the company issued new shares in the business. How can you see this from that part of the balance sheet shown in Table 26.4?
3 Emap has grown in size partly by buying up other companies. If it paid £100 million for a company in 1998, how might this affect: (a) the retained profit and reserves of the company in 1998; and (b) the future profit of the company?

key terms

Assets - what is owned, for instance, by a business.
Balance sheet - the part of a business' accounts where the assets and liabilities of the business are recorded.
Creditors - the individuals, other businesses and governments to which the business owes money.
Current assets - liquid assets of the business.
Current liabilities - what the business owes and will have to pay within the next 12 months.
Debtors - people, other businesses or governments which owe a business money.
Fixed assets - what is owned by a business which it uses over a long period of time, such as buildings or machinery. Fixed assets include tangible and intangible assets.
Goodwill - the value of the customer contacts of a business.
Liabilities - for a business, the monetary value of what it owes, for instance, to other businesses or to the government.
Liquid assets - assets of the business which can easily be turned into cash or which are cash.
Long term liabilities - what the business owes and will have to pay in more than 12 months time.
Net current assets or working capital - current assets minus current liabilities.
Security - an asset, like property, which can be sold if a borrower fails to repay a loan and the money used to pay off the rest of the loan.
Tangible assets - assets which exist in a physical sense, such as buildings or machinery, as opposed to intangible assets, such as goodwill which don't exist in a physical sense.

Checklist ✓

1 What is the difference between the assets and the liabilities of a business?
2 List FIVE fixed assets of a garage business.
3 What is the difference between the fixed assets of a business and its current assets?
4 Who might be the debtors of a business making jeans?
5 Who might be owed the money which appears as a current liability on a business' balance sheet?
6 Why is a mortgage a long term liability for a business?
7 Why is share capital a liability for a business?
8 For what might a business use its retained profit?

JUSTYOU LTD

SUMMARY CASE STUDY

JustYou is a fashionable nightclub in a smart area of Manchester. The company was founded by 4 people, each of whom put up £50 000 to finance the 200 000 shares in the company priced at £1. They bought a smart nightclub and today, together with fixtures, fittings and equipment, the premises are valued at £320 000. They had to take out a mortgage to finance buying the club and there is still £110 000 to pay on it. They also have a long term £20 000 bank loan which they used to buy some of the fixtures and fittings.

The nightclub is very successful. This year, the owners were able to retain £70 000 profit for investment in the business. The company also has £55 000 in the bank. Drink is always popular amongst the customers and most of the company's £90 000 stock is made up of drink. Some customers run credit accounts and the club is owed £20 000 by them. Current liabilities are £85 000.

1 Draw up a balance sheet for JustYou.
2 A year ago, the mortgage was £120 000, the premises, fixtures and fittings and equipment were valued at £300 000, the club had £100 000 worth of stocks of drink and was owed £30 000 by its creditor customers. Explain which of these figures you think show that the company is doing (a) better; and (b) worse today than a year ago.

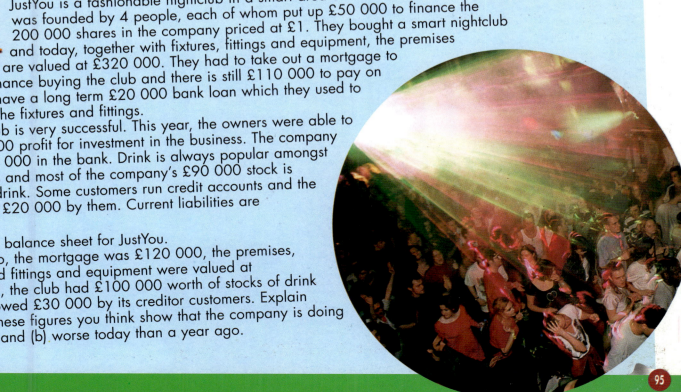

Making decisions

How well is a business doing? There is a large number of ways of answering this question. Looking at profit and loss figures or studying the balance sheet are possible ways. Another is to use financial ratios. Having looked at the figures, the business needs to decide whether it is going to change its strategy. Could it perform better?

Hamley's is one of Britain's best known toy retailers. Its flagship store in Regent Street, London, is internationally renowned for its range and quality of toys. It has a number of branches in the UK and is a growing business. In the 1997 financial year, its sales turnover was £30.5 million and it made a net profit of £6.6 million.

Gross profit

Table 27.1 shows that between 1993 and 1997, Hamleys increased its **sales turnover** from £17.9 million to £30.5 million. So, looking just at sales turnover, Hamleys has performed extremely well over the period.

However, the **cost of sales** has also risen from £8.8 million to £14.5 million. Does Hamleys need to worry about this increase in the cost of sales?

- No. There was a 70 per cent increase in sales turnover during the five year period. So an increase in the cost of sales was almost certain.
- Yes. The figures might show that the cost of sales has been

increasing at a faster rate than the sales turnover. Then the rise in sales will not be matched by a similar rise in **gross profit**.

One way to find out what happened to turnover in relation to costs of sales is to calculate the RATIO OF GROSS PROFIT TO SALES TURNOVER (often called the GROSS PROFIT MARGIN) where:

Ratio of gross profit to sales or gross profit margin (as a %)

$$= \frac{Gross\ profit}{Sales\ turnover} \times 100$$

Remember, gross profit is sales turnover minus costs of sales. So if the gross profit margin is

Table 27.1 *Hamleys plc: trading account.*[1]

	1993	1994	1995	1996	19 (£ milli)
Sales turnover	17.9	20.9	26.2	30.1	30
Cost of sales	8.8	10.2	13.1	15.1	14
Gross profit	9.1	10.7	13.1	15.0	16
Ratio of gross profit to sales	51%	51%	50%	50%	52

1 Figures rounded to the nearest £0.1 million.

increasing, sales costs must be falling in relation to the value of sales. This is usually a good indicator for the company. If the ratio is falling, sales costs are rising in relation to the value of sales and this could be a worrying trend for a business.

Table 27.1 shows that, at Hamleys, the ratio of gross profit to sales was fairly constant between 1993 and 1997. The slight fall between 1994 and 1996 could have been due to a number of factors.

- Costs may have risen more than prices. For instance, the cost to Hamleys of buying in toys for sale may have risen slightly faster than the price at which they sold them.
- Revenue may have fallen. Increased competition may have forced Hamleys to reduce its prices by more than it would have liked. Or the company may

Expro International Group PLC

Expro International Group provides a range of specialised services and products to companies involved in oil and gas exploration and production.

1 Look at Table 27.2. Do sales revenue figures indicate that Expro International has been doing well or badly? Explain your answer.

2 Now look at the cost of sales as well as the revenue.
(a) Calculate for each year: (i) the gross profit;
(ii) the gross profit margin.
(b) Do you think the business has been doing well? Explain your answer.

Table 27.2 *Sales revenue and cost of sales.*[1]

	1993	1994	1995	1996	1997 (£ million[2])
Sales revenue	51	66	70	82	105
Cost of sales	37	49	51	60	76

1 For the financial year to 31 March.
2 Rounded to the nearest £ million.

Source: adapted from Expro International Group PLC, *Annual Report and Accounts*, 1997.

Table 27.3 *Danka Business Systems PLC: profit and loss account.[1]*

					£ million
	1993	1994	1995	1996	1997
Sales turnover	186	347	516	793	1 324
Gross profit	69	132	197	297	489
Overheads	51	100	152	243	460
Net profit[2]	18	32	45	54	29

1 Figures rounded to the nearest £million.
2 Profit on ordinary activities before taxation.

have wanted to increase its share of the market, doing this by offering lower prices than those of its competitors.

- If sales of low profit margin toys increased, but sales of high profit margin toys fell, the average profit would fall.

The company saw gross profit margins increase in 1997. This was a good sign for the company. It could indicate better control of costs. It could be that it was able to increase its prices. Or it could be that it sold a larger proportion of higher profit margin toys.

Net profit

Gross profit is important, but it doesn't include overhead costs. For the owners of a business, the final net profit figure is more important. Table 27.4 shows that net profit at Hamleys rose between 1993 and 1997. The success of the company is backed up by another indicator, the RATIO OF NET PROFIT TO SALES TURNOVER or NET PROFIT MARGIN.

Ratio of net profit to sales or net profit margin (as a %)

$$= \frac{Net\ profit}{Sales\ turnover} \times 100$$

It shows how much net profit a business is making per £ of product sold. The higher the profit per £ and therefore the higher the ratio, the more profitable a

Table 27.4 *Hamleys plc: profit and loss account.[1]*

					£ million
	1993	1994	1995	1996	1997
Sales turnover	17.9	20.9	26.2	30.1	30.5
Gross profit	9.1	10.7	13.1	15.0	16.0
Overheads[2]	7.9	8.0	7.4	8.6	9.1
Net profit[3]	1.2	2.7	5.7	6.4	6.9
Ratio of net profit to sales turnover	7%	13%	22%	21%	23%

1 Figures rounded to the nearest £0.1 million.
2 Distribution costs, administration costs exceptional items and net interest.
3 Profit on ordinary activities before taxation.

business is likely to be. On the other hand, a lower ratio is often a sign that the business is not doing well.

The net profit ratio at Hamleys rose between 1993 and 1995 from 7 per cent to 23 per cent. This was a substantial increase. It could indicate that Hamleys had been cutting overhead costs per unit sold. This would suggest that Hamleys became more **efficient** over the period. Maintaining a high net profit margin in 1996 and 1997 is a good sign too. A possible danger for Hamleys is if it fails to control its overhead costs as the company grows. This could result in a fall in the net profit margin - a sign that the company was becoming less efficient.

Return on capital employed

A third ratio which is useful when looking at how well a business has performed is the RATE OF RETURN ON CAPITAL EMPLOYED (ROCE). Say you received £10 interest on money you had put into a bank account a year ago. You can't say whether you have invested your money well until you know how much you had in the account (your **capital**). If you had £20 in the account, you would have made 50 per cent on your money - a very good rate of return. If you had £1 million in the account, then you would have done badly.

Similarly, a business can't say how well it has done until it compares its profit with the amount of capital in the business. This is what ROCE shows.

$$ROCE\ (\%) = \frac{Net\ profit}{Capital\ employed} \times 100$$

The **capital employed** is defined as the **fixed assets** and the **net current assets**, minus any amounts that must be repaid (including borrowing) in over a year's time (shown on the balance sheet ☞ unit 26).

Table 27.5 *Hamleys plc: rate of return on capital employed.[1]*

£ million

	1993	1994	1995	1996	1997
Net profit	1.2	2.7	5.7	6.4	6.9
Capital employed	(12.6)	(10.7)	4.1	6.6	9.1
Rate of return on capital employed	–	–	139%	97%	76%

Figures in brackets are minus numbers.
1 Figures rounded to the nearest £0.1 million.

Table 27.5 shows that in 1993 and 1994, Hamleys had negative amounts of capital employed in the business. This means that it owed more than the assets of the business. So it is not possible to calculate the ROCE. However, in 1995 the ROCE was 139 per cent, an exceptionally high figure. In 1996 and 1997, it was 97 per cent and 76 per cent.

Making comparisons

So far in this unit, we have compared one year's figures of Hamleys with another year's figures. Making comparisons over

Table 27.6 *Accounts.*

	House of Frazer to 25 Jan	Moss Bros Group plc to 25 Jan	Hamleys plc to 1 Feb
	£m	£m	£m
Sales turnover	781.4	121.9	30.5
Cost of sales	559.4	59.6	14.5
Gross profit	222.0	62.3	16.0
Operating expenses	260.4	46.4	9.4
Net profit	(38.4)	15.9	6.9
Capital employed	211.9	51.2	9.1
Ratio of gross profit to sales turnover	28%	51%	52%
Ratio of net profit to sales turnover	- 5%	13%	23%
Return on capital employed	-18%	31%	76%

Figures in brackets are minus numbers.
Source: adapted from 1997 company *Report and Accounts* of House of Frazer plc, Moss Bros Group plc and Hamleys plc.

time is very helpful to a business and its management accountant. However, a business can also compare itself with another similar business to see whether or not it is doing well or badly.

Look at Table 27.6. It shows the accounts for Hamleys and another two retailers. House of Fraser is a department store group. In 1995 and 1996, Hamleys sold toys through House of Fraser under the 'House of Toys' name. Moss Bros is a chain of shops which specialises in hiring clothes for special occasions like weddings. It is also a major retailer of clothes for men. How do these companies compare?

Starting from the top of the set of accounts, you can see that House of Fraser has a higher turnover than both Moss Bros and Hamleys. In fact, sales revenue at House of Fraser is over 25 times as large as at Hamleys. However, cost of sales is also much higher at House of Fraser. The gross profit figure might seem to show that House of Frazer is more profitable than the other two companies. But the ratio of gross profit to sales turnover tells a different story.

House of Fraser has the lowest figure of the three. Moss Bros and Hamleys have similar gross profit ratios. Looking at the net profit figures, House of Fraser is making a loss. Although Hamleys is making less than half the net profit of Moss Bros, its net profit ratio is almost twice as high. Equally, Hamleys comes out best on return on capital employed, making 76 per cent compared to Moss Bros with 31 per cent and House of Fraser with -18 per cent. These statistics would suggest that

Capital Radio

Capital Radio is a commercial radio group broadcasting in London, Birmingham, Kent, Sussex, Hampshire and Oxford. It is involved in radio broadcasting as well as in advertising, where it sells clients' airtime to national advertisers.

Table 27.7 *Capital Radio plc: profit and loss account.[1,2]*

£ million

	1992	1993	1994	1995	1996
Sales turnover	28.4	36.0	51.7	67.4	77.8
Net profit[3]	11.0	11.7	22.1	39.9	32.1
Capital employed	25.9	20.5	7.8	28.9	39.5

1 Figures rounded to the nearest £0.1 million.
2 Financial year to 30 September
3 Profit on ordinary activities before taxation

Source: Capital Radio, *Annual Report and Accounts*, 1996.

1 How did the company perform over the period 1992 to 1996 according to: (a) its sales turnover figures; and (b) net profit figures?
2 (a) Calculate the rate of return on capital employed (ROCE) for each year between 1992 and 1996. (b) How well did the company perform as measured by its ROCE over the period?
3 In 1995, Capital Radio sold its shareholding in a company, Metro Radio Group, which it part owned. It received £13.4 million which was added to its profit for that financial year. What might be the advantages and disadvantages to shareholders if Capital Radio sold other companies which it part owned?

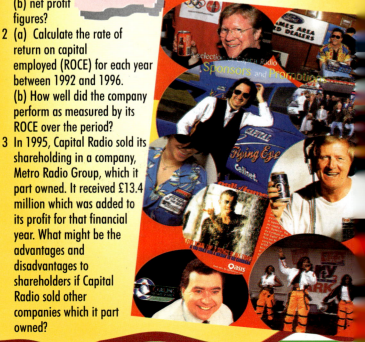

House of Fraser has problems. It needs to become profitable if it is to have a long term future. Hamleys would seem to be performing better than Moss Bros. However, Moss Bros is still performing well with a good return on capital employed.

Because these three companies are plcs, stock market investors can look at these statistics when deciding whether to buy or sell shares. House of Fraser shares in 1996 were likely to be relatively low because of the poor profitability of the company. On 25 January 1997, House of Fraser shares were being sold at a lower price than Hamleys' shares. This is despite the fact that House of Fraser is a larger company on most measures than Hamleys. If a company has a low share price, this might attract another company to buy it up and make it more efficient.

Source: adapted from Hamleys, *Annual Report and Accounts*,1997; Moss Bros Group PLC, *Annual Report and Accounts*,1996-7; House of Fraser, *Annual Report and Accounts*,1996-7.

Checklist ✓

1 The sales turnover of a private limited company importing cycle parts went up from £2m to £5m whilst cost of sales increased from £1m to £2m. What has happened to: (a) gross profit; (b) the gross profit margin?
2 Explain whether an increase in the gross profit margin is likely to be a good indicator of the performance of a business or a bad one.
3 What is the difference between gross and net profit?
4 The net profit of a plc went up from £2m to £5m whilst sales turnover increased from £20m to £100m. (a) What has happened to the net profit margin? (b) Explain whether this is a good indicator for the business.
5 Explain, using examples, what the rate of return on capital shows about the performance of a business.
6 Andrew's Ltd has a higher rate of return on capital than Maine's Ltd. Who might be interested to know this information?

Dixons Motors PLC and **Dagenham Motors Group PLC** are both vehicle distributors operating new and used car and commercial vehicle showrooms. They also service vehicles. Table 27.8 shows their 1996 results to 31 December.

1 Write a report comparing the two companies. Which company do you think, from the limited information presented, is doing better?

Table 27.8

	Dagenham Motors Group £m	Dixons Motors £m
Sales turnover	291.8	262.6
Cost of sales	252.8	223.6
Gross profit	39.0	39.0
Operating expenses and interest	33.9	33.5
Net profit	5.1	5.5
Capital employed	41.4	44.3
Ratio of gross profit to sales turnover	13.4%	14.9%
Ratio of net profit to sales turnover	1.7%	2.1%
Return on capital employed	12.3%	12.4%

Source: adapted from Dixons Motors PLC and Dagenham Motors Group PLC, *Annual Report and Accounts* 1996.

SUMMARY CASE STUDY

ETAM

Etam is a company which operates a chain of clothes shops found on most high streets in the UK. In January 1997, it operated from 216 sites in the UK.

1 (a) What has happened to sales turnover between 1993 and 1997?
(b) Are these figures likely to be a sign that the company is doing well or doing badly and why?
2 (a) Describe and (b) comment on what has happened to gross profit and net profit over the period.
3 (a) Calculate the ratio of net profit to sales for each year.
(b) What do these figures suggest about the performance of the company?
4 Calculate the rate of return on capital employed for each year and comment on its significance.
5 The Interim Results to 9 August 1997 stated that 'trade in the first half of 1997/98 was unsatisfactory'. It was reported that other companies might offer to buy Etam. Discuss TWO ways in which a company taking over Etam might improve its performance.

Table 27.9 *Etam plc: profit and loss account.*[1,2]

£ million	1993	1994	1995	1996	1997
Sales turnover	221	220	218	202	187
Gross profit	17	19	17	7	2
Net profit[3]	11	14	11	0	2
Capital employed	18	32	45	54	29

1 Figures rounded to the nearest £million.
2 Financial year to 25 January.
3 Profit on ordinary activities before taxation.

Source: adapted from Etam, *Annual Report and Accounts*, 1997.

unit 28

CASH FLOW

Making decisions

Businesses need to make profit to survive in the long term. In the short term, they also need to be able to manage their day to day flows of cash. They have to decide how they can manage receipts and payments so that there is always enough cash to pay the bills of the business. Looking at how cash has flowed through the business in the past and predicting how it will in the future are both important aids to effective decision making.

Jordan Banks graduated from Design College 8 years ago. Since then he has worked in the textile industry, often using the latest technology. He thinks, however, that he has spotted a gap in the market for knitwear. He wants to set up his own business, Variety Socks, making traditional high quality socks. Most pairs will be sold through mail order. He has drawn up a business plan (☞ unit 22). Included in that is a CASH FLOW FORECAST.

Disc-Pro

Disc-Pro is a manufacturer of hard discs. Next year, it predicts that:
- its wage bill will be £1 million;
- sales of products will be £7 million;
- the cost of parts and raw materials will be £3 million;
- advertising and other marketing costs will be £1 million;
- all other costs will be £1 million;
- interest received on investments will be £0.2 million.

1 (a) Which of these are receipts for the business? (b) What is the total value of receipts forecast?
2 (a) Which of these are payments or outgoings for the business? (b) What is the total value of payments forecast?
3 What is the forecast net cash flow of Disc-Pro?
4 If Disc-Pro had cash of £1 million at the start of the year, how much would it have at the end of the year?

Surviving the first month

Jordan has thought for some time that he would like to start his own business. So he saved up £14 000 to invest in the business. This is a RECEIPT for the business in the first month. Receipts are the cash flowing into a business. In later months, his receipts will be the money he gets from sales of socks.

His OUTGOINGS or PAYMENTS are the monies which he has to pay out. In his first month, he has to find some premises from which to operate. The premises will need to be equipped with furniture. Some raw materials have to be bought to make the socks. He will need to recruit part time outworkers to knit the socks and spend some time training them to make the patterns he has already designed. (Outworkers are workers who work in their own homes. In the textile industry, they tend to earn very low wages.)

So in his first month, July, he forecast his outgoings would be £3 300, made up of:
- £2 000 setting up costs such as buying furniture;
- £800 for production costs such as the rent of business premises and materials like wool;
- £500 for other expenses such as travelling and postage.

Table 28.1 shows the cash flow forecast for the first month, July. His receipts are put first. Then comes his payments. **Net cash flow**, £10 700, is the difference between **receipts** of £14 000 and **payments** of £3 300. A positive net cash flow shows that more money will come into the

Table 28.1 *Cash flow forecast for Variety Socks, July (£).*

	July
Receipts	
Cash injection	14 000
Total	14 000
Payments	
Setting up costs	2 000
Production expenses	800
Other costs	500
Total	3 300
Net cash flow	10 700
Opening bank balance	0
Closing bank balance	10 700

The Bristol Better Crust

The Bristol Better Crust is a bakery run by two partners. They specialise in baking high quality breads for sale to hotels, restaurants and delicatessans. Table 28.2 shows their cash flow for February.

1 (a) Copy out Table 28.2 and fill in and calculate the cash flow figures for March assuming that: wages are £21 000; van expenses are £2 000; sales of bread are £110 000; drawings of the partners (the amount they pay themselves from the business) are £5 000; flour and other materials are £55 000; rent and rates are £5 000; and other costs are £18 000.

2 Fill in the table for April assuming that: wages are £22 000; van expenses are £1 500; sales of bread are £105 000; rent and rates are £5 000; drawings of the partners (the amount they pay themselves from the business) are £5 000; flour and other materials are £52 000; and other costs are £26 000.

Table 28.2 *Cash flow forecast for The Bristol Better Crust (£).*

	February	March	April
Receipts			
Sales of bread	100 000		
Total	100 000		
Payments			
Flour and other materials	50 000		
Wages	20 000		
Rent and rates	5 000		
Van expenses	1 000		
Other costs	15 000		
Drawings of the partners	5 000		
Total	96 000		
Net cash flow	4 000		
Opening balance	22 000		
Closing balance	26 000		

business in his first month than goes out.

His **opening balance** would be £0. This is the amount of money in the business at the start of the month. During the month his net cash flow is £10 700. So by the end of the month he will have £10 700 (the opening balance, £0, plus the net cash flow, £10 700) left in the business. This is his **closing balance.**

His second month

In the second month, he plans to order his stock of mail order catalogues. These will be expensive because he wants them to bring out the high quality nature of the socks he is making and selling. But he won't need to pay for them till later.

He also has to pay his outworkers who are beginning to produce socks. More raw materials will need to be bought and other costs like rent will have to be paid. He still won't have sold a single pair of socks though. Table 28.3 shows his cash flow forecast for the second month.

He has no receipts for the month because he has no sales yet. His payments total £1 300. So his net cash flow, the difference between receipts and payments, is - £1 300. Money is therefore going to flow out of the business. His opening balance for the month is £10 700 (equal to last month's closing balance). His closing balance is £9 400 (£10 700 - £1 300).

September to December

At the beginning of September the catalogues will arrive from the printers. This is the first month he plans to advertise his socks. Advertisements in national magazines and newspapers are costly. He will only be able to afford four small boxed adverts. However, he forecasts they

will bring in some requests for catalogues and that this will lead to orders in October. The catalogues will have to be paid for at the beginning of October. More advertising in October and November in the run up to Christmas will lead to more catalogues going out and orders coming back. His outworkers will be making the socks whilst he is dealing with the orders and doing everything else associated with running the business. In December he stops advertising, but orders are still coming in from the catalogues he has already sent out.

Table 28.4 shows his cash flow forecast for the whole period from July to December. Under receipts, the sales of socks are shown in October, November and December. Under payments, he has to continue paying for rent, new materials and the wages of his outworkers. He assumes that these will be the same £800 each month. The mail order brochures and advertising are by far the largest cost he faces. Other costs are estimated at £500 per month.

The net cash flow is negative between August and November. This means that money will be flowing out of the business in these months. By the end of November, he has run out of money because his

Table 28.3 *Cash flow forecast for Variety Socks, August (£).*

	August
Receipts	
Total	0
Payments	
Production expenses	800
Other costs	500
Total	1 300
Net cash flow	-1 300
Opening bank balance	10 700
Closing bank balance	9 400

Table 28.4 *Cash flow forecast for Variety Socks for July to December(£).*

	July	Aug	Sep	Oct	Nov	Dec
Receipts						
Cash injection	14 000	0	0	0	0	0
Sales	0	0	0	2 000	2 500	2 500
Total	14 000	0	0	2 000	2 500	2 500
Payments						
Setting up costs	2 000	0	0	0	0	0
Production expenses	800	800	800	800	800	800
Mail order brochures and advertising	0	0	2 000	6 500	2 000	0
Other costs	500	500	500	500	500	500
Total	3 300	1 300	3 300	7 800	3 300	1 300
Net cash flow	10 700	- 1 300	- 3 300	- 5 800	- 8 00	1 200
Opening balance	0	10 700	9 400	6 100	300	- 500
Closing balance	10 700	9 400	6 100	300	- 500	700

Sam Walker was unemployed. He decided to set up in business as a market trader dealing in antiques. Table 28.5 shows how well he did over the first seven months of running the business. He received a grant from his local TEC (Training and Enterprise Council) of £1 000 to set up the business. He also arranged an overdraft facility, which allowed him to borrow up to £300 from his bank account. Each month, his drawings from the business, the amount he paid himself in wages, were £200. Look at the figures carefully.

1 (a) What happened to: (i) sales; and
   (ii) costs over the seven months?
   (b) Explain whether these figures showed that the business was doing well or badly.
2 (a) What happened to cash flow during this time?
   (b) Do these figures indicate the business was doing well?
3 When did Sam Walker have to use his overdraft facility?
4 Explain whether the business: (a) has made a profit over its first seven months; and (b) is likely to make a profit in the future.

Table 28.5 *Cash flow forecast for Sam Walker (£).*

	June	July	Aug	Sept	Oct	Nov	Dec
Receipts							
Grant	1 000	0	0	0	0	0	0
Sales	500	600	700	800	900	1 000	1 000
Total	1 500	600	700	800	900	1 000	1 000
Payments							
Setting up	300	0	0	0	0	0	0
Rent	120	120	120	120	120	120	120
Stock	500	350	400	450	500	550	500
Drawings	200	200	200	200	200	200	200
Other exps.	100	110	120	130	140	150	150
Total	1220	780	840	900	960	1020	970
Net cash flow	280	-180	-140	-100	-60	-20	30
Opening bank balance	0	280	100	-40	-140	-200	-220
Closing bank balance	280	100	-40	-140	-200	-220	-190

- He needed it for his own planning. From his forecast, he can see that he will not be able to pay himself any wage at the start. He will also have spent £14 000 of his own money on the business and yet only has £2 700 in cash left after 18 months. However, he will have seen growing sales. If he could double sales in the third year, he would have a strong positive cash flow and be able to pay himself a much bigger wage.
- He needed it for the bank. In November of the first year, he needed to borrow some money. It was important for the bank to see how cash would be managed in the business to see whether the business had a chance of survival. Without a cash flow forecast, he would not have got an overdraft from the bank.
- He would also have needed it had he applied for a grant to set up the business from, say, his local **Training and Enterprise Council (TEC)** (☞ unit 52 and 58).

closing balance becomes negative. He has to find this money from somewhere. He plans to borrow money from the bank through an **overdraft** (☞ unit 31). In December, though, the closing balance is positive again after a positive inflow of cash in that month.

The next year

By 31 December, Jordan has put £14 000 of his own money into the business. He only has £700 of that money left in cash. What is more, he has worked for six months and not paid himself anything. This might seem disastrous. However, Jordan knows that it can be difficult to establish yourself in the clothing business. The following year, he plans to develop his mail order business.

He knows that customers who place orders are likely to reorder again. Existing customers will tell their friends and this will generate further orders. So, in a full year, he hopes to sell £30 000 worth of socks by mail order. He also plans to start selling to design houses and shops. He predicts these trade sales will be £20 000. The **profit margin** (☞ unit 27) will be lower than on mail order, but it will help increase profits.

Advertising and the printing of more brochures will remain a heavy cost. Materials and wages will increase because he is making more socks. He also plans to pay himself £6 000. These payments are called **drawings** from the business. So his total payments are forecast to rise too from the first year.

His net cash flow over the year is forecast to be positive (£2 000). Overall, he predicts that he will end the year with £2 700 in cash. This is shown in Table 28.6.

The use of a cash flow forecast

Jordan needed to make a cash flow forecast for a number of reasons.

Cash flow statements

Jordan made his cash flow forecast before he set up in business. Once he started operating, he kept monthly CASH FLOW STATEMENTS. These showed how much money was actually flowing into and out of the business each month. He kept these for a number of reasons.

Table 28.6 *Cash flow forecast for Variety Socks for January to December of the second year of operation (£).*

Receipts	
Cash injection	30 000
Trade sales	20 000
Total	50 000
Payments	
Production expenses	24 000
Mail order brochures and advertising	12 000
Other costs	6 000
Drawings	6 000
Total	48 000
Net cash flow	2 000
Opening bank balance	700
Closing bank balance	2 700

- It was one way of monitoring the performance of the business. If sales were down, for instance, this could show up as a worsening of the cash flow.
- It helped him identify crisis points. If the cash in the business were falling much more rapidly than his cash flow forecast predicted, he knew he would have to do something immediately to stop the fall.
- He used it to compare performance from month to month and year to year. For instance, he could see that his cash flow position was better in December than in November because in December it was positive whilst it was negative in

November. In his second year of trading, sales increased and he was able to see improvements month by month compared to the previous twelve months.

Cash flow and profit

Profit and cash flow are different. For instance, Jordan aimed to make a **gross profit margin** (his sales divided by his production expenses, ☞ unit 27) of about 100 per cent. This meant that the price he sold his goods at was twice the cost of the raw materials and wages used in making them. Most of the rest went on his **overheads** such as the cost of the brochure. What was left was profit.

The cash flow position, though, was different. He had to pay for materials and wages before he received money from orders sold. He also had to pay his overheads. Without enough cash in the business, he would never have survived to earn the profit. The business would have collapsed under debts before it was able to collect the money from sales.

This shows that businesses can potentially be profitable but collapse because they have cash flow problems. Equally, a business can have a stable cash flow position from month to month. However, unless receipts are greater than payments, the business will not make a profit.

PARINDER KAUR

Parinder Kaur wants to set up in business making soft furnishings for customers on an individualised basis. In her business plan, she predicts that to start with nearly all her orders will be for curtains and pelmets. Later on, she hopes to branch out into more complicated work.

She is going to work from home, so her fixed costs will be low - just £200 per month. One main fixed cost will be adverts in the local newspaper. The main variable cost will be the cost of material for the curtains. On average, she expects her variable cost to be half the amount she charges her customers for a particular job. For instance, on a job where she charges £200, she expects £100 of that to be the variable cost of materials.

Every order is individual and so she keeps no stocks. When she buys material, it is immediately made up into the order. She also expects her clients to pay immediately the order is fulfilled.

Spreadsheet
(The cash flow forecast which you are asked to prepare in questions 1-5 could be more easily done using a spreadsheet package.)

1 She is prepared to put £200 into the business in the first month to start it up. She predicts sales in the first month, March, will be £200 whilst material costs will be £100. Fill in her cash flow forecast for March in Table 28.7.
2 In April, she expects to pick up more orders. She thinks sales will be £300 whilst material costs will be £150. Complete her cash flow forecast for April.
3 In May, June and July, she expects to have sales of £400 per month with material costs of half that amount. Complete her cash flow forecast for these months.
4 In August, with so many people on holiday, she expects to get only £200 worth of orders with £100 material costs. (a) Complete her cash flow forecast for the month. (b) She faces an important problem in this month. What is it?
5 In the remaining four months of the year, she forecasts £600 worth of sales and £300 worth of material costs per month. Complete Table 28.7 for these months.
6 Is the problem in August important given what she predicts will happen in the last four months of the year?
7 Parinder expects to work 20 hours a week on her business between September and December. The only money she receives is the profit made by her business.
(a) Do you think that her business is successful?
(b) Suggest TWO ways in which Parinder might increase her profits.

Table 28.7 *Cash flow forecast for Parinder's soft furnishing business (£).*

	Mar	Apr	May	Jun	Jul	Aug	Sept	Oct	Nov	Dec
Receipts										
Cash inflow	200									
Sales										
Total										
Payments										
Fixed costs										
Material costs										
Total										
Opening balance										
Closing balance										

key terms

Cash flow forecast - a prediction of how cash will flow through a business over a period of time in the future.
Cash flow statement - a statement showing how cash has flowed through a business over a period of time. It includes a summary of receipts and payments during each period of time.
Receipts - the monies flowing into a business.
Payments - the monies flowing out of a business.

WORKING CAPITAL

Making decisions

Businesses need assets to produce goods and services. They need fixed assets like offices, factories and vehicles. They also need circulating assets (or working capital) such as cash, stock or payments due shortly. A business doesn't want too much tied up in working capital. Money invested in stocks could be earning interest in a long term investment, for instance, or it could be used to buy a new machine. On the other hand, too little working capital could lead to it going out of business. A shop with no stock to sell isn't going to earn any profit. So the business has to decide how much working capital it needs to be successful.

Spirax-Sarco is an engineering company which specialises in providing knowledge, service and products for the control and efficient use of steam and industrial fluids. Steam power is used in many industries. Spirax-Sarco makes a range of products such as valves, boiler controls and flow meters which allow steam power to be used safely and efficiently.

Working capital

Spirax-Sarco needs **fixed assets** to manufacture products. These are the machines, factories, offices, etc. which the company owns. But it also needs WORKING CAPITAL to pay for day to day expenses, such as bills. Working capital is what the business owns which is either cash or could easily be turned into cash minus what it owes and which needs paying shortly. For Spirax-Sarco, working capital is:

- the value of the cash in the business as well as cash held in the bank;
- the stocks (☞ unit 46) of the company, such as steel waiting to be turned into valves and finished valves waiting to be sent to customers;
- the debtors (☞ unit 26) of the company, the businesses which have received goods from Spirax-Sarco but have yet to pay for them;

minus

- money owed to the bank which might be repaid within the next 12 months;
- what it owes to other businesses for goods and services that it has received but not yet paid for (its creditors ☞ unit 26);
- other monies owed which are payable within a year, such as to the government in tax or to its shareholders in dividends.

There is a formula to calculate working capital. It is defined as the difference between **current assets** and **current liabilities** (terms which are found on the balance sheet of the business ☞ unit 26). So working capital is:

current assets - current liabilities

or:

*(cash + debtors + stock) -
(bank overdraft + creditors + other monies owed)*

Working capital is the value of **net current assets**. This is the current assets of the business left over after the current liabilities have been taken away.

The working capital cycle

Every business has a working capital cycle. Look at Figure 29.1. Spirax-Sarco manufactures products using materials and components. Some are bought with cash. Some are delivered now by **creditors** and paid for 30 days later. It also hires workers and equipment. The products are sold to customers who usually get 30 days to pay for them. So customers become **debtors** for Spirax-Sarco. The customers will then pay Spirax-Sarco. The cash coming into the company has to pay for the raw

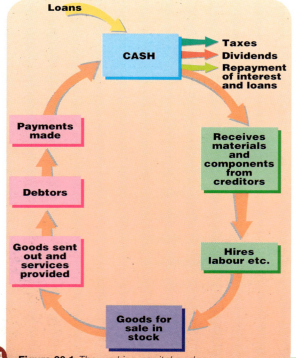

Loans

CASH → Taxes / Dividends / Repayment of interest and loans

Payments made

Debtors

Goods sent out and services provided

Receives materials and components from creditors

Hires labour etc.

Goods for sale in stock

Figure 29.1 *The working capital cycle.*

Bisco

EITHER chart the flow of working capital round your business and estimate or record the level of working capital in the business at a point of time in its operation, OR complete the following case study.

Bisco is your mini-company. You plan to make and sell biscuits within your school. For your first day, you plan to make 90 Shrewsbury biscuits. The four members of the business have each put £0.50p into the mini-company as start-up capital, but you know this won't cover the cost of the ingredients to make the first batch of biscuits. So you have persuaded your parents to lend you all the money to buy the ingredients and you have promised to pay back the money once you have sold the biscuits. To make the 90 biscuits, you need 350 gm of margarine, 350 gm of castor sugar, 3 small eggs, 700gm of plain flour, and 2gm of ground cinnamon. Unfortunately, when you come to buy the ingredients, you find you can't buy 350 gm of margarine, 350 gm of castor sugar etc. - you to have buy bigger packs. The size of packs and their prices are shown in Figure 29.2.

You sell each biscuit for 5p. On your first day, you sell 80 out of the 90 biscuits. Two people buy a biscuit and promise to pay you the next day.

1 Calculate your current assets at the end of the first day. Record your answers by copying out Table 29.1.
2 Calculate your current liabilities at the end of the first day.
3 At the end of the first day, what is the value of: (a) your working capital; (b) the total amount of cash that you have?
4 Why does your business need working capital to carry on trading?

Table 29.1 *Current assets for Bisco.*

	(£)
Cash	
Start up capital	?
First day's takings	?
Total cash	?
Debtors	?
Stock	
Unsold biscuits	?
Ingredients	?
Total stock	?
Total current assets	?

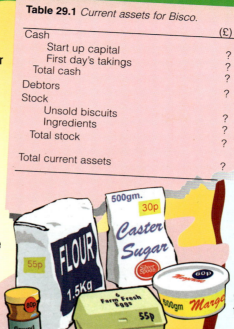

Figure 29.2

bills, then it faces a cash flow problem.

On the other hand, a business might have £100 million in the bank in cash today. It is cash rich today and it has no cash flow problem. But if it has to pay a bill for £200 million in a week's time and its other current assets like stocks are worth only £50 million, then it has a working capital problem today. It doesn't have enough current assets to cover its current liabilities. As a result, it is likely to get into financial difficulties in the future.

Current ratio

Another way in which Spirax-Sarco can find out whether it has enough working capital is for it to work out its CURRENT RATIO. This is the ratio of current assets to current liabilities:

$$\text{Current ratio} = \frac{\text{Current assets}}{\text{Current liabilities}}$$

The higher the ratio of current assets to current liabilities, the higher the amount of working capital in the business. The higher the ratio, therefore, the safer is the business.

The part of the balance sheet which shows the working capital for Spirax-Sarco is shown in Table 29.2. At 31 December 1996, the current ratio for the company was £162.7 million ÷ £64.2 million, which is

materials that it originally bought. It also has to pay for the wages of its workers, its overheads, taxes, repayments on loans and dividends to shareholders. So current assets and liabilities like cash, stocks, debts, credits and bank loan repayments are constantly going round the financial system of the business.

bankers of Spirax-Sarco might suddenly decide to 'call in' its overdraft (i.e. ask for it to be repaid). Or a major customer might go out of business leaving unpaid bills with Spirax-Sarco. If it has enough current assets compared to current liabilities, it will be able to carry on paying its day to day bills, even though working capital is reduced.

The need for working capital

To survive, businesses need working capital. They need enough current assets left over, after allowing for current liabilities, to pay for the day to day bills of the business.

It is considered good practice in the average business for current assets to be between $1\frac{1}{2}$ and 2 times the value of current liabilities. This allows a business to cope with a sudden crisis. For instance, the

Working capital and cash flow problems

Problems with shortages of working capital can be different from cash flow problems (☞ unit 28). A business, for instance, might have a large amount of working capital if its stock levels are very high and it owes little to the bank. But if it doesn't have enough cash to pay its day to day

Table 29.2 *Working capital, Spirax-Sarco Engineering plc, 31 December 1996.*

	£	£
Cash	35.6	
Debtors	75.2	
Stock	51.8	
Current assets		**162.7**
Bank overdraft	3.9	
Bank loans	4.7	
Trade creditors	13.8	
Other creditors	41.8	
Current liabilities		**64.2**
Working capital		**98.5**

Andy Clarke doesn't always get things right. His small engineering business is not doing as well as he had hoped. He wanted it to make enough money for him to buy a Mercedes. Instead, he has to drive around in the ten year old van belonging to the business. He has written you a letter saying that he has found the solution to his problems -increase the working capital of the business. To achieve this, he intends to get more cash in the business by:

(i) increasing his overdraft with the bank;

(ii) reducing his stocks by 50 per cent;

(iii) delaying paying his bills (his creditors) by a month.

Wordprocessing

Write a letter back to him, explaining:

(a) the difference between cash and working capital;

(b) why none of these three measures will increase his working capital;

(c) the possible effects of the measures on (i) the costs and (ii) the revenues of the business and therefore on (iii) the profit of the business.

equal to 2.5 to 1. As already mentioned, accountants usually advise that a **typical** business should have a current ratio of 1.5 to 1 to 2:1. If it is less than this, the business runs the risk of not being able to pay its bills and going out of business. Spirax-Sarco looks a very safe business with a current ratio of 2.5 to 1. However, the business doesn't want too high a current ratio because current assets earn little or no interest and money might be better used elsewhere.

The acid test ratio

Stock is part of the working capital of the business. However, it might be difficult to sell off stock quickly if the business faced a cash crisis. For instance, Spirax-Sarco might find it difficult to sell quickly half its stock valued at £51.8 million for £25 million if it needed the cash. Even if it succeeded, it might have to sell it at such a low price that it didn't get anywhere near £25 million for the sale.

So a better measure of whether a business has enough working capital might be the ACID TEST RATIO. This excludes stock from current assets in calculating the ratio of current assets to current liabilities:

$$\text{Acid test ratio} = \frac{\text{Current assets - stock}}{\text{Current liabilities}}$$

Like the current ratio, the higher the acid test ratio, the safer is the business and the less likely it is to become insolvent. At 31 December 1996, Spirax-Sarco's current assets minus stock were £162.7 million - £51.8 million = £110.9 million. The acid test ratio was £110.9 million ÷ £64.2 million, which is equal to 1.7:1. This is very different from its 2.5:1 current ratio. A typical business should have an acid test ratio of between 0.5:1 and 1:1. Again, Spirax-Sarco looks a very safe business with its acid test ratio above the textbook norm.

Source: adapted in part from Spirax-Sarco, *Annual Report and Accounts*, 1996.

Walker Greenbank PLC

Walker Greenbank PLC is a major UK manufacturer of wallpaper. It designs, manufactures, markets and distributes wall coverings, furnishing fabrics, display materials and luxury carpets for the commercial and top-end consumer markets.

Table 29.3 *Walker Greenbank PLC, working capital at 31 January[1].*

	£m	
	1996	1997
Stocks	18.1	20.4
Debtors	21.9	22.7
Cash at bank and in hand	2.0	2.2
Bank overdraft	0.3	3.4
Trade creditors	9.5	10.0
Other creditors	12.9	11.9

[1] Figures rounded to the nearest £0.1 million.

Source: adapted from Walker Greenbank plc, *Annual Report and Accounts*, 1997.

1 What is the difference between: (a) a debtor and a creditor; (b) 'cash at bank and in hand' and an overdraft?

2 Calculate: (a) the current assets; (b) the current liabilities; (c) the working capital of the company in 1996 and 1997.

3 (a) What has happened to the company's working capital between 1996 and 1997?

(b) Do you think, looking at Table 29.3, that the company is in a better financial position in 1997 than in 1996? Give at least TWO reasons to back up your answer.

Galliford and Alfred McAlpine are two of the UK's leading building companies.

Table 29.4 *Working capital of two building companies.*

	Galliford plc[2]		Alfred McAlpine[3]	
	£m[1]			
	1995	1996	1995	1996
Current assets				
Stocks	35.2	35.1	157.9	143.7
Debtors	33.2	29.2	172.6	150.3
Cash	3.1	4.4	28.1	27.6
Current liabilities	51.7	48.0	181.7	168.2

[1] Figures rounded to the nearest £0.1 million.
[2] at 30 June.
[3] at 31 December.

Source: adapted from Galliford plc and Alfred Mc Alpine, *Annual report and Accounts*, 1997.

1 Calculate from Table 29.4:
   (a) total current assets; (b) the current ratio; and (c) the acid test ratio; for both companies in 1995 and 1996.
2 (a) Which company has: (i) the highest current ratio; and (ii) the highest acid test ratio? (b) There is sudden downturn in the UK economy and the construction industry is very badly affected through loss of orders. Discuss which of the two companies in Table 29.4 you think might find it easiest to survive this situation.

Checklist ✓

1 What is the difference between the current assets of a business and its current liabilities?
2 Explain what will happen to a business' working capital if: (a) its cash increases; (b) its stocks rise; (c) its creditors rise; (d) its debtors fall; (e) it increases its bank overdraft by £1 000 and uses the money to buy extra stock; (f) it sells £1 000 of stock for cash; (g) it reduces its bank overdraft because it has increased the prices of its products for sale.
3 What is the difference between cash and working capital?
4 What is the difference between the current ratio and the acid test ratio?
5 A manufacturing business finds that its current ratio falls from 2.5:1 to 1:1. (a) Why does this suggest that the business is in trouble? (b) What might have caused this fall?
6 A manufacturing business has a current ratio of 3:1 but an acid test ratio of only 0.5:1. (a) What must be its most important type of current asset? (b) Why might the business face problems in the future?

key terms

Acid test ratio - the ratio of current assets minus stock to current liabilities.
Current ratio - the ratio of current assets to current liabilities.
Working capital - current assets minus current liabilities.

SUMMARY CASE STUDY

VITEC GROUP

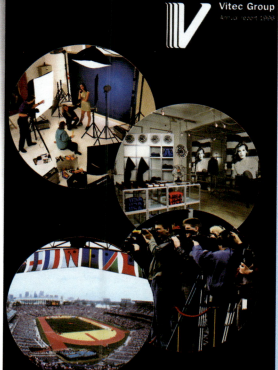

Vitec Group plc has two main groups of businesses. First, it owns a number of businesses in the photographic industry, including the world's leading manufacturers of camera mounting and lighting support equipment for professional photographers. Second, it has businesses in broadcast services, including rentals of broadcasting equipment and internet provision.

Table 29.5 *Vitec Group plc, current assets and liabilities.*

	£m[1]	
	1995	1996
Current assets		
Stocks	32.0	25.5
Debtors	31.0	27.1
Cash[2]	21.0	54.5
Current liabilities		
Borrowings	10.2	16.3
Trade creditors	11.1	8.4
Other creditors	20.3	17.5

[1] Figure rounded to the nearest £0.1 million
[2] including investments.

Source: adapted from Vitec Group plc, *Annual Report and Accounts*, 1997.

1 (a) What is a 'current asset'? (b) Give FOUR examples of stocks which Vitec Group is likely to hold. (c) Debtors of Vitec include television companies. Why is this the case? (d) From Table 29.5, calculate the value of current assets for: (i) 1995; and (ii) 1996.
2 (a) What is a 'current liability'? (b) If the company had a loan which must be repaid in 6 months time and one which must be repaid in 5 years time, which of these is a current liability and why? (c) Electricity companies are trade creditors for Vitec Group. Why is this true? (d) From Table 29.5, calculate the total value of current liabilities for: (i) 1995; and (ii) 1996.
3 Calculate, for: (i) 1995; and (ii) 1996; Vitec Group's: (a) working capital; (b) current ratio; and (c) acid test ratio.
4 Explain whether you think Vitec Group's current ratio and acid test ratio would suggest that the company is a safe company in which to buy shares and invest.
5 Vitec Group is continually expanding and launching new products. For instance, it opened a new factory in 1997 to produce photographic equipment for its Alu range. Explain why Vitec Group needs more working capital if it is to expand its business.

FINANCING THE BUSINESS THROUGH CAPITAL

Making decisions

Businesses need money to start up and run their operations. One way of getting this money is for the business to attract capital - where another business or individual puts money into the business in return for a share of the ownership. If the business is already in existence, it can put back any profits made to pay for investment. The business needs to decide which is the best way of obtaining money. For instance, should a sole proprietor put in savings? If a partner or new shareholder is brought in, what will be his or her share of the profit and how much control will be left in the hands of the original partners or shareholders?

Jamie Picton is a dentist. He has worked for six years in two dental practices and now wants to set up on his own. Most dentists join existing practices and put money into them. But he decided he wanted to start from scratch so that he could have complete control over equipment and premises. The risk, though, was that he wouldn't build up a patient list quickly enough to make a profit. He knew that he would need a lot of financial capital to start the business.

Getting started

Jamie drew up a **business plan** (☞ unit 22). He calculated that he would need £150 000 in total. The dental equipment would cost £60 000. Redecorating and refitting the rented premises would cost £30 000. He would then need £60 000 in **working capital** to cover day to day expenses like wages for the receptionist, laboratory bills and the rent.

Jamie hoped to borrow £50 000 of this from a bank. The other £100 000 he hoped would come from raising capital for the business. Raising capital (sometimes called EQUITY or EQUITY CAPITAL) means:

* Jamie putting his own money into the business;
* finding people who are prepared to become joint owners of the business. These could be either **partners** (in a partnership ☞ unit 11) or **shareholders** (in a limited company ☞ unit 12).

Raising capital for a small business

It is sometimes very difficult for small and medium sized businesses (like partnerships or private limited companies) to find someone prepared to become joint owners. When found, they are often:

* members of the family, like a parent or an uncle;

Turbowash

Kerry had worked at the dry cleaners for five years. She was 23 and felt that she didn't want to work for someone else for the rest of her life. She thought she could do everything that her current boss, Della, was doing in running a small business. Buying a dry cleaners of her own was out of the question. It would cost her tens of thousands of pounds. However, Kerry estimated that if she could rent a place, then she would only need about £10 000 to start the business. She had £5 000 in savings. Her mum said she would lend her £1 500. She needed more than this though.

Della got to hear about her plans. To Kerry's surprise, she suggested they might go halves on a new dry cleaners. Della would put in £5 000 and they would become equal partners. She would give Kerry advice on how to manage the business. She was also thinking of refurbishing her existing dry cleaners. Most of the equipment was almost worthless if sold second hand, but it was still in good working order.

The new dry cleaners would then start off with this equipment, which would cut down on the £10 000 start up cost. What's more, Della was prepared to lend the new business money in the first few months until it established itself.

1 (a) What skills did Kerry have which would help her in her new business?
   (b) What skills would she have had to learn if she opened the business?
2 What financial problem did Kerry face in trying to start up on her own?
3 Why do you think Della was interested in helping Kerry set up a new salon?
4 What advantages and disadvantages were there for Kerry in having Della as a partner?
5 Should Kerry accept Della's offer? Explain your answer.

Streamline

Streamline Holdings is to be floated on the London Stock Exchange. The company is the largest supplier of traffic signs and road marking materials in the UK and France. It also manages highway maintenance contracts for local authorities. 22 million shares will be sold at 180p. The rest of the 40 million shares will be kept by existing investors, including the directors of the company who hold 14.4 per cent of the total shares.

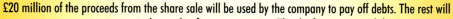

£20 million of the proceeds from the share sale will be used by the company to pay off debts. The rest will be used to finance expansion. The chief executive said the company was close to buying two companies. 'This will enable us to continue to build up our business of providing solutions to traffic management.'

Source: adapted from the *Financial Times*, 23 February 1996.

1 What does Streamline Holdings make?
2 What does 'floated' mean?
3 How much money will the company raise by issuing new shares?
4 What does the company plan to do with the money raised?
5 (a) What will happen to the share of the total profits going to the directors who own shares in the company after the flotation? (b) Suggest why, despite this, they chose not to sell any of their shares at the time of the flotation.

- friends who can see a good business opportunity;
- people known through work;
- people who want to set up in business and also need to find someone prepared to invest in the business.

Jamie's father was a dentist who owned a practice ten miles away from where Jamie was going to set up. He was prepared to put up £50 000. Jamie also had a friend from his days at dental school who had done very well in her first six years of work. She was prepared to put in £30 000 on the understanding that she might work in the practice in future if it attracted enough patients. Jamie had put his flat up for sale and hoped to have £20 000 once the mortgage had been paid off.

Jamie would then have owned 20 per cent of the practice, his friend 30 per cent and his father 50 per cent. This is because the ratio of capital put into the business would have been £20 000 to £30 000 to £50 000. Jamie would have had the least say in how the business was run if there was any

disagreement. He was unhappy about this.

In the end, he persuaded his father to lend him the £50 000 instead. His friend then owned 30 per cent (with £30 000) and Jamie owned 70 per cent (£50 000 loan plus his own £20 000 = £70 000). As dentists, Jamie and his friend set up a partnership. They had to accept the risk of unlimited liability. However, if can sometimes be easier to find new capital for a small business if it is a private limited company, where shareholders have limited liability.

Share capital for larger businesses

Jamie Picton's problems were typical of those faced by small businesses starting up or wanting to grow. One of the reasons why larger businesses become **public limited companies** is because they find it easier to sell (or **float**) new shares in the business. A business, for instance, can raise new money through **going public**

(i.e. becoming a public limited company). Later on, it can make a **share issue** (i.e. sell extra shares in the company) to raise more finance.

A new share issue by a public limited company is likely to be organised by a bank or a merchant bank. It might offer the shares for sale to the general public, or it could sell the shares to existing shareholders. It might also **place** the shares (i.e. sell them) with other financial organisations like assurance companies, unit trusts or pension funds which invest in shares on behalf of their savers.

One reason why investors are far more prepared to buy shares in a public limited company than in, say, a private limited company is because there is an organised market for the buying and selling of second hand shares. This market is the **stock market**.

Types of share

Most shares issued by **private** and **public** limited companies are ORDINARY SHARES. The owners of the shares, the shareholders of the company, are entitled to receive a share of the profits. This share of the profits is called a DIVIDEND. The dividend can go up and down from year to year depending upon how much profit the company has made and how much it decides to give to its shareholders.

Limited companies can also issue PREFERENCE SHARES. These carry a fixed rate of dividend

Second hand shares are traded on the stock market.

and so shareholders don't benefit from any increases in profits made by the company. However, they also don't suffer as much if the company has a bad year. Ordinary shareholders may receive no dividend that year, but preference shareholders may be paid because they are entitled to get the first share of any profits made by the company.

Venture capital

Jamie Picton's business would have been too small to be of interest to a VENTURE CAPITALIST. Venture capital companies specialise in buying a share of small but growing businesses, most of which are private limited companies. The venture capitalist hopes that in about 5 years the business will have grown and its stake in the business can then be sold at a profit.

Retained profit

In any year, only a few per cent of all the money to finance investment in the UK comes from raising new capital. The most important source of finance is RETAINED or UNDISTRIBUTED PROFIT. This is profit which has been made by the business and is not distributed to the owners of the business. Instead, it is kept back, or retained.

Jamie Picton, for instance, hopes to be able to expand his business once it becomes profitable by taking on another dentist to work with him. He will therefore need more equipment, another room refurbished and more working capital. A large public limited company is no different. It ploughs back profits to finance growth of its business.

Retained profit is an INTERNAL SOURCE OF FINANCE because the money has come from within the business. New capital, in contrast, is an EXTERNAL SOURCE OF FINANCE because the money comes from outside the business.

The great advantage to Jamie of retained profit as a way of financing investment is that he doesn't have to pay interest or dividends on the money. It also means that he doesn't have to find banks, new partners or shareholders, or anyone else who would be prepared to lend money or invest in the business.

Other internal sources of finance

Another way for a business to raise money internally is to sell assets. For instance, in ten years time, Jamie might have bought his own premises. He may decide to move to bigger premises. He could then sell his existing premises to raise money to pay for the new building.

Larger businesses might be able to negotiate a **sale and lease-back** scheme. Here, the business sells some or all of its property to another company, like a property company. At the same time, it signs an agreement to lease (i.e. rent) back the property for a fixed annual rent. The business receives a lump sum of money which can be used to pay for expansion. The drawback is that the business now has to pay rent on the property.

Raising finance - The Print Company

The Print Company is a mini-company which plans to sell photographs of its school. It has a print of an aerial shot of the buildings and one of the directors of the company, who is a keen photographer, plans to take a number of other shots of the school. Six photographs will be mounted into a frame made by two other directors of the company with the help of their technology teacher. They are going to charge £5.99 for a set of photographs plus the frame. For £7.99, they will include a picture of any pupil or group of pupils, the photograph being taken by the photographer in the company.

In its business plan, the board of directors states that most of the frames produced will be produced to order. People will pay their money and the frames will be delivered later. However, they need to produce at least one frame for display purposes. They also want to produce another 10 for immediate sale at the next parents' evening. They calculate they need £40 for this and to cover advertising costs. They decide to make a share issue of forty £1 shares.

Read through the case study. EITHER use it to think about how you would raise capital for your mini-enterprise OR answer the following questions.

1 Who could the company get to buy the shares?
2 Why might people want to buy the shares?
3 The company successfully sells a number of photographs and makes £50 profit. Another parents' evening is coming up and the company decides that it would like to make another 10 frames for immediate sale.
   (a) Where could it get the money from to finance this? (b) Discuss which would be the best way of financing the deal.

Games Workshop

Games Workshop is a company which manufactures and sells model soldiers used for playing 'war games'. A highly successful company, it is planning to move into all of the world's major countries to sell its products.

Wordprocessing/Graphics

A shareholder has written to Games Workshop to question why more profit has been retained in 1996 than has been paid out in dividends. Write a letter (which could be wordprocessed) to the shareholder explaining why Games Workshop needs to retain profits and why this might benefit shareholders in the long term. Structure your letter as follows.

1 Thank the shareholder for her letter.
2 Explain that she is correct to say that retained profits were larger than dividends in 1996. Construct EITHER two pie charts OR a single bar chart to illustrate this point. If possible, use a graphics package to do this.

Table 30.1 *Games Workshop Group PLC - where its profits went.*

	1996
Tax profit before tax	8 865
distributed as	
Tax on profit on ordinary activities	3 200
Dividends	2 113
Profit retained	3 552

Source: adapted from Games Workshop Group PLC, *Annual Report and Accounts*, 1996.

3 Explain what retained profit is used for.
4 Point out that investment in the company will now enable the company to grow and pay bigger dividends in the future.
5 End the letter by thanking the shareholder for her interest and saying that you hope this letter answers all her concerns.

key terms

Dividend - a share of the profits of a company received by people who own shares.
Equity or equity capital - the monetary value of a business which belongs to the business owners. In a company this would be the value of their shares.
Internal and external sources of capital - finance which is obtained from within the business (internal) or from outside the business (external).
Ordinary shares - shares in a limited company where the company can vary the amount of dividend paid to shareholders each year depending upon the amount of profit made.
Preference shares - shares in a limited company where shareholders receive a fixed amount in £s in dividends each year. The company can choose not to pay a dividend in any one year if it feels it has not made enough profit. If dividends are paid, preference shareholders take priority over ordinary shareholders.
Retained or undistributed profit - profit which is kept back by a business and used to pay for investment in the business.
Venture capital - money which is used by a venture capitalist to buy a share of what is hoped to be a growing business.

Checklist ✓

1 Why might capital be needed to start up and run a business?
2 Who might be willing to put capital into a small business?
3 A friend of the family mentions that he is looking for someone to take a 40 per cent stake in a limited company he is setting up. You have the £10 000 he is looking for saved in a building society account. What might be: (a) the advantages; and (b) disadvantages for you of investing money in the new company?
4 Explain the meaning of: (a) share issue; (b) going public; (c) placing shares.
5 Why are investors much more willing to invest in shares of a public limited company than in a private limited company?
6 What is the stock market?
7 What is the difference between an ordinary share and a preference share?
8 How might a venture capitalist be of help to a growing company?
9 (a) What is undistributed profit? (b) What are the advantages to a business of using retained profit to finance investment?

SUMMARY CASE STUDY

INNOVATIVE TECHNOLOGIES GROUP PLC

Innovative Technologies, the health care company, is to issue 10.4 million new shares at 70p each. This will increase the number of issued shares in the company to 31.2 million.
The company is a young medical company which wants to move on from research to the manufacturing stage. It has patented a number of innovative woundcare products including Hollister and Bioderm. The money will be used to provide working capital for this next stage of its development as a company.

Source: adapted from the *Financial Times*, 23 January 1996.

1 How many new shares were Innovative Tech issuing for sale?
2 Calculate how much money they were raising as new equity.
3 What did Innovative Tech plan to do with the money raised?
4 Why might anyone have wanted to buy shares in the company?
5 (a) Give TWO other ways in which the company could have raised money.
(b) Write a short report suggesting why issuing new shares might have been better for the company than the other two sources of finance that you have suggested.

FINANCING THE BUSINESS THROUGH BORROWING

Making decisions

Businesses need money to start up and run their operations. They can choose to get the money by borrowing it. The business needs to decide which is the most appropriate way to borrow money. In particular, it needs to consider the rate of interest, when the money needs to be repaid, whether or not it is possible to arrange the finance and what are the implications if the business gets into difficulty repaying the loan.

Horobin Ltd is a manufacturer of packaging for the food industry. It makes plastic containers for everything from cakes and biscuits to vegetables to chocolates. It needs money to pay for the day to day running of the business, like paying the bills and the wages. It also needs money for long term finance. It is a growing company and needs money to pay for new equipment and extensions to its factory.

External and internal sources of finance

In unit 30, two ways of raising finance for a business were explained. These were finding **equity capital** (an external source of finance) and using **retained profit** (an internal source of finance). In this unit, other external sources of finance will be covered.

Bank overdrafts

Horobin, like nearly all businesses, has a current account at a bank. It uses the cash in the account to pay its day to day bills using **cheques**. A bank might also give the business an OVERDRAFT. This means that the bank will allow it to draw out more money than it has in its account. The maximum amount it can be overdrawn (i.e. borrow) is called its **overdraft limit**. For instance, Horobin has an overdraft limit with its bank of £400 000. It uses this to pay for the day to day running of the business, including paying for materials. Sales are higher in the winter months than in the summer months, partly because food sales are particularly high at Christmas. Horobin's current account tends to be far more **in the red** (i.e. overdrawn) in the winter months than in summer months.

The great advantage of an overdraft is that money is only borrowed when it is needed. This cuts down on the interest bill. Horobin borrows far more in the winter months than in the summer

Wagner's

Tom and Jill Wagner ran a successful business making cider from their own farm. They decided to expand the business by opening a bar and restaurant. They built the premises on their own land from an old barn which had been dismantled on a neighbouring farm. The cost was financed by a loan of £150 000.

They opened in September, employing a chef and an assistant chef. There was a lot of interest to start with but business dropped dramatically in November and December. This was just the time when the restaurant should have been full with Christmas parties. The bar and restaurant part of the business began to lose on average £3 000 a month.

Within six months, they had run up an overdraft of £18 000.

With an overdraft limit of just £20 000, the Wagners had to act. The two chefs left and were replaced by one chef. He altered the menu considerably, making it much more linked to the Wagner's organic farming and cider activities. The number of customers doubled very quickly and the restaurant became profitable.

1 What is an overdraft?
2 On what do you think the Wagners were spending the money they were borrowing through their overdraft?
3 Explain why the Wagners 'had to act' when their overdraft was £18 000 and still rising.
4 Do you think the Wagners acted quickly enough to solve their problems? Explain your arguments carefully.

months. It doesn't want to be borrowing money in the summer months which it doesn't need and paying interest on that loan.

Overdrafts, though, can be more expensive than they seem, particularly for small businesses. Banks often charge an arrangement fee to give the overdraft and then make a charge per quarter (three months) to maintain the overdraft limit. Banks may make higher charges for cheques issued when the account is overdrawn.

Another disadvantage is that an overdraft is also repayable on demand. The bank can **call in** an overdraft (i.e. insist that the money borrowed is repaid immediately). This means that there is a risk involved in this type of borrowing.

Pike is a private limited company in the engineering industry. At the moment it employs a full time worker to collect money from sales invoices. It would like to increase its cash and stocks in the business because it is growing.

1 How could Lombard NatWest help Pike?

2 What disadvantages would there be for Pike if it used Lombard NatWest's services?

3 An alternative way of increasing the amount of cash in the business would be for Pike to increase its overdraft with its bank. Do you think this would be better for the company rather using Lombard NatWest's services? Explain your reasons carefully.

KeyCash

Key*Cash* has been designed to provide finance and a basic sales ledger service to growing businesses which are forecasting sales of between £50,000 and £300,000 per year and create suitable trade debts by selling on credit terms to other businesses (not directly to the public).
Key*Cash* offers a solution to the problems caused by rapid growth. The client sells unpaid trade debts to Lombard NatWest, who immediately make available finance of up to 80% of the value of all approved invoices. The balance, less charges, is paid as each debtor settles an invoice.

Charges and termination period

Lombard NatWest charge an initial arrangement fee of £200 and a service fee, which is usually 1% of the value of all invoices (minimum £1200 per year). They also make a discounting charge on all finance drawn by the client at a rate similar to the interest charged on a business overdraft. The **Key***Cash* agreement can be terminated by giving 3 months notice in writing (similar services may involve 6 or 12 months notice of termination).

What would I gain from using KeyCash

• An immediate injection of finance based on the value of the trade debtors on the day your **Key***Cash* agreement starts.
• Access to ongoing finance based on the current value of your trade debtors.
• Our computer based sales ledger service, which would assist you with the task of chasing customers for payment.
• A computer link with Lombard NatWest, which enables you to see, on your own PC, how much finance is available from us, to draw finance, and see details of individual customer accounts and reports on the whole sales ledger.

Source: adapted from **Key***Cash*, Accelerated Cash flow for Growing Businesses, Lombard NatWest.

Trade credit

Horobin gets **trade credit** from the businesses from which it buys its

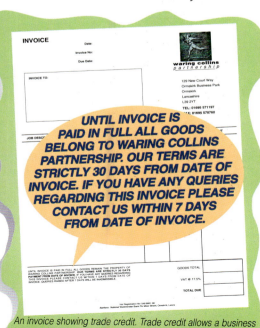

An invoice showing trade credit. Trade credit allows a business to pay for goods or services at a later date.

supplies. It doesn't have to pay for goods until at least one month after they have delivered. The advantage is that other businesses lend money to Horobin for at least one month 'free' of charge. The more Horobin produces, the more trade credit they are likely to get as their need for supplies rises. Hence, trade credit is a way of increasing the cash in the business (☞ unit 28).

However, trade credit is not always free. Some businesses give discounts if their customers pay bills immediately. Another disadvantage of trade credit is that suppliers may stop selling goods to a business if it owes too much money through trade credit. The supplier will be afraid that the business owes too much money and may be in danger of going bankrupt or into liquidation, leaving its debt unpaid.

Factoring

Horobin uses a FACTOR to reduce the amount of money it

has to borrow on overdraft. A factor is a specialist finance company. It collects the money which is owed to Horobin by other businesses and charges a fee. (Remember, although Horobin gets trade credit from its suppliers, it in turn is forced to give trade credit to its customers like supermarkets and food manufacturers.)

The factor will pay Horobin even if an **invoice** (a bill) hasn't been paid by a customer. Horobin is therefore guaranteed regular payment of its invoices. It also doesn't have to employ staff to chase and collect those bills. However, a factor will only give the business a percentage of the bill, usually 80 per cent. The other 20 per cent is paid to Horobin when its customers pay the factor. The great advantage of using a factor is that it speeds up the flow of cash through a business.

Bank loans

Overdrafts, trade credit and factoring are different ways in which a business like Horobin can increase the cash and working capital flowing round the business. However, they are not suitable ways of raising money to finance the replacement of, say, £200 000 of outdated machinery. This needs some form of longer term finance like a bank LOAN.

With a bank loan, the business usually borrows a fixed amount of money and then pays it back in regular fixed instalments. These repayments include the interest on the outstanding money owed. The bank may demand security on the loan. This means that the business has to pledge assets to the bank which the bank can sell if the business fails to repay the loan. For instance, Horobin could offer its factory as **security** or **collateral.**

A MORTGAGE is a type of long term loan. The money borrowed is usually used to pay for the purchase of property, such as a new buildings or land. The property is then used as security for the loan.

Leasing and hire purchase

Horobin has a number of photocopiers in its offices. It could have bought them outright, but it would have to borrow the money to do that. Instead, it has LEASED (i.e. rented) the photocopiers from a leasing firm. Many leasing contracts also include maintenance contracts where the leasing company maintains and repairs the machines as part of the price of the rental. Leasing equipment is usually more expensive over the lifetime of the machine than buying it outright. On the other hand, it could work out cheaper if the leasing firm can buy machines in bulk and pass on the discount to its customers. There can also be important tax advantages to renting equipment rather than buying outright. Maintenance contracts included in a leasing deal, whilst often expensive, reduce the risk of sudden large unexpected bills if the machine breaks down.

HIRE PURCHASE is an alternative way of borrowing money. If Horobin bought a photocopier on hire purchase, it would pay a fixed number of instalments to buy the photocopier. Legally, each instalment is a rental payment and the finance house, a type of bank which specialises in hire purchase deals, would own the photocopier until the last instalment is paid.

Debentures

Large public limited companies can borrow money through the City of London by issuing DEBENTURES (also called **stocks** or **bonds**). These are usually long term loans, normally for between 5 and 25 years. Interest has to be paid on the loan. A debenture where the money borrowed is in another currency is called a Eurobond. For instance, ICI, a UK company, might borrow German deutschmarks to finance the building of a chemical plant in Germany. Private limited companies, like Horobin, can also issue debentures which are typically bought by banks.

Grants

Grants to businesses are given by a wide number of bodies including the UK government through local Training and Enterprise Councils (TECs) and the European Union.

Grants are offered by TECs to unemployed people who set up their own businesses. The TEC provides training and support. If the person prepares a business plan which shows that the business is likely to succeed, a 'grant' may be given for a period of time.

Stuffed shirts

John Pease runs the Stuffed Shirt Company. He was an oil executive who was constantly going from oil sites to business meetings. Smart, clean clothes were essential but ordinary suitcases or bags tended to crease clothes. So he designed a set of frames which would keep clothes, like shirts, crease free.

In 1993, he set up his company to manufacture the frames and luggage, putting in £100 000 of his own money. The following year, two friends joined him, putting in £75 000 each. £120 000 of this was used just to patent the designs and trademarks in 26 countries. The rest was spent leasing premises in Sedbergh, Cumbria, paying wages and seeing to all the other start up costs of a business.

Cash flow was rarely a problem. Overseas customers had to pay on delivery. The Stuffed Shirt Company used a factoring firm for its UK customers. The frames were made by a manufacturer in Bradford whilst the covers for the frames were manufactured in China and Egypt. The company received 30 days trade credit from these suppliers.

With the business expanding, the company gained a £50 000 working capital loan in April 1996 from the Rural Development Commission, a government organisation. Later on that year, another investor bought £150 000 worth of shares in the business, bringing the amount of share capital to £400 000.

Source: adapted from the *Financial Times*, 18 January 1997.

1 How much money did John Pease use to start his business?
2 What was this start up capital used for?
3 The Stuffed Shirt Company: (a) used a factor; and (b) received a loan from the Rural Development Commission. Suggest why it used these two sources of finance.
4 The company has relatively low borrowings. Instead, it chose to obtain finance by raising new share capital. Suggest what would have been the disadvantages to the company of financing expansion through heavy loans from a bank.

Bliss Bridal Wear

After help from Business Link, two Doncaster businesswomen put together a deal to expand their bridal wear company - investing over £250 000 and creating 14 new jobs in the process. For the past six years Anita Coates and daughter Amanda Carr combined their business and design talents to successfully run the Bliss Bridal Wear retail company. Following advice from Business Link Doncaster they have recently been able to combine a number of grants and loans with existing company resources to take their business further forward. This combination of different funding sources has allowed Bliss to establish a manufacturing base in Doncaster. They now have the capacity to produce 3 500 brides' and bridesmaids' dresses in the first year and will supply all three Bliss retail outlets in South Yorkshire. Plans are also in place to develop links with 20 other retailers across the country. Both of Bliss' partners felt that the Business Link actively helped them achieve their view of the company's future strategy. Amanda Carr commented: 'We knew where we wanted to be and turned to Business Link Doncaster to help us get there. They have supported us all the way - helping to bring our business plan to life and secure the funding to make it work.'

The importance of funding

Funding is a major concern for businesses. It forms the lifeblood of any company, providing the most essential resource for development. Business Link can help find out exactly what your business needs are and tailor a package of support ideally suited to meet those needs, financial or otherwise. Business Links can advise about local and regional grants and financial assistance.

Source: *Helping You Get The Best From Your Business*, Business Link.

1 Why did Bliss Bridal Wear need extra funding?
2 Explain the THREE types of finance the owners used to expand the business.
3 How did Business Link Doncaster help the business?
4 Discuss THREE risks that the business faced because it expanded.

Checklist ✓

1 What does it mean if a business with a bank account has: (a) a £5 000 overdraft limit; (b) its overdraft called in?
2 Explain how a business can borrow money free of interest from other businesses.
3 How can a factor help a business increase the amount of cash it holds?
4 (a) Outline the differences between a bank loan, a mortgage and an overdraft. (b) A business wishes: (i) to expand turnover by buying in more stock for sale; (ii) buy a new machine; and (iii) purchase a new office building. Explain which of the three methods of financing in (a) might be most appropriate for each of these projects.
5 (a) What are the differences between leasing and hire purchase? (b) Explain which of the following a business might consider financing through a leasing agreement: (i) a photocopier; (ii) a company car; (iii) an increase in stocks; (iv) a computer system; (v) an increase in creditors.
6 What is the difference between a debenture and a share?
7 Who might give a grant to a business?

Key terms

Debenture - a long term loan to a business.
Factor - a business which collects the debts of other businesses, for which it charges a fee.
Hire purchase - legally, renting equipment prior to buying it. In effect, it is a type of loan.
Leasing - renting equipment or premises.
Loan - borrowing a sum of money which then has to be repaid with interest over a period of time like 1-5 years, typically in fixed monthly instalments.
Mortgage - a loan where property is used as security.
Overdraft - borrowing money from a bank by drawing more money than is actually in a current account. Interest is charged on the amount overdrawn.

SUMMARY CASE STUDY

SMALL BUSINESS FINANCE

Wordprocessing

1 Write a report to be read by clients interested in setting up their own business. In the report explain how small businesses raise finance. Comment on the possible advantages and disadvantages of the main forms of finance. Use the data in Figures 31.1 and 31.2 to support your answer. If possible, word process your report.

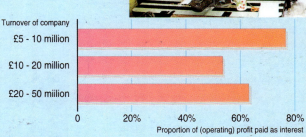

Type of finance (% of respondents)

Overdraft	79.9%
Term loan	39.7%
Leasing	38.1%
Hire purchase	32.8%
Factoring and invoice discounting	6.3%
Share issues	5.8%
Other	5.8%

Source: adapted from *Business Banking Review*.

Figure 31.1 *How small businesses raise finance.*

Turnover of company

£5 - 10 million	
£10 - 20 million	
£20 - 50 miilion	

0   20%   40%   60%   80%
Proportion of (operating) profit paid as interest

Source: adapted from Touche Ross.

Figure 31.2 *The cost of depending on debt.*

WHICH SOURCE OF FINANCE?

Making decisions

Businesses need to find the right type of financing for their situation. Which type of financing would be cheapest? Which would be the most suitable? Would it put the business at any risk? What sources of finance are available?

What is the money needed for?

Jamie Picton, the dentist described in unit 30, would not take out a 5 year loan to pay for an increase in the electricity bill. Equally, Horobin Ltd, the manufacturer of packaging for the food industry described in unit 31, would not finance the building of a new factory by taking out an overdraft. In general, short term financing is used to pay for an increase in **cash** and **working capital**. For instance, when Horobin gets an increase in orders, it is likely to increase its overdraft and trade credit to pay for this.

The purchase of equipment or buildings (**fixed capital** for the business) is generally financed using longer term methods. Taking out a loan may be suitable for buying a company car or a new dentist's chair. Issuing new shares could be suitable for a large expansion project by Horobin.

Cost

Different types of financing have different costs. Borrowing money means that interest has to be paid. Leasing a company car costs the hire of the lease. Issuing new shares means that extra dividends will have to be paid. For Jamie Picton and

Horobin, cost would be an important element in deciding which type of finance to choose.

Risk

Horobin, a limited company, can issue new shares and retain profit to increase its capital. Unlike a loan, where interest has to be paid, dividends to shareholders don't have to be given if profits fall or the company makes a loss. So borrowing is perhaps riskier than increasing the capital of the business. One way of measuring this risk is to calculate the GEARING RATIO, the ratio of loans to share capital. A company with more loans than share capital (i.e. a gearing ratio of over 100 per cent) would be risky. Horobin, with loans equal to 25 per cent of share capital (a gearing ratio of 25 per cent), is relatively safe.

Availability of finance

Some types of finance are available to most businesses.

- Businesses, except those starting up, can use retained profit.
- Bank loans and overdrafts are frequently used. Small businesses, such as sole proprietorships, often complain though that they are charged much higher rates of interest on loans and overdrafts than larger

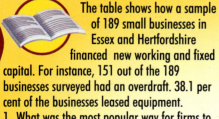

The table shows how a sample of 189 small businesses in Essex and Hertfordshire financed new working and fixed capital. For instance, 151 out of the 189 businesses surveyed had an overdraft. 38.1 per cent of the businesses leased equipment.

1 What was the most popular way for firms to finance themselves?

2 What is the difference between leasing and hire purchase?

3 What 'other' methods of finance might there be which 11 of the businesses surveyed used?

4 The shareholders of a small furniture manufacturing business need money to finance expansion of their private limited company. They were thinking of issuing more shares in the business but then read the report in the *Business Banking Review* and saw the above table. They notice that very few businesses use share issues as a method of financing. Write a report (a) explaining why this might be the case and (b) arguing that share issues have many advantages over other methods of financing.

Table 32.1 *Financing methods.*

Type of finance	Number	Per cent
Overdraft	151	79.9
Loan	75	39.7
Leasing	72	38.1
Hire purchase	62	32.8
Share issues	11	5.8
Factoring	5	2.6
Other	11	5.8

Source: Survey of small companies in Essex and Hertfordshire, *Business Banking Review*.

businesses. Banks justify this by arguing that small businesses are more likely to go bankrupt or into liquidation than large businesses. Hence, lending to small businesses is more risky and they have to charge higher rates of interest to make the same rate of profit overall compared to lending to larger businesses.

- Trade credit, hire purchase, leasing and factoring are also possibilities.
- Smaller businesses, like sole proprietors or partnerships, have difficulty finding people or other businesses who might inject money as equity capital into their business. So they tend to rely on borrowing money rather than raising equity (☞ unit 30).
- Private limited companies can issue equity capital in the form of shares, but they tend to be sold to a small number of people, often family or friends. Plcs can issue shares on a stock exchange, which puts large numbers of potential investors into contact with businesses.

Key terms

Gearing ratio - the ratio of long term borrowings of a company to its share capital.

(☞ unit 30).

Table 32.2 Sources of finance.

	Retained profit	Bank overdraft	Bank loan	Leasing & hire purchase	Debentures	Shares	Shares on the London stock market
Sole proprietorship	✔	✔	✔	✔	x	x	x
Partnership	✔	✔	✔	✔	x	x	x
Private limited company	✔	✔	✔	✔	✔	✔	x
Public limited company	✔	✔	✔	✔	✔	✔	✔
Retail co-operative	✔	✔	✔	✔	✔	✔	x
Worker co-operative	✔	✔	✔	✔	✔	✔	x
Public corporation	✔	✔	✔	✔	✔	x	x

Checklist ✓

1 A business has the following finance needs. Explain what type of finance would be most suitable for: (a) a new factory; (b) a company car; (c) an increase in purchases of components; (d) the take-over of another company; (e) an increase in the number of workers employed; (f) the setting up of a new subsidiary company.

2 Explain why the following might be considered poor business practice. (a) A small business buys a £50 000 new machine and finances it by increasing its overdraft. (b) A hotel business takes out a loan for £30 000 repayable over five years to pay for increased staff costs during very busy holiday months in July and August. (c) A business takes out a mortgage on its factory repayable over fifteen years to pay for a £30 000 company car for the chairperson. (d) A business which has made losses for the past three years and is close to going into liquidation takes out a five year loan to pay off some of its other debts.

3 Why wouldn't the following happen? (a) A sole proprietor issues shares in her company to finance an increase in working capital. (b) A partnership issues debentures on the Stock Exchange. (c) A public limited company negotiates a £400 loan from its bankers.

4 Explain why large businesses are likely to have a greater choice of finance than small businesses.

SUMMARY CASE STUDY

MANGLING PRAWNS

Adrian Weaver has always loved messing around with machinery. He is constantly modifying bits and pieces to make them work better. His prawn mangle idea came after a holiday where he talked to some local fishermen. The problem was how to de-shell prawns on a large scale basis. Existing technology involved taking the prawn and squirting it with a jet of water. The prawn meat would then be forced out of the shell. But the process was labour intensive and, with so much water being used, working conditions were poor. Adrian invented a machine which operated like a mangle, forcing the prawn meat out mechanically rather than using a jet of water.

After a great deal of work, he set up a company, Weaver Seafood Associates Ltd, to exploit the invention. He was joined by two other friends and between them they put up £30 000 in share capital. The company secured a bank overdraft of £50 000 and received a £20 000 innovation grant from the Scottish Development Agency. In their first year, the company had to spend £20 000 patenting the machine. It employed a worker to assemble machines and be a technician costing £15 000. Components to make machines came to £10 000. Renting premises cost £5 000. Interest on the overdraft was £2 000. Marketing and other costs were £15 000. The three associates didn't pay themselves anything either in wages or in dividends.

But they didn't sell a single machine in that first year. Seafood processors, the businesses that were the potential customers, were deeply suspicious of the machine. They had bought machines based on similar technology in the past which hadn't worked. So in the second year, the company decided to install machines free of charge in the factories of potential buyers. They would try them out and, hopefully, see for themselves that there were large cost savings to be gained by using the machines. Then they would buy.

1 With how much: (i) equity; (ii) loans; and (iii) grants did Weaver Seafood Associates start the business?

2 In its second year of operation, the company failed to win a single order for its machines. Why did it face a crisis?

3 Adrian Weaver is convinced that customers will shortly place orders for the machines. They have been working extremely well in the factories where they were placed. Would it be better for his company to raise new equity or get a loan? Explain your reasons carefully.

unit 33

THE ROLE OF PROFIT

Making decisions

Businesses have to pay great attention to profit figures. If they make losses over a period of time, they are likely to be forced out of business. When they make a profit, they have to decide what to do with it. They could, for instance, pay it out to shareholders, buy new machinery or acquire another business. If there are high profits to be made in a market, then a business might be tempted to enter the market or expand existing production.

Taking 3,00 water qualit tests a day

United Utilities PLC is a group which includes North West Water, a water company, and NORWEB, an electricity company. Both these companies serve customers in the North West of the UK. The group also has an international division where it it competes for work with other companies. In 1997, the group's sales turnover was £2 377 million whilst its profit before tax was £284 million.

Telephones

Telephones are almost one hundred years old, but the telephone market is still expanding. In the UK, nearly all households now have a fixed line telephone. Only one in five though has a mobile telephone. So mobile phone companies are still investing hundreds of millions of pounds each year to expand their highly profitable networks.

However, there are big profits to be made too from traditional fixed line telephones. Cable companies have long offered an alternative to British Telecom lines, sending telephone messages down their television cable lines. The National Grid has laid a network along its pylon network which is now managed by Energis. All the competitors to British Telecom rent British Telecom lines to complete their door to door networks.

There is satellite telephony too. Ionica is a UK company which installs a dish on your house and beams your telephone message out into space and back again before being taken by another dish or land line to its final destination.

1 The cost of telephone calls has been going down over the past ten years but the number of telephone calls made has risen. Explain: (a) who you think has benefited from these trends; and (b) why it has encouraged businesses like Ionica to enter the telephone market.
2 Discuss whether the shareholders of British Telecom, the largest telephone company in the UK, are likely to gain or lose out from the extra competition in the future.

Who gets profit?

Profit is the reward paid to the owners of a business for risking their money. United Utilities shareholders, for instance, could put their money in a bank account and earn interest instead of buying shares. They need the **incentive** of **dividend payments** (☞ unit 30) and the possibility of increases in the price of the shares to persuade them to own the shares.

Profit is also kept back by the business to finance investment (☞ unit 30). In 1997, for instance United Utilities retained £40 million to invest in its businesses.

Allocating resources

In a **market economy** (☞ unit 3), profit acts as a signal in allocating resources. Businesses which make losses will, in the long term, go out of business. The workers, factories and offices they used will then be bought by other more successful businesses.

On the other hand, businesses which make high profits are likely to expand. For instance, in 1995 North West Water expanded by buying NORWEB, attracted by the

Definitions of profit

Profit is the difference between revenues and costs (☞ unit 23). However, there are many different types of profit depending upon what measure of revenue and measure of cost are used. For instance:
- **gross profit** (☞ unit 25) is the

difference between sales revenue and the direct cost of sales;
- **net profit i**s the difference between revenue and both the cost of sales and overhead costs;
- **profit before tax** is net profit before corporation tax, a tax on company profits, has been paid.

possibility of earning higher profits. Making greater profits is an important incentive to expand. Other businesses may also be attracted to set up in the industry if they can see an existing business earning high profits. So, in 1998, NORWEB has expanded its business by offering to supply electricity to households outside its traditional North West area.

Efficiency

Businesses which make profits are able to stay in business. They are the businesses which are selling a product to customers at an affordable price. In a **competitive market** (a market where there are a number of businesses competing against each other for the same customers), these businesses must be providing customers with products which are as good value, if not better value, than other businesses in the market. Increasing profit is a sign that:

- either the business is selling a product which customers particularly want to buy and are prepared to pay a high price for;

- or the business has been successful at cutting its costs.

Both of these suggest that profit is linked to the **efficiency** of a business. The international businesses of United Utilities operate in a competitive market. From 1998, NORWEB is operating in a competitive market too. Other electricity companies are competing for its customers in the North West of England. NORWEB, on the other hand, will be offering to supply electricity to households outside the North West. Profit is a key indicator of the efficiency of these businesses.

Market power

About one third of the sales revenues of United Utilities in 1997 came from supplying water and its wastewater operations. Much of this business is **non-competitive.** Households in the North West have to buy their water from United Utilities. The company therefore has a great deal of **market power.** In theory, it can charge what prices it likes because customers have no alternative to buying water from United Utilities.

In practice, United Utilities is limited in the price increases it can set for water and sewerage services. This is because OFWAT (the Office of Water Services) was set up at the time that North West Water was **privatised** (☞ unit 16). OFWAT has a duty to fix maximum price rises for water. The price increases are expressed in terms of 'K' factors. K is the inflation rate, the average increase in prices for all products in the UK over a year. North West Water has been allowed by OFWAT to increase prices by at most K + 2.5 per cent for the period April 1998-99 (2.5 per cent above the inflation rate of 3.7 per cent).

These maximum prices encourage North West Water to reduce costs, since this is the only way that it can increase profits. Cutting costs leads to greater efficiency. OFWAT takes this into account when deciding future maximum water prices. Regulation of water prices benefits customers in the long run.

OFWAT is not just responsible for fixing maximum prices. It is also responsible for monitoring the service given by water companies to their customers. In addition, the Drinking Water Inspectorate monitors drinking water quality, whilst the National Rivers Authority is responsible for monitoring effluent quality.

North West Water's water and effluent quality are among the highest in the UK and Western Europe.

Source: adapted from United Utilities PLC, *Annual Report and Accounts*, 1997.

SUMMARY CASE STUDY

THE PRICE OF PETROL

In 1997, the government launched an inquiry into the price of petrol. In the 1990s, more and more petrol has been sold by the supermarket chains. They have sold petrol at rock bottom prices. They can still make a profit on it because they can sell high volumes from sites which are relatively cheap to set up and operate. They can make extra profit from customers who decide to do their shopping at the same time.

In 1996, Esso decided to fight back. It launched 'Price Watch'. This promised that the price of Esso petrol would be as low as any competitor in the local area. Why should Esso cut prices?

First, schemes like Price Watch are driving independent petrol stations out of business because they can't compete. In 1996 and 1997, an estimated 3 000 petrol stations nationally stopped selling petrol. Some of the customers who used to buy from these petrol stations are now buying Esso petrol. Second, the petrol station owners who sell Esso petrol are complaining that they are the ones who are paying for the low prices. Esso has raised its rent on the sites which Esso owns. It has also forced the petrol stations to pay for part of the Price Watch scheme by reducing the profit that they make make on each litre sold. If Esso can sell a lot more petrol to its petrol stations at slightly reduced prices, its profit will increase.

Source: adapted from the *Financial Times*, 12 June 1997.

1 According to the article, why do supermarkets sell petrol at low prices?
2 Esso has responded to the supermarkets by cutting prices at Esso petrol stations. Explain how these price cuts can lead to higher profits for Esso.
3 You own a local independent petrol station. Write a letter to your local newspaper explaining why the price war between the supermarkets and the major oil companies like Esso is driving independent petrol stations out of business and why this might be bad for the motorist in the long term.

Checklist ✓

1 Describe THREE different measures of profit.
2 Who receives a share of the profit in a limited company?
3 Explain how profits act as a signal in allocating resources in an economy.
4 Business X, a leisure company, is making very high profits. Business Y, a shipbuilder, is making a loss. Explain what is likely to happen in (a) the leisure industry and (b) the shipbuilding industry.
5 Why might high profits be an indicator of a business exploiting its customers?

unit 34
MARKETING

Making decisions

Businesses have to sell what they produce. So they have to make marketing decisions. These include:

- what product will be sold;
- what price it will be sold at;
- how the customer will get to know about the product;
- where the best place to sell the product to the customer will be.

In 1989, PepsiCo, the US drink and snack food manufacturer, bought Walkers and Smiths, two UK crisp manufacturers. Through careful marketing in the 1990s it has transformed Walkers. In 1997 it was a high growth, high profit brand of upmarket crisps.

Marketing

MARKETING is not just about selling. It involves:

- researching the market and finding out what customers want to buy (☞ units 35 and 36);
- developing and designing a **product** that satisfies customers' needs and wants (☞ units 37 and 38);
- producing the right amount and to the right quality specification (☞ unit 38);
- getting the **price** right so that the product is affordable to customers, but also allows the business to make a profit (☞ units 39 and 40);
- making sure that the customer knows about the product through **promotion** (☞ unit 41);
- ensuring that the product is on sale in **places** convenient for the customer to buy it (☞ units 42 and 43).

Sometimes, this list is known as the MARKETING MIX or 'the 4 Ps'. The 4 Ps are product, price, promotion and place.

The need for marketing

Each year, millions of new products are launched worldwide. Most are unsuccessful and they stop being produced after a while. Buying a business which owned well known brands, like Walkers crisps, meant that PepsiCo could avoid the risk of trying to launch a new product which then failed.

In 1989, though, Walkers was not

?
1 Why do you think these products need to be marketed?
2 (a) What is meant by 'the marketing mix'?
   (b) How do you think these products could be marketed? To answer this question, you need to comment on each of 'the 4 Ps'.

anywhere near as successful as it is today. It was a regional brand that was not sold everywhere in the UK. Walkers crisps only came in a narrow range of flavours and packets. Sales to retail outlets, such as local corner shops, were weak.

PepsiCo set about transforming the brand. Market research showed that customers wanted crisps that were crisper. So in 1992 it switched from plastic to foil bags, helping to keep air out of packets. In 1996, it started to pack crisps in nitrogen-filled bags. Other improvements in the product include continuing research into the best type of potato with which to make crisps.

PepsiCo also was careful about pricing the product. Between 1992 and 1995, for instance, it didn't raise its price. This is because the economy was only slowing coming out of recession (☞ unit 6) and customers were being very careful about how they spent their money.

Spending on advertising and other types of promotion was increased. For instance, spending rose by one quarter between 1992 and 1995 when the price of a packet of crisps stayed the same.

Finally, PepsiCo turned Walkers into a national brand. It increased its sales force to make sure that Walkers crisps were being sold in corner shops as well as supermarkets.

Businesses need to market their products because there is so much choice in the market. There are so many different ways in which customers can spend their money. A business would like to be in a **sellers' market** where customers have little choice but to buy from them. In a **buyers' market**, though, businesses have to compete against other businesses for sales. The greater the competition, the more businesses have to be **market orientated** (☞ unit 36) and the greater is the need for effective marketing.

Source: adapted from the *Financial Times*, 5 February 1996 and updated to 1998.

key terms

Marketing - the management process which is responsible for identifying potentially profitable products and then selling them to customers.

The marketing mix - the combination of factors which help the business sell a product - usually summarised as the 4 Ps, which are price, product, promotion and place.

Checklist ✓

1 List FOUR different aspects of marketing a product.
2 What are the 4 Ps?
3 Why do businesses have to market their products?
4 What is the difference between a buyers' market and a sellers' market?

Summary Case Study

HOLLYWOOD MARKETING

For every $3 that it costs to make a film, a Hollywood studio expects to have to spend $2 promoting its release. Films have short lives. Most of the revenue to cover these costs will be earned in the first six months of release. Box office receipts are important. But royalties on product licences can be even more important for big blockbuster films. For instance, Disney received $135 million from other businesses on its 1996 version of 101 Dalmations. McDonald's alone paid $35 million for the right to advertise the film on television with its name attached. It then promoted the film in its restaurants. Dreamworks, makers of Jurassic Park, spent two years signing up licensees before the sequel, The Lost World, was launched. 800 businesses paid royalties to sell food, T shirts, toys and burgers associated with the film.

Source: adapted from the *Financial Times*, 4 February 1997.

1 Why does a film like 101 Dalmations or Jurassic Park need marketing?
2 McDonald's is one business which regularly promotes films.
  (a) How does it use films as part of its marketing?
  (b) Why is McDonald's prepared to pay film studios for the right to use films in promoting its food?
3 A toy manufacturer has won the right to sell toys featuring Batman. Discuss, using 'the 4 Ps', how it might market its range of products.

Making decisions

Businesses have to decide what to make and sell. This involves finding out who are the likely customers of the business. For instance, are they old or young, rich or poor, or Northerners or Southerners? Businesses with this sort of information are far more likely to be successful than ones who have little knowledge of their market.

The Simpsons - Sky 1

MATT GROENING

Dream Team - commissioned by Sky 1 as part of its commitment to home produced entertainment.

Sky Television is the UK's only satellite broadcasting service. In March 1998, it had 4.1 million subscribers. In addition, 2.5 million cable television viewers also subscribed to Sky channels. Sky earns revenues partly by charging viewers but also by selling advertising time to businesses. It is essential for the success of both of these that Sky analyses its viewing market.

Market segments

Sky knows that different viewers want to watch different programmes. Young males aged 18-25 might want to watch sport.

1 (a) Make a list of as many magazines and comics as you can think of which are bought by or for children and teenagers. (b) By the side of each magazine or comic, write down the market segment which it targets.
2 A publishing company wants to launch a profitable new children's or teenage magazine. Which segment of the market would you suggest and why?

Children might want to watch cartoons. Females aged 40-50 might want to watch a movie. Sky therefore tries to cater for different MARKET SEGMENTS. A market segment is a part of a market which contains a group of buyers with similar characteristics.

For instance, Sky Sports 1 is watched mainly by males. Between March 1997 and March 1998, 71 per cent of the viewers were males. Of these males, 39 per cent were aged 16-34 and 38 per cent were aged 35-54. So Sky Sports 1 appeals mainly to the male segment of the market.

Some businesses make products which they hope will appeal to the whole market. Birds Eye Wall's, for instance, hopes that everyone, whether young or old, male or female, rich or poor, will want to buy a Cornetto ice cream. Many products, though, are aimed at a segment of a market, like the Sky Nickelodeon channel aimed at children.

Knowing who are its possible customers helps Sky to decide the programming for existing channels. It also helps it to market its channels. For instance, Sky is unlikely to advertise its Sky Sports 1 in a magazine read mainly by women aged over 60. Instead, it may target magazines like *FHM* which are read by younger males.

Age, gender, income, area, ethnic group and occupation

Markets can be segmented according to the characteristics of buyers.

Age Sky offers channels which will appeal to people of certain ages. Children might watch Nickelodeon or TCC. Older people may watch Sky news, a 24 hour news channel. MTV is a music channel aimed at younger people whilst VH1 targets adult music fans.

Gender Males are three times as likely to watch Sky Sports 1 as females. On the other hand, females are more likely to watch Sky 1, a channel which broadcasts

Table 35.1 *Socio-economic groups.*

Social grade	Social status	Head of household's occupation	% of total UK population (approx.)
A	Upper middle class	Higher managerial, administrative or professional such as doctors, lawyers and company directors	3.5%
B	Middle	Intermediate managerial, administrative or professional such as teachers, nurses and managers	12-13%
C_1	Lower middle class	Supervisory or clerical and junior managerial, administrative or professional such as shop assistants, clerks and police constables	22%
C_2	Skilled working class	Skilled manual workers such as carpenters, cooks and train drivers	32-33%
D	Working class	Semi-skilled and unskilled manual workers such as fitters and store keepers	19-20%
E	The poorest in society	State pensioners or widows, casual or lower grade workers, or long term unemployed	10%

Sky Scottish is aimed at viewers in Scotland.

first showings of popular series like Friends, ER and The X Files. It shows a range of programmes including comedy, drama and documentaries.

Income Cable and satellite homes have above-average income. They are 23 per cent more likely to be in full-time employment. These statistics are important when Sky wants to sell advertising opportunities to companies like Ford or Kelloggs. The higher the income of the viewers, the more companies are usually prepared to pay for advertising slots.

Area Shoppers in the North East of England might have different tastes from those in the London area. People In Yorkshire and Humberside eat more fish than those in any other region in the country, for example. Businesses need to be aware of these differences when deciding what to sell and how to sell. For instance, Sky runs Sky Scottish, a channel with Scottish sports and entertainment aimed at Scottish viewers.

Ethnic, cultural and religious groups In 1997 Sky did not offer a channel aimed at religious groups. However .[tv] is aimed at people with an interest in computers and CMT is for those who enjoy country music. The introduction of

Supermarket loyalty cards

In February 1995, Tesco launched Clubcard, a loyalty card for shoppers at Tesco. For every £1 that customers spend, they get 1p back on the card. The cards were highly successful and soon all the large supermarket chains had launched cards.

Their main purpose was to encourage customers to shop only with one supermarket and to spend more money. However, they can serve another purpose. The supermarkets can now get information about the spending habits of every individual loyalty card shopper if they want. If you buy two bottles of wine every week, or three frozen pizzas, then the supermarket will know because your itemised bill is recorded on its computer system along with the information of your loyalty card. It can know where you shopped and when and whether you paid by card or cash.

The supermarkets are faced with information overload at the moment.

How do they make best use of all this information which is available to them? Tesco, for instance, has experimented with identifying different types of shopper. Big spending customers in some stores who regularly shop for wine have been invited to wine and cheese evenings. It has also sent mailshots targeting vegetarians, diabetics, students, pensioners and others identified from the Clubcard data. In future, supermarkets may pinpoint customers who are irregular shoppers with them. They might be targeted with money-off vouchers to bring them more regularly into the store. Or they may target pensioner customers who are shopping at times of the week when the store is very crowded. They may be offered a reduction on their shopping bill if they shop at times when the store is less crowded.

Source: adapted from the *Financial Times*, 18 May 1995.

1 What is a supermarket loyalty card?

2 How can supermarkets know whether or not you bought a packet of cornflakes this week if you have a loyalty card?

3 Loyalty cards can be used to provide information about different segments of the market. For instance, it can provide information about the average age of shoppers at a particular supermarket, or what proportion of shoppers at a supermarket is aged over 60.
(a) Give FOUR other examples of information which loyalty cards can give.
(b) For each example, explain how a supermarket could target these shoppers to persuade them to spend more money in the store.

4 Some supermarkets are very crowded at certain times of the week. A supermarket offers to give extra points on the loyalty card to shoppers who always shop in off peak hours. They identify shoppers who sometimes shop at peak times and sometimes at off peak times and send them a leaflet explaining the offer. What would be: (a) the advantages; and (b) the disadvantages to the supermarket of doing this?

digital television in the future may mean that more niche channels become available. In the UK it is possible to receive channels broadcast in German and Spanish.

There are radio and television programmes aimed at religious groups, such as the Sunday programme on Radio 4. NWK, a radio station aimed at African-Caribbean groups operated till 1994.

Different groups can give opportunities for businesses to sell products and services. Equally, businesses need to be careful when selling products. For example, an orthodox Jew would not buy pork and Hindus would not buy beef.

Socio-economic groupings

One of the most important ways of dividing up the market is to split consumers into SOCIO-ECONOMIC GROUPS. This divides people up according to their occupation (i.e. job) or the occupation of the head of the household (such as the mother or father in a family).

Table 35.1 shows that households are split into five categories from A to E. The C category is divided into C1, lower middle class, and C2, skilled manual workers. So, for instance, Sky knows from its subscription information that 47 per cent of those in socio-economic groups A, B and C1 subscribe to Sky Sports 1. Further down the socio-economic scale, this falls to 23 per cent of C2s, but rises to 30 per cent of groups D and E (BARB/RSMB estimates).

Other ways of segmenting the market

Businesses can analyse their markets in a large number of different ways other than just by type of consumer. One way is whether customers are repeat customers or one-time customers. Repeat customers are those who keep on buying the product. They have brand loyalty. A one-time

customer is a customer who buys the product once but is unlikely to do so again. For instance, for Sky, a repeat customer might be somebody who has paid to receive every pay-per-view sporting event offered over the past two years. A one-time customer might be somebody who has only subscribed to one pay-per-view event during this period.

Another way of analysing the market is to find out whether customers buy the product on impulse or whether the purchase was planned. For instance, Sky publishes a magazine which lists satellite programmes for the next month. One customer may make a planned purchase

every month. Another customer may be attracted by the front cover one month and make an on-the-spot decision to buy it.

Source: adapted from information provided by British Sky Broadcasting Ltd.

Telephone banking

Telephone banking is part of the future of banking. Fewer and fewer people will want to go into the branch of a bank on a high street because they will deal with their banking needs over the phone. Already, two million bank transactions are made per year by telephone, with the number expected to grow to nearly 10 million by the year 2000.

The current typical telephone banking customer is male, owns his own home, and is aged between 24 and 54. He earns at least £20 000 a year. If telephone banking is to grow, it must attract new customers with different customer profiles. The Co-operative Bank, the current market leader with about 750 000 customers, is confident that 'telephone banking is the face of the future, and it is here to stay'. With branches on the high street more expensive to run per customer than large regional call centres dealing with telephone customers, the banks have every incentive to make sure this comes about.

Source: adapted from *The Times*, 10 February 1996.

1 What is 'telephone banking'?
2 Who is the typical customer of telephone banking services?
3 Suggest why the typical customer of telephone banking services is NOT: (a) aged over 70; (b) earning less than £6 000 a year; (c) renting a house; (d) a female.

Wordprocessing

4 You work for the Co-operative Bank. You have been asked to draw up a short report on telephone banking and female customers. In your report:
(a) explain why it is important for the bank to get more female customers using telephone banking services;
(b) discuss TWO suggestions about how more females could be attracted into using the service.

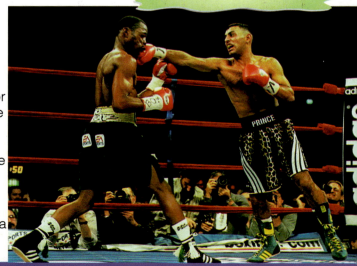

Naseem Hamed vs Kevin Kelly - a pay per view event on Sky Box Office.

EITHER answer questions 1 and 2 for your mini-company OR answer all the questions based on the Dry Flower Company.

The Dry Flower Company

Your business idea has been to make dried flower arrangements. One member of the company has a parent who is a well known local expert on dried flower arrangements. She has shown you how to make them and has promised help if you run into any problems. She has also talked to you about where to get all the dried flowers from and the baskets needed to make the arrangements.

It is the Autumn term. You have decided to sell your product, ...d at £4.99, in two ways. Firstly, you have run off leaflets advertising the dried flower arrangements. ...have asked your teachers/lecturers to give one leaflet to each student in their tutor group to take home ...eir parents. Secondly, there is an important Christmas Bazaar in November which is very popular with ...nts. You have been allowed to have a stall at the bazaar.

...hat is the product that you are selling?

...ho are your customers likely to be? For instance, are they likely to be men or women, older people or ...ounger people, people with a high income or people with a low income?

...hich method do you think is most likely to result in sales from your targeted customers - the ...aflet or the Christmas Bazaar? Explain your answer.

...u have decided that you want a second product to sell alongside your existing product.

..) How could you adapt your existing product to make it appeal to a different segment of the market?

..) Explain why it might appeal to a different market segment.

key terms

Market segment - part of a market which contains a group of buyers with similar characteristics, such as age or income.

Socio-economic groupings - division of people from A to E according to the occupation (job) of the head of the household in which they live.

Checklist ✔

1 Why is it important for a business to know at which segment of the market to aim its products?
2 Explain what type of person by (i) age, (ii) gender and (iii) income you think is likely to buy: (a) clothes from Tammy Girl; (b) a pair of ladies shoes from Marks & Spencer; (c) a pint of beer in a pub; (d) a copy of the *Financial Times*; (e) a £5.99 spaceman Lego set; (f) a Porsche car; (g) a month's holiday in Spain in February.
3 What is the difference between an A and a C_1 in terms of socio-economic grouping?
4 Socio-economic group E is not usually a sales target for businesses. Why not?
5 A person in socio-economic group B might go touring in France in the summer. A person in socio-economic group C or D might go to Benidorm on a package tour. Why do you think there is a difference in the holiday destinations of the two groups?
6 What is the difference between a repeat customer and a one-time customer?
7 What is an impulse purchase?

SUMMARY CASE STUDY

SPORTS EQUIPMENT

A manufacturer of sports equipment is studying its market.
1 What is meant by 'socio-economic groupings'?
2 It wants to target advertising for its range of: (i) darts equipment; (ii) soccer equipment; and (iii) golf equipment. How might the information about socio-economic groupings in Table 35.2 help?
3 The manufacturer is launching two new ranges: a swimwear range and a keep fit/yoga range. (a) Who are likely to be its customers? (b) How would it market the range of products to target these customers? Base your answer around the '4 Ps' of marketing.

Table 35.2 *Participation in sports and games.*

Percentage in each group participating in each activity in the 4 weeks before interview

	Professional	Employers and managers	Intermediate & junior non-manual	Skilled manual & own account non-professional	Semi-skilled manual and personal service	Unskilled manual
Snooker, pool & billiards	11	12	8	17	10	9
Darts	6	5	4	8	6	6
Swimming	27	19	18	10	11	6
Keep fit, yoga	13	12	18	6	9	8
Soccer	6	3	3	6	3	3
Golf	9	10	5	6	2	2

Source: adapted from ONS, *Social Trends*.

MARKET RESEARCH

Making decisions

Businesses need information if they are to make good decisions. One way of gaining that information is by carrying out market research. There are various types of market research. Businesses need to decide what market research methods are most likely to give them the information they need.

Cadbury Limited is the UK's chocolate manufacturing arm of Cadbury Schweppes, the large multinational food and drinks company. In 1996, it had a 30 per cent market share of the £3.4 billion chocolate market in the UK. It regularly launches new products. Each launch is carefully researched to reduce the risk of failure. In September 1996 it launched a new chocolate bar, Fuse, with enormous success.

Product and market orientation

Many businesses are PRODUCT ORIENTATED. This means that they design and make a product, and then try to convince consumers to buy it. An example might be a drug company, like Glaxo, developing a product to help consumers with an illness and then advertising it.

Businesses can also be MARKET ORIENTATED. This is where they try to find out what consumers want **before** making the final product. In 1996, Cadbury launched Fuse, a new chocolate bar. Before the launch, Cadbury tried to find out the type of product consumers wanted. Finding out about what consumers want and need, and what makes them buy, is called MARKET RESEARCH.

Why research the market?

Businesses which are mainly product orientated risk spending a large amount of resources launching a product which proves to be a failure. Researching the market helps reduce this risk. It should focus research and design effort onto products which have a chance of success in the market place. When the product is launched, a carefully researched product stands less change of failing.

Stages of market research

Market research attempts to find the answers to questions a business might have about its market. For example, the development of Fuse began with the question of how Cadbury could expand both the market for chocolate confectionery and its own share of the snacking sector of the market.

The market researcher must then decide what information might help answer this question. Cadbury

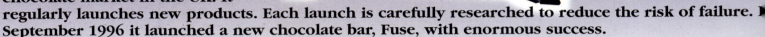

An electronics company is considering entering the white goods sector of the market (i.e. it is considering manufacturing goods such as deep-freezers, washing machines and dishwashers).

1 Table 36.1 shows that 96 per cent of skilled manual workers owned a washing machine in 1995. Give THREE other facts which the table shows.

2 The design of the product and its advertising have been aimed at professional people and employers and managers. Do you think this is a good strategy? Give arguments for and against, using evidence from the table.

3 One manager has suggested that the company should target unskilled manual workers and households where the head of the household is unemployed.
(a) Why do you think this might have been suggested?
(b) Explain whether you think this would be a good idea or not.

Table 36.1 *Households with durable goods: by socio-economic group of head, 1995.*

Great Britain | | | | | | Percentages

	Economically active					Economically inactive heads of households
	Professional	Employers and managers	Other non-manual	Skilled manual	Unskilled manual	
households with:						
Deep/fridge freezer	96	95	92	94	86	83
Washing machine	98	98	94	96	88	83
Tumble drier	65	71	57	61	44	37
Microwave oven	84	83	75	82	65	55
Dishwasher	45	45	27	19	5	9

Source: adapted from General Household Survey.

wanted information about the existing pattern of sales in the market and how the market was changing. It needed to identify a **segment** of the market (☞ unit 35) which it could sell to. Cadbury also wanted consumers to tell it about the sort of new product they wanted to buy. The market researcher then decides how best to collect this information.

The information is then collected and analysed. Finally, the business has to make a decision about what to do in the light of the information gained. Cadbury decided to launch a new product nationally.

Desk research

DESK RESEARCH involves the use of SECONDARY DATA. This is information which is already available, both within and outside the business.

Information within the business

Businesses collect information routinely. Invoices, for instance, will tell them how much they sell and who they are selling to. Cadbury knew the sales figures for its snacks, including chocolate bars. It could see the trends in sales which pointed to the increasing demand for 'foody' type snacks which might replace a meal.

Information from outside the business

Businesses can also collect information which is available from sources outside the business. Figure 36.1 shows some of these

○ **Internal sources** - such as sales invoices, reports, accounts.

○ **Government** - published statistics, such as consumer spending figures; reports such as Monopolies and Mergers Commission Reports

○ **The media** - reports in newspapers, magazines, on radio and on television.

○ **Trade associations** - statistics or reports published by national organisations such as the TUC, the CBI or chambers of commerce, or industry associations such as the Engineering Employers Federation or the National Farmers Union.

○ **Research organisations** - reports prepared by specialist market research organisations such as Mintel or Mori; articles published in academic journals such as university journals.

Figure 36.1 *Sources of secondary data.*

sources. Cadbury made use of market research reports which discussed trends in the snack market and which gave figures for sales of products from rival companies like Mars and Nestlé. Table 36.2 over the page, for instance, shows the 20 top selling brands of chocolate one month before the launch of Fuse.

Field research

FIELD RESEARCH involves the collection of PRIMARY DATA - information which no one has yet collected. It is collected specially for the particular piece of research. Primary data is collected through direct investigation, usually through observation, survey or experiment.

Observation

Looking at and recording what people do and **how** they behave can be important. For instance, a supermarket may find that sales in one aisle in the store are very poor. By observing people, it would be possible to see whether the problem was that shoppers were avoiding the aisle. However, observation can't tell the supermarket anything about **why** shoppers are behaving in this way.

Surveys

A SURVEY usually involves asking

In 1993, the advertising agency Ogilvy and Mather conducted a survey about women. It got twelve groups of women to keep a diary for a week.

In their diary, the women had to note down the adverts they had watched and their reactions to them. Then in groups they discussed how they saw themselves, their lives and what was important to them. They also discussed their views on brands and advertising.

The survey found that women were like onions, made up of a number of layers. In the centre is 'me within'. As the woman passes from young single working woman to mother and housewife and back to older working woman, the 'me' stays the same.

Some of the 'me' aspects of women include:
- the free woman - independent, happy, in control;
- the woman on top - being the boss, even when it is not expected;
- the pampered woman - romantic, indulging, relaxed;
- the wild woman - outrageous, rebellious and sexy.

Successful adverts aimed at women had to appeal to the 'me'. Adverts which patronised women, like so many washing powder adverts, irritated the women in the survey.

Source: adapted from the *Financial Times*, 3 February 1994.

1 (a) What is field research and (b) why was this survey an example of field research?

2 Conduct your own desk research. Find and describe FOUR advertisements which you think might appeal to: (a) the free woman; (b) the woman on top; (c) the pampered woman; (d) the wild woman.

DTP

3 Design TWO advertisements (if possible, using a DTP package), (i) as a drawing for a magazine advert, (ii) as a story line for a TV commercial. You can choose to advertise any product you want. The adverts should be targeted at women. (a) The first should be an advert which you think would be successful, appealing to the 'me' in women. (b) The second should be an advert which you think would be a failure, putting women off buying the product. (c) Explain briefly why you think your adverts would have these effects. (d) How might you find out whether your first advert would be successful in appealing to women?

questions of RESPONDENTS - people or organisations who reply to the questions asked. Cadbury, for instance, used a survey to find out about the snacking habits and preferences of consumers. The survey showed that snack foods often were used as meal substitutes. Compared to traditional confectionery products, like a pure chocolate bar, snacks were seen to have 'foody' ingredients such as cereal, wafer, biscuits, peanuts and fruit.

There are different ways of conducting surveys. A **postal survey**, where QUESTIONNAIRES are sent through the post, or **newspaper surveys**, where readers are invited to fill in and return a questionnaire in a newspaper, are cheap. **Telephone surveys**, **personal interviews**, and **consumers' panels** are more expensive because an interviewer has to be employed to interview customers. However, only a fraction of customers sent a postal survey will respond. A much larger proportion of those approached will take part in telephone and personal interviews. The interviewer can also help the respondents understand what questions mean and how they should be answered.

If the interview is in a person's home, products, packaging, etc. can also be shown so that reactions can be recorded. A consumer panel, where a group of people meet together, allows researchers to see how people react in a group situation to a product or idea. In the case of Fuse, Cadbury put the product through two extensive 'in home placement' tests. This is where consumers are asked to use the product in their homes over a period of time. Their actions and opinions are monitored and recorded. Cadbury then used the results of these tests to calculate the likely **repeat purchase** (whether consumers would buy another Fuse after they had tried it out once) and **purchase frequency** (how often consumers would buy a Fuse bar) figures for Fuse.

Surveys can only be useful for market research purposes if the questions asked are appropriate. For instance, sometimes it is important to ask **closed questions**. These are questions which have a definite answer. An example would be: 'How many chocolate bars did you buy last week?'. Other times, the market researcher might want to find out about opinions and allow the

respondent to develop an answer. It is best then to ask **open questions**, which have many possible answers. For instance, 'Why do you like the packaging of Fuse?' is an open question.

Sampling

A survey cannot ask every customer for their opinion. Only a fraction or SAMPLE of customers can be surveyed. To be useful, the sample chosen must be representative of all consumers (the **population**).

In a **random sample**, every potential respondent has an equal chance of being chosen. Random numbers can be used to do this or it can be done by 'picking people out of a hat'. It is often quite difficult to construct a truly random sample. So a cheaper and quicker method is to use a **systematic sample**. This is where, say, every 100th or 1 000th person on a list like a telephone directory or the electoral register is chosen. A systematic sample is not truly random though and therefore the results may be less reliable.

In a **quota sample**, the sample is broken down (or stratified).

Cadbury wanted to target 16-24 year olds in particular and 16-34 year olds more generally with its Fuse bar. It might know that 2 out of ten people who bought chocolate bars were aged 0-15, 7 out of ten were aged 16-34 and the rest were over 34 years old. So out of a sample of 100, Cadbury would ask 70 people (7 out of 10) aged 16-34 to complete a survey.

One problem with a quota sample is that any people who fit the description can be asked to complete the survey. So Cadbury wanting to find seventy people aged 16-34 to complete a survey, could ask the first seventy 16-34 year olds who came out of a McDonald's in London. This may not be very representative of all 16-34 year olds nationally.

A **stratified random sample** may get round this problem. It is a quota sample where all the

Table 36.2 *Top selling chocolate brands before the launch of Fuse.*

1. Cadbury's Dairy Milk Megabrand	11. Cadbury's Wispa
2. Kit Kat	12. Cadbury's Time out
3. Mars	13. Smarties
4. Galaxy	14. Cadbury's Crunchie
5. Cadbury's Roses	15. Cadbury's Milk Tray
6. Snickers	16. Cadbury's Creme Egg
7. Quality Street	17. Bounty
8. Twix	18. Milky Way
9. Maltesers	19. Cadbury's Caramel
10. Aero	20. Yorkie

Source: adapted from *General Household Survey.*

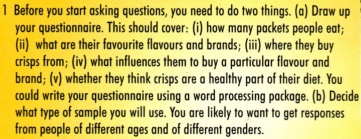

 Database and wordprocessing

Conduct a survey about crisps.

1 Before you start asking questions, you need to do two things. (a) Draw up your questionnaire. This should cover: (i) how many packets people eat; (ii) what are their favourite flavours and brands; (iii) where they buy crisps from; (iv) what influences them to buy a particular flavour and brand; (v) whether they think crisps are a healthy part of their diet. You could write your questionnaire using a word processing package. (b) Decide what type of sample you will use. You are likely to want to get responses from people of different ages and of different genders.

2 Conduct your survey.

3 You now need to analyse your findings. You could enter your results on a computer database and the program would then do much of the work for you.

4 Write a short report. You could use a wordprocessing package for this. (a) The report should outline briefly the questionnaire and the sample you chose to use. Were there any problems you found with the survey? (b) Briefly present the main findings of the survey. (c) A small but growing chain of supermarkets is thinking of launching own brand crisps. What does your survey suggest is important if sales are to be high?

respondents, the people being interviewed, must be chosen at random. For the sample to be random, Cadbury would have to find some way of selecting 70 people aged 16-34 through pure chance.

Experiments

Market researchers can use experimental techniques. To launch a new product is often very costly. Fuse, for instance, cost £10 million to develop and the launch advertising campaign was £4 million. Manufacturers like Cadbury therefore test products as they are being developed to check that they are likely to succeed. More than 250 different ingredients were tried and tested before the recipe for Fuse was finalised. The product was tested in the 'home placement' tests described earlier. New chocolate bars are also usually **test marketed** in an area before being launched nationally.

However, Cadbury decided that the results of the rest of its market research were so positive that it would go for a national launch immediately. This increased the risk if the product were to be a failure. On the other hand, it would gain from having higher sales immediately rather than wait and launch the product nationally at a later date.

Decisions

The purpose of market research is to help a business come to a decision. Cadbury thought that there was the potential to launch a new chocolate confectionery product. It found out what consumers wanted from any new product. It then created the product. Consumer trials showed that the new product would be a success. Finally, Cadbury took the risk of launching the product nationally in September 1996. All the careful market research paid

off because Fuse was a bigger success than Cadbury had predicted.

Source: adapted from *Launching a New Product into a Developed Market*, Cadbury Schweppes.

Key terms

Desk research - finding out information from secondary data.
Field research - the process of collecting primary data.
Market orientated business - a business which develops products which have been researched and designed to meet the needs of cunsumers.
Market research -the process of gaining information about customers, competitors and market trends through collecting primary and secondary data.
Primary data - information which has been gathered for a specific purpose through direct investigation such as observation, surveys and through experiment.
Product orientated business - a business which develops products with little or no market research and which it hopes will prove successful in the market.
Questionnaire - a list of questions to be answered by respondents, designed to give information about consumers' tastes.
Respondent - person or organisation answering questions in a survey.
Sample - small group out of a total population which is selected to take part in a survey.
Secondary data - information which already exists, such as accounts and sales records, government statistics, newspaper articles or reports from advertising agencies.
Survey - research involving asking questions of people or organisations.

MARKETING WAKE-UP

Graham West founded his company, Belgrade Insulations, 20 years ago. It is a manufacturer of plastics and vacuum-formed products. Until the early 1990s, it was highly dependent on the building industry for orders. For instance, one of its products was plastic lids for cold water tanks. No less than 60 per cent of its sales in the early 1990s went to one customer.

The recession of the early 1990s hit the building industry and Belgrade Insulations badly. The company needed to find new markets. It was then that the company took part in the Investors in People scheme. An outside marketing consultant helped the company identify its strengths and weaknesses and what it could offer that was better than its competitors. The answer was 'actually very little'. One outcome was that the car components industry was targeted. A telephone survey was conducted about what products car component manufacturers might be interested in buying. Every sales enquiry was followed up, however small. The company began to produce prototypes from customers' requests. Many orders produced little or no profit. But there was a steep learning curve with the company eventually being able to produce a prototype in a week or less compared to the month or two it had taken previously.

In 1996, the company hired a full time marketing executive to hunt out growth industries where the company's skills, including its sharper research and development capabilities, could be used.

In addition to car components, Belgrade Insulations is now selling to the leisure industry, to heating and ventilation companies and to the general engineering sector. It has recently focused on waste disposal as another growth area.

Source: adapted from the *Financial Times*, 3 June 1997 and information provided by Belgrade Insulations Limited.

1 What does Belgrade Insulations make?
2 Why did it need to research its markets in the early 1990s?
3 (a) What is a 'telephone survey'? (b) What did Belgrade Insulations find out from its telephone survey? (c) How did it follow up the telephone survey?
4 Suggest THREE ways using either desk or field research that Belgrade Insulations could find out about other 'growth areas' for its products.

Checklist ✓

1 Explain the difference between a market orientated and product orientated business.
2 What is the purpose of market research?
3 List the stages of market research.
4 What sources of information are available to someone undertaking desk research?
5 Distinguish between field research and desk research.
6 A shopping centre wants to find out how many shoppers visit the centre. How could it gather this information?
7 What differences are there between a postal survey and personal interviews in surveys?
8 A business wants to take a random sample of people in the London area. How could it do this?
9 A chocolate manufacturer wants to find out if a new bar of chocolate is going to sell well in the UK. How could it find this out without having to go to the expense of launching the product nationally?

Making decisions

Businesses have to decide what product or range of products they are going to sell. They also have to decide what quality of product they wish to make and sell, what name to give to the product and how it is to be packaged. A further decision is whether to attempt to brand the product.

Nestlé is one of the world's largest food manufacturing companies. In 1996, its sales were over £25 billion. It employed over 221 000 workers worldwide and operated 489 factories.

The product range

Nestlé sells a RANGE of coffee. In 1938 it invented Nescafé, still the world's best-selling brand of coffee. This range is part of the company's total PRODUCT MIX. Nestlé is the world's largest producer of mineral waters like Perrier. It also sells more chocolate drinks than any other world manufacturer. Other important parts of Nestlé's product mix are milk products and ice cream, chocolate and confectionery, cooking products and pharmaceuticals.

Nestlé produces a range of coffees because different consumers want different products. Nestlé can then sell more and make more profit by satisfying consumers' wants (☞ unit 1).

Product differentiation

Producing a range of coffees allows Nestlé to DIFFERENTIATE its products. Each coffee is different. For instance, Nescafé is the leading brand and is bought by a wide range of people. However, Gold Blend is aimed at consumers who want a coffee which is more mellow. Alta Rica and Cap Colombie are more upmarket, expensive instant coffees aimed at consumers who want a coffee which tastes more like fresh coffee. Decaffeinated Nescafé is bought by consumers who want to drink less caffeine, the stimulant in coffee. Nespresso is an upmarket espresso coffee and Caffèpresso is designed for offices so that workers can prepare individual cups of coffee.

Ways of differentiating the product

There is a number of important ways in which businesses make their products different from each other.

Design and formulation Every coffee produced by Nescafé is differently formulated. It uses different mixes of beans and the roasting process is different. Nescafé 1&2, sold in Japan, is different from other coffees as it combines coffee, milk and sugar. Similarly, car manufacturers produce a range of cars. Each car model may have hundreds of different

1 How are these four products differentiated from each other?
2 What consumer needs and wants does each product satisfy?
3 There has been a suggestion that burger chains, like McDonald's or Burger King, should sell ethnic food, such as Chinese spring rolls or Indian curries. Explain whether you think these would be as popular and as profitable as the food in their current product mix.

Vegeburger £1.74
Big Mac £1.84
Cheeseburger £0.69
Burger £0.59

Beverages
Soluble and instant coffee: eg Nescafé,
Mineral and spring water: eg Perrier
Chocolate-based and malted drinks: eg Nesquik/Nestlé
Quik
Roasted coffee: eg Nespresso
Fruit juices: eg Libby's
Tea-based drinks:
eg Nestea

Milk products, dietetics and ice cream
Condensed, evaporated and powdered milk: eg
Carnation
Foods for young children: eg Petits Pots
Chilled dairy products: eg Nestlé fruit yogurts
Adult nutrition: eg Nestlé Slender
Ice cream: eg Maxibon

Prepared dishes and cooking aids
Frozen products: eg Findus
Canned products: eg Buitoni
Pasta: eg Buitoni
Oriental noodles: eg Maggi
Cold sauces: eg Thomy
Cat and dog food: eg Friskies

Product range

Chocolate and confectionery
Chocolate: eg Kit Kat
Sugar confectionery:
eg Fruit Pastilles
Biscuits: eg São Luiz

Pharmaceutical products
Alcon Laboratories is divided into three
sections
Ophthalmic therapeutic drugs:
eg Betopic
Contact lens care: eg Opti-clean,
*Instruments for ocular surgery and
preparations for dental surgery:*
eg Legacy

Figure 37.1 *The Nestlé product mix.*

Sellotape

Before the mid-1990s, Sellotape Ltd had a problem. In the UK, Sellotape is not just a brand name for a single sided, sticky, clear tape produced by Sellotape Ltd. It is the name consumers tend to give to any clear, sticky tape produced by any company. For your brand name to become the name of the product in general should be a company's dream. But in this case, too many consumers were buying 'Sellotape' which was not made by Sellotape Ltd. What's more, Sellotape Ltd was finding it difficult to get consumers to buy other products made by the company and sold under the Sellotape name. Consumers tended to think that anything with Sellotape on the packet would contain sticky, clear tape.

To get around these problems, the company has adopted a number of strategies. It has changed the company name from Sellotape Ltd to The Sellotape Company. This aims to show that it makes more than just clear, sticky tape. Different colour packaging is to be used for non-Sellotape products, with much bolder lettering to emphasise the product. The 'Sellotape' company logo on packaging is to be given less emphasis except on Sellotape packets. This was done on 'Elephant Tape', a grey cloth tape aimed at the DIY market. It was the company's fastest selling new product in 1995. Sellotape Company products sold in the DIY market will have a completely different design of packaging from office stationery products. A range of sub-branded products for children called 'Stick It!' has also been introduced.

Source: adapted from the *Financial Times*, 23 November 1995.

1 Why did Sellotape Ltd have a problem differentiating its products?
2 How might: (a) repackaging; (b) renaming; and (c) new designs help to differentiate Sellotape's products?
3 Discuss whether: (a) total sales and (b) total profits would increase if the company name of 'Sellotape' were removed from all products other than Sellotape.

---

feature combinations, from the colour of the car to the engine size to whether or not it has a fitted sunroof. McDonald's sells a variety of foods, from Big Macs to Chicken Nuggets to coffee. More expensive **up-market** products are likely to be better quality than a better selling but cheaper **mass market** product.

Name Different products have different names. The name of the product is very important if it is to sell. Calling a coffee 'Yukcoff' or 'Cafe stink' is likely to be a disaster in sales terms. New products generally have short names which are easy to pronounce and to remember. They should say something positive about the product. 'Gold Blend', for instance, links something valuable (gold) with a soft word (blend) which implies smoothness and mellowness. Polo, the mint sweet, also produced by Nestlé, has two 'o's in the name linking it with the hole in the product.

However, the name is only a small part of the marketing mix of the product. No marketing company would have advised a UK baked bean manufacturer to brand its product 'Heinz', and yet Heinz

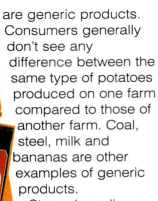

Baked beans: brands vs own brands

Your task is to compare branded baked beans with own brands and write a report. Your aim is to find out whether branded products are worth the higher price usually charged for them. You may find it easier to do this working as part of a group.

In school
1 Make a list of the different brands of baked beans; then list the own brands you know.
2 Which do you think is the leading brand in the UK and why?
3 Decide which shops you will survey to find out about the prices of cans of baked beans. You should survey at least one supermarket and one local small shop. The more shops and supermarkets you can survey the better.
4 You need to buy different brands of baked beans for a tasting session. Decide who in your group is going to buy which brand.

In the shops
1 Note down the prices of the brands and own brands on your list. There will be different sizes of cans. You need to note down the weights and prices.
2 If there are any brands which you do not have on your list, record those too.
3 Buy the brands or own brands which you have agreed to use in the tasting.

Back in school
1 Organise a blind tasting with the rest of your group. One person needs to prepare the food and put it into bowls each with a number. The tasters need to record what they liked and disliked about each variety. For instance: 'too sweet', 'too chewy', 'just the right colour'. Give an overall mark out of 5 (5 = top mark) for each variety.
2 At the end of the tasting, the cans can be put by their bowls. Did you pick out as your favourite variety the one you thought you would?
3 Now look at the packaging on the cans. Comment on how effective it is.
4 Compare the ingredients by looking at the labelling.
5 Were branded baked beans better than own brands? In your report, compare price with taste, packaging and ingredients.

Database/Spreadsheet/Graphics/DTP
The results of the survey and the blind tasting can be recorded and analysed on a database. Results may also be recorded on a spreadsheet and graphs and charts produced from the data with a graphics program. The final report can be produced with a DTP package.

baked beans is the most successful brand name for baked beans in the UK today.

Packaging Packaging is used to deliver products safely to the consumer. For instance, putting tin foil round a KitKat, another Nestlé product, keeps the bar fresher and prevents deterioration. Instant coffee tends to be sold in jars to prevent spillage and because glass is a strong material. Nescafé Espresso Roast is sold with a 'click lock closure' which makes the jar easy to open.

Packaging should also help businesses and consumers store the product. Bottles need flat bottoms for stability, for instance. Packaging gives information to the customer about the product. On Findus frozen products, another Nestlé brand, cooking times are given as well as how long the packet can safely be kept.

Packaging has other uses though. It is a way of **promoting** the product (☞ unit 41). Colours, designs and letters attract the customers' attention. Smarties packets, for instance, are brightly coloured because they are sold mainly to children.

Branding

Every business would like its products to be strong BRANDS. A brand is a product which in the eyes of customers is seen to be different from other, often similar products. For instance, consumers see Nescafé and Nescafé Gold Blend as two separate products even though they are both instant coffees.

The opposite of a branded product is a GENERIC PRODUCT. Potatoes are generic products. Consumers generally don't see any difference between the same type of potatoes produced on one farm compared to those of another farm. Coal, steel, milk and bananas are other examples of generic products.

Strong branding means that a business can charge a PREMIUM PRICE for the product. This is a price which is higher than the price charged for similar products in the market. For instance, in October 1997, a jar of Nescafé was £3.89 at Kwik Save. The same size packet of Kwik Save's 'No Frills' coffee was £1.29.

There are two reasons why customers are willing to pay premium prices for branded products. First, the quality of the product is usually higher. For instance, Nestlé would claim that Nescafé was a much better tasting coffee than Kwik Save's No Frills coffee. Second, brands tend to be advertised heavily. Advertising and other forms of promotion mean that customers are more aware than they would otherwise be of the claimed advantages of the product.

Own brands

Maintaining the brand through

Differentiating by packaging and ingredients. Nescafé Espresso Roast has a jar with a 'click lock' lid. Nescafé 1+2 is coffee, milk and sugar combined.

promotion and improvement in the product is essential if the brand is to survive. Today, many brands are faced with strong competition from OWN BRANDS. These are products which carry the brand labels of retailers such as Sainsbury's, Dixons or Woolworths. Nestlé faces competition from supermarket own brands of coffee, like those of Sainsbury's or Tesco's. Own brands are usually cheaper than the branded products from manufacturers.

The great danger for businesses like Nestlé is that customers might also see own brands as being of just as high quality as more expensive manufacturers' brands. If this happens, the customers could choose the own brands simply because they are cheaper.

Source: adapted in part from Nestlé, *Annual Report and Accounts*.

Key terms

Brand - a named product which customers see as being different from other products.

Generic product - a product made by a number of different businesses in which customers see no difference between the product of one business compared to the product of another business.

Own brand - a product which is sold under the brand name of a supermarket chain or other retailer rather than under the name of the business which manufactures the product.

Premium price - a price which is above the average for products of a particular type.

Product differentiation - making one product different from another, for instance through the quality of a product, its design, packaging or advertising.

Product mix - the combination of products that a business sells, like soap powders, cosmetics and medicines.

Range of products - a group of similar products made by a business, like a number of different soap powders.

Have you ever bought a Puffin biscuit from Asda? It is Asda's own brand of the much more famous branded Penguin biscuits. In 1997, United Biscuits, the makers of Penguin, won a court case against Asda which declared that the packaging of Puffin was too similar to that of Penguin. This could cause confusion amongst customers. Someone could pick up a Puffin when they thought they were picking up a Penguin. United Biscuits also wanted the court to ban Asda from using the Puffin name. But the court decided that Puffin did not violate the Penguin trade mark and so Asda could continue to use it. The Puffin case highlights the problems of lookalikes. Supermarket chains have increasingly been putting their own label products into packaging which looks like that of a well known brand. Names are often very similar.

Source: adapted from the *Financial Times*, 25 March 1997 and 19 May 1997.

1 What is the difference between a brand and an own brand?

2 Choose THREE supermarket own label products which you think look similar to a branded product. Describe the similarities.

3 Explain why: (a) supermarkets produce lookalike own label products; and (b) why manufacturers object to this.

Checklist ✓

1 Give THREE examples each of products in: (a) the Birds Eye Wall's ice cream range; (b) the Vauxhall car range; (c) the Cadbury's range of chocolate.

2 Why do businesses usually sell ranges of products rather than just one single product?

3 How do the following businesses differentiate their products: (a) a multi-screen cinema; (b) a record company; (c) a manufacturer of crisps?

4 Why do you think the following brand names help sell their product: (a) Cadbury's Flake; (b) Kellogg's Frosties; (c) Bold, manufactured by Procter & Gamble?

5 Why do manufacturers use packaging?

6 What is the difference between a branded product and a generic product?

7 'Brands are sold at premium prices.' Explain what this means.

8 Why do own brands compete successfully against branded products?

STRETCHING THE BRAND

Persil, the soap powder, became Persil the washing up liquid. Virgin, the record label, became Virgin the record store, Virgin the airline, Virgin the pension, Virgin the cola, Virgin the cinema and Virgin the railway company. Sainsbury's the supermarket became Sainsbury's the petrol retailer and Sainsbury's the bank. Why take a brand name for one product and spread it to other products? One reason is that it is so difficult to establish a new best-selling brand in the market. Of Britain's 50 top selling grocery brands, 4 were launched before 1900, 16 between 1900 and 1950, 21 between 1950 and 1975 and only 9 since then.

Spreading a name across a range of products is a dangerous strategy. Imagine having a best selling brand of quality chocolate and launching a cheap low quality ice cream with the brand name on it. Not only could the ice cream be a failure, but it could reduce sales of the chocolate. Equally, it can be a cheap way of expanding the product mix. Persil washing up liquid was a success because consumers instantly recognised the name and associated it with a quality washing product. They carried on buying it because it was a high quality product.

Source: adapted from *The Sunday Times*, 3 November 1996.

1 Describe Virgin's product mix.

2 In 1997, Heinz produced 15 varieties of baked beans. Why does it have such a large product range of baked beans?

3 What do you think were the advantages to Unilever, the manufacturer of Persil, of taking the Persil brand name and extending it to washing up liquid? Explain your answer referring to the effects on: (a) sales; (b) costs; and (c) profits.

4 A consultant suggests that Nestle, the maker of Nescafé, should produce a 'Nescafé washing powder'. Explain whether or not you think that this would be a success for Nestlé.

Making decisions

Businesses sell products. The products they sell go through a life cycle. At each different point of the life cycle, the business needs to make decisions about how the product is to be priced, how it should be promoted and how it should be distributed. It also needs to consider how the product could be developed to extend the life of the product.

BMW owns Rover Group, the UK based car manufacturer. In buying the Rover Group in 1994, BMW bought one of the world's most innovative cars - the Mini. Still in production more than three decades after it was first produced in 1959, the Mini is a 'classic' car.

The product range

The PRODUCT LIFE CYCLE shows the stages through which, it is argued, a product passes over time. A normal product life cycle is illustrated in Figure 38.1. The product life cycle of the Mini, shown in Figure 38.2, is very similar to this.

The development stage

Products start life at the **development** stage. The Mini, for instance, first started life in 1956. Sir Leonard Lord, chairman of the British Motor Corporation (BMC) ordered his designers to come up with a new small car. The **research and development** (☞ unit 46) of the car took three years for the designer, Sir Alec Issigonis, and his team. This included the time needed to adapt the Longbridge and Cowley car plants to manufacture the Mini. Today, any development of a car would also be heavily influenced by **market research** (☞ unit 36).

Launching the product

The product is then ready to be launched. Most products coming on the market will be backed up by some advertising and other forms of promotion. The Mini came onto the market in August 1959. It was advertised in newspapers and specialist car magazines. BMC's car dealer network were given **point of sale** promotional material (☞ unit 41). Models were in the car showrooms so that customers could see the car.

The growth phase

In the **growth** phase of the cycle, sales and profits will be rising. In 1960, the first full year of production, 116 677 Minis were produced. In 1961, this increased to 157 059.

Product maturity

In the **maturity** stage, the product reaches a peak in terms of sales. Research and development costs are likely to have been paid off. The product is profitable enough to be financing the development of new products. For the Mini, the maturity

In the first half of the 1990s, the world's number one games machine was the Nintendo Super Famicon. It used 8 bit technology. By 1994, the product had reached saturation point and was vulnerable to attack. It seemed that the battle might be won by Sega, long rivals of Nintendo. They launched a superior 32 bit machine in 1994. The Sega Saturn was capable of playing faster and better games than Nintendo's 8 bit technology.

But one month after the Saturn was launched, Sony launched its PlayStation. Like the Saturn, it used 32 bit technology. Sony, though, was able to take a clear market lead. Much of this was due to a superiority in the games being offered. Most games are produced by independent manufacturers who licence the technology of a games machine. Sony offered much better terms than Nintendo or Sega with the result that many independents started making games for the PlayStation rather than the two more established producers. When Nintendo leapfrogged Sony and Sega by offering a 64 bit machine, it found that lack of software was a crucial factor in its failure to regain market leadership from Sony.

Source: adapted from the *Financial Times*, 7 March 1997.

1 Describe, using a diagram, the likely product life cycle of the Sony PlayStation.
2 Explain why a product like the Nintendo Super Famicon becomes vulnerable when it reaches saturation point in the market.
3 Launching new software games can be seen as an extension strategy for the PlayStation. Explain why.
4 How might Nintendo regain market leadership of the games market in the future?

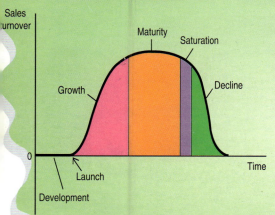

Figure 38.1 *The product life cycle.*

Figure 38.2 *The product life cycle of the Mini.*

Saturation

Towards the end of the maturity phase, the market becomes **saturated**. Competitors bring out products to try to take sales away. For the Mini, saturation perhaps occurred in the 1970s. Other car manufacturers began to bring out their own version of a small car to compete with the Mini.

Decline

Eventually, a product is likely to go into **decline**. The key event which took the Mini into decline was the launch of the Metro in 1980. This was a super-mini produced by the Rover Group, the car company that now produced the Mini and was the successor of the BMC. The new car took large numbers of sales away from the Mini. However, the Rover Group continued to produce new variations of the Mini in order to extend the life of the product.

Source: adapted from information provided by Kevin Jones, Rover Group Ltd.

stage probably lasted for most of the 1960s and the early part of the 1970s.

Manufacturers are likely to try to extend the maturity stage of the product for as long as possible. Producing a completely new product would involve all the start up costs again. So businesses try to make use of **extension strategies**. This involves slightly changing the product to give it fresh appeal to its target market. Extension strategies can also help a product appeal to a new **segment** (☞ unit 35) of the market.

The Mini has been constantly changed during its life. For instance, in 1961, a version called the Mini Cooper was launched with a more powerful engine. In 1964, a jeep-type version called the Mini Moke was first put on sale. 1967 saw a facelift of the Mini range with the new cars being called Mark II Minis. New variants of the Mini have in fact been launched in most years of its existence.

key terms

Product life cycle - the stages through which a product passes from its development to being withdrawn from sale.

SUMMARY CASE STUDY

COCA COLA

Coca Cola has been an astonishing success story. After 100 years, the drink still continues to sell more each year. It is the world's number one cola drink and the world's number one carbonated drink. Why has the drink not gone into decline decades ago?

One reason in world terms is that Coca Cola is constantly pushing its drink into new areas. China, for instance, per person drinks almost no Coca Cola. Partly this is because Coca Cola was banned until recently by the Chinese government. Partly it is because much of China is still very poor and can't afford luxuries like fizzy drinks. But Coca Cola is in the Chinese market, exploiting whatever marketing opportunities it can. With a quarter of the world's population living in the country, the potential growth is huge.

Another reason for Coca Cola's continued success is that it is prepared to innovate. Over thirty years ago, for instance, it put Coca Cola into cans for the first time. In 1993, it put Coke into 20oz plastic contoured bottles, mimicking the famous shaped glass Coca Cola bottle. This increased Coke sales. In 1997, it launched a contoured can, again mimicking the glass bottle.

Putting Coke into different types and size of container might not seem important. But the packaging is a vital part of the marketing mix of any soft drink. Coca Cola has to respond to what the market wants or else a competitor will take market share away from the market leader.

Source: adapted from the *Financial Times*, 10 December 1996, 3 March 1997.

1 (a) Draw and label a product life cycle diagram.
  (b) Explain where in the product life cycle is Coca Cola in:
  (i) China; and (ii) the United States.
2 What extension strategies have Coca Cola used?
3 Discuss TWO other extension strategies that you think might increase sales of Coca Cola.

Checklist ✓

1 What happens during the development stage of a product's life?
2 Why is a product likely to need advertising and promotion when it is launched?
3 Profits for a product which is a market leader in its maturity stage tend to be very high. Why is this?
4 What is an extension strategy?
5 What happens to a product in the decline phase of its life cycle?

PRICING

Making decisions

Price is one element of the marketing mix. A business must decide how to price its product. In making this decision it needs to consider:

- what are the prices charged by competitors;
- how price can be used to increase sales of the product;
- whether the price will cover costs of production.

The record industry is big business. 71 million singles were sold in 1996. CD sales were nearly 140 million. In 1996, 52 per cent of the population owned a CD player compared to 27 per cent in 1992. A record company like EMI or Sony will sell its CDs to retailers (shops), where most people buy them. How does a record company decide what price to charge retailers for its CDs? How does a retailer decide what price to charge consumers?

Competition based pricing

One way in which record companies decide at what price to sell their CDs is to look at prices charged by other companies. This is known as COMPETITION BASED PRICING. Selling a CD to retailers for £20 when other full priced CDs are around £10 is likely to lose sales. On the other hand, selling a new CD for £3 may give the message that the CD is not as good quality.

Setting the price at the market average avoids price competition and is a safe strategy. The record company can then compete using other strategies, like advertising or putting out CDs by new bands that it thinks will be popular.

Market orientated pricing

An alternative to competition based pricing is MARKET ORIENTATED PRICING. This is where the price charged is based upon an analysis of the market and its characteristics.

Discounts, special offers and sales A record company may give retailers a special discount for a period on certain CDs to increase their sales. For example, from August to the end of the year retailers may be given a discount on large orders placed for older CDs of well known artists. In the Summer and in January, retailers often hold sales. They are a way of getting rid of stock that hasn't sold well at its usual price at other times in the year. Retailers may also offer **loss leaders**. These are products which are priced so cheaply that the retailer makes no profit or even a loss on every sale. But they attract customers into the store who then buy other full priced products.

? 1 Suggest why the drinks shown in the photograph might all have a similar price.

British Telecom

British Telecom has a complicated pricing structure for its business and residential customers. The tables below show the charges for local, regional and national calls in the daytime, in the evening and at weekends. VAT at 17.5 per cent has to be added to all the prices in the tables.
Households can opt to pay a higher fixed line rental charge and get lower call costs. The Friends and Family scheme offers 25 per cent off calls made to up to 10 designated numbers. Customers who have very low phone bills can get a rebate.
(Prices at 31 October 1997)

1 How much would it cost a small business based in London to ring Glasgow for 10 minutes excluding VAT?
2 Excluding VAT, how much would it cost a residential customer in London to ring someone a few streets away for ten minutes at: (a) 10.a.m. Monday morning; (b) 7 p.m. Tuesday evening; and (c) 1 p.m. Sunday afternoon?
3 Suggest why British Telecom has such a complicated price structure.
4 British Telecom is told by its regulator that it has to reduce its prices by an average of 5 per cent. A competing telephone company has just cut its prices to its business customers by 10 per cent. Discuss whether BT should cut all its prices by 5 per cent, cut prices to business customers by more than 5 per cent and to residential customers by less than 5 per cent, or vice versa.

Table 39.1 *The price of UK calls for business users.*
Line rental for a single line £35.84 per quarter (3 months).
All calls are subject to a minimum charge of 4.2p.

daytime (mon to Fri 8am-6pm)

	local	regional (up to 35 miles)	national (over 35 miles)
Pence per minute	3.36p	6.73p	6.73p

evenings & night-time (Mon to Fri before 8am & after 6pm)

	local	regional (up to 35 miles)	national (over 35 miles)
Pence per minute	1.4p	3.36p	3.95p

weekend (Midnight Fri - Midnight Sun)

	local	regional (up to 35 miles)	national (over 35 miles)
Pence per minute	0.85p	2.80p	2.80p

Source: adapted from *UK Call Prices for Business*, BT.

Table 39.2 *The price of UK calls for residential users.*
Line rental for a single line £26.62 per quarter (3 months).
All calls are subject to a minimum charge of 5p.

daytime (mon to Fri 8am-6pm)

	local	regional (up to 35 miles)	national (over 35 miles)
Pence per minute	3.95p	7.91p	7.91p

evenings & night-time (Mon to Fri before 8am & after 6pm)

	local	regional (up to 35 miles)	national (over 35 miles)
Pence per minute	1.65p	3.95p	4.18p

weekend (Midnight Fri - Midnight Sun)

	local	regional (up to 35 miles)	national (over 35 miles)
Pence per minute	1p	3.29p	3.29p

Source: adapted from *UK Call Prices*, BT.

Selling singles for £1.99 at the start is an example of penetration pricing.

Price discrimination

Record companies sell CDs at different prices in different areas of the world. Selling the same product at different prices to different **segments of the market** (☞ unit 35) is known as PRICE DISCRIMINATION. The record company may attempt to charge what the market will 'bear' in order to earn the highest profit possible in each market. For instance, it may charge more in the UK than in US markets if British buyers are prepared to pay higher prices than American buyers. Many record companies also have a lower price or a 'mid-price' range. This is where they will charge a lower price for well known, older CDs by artists, whilst more recent CDs remain at full price.

The car insurance revolution

Car insurance used to be a fairly sleepy business. Loyal motorists tended to renew their insurance year after year without checking whether there were cheaper alternatives.

Peter Wood changed all that. He founded Direct Line. It revolutionised the insurance industry in two ways. First, it competed on price, aiming to give the lowest price for safe motorists. Second, it sold its insurance direct to the motorist over the phone. Before, insurance companies tended to use brokers - businesses in the middle between customers and insurers, which usually had branches in the high street.

Direct Line could afford to offer lower prices. It wouldn't insure high risk motorists. It didn't have to pay a commission to brokers to sell its insurance on to motorists. Its own organisational costs were very low. With low costs, it could afford to charge a mark up which allowed it to become highly profitable. Its competitors were forced to change, cutting their costs and setting up their own direct selling organisations.

Source: adapted from *The Sunday Times*, 17 November 1996.

1 What is the product that Direct Line sells?
2 Suggest what are: (a) the variable costs; and (b) the fixed costs of Direct Line.
3 'Direct Line adopts a full-cost pricing policy.' What does this mean?
4 Other insurance companies have been forced to cut their premiums (their prices) to motorists. Explain what type of pricing policy they have adopted.
5 A very bad winter increases the number of accident claims by 30 per cent. What premiums (prices) should Direct Line now set? Explain your answer.

DIRECT LINE
INSURANCE

Penetration pricing

Singles are now typically discounted during the first week of sale. A £3.99 single may be sold for £1.99. This is because the record companies want to maximise early sales so that the single can get into the charts. Getting into the charts means that it will be played more often on radio, which will lead to further sales. Charging a lower price for a product at the start in order to gain **market share** (☞ unit 18) is known as PENETRATION PRICING. One problem with this strategy is that consumers may refuse to buy at the higher long term price. They might see the initial price as a 'fair' price and the more expensive price as not representing value for money.

Figure 39.1 *CD pricing: where the money goes.*

CD Selling price £13.99

- Profit before interest & tax £0.65
- VAT £2.08
- Retailer's margin £4.67
- Other overheads £1.32
- Other artists & repertoire costs £1.61
- Songwriter/ publisher £0.68
- Artists' royalty £1.61
- Physical manufacturing costs £0.65
- Distribution costs £0.72

Source: adapted from Media Research Publishings Ltd.

Creaming

CREAMING (or SKIMMING) is the opposite of penetration pricing. It is setting a high price for a product initially and lowering it later on. It is used, for instance, with hi-fi products. When CD players were first marketed in the early 1980s they were typically priced at £200-£300. Today, despite inflation (☞ unit 6), a CD player with better features is typically priced at £100-£200. In the early days, hi-fi enthusiasts were prepared to pay a high price to get a new product. However, to create a mass market for CD players, manufacturers had to lower their prices even though they put more features onto machines.

Cost based pricing

Record companies are in business to make a profit. Charging a price similar to competitors is one way to set prices but might lead to losses. Another way would be to base price on costs of production.

A retailer selling CDs might use COST PLUS PRICING. It could calculate the cost of selling the CD and then add a MARK-UP or PROFIT MARGIN (☞ unit 27 for a discussion of gross profit margins and net profit margins). The price of the CD would then be the cost plus a profit for the retailer.

The cost is the average cost and is made up of:
- the variable cost - mainly the cost of buying the CD from the record company;
- the fixed cost - such as the wages of staff, the rent of the shop and heating and lighting.

When the price covers both the average fixed and variable cost of the product, the business is said to be **full-cost pricing**.

Sometimes it is difficult to sell certain CDs. Some CDs take longer to sell than others. Some artists are only bought by a small number of people. Tastes may change and an artist may become unpopular. The retailer may have to cut the price to below the full cost price to sell these CDs. So long as the new price more than covers the variable cost, it will at least make some **contribution** (☞ unit 23) towards the fixed costs of the business. In the long term, the retailer has to cover all its costs to survive. In the short term, charging a price above variable cost may make sense.

Source: adapted from the *Financial Times*, 12 April 1997; Paul Quirk, Quirk's Records, Ormskirk.

The Delicious Cake Company

The Delicious Cake Company is a mini-enterprise company. The board of directors has decided that its business will make cakes and gateaux and offer a free delivery service to the door of the customer.

.The board is now meeting to decide what price the Company should charge for its cakes. The first cake on their list is a gateau with icing on top. Ingredients for one gateau cost £1.36. The box to put it in will cost 15p. The school is charging the company a flat £20 fee for the use of rooms etc. whilst the company is operating. Parents have agreed to lend baking tins and other equipment free. Parents have also agreed not to charge for the use of ovens to bake the cakes. It is estimated that a cake would take an hour to make. They haven't quite worked out how they will arrange the door step delivery.

1 What price do you think the Delicious Cake Company should charge for its gateaux? Explain your reasons carefully.
2 The company sends out a price list for its cakes to parents. It also advertises in local shops. It finds that its cakes aren't selling well, but it is making a substantial profit on each cake. Do you think that the company should reduce its prices? Consider as many arguments for and against as possible.

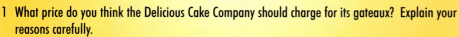

Key terms

Competition based pricing - setting a price based on the prices charged by competitors for similar products.
Cost plus pricing - fixing a price by adding a percentage profit margin to the cost of production of the good or service.
Creaming or skimming - selling a product at a high price, sacrificing high sales in order to earn high profits.
Market orientated pricing - setting a price based on an analysis of the market.
Mark-up or profit margin - the percentage added to the cost of production which equals the profit on the product.
Penetration pricing - setting an initial low price for a new product so that it is attractive to customers. The price is likely to be raised later as the product gains market share.
Price discrimination - setting a different price for the same product in different segments of the market.
Profit margin - the extra which is added to the cost of a product to cover the profit to be made.

SUMMARY CASE STUDY

THE HISTORY OF FASHION

A magazine publisher is bringing out a 60 part series on the history of fashion. It will link past fashion with today's latest fashion ideas. Each issue, costing £2.99, will include a free pattern for an up to date item based on the fashion ideas in that issue. Binders will also be available. The readers can place each edition in the ring binder so that the magazine can be built up into a comprehensive guide to fashion.

1 What pricing strategy might the publisher have used when fixing the price for the magazine? In your answer, give the advantages and disadvantages from the publisher's viewpoint.
2 Explain how you think the binders should be priced.
3 The final cost to the customer of buying 60 parts will be £179.40 plus the binders. Discuss why the publisher doesn't publish a set of books with all the material in for £179 instead of publishing it as a 60 part series.

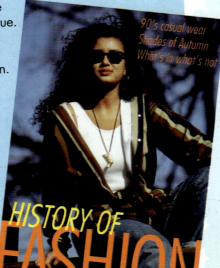

90's casual wear
Shades of Autumn
What's in what's not

HISTORY OF
FASHION

Checklist ✓

1 Explain, using teenage magazines as an example, what is meant by 'competitive pricing'.
2 Why do shops have sales?
3 How might a hairdresser price discriminate?
4 Why might penetration pricing be a good price strategy to use when launching a new brand of yogurts?
5 'Mobile phone networks have used price creaming strategies when setting prices.' Explain what this means.
6 Calculate the price of a product if its cost of production is: (a) £10 and the mark up is 50 per cent; (b) £100 and the mark up is 10 per cent; (c) £5 and the mark up is 100 per cent.
7 What is meant by a 'contribution' in pricing?

Making decisions

Businesses have to decide what price to set for their products. The higher the price, the lower will be the demand for their product and the less they will be able to sell. Some businesses have to accept the market price for their product if they are to sell at all. They have no control over the price they receive. Their prices are set completely by the forces of demand and supply. With a fixed price, these businesses need to decide whether their costs will be low enough to make it worthwhile carrying on in business.

Meridian Mining is a British mining company specialising in tungsten and gold. It owns a gold mine in Ghana. The profit it makes depends on the world price for gold.

Price takers

Meridian Mining is a **price taker**. This means that it can't fix the price of the gold that it sells. One reason for this is that gold is not branded. It is a **commodity** or **generic** product (☞ unit 37). Businesses that buy gold see no difference between gold that comes from the Meridian mine in Ghana or gold from a mine in South Africa.

Meridian Mining is also in competition with thousands of other gold mining companies round the world. Its business is not, for instance, like that of Proctor & Gamble, which sells about half of all washing powder bought in the UK. If Meridian Mining were to charge a higher price for its gold than other mining companies, then no one would buy the gold. It either accepts the going market price or doesn't sell at all.

Demand

The MARKET PRICE for gold is fixed by the forces of demand and supply. DEMAND is how much customers will buy at any given price. The higher the price of gold, the less will be the quantity demanded of gold. This relationship between demand and price is shown in Figure 40.1.

Price is one factor affecting demand for a commodity like gold. There are other factors. For instance, as incomes rise worldwide, more gold jewellery is bought and so the demand for gold will rise. If the price of a competing product like silver falls, then gold becomes less attractive. A fall in the price of silver jewellery is likely to mean that less gold jewellery will be bought. Equally, a rise in the world's population means there are more potential customers for gold.

Changes in factors other than price will lead to shifts in the demand curve. In Figure 40.2, for instance, the demand curve has shifted to the right. This means that at any given price, more is demanded. In the gold market, it could be that the Japanese, major buyers of gold jewellery, have seen their incomes rise very fast this year. Or it could be that a new industrial use for gold has been found and put into operation.

Supply

SUPPLY is the quantity that producers are prepared to sell at any given price. The higher the price, the greater the incentive for producers to make and sell. So a rise in price increases the quantity supplied. This is shown in Figure 40.3. Other factors also affect supply. For instance, if miners' wages throughout the world go up, then the cost of mining gold will rise. Gold mining companies like Meridian Mining will need higher prices to cover this. On the other hand, changes in technology might allow mining companies to produce more gold with less equipment. This will mean that they are prepared to sell gold at a lower price than before. Changes in factors other than price

Peanuts

Peanuts are growing in popularity worldwide. As world incomes rise, consumers are crunching, grinding, spreading and chewing more nuts every year.

But prices in the shops could be set to rise soon. Drought in Argentina has led to a very disappointing peanut crop, with yields down by a third. As a result, the auction price of peanuts rose from $700 a tonne in January to $900 a tonne in May. For Billy Carter, a peanut farmer in Georgia, USA, this could be good news. He will be able to sell his crop at a higher price. The customers in his local supermarket might not be so pleased.

Source: adapted from the *Financial Times*, 1 May 1997.

1 Why is the demand for peanuts rising worldwide?
2 (a) Explain what happened to the supply of peanuts from Argentina. (b) What effect did this have on: (i) the world supply of peanuts; and (ii) the world price of peanuts?
3 What is likely to happen to peanut prices next year?

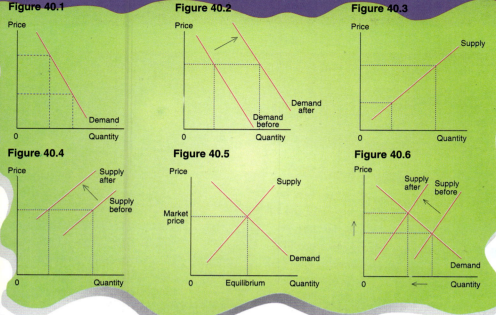

Figure 40.1 to **Figure 40.6**

Price

The world price of gold is fixed by demand and supply. In Figure 40.5, the market price is shown where the demand and supply curves cross. This is the price where what is offered for sale equals the amount that customers want to buy.

The price of gold changes from day to day and from year to year. This can be caused either by changes in demand or by changes in supply. For instance, assume that gold mining companies see a rise in production costs. This will shift the supply curve to the left as shown in Figure 40.6. This fall in supply leads to higher world prices for gold with less being bought and sold.

will shift the supply curve. In Figure 40.4, the supply curve has shifted to the left. At any given price, less is supplied. In the gold mining industry, this could be because costs of production have risen, or because workers striking for better wages have reduced output.

Key terms

Demand - how much will be bought of a product at any given price.
Market price - the price where the demand for a product equals its supply.
Supply - how much producers of a product will sell at any given price.

THE MANOR HOTEL

Jill Baldwin is owner of the Manor Hotel in the tourist heartland of central London. There are nearly 1 000 hotels, motels, inns, guest houses and B&Bs registered as members of the London Tourist Board and many more which aren't. Nearly 137 000 rooms are available in registered establishments. Jill had a good year in 1997. The prices she was able to charge per room went up for the fourth year in a row. With the economy growing strongly, people had more money in their pockets to spend on items like holidays and short breaks. The low value of the pound between 1994 and 1996 pulled in record numbers of foreign tourists. The memory of the bad times in the hotel trade in the early 1990s also stopped many hotel chains expanding and building new hotels. So competition didn't increase very much.

In 1998 she was worried because planning permission had been given to convert the large house next door into a hotel. It opened in May 1998. The street already had three hotels including hers. She was also worried because it was very difficult to get hold of staff. She lost an excellent chamber maid in March who moved to a hotel paying better wages. Jill decided she would have to give a fairly substantial pay rise later in the year because she feared losing more staff.

Source: adapted from the *Financial Times*, 18 December 1996; British Tourist Authority, 1997.

Figure 40.7 *Average nightly room rate in London.*

Average nightly room rate (£)

1988 89 90 91 92 93 94 95 96 97

1 What happened to average prices for hotel rooms in London between 1988 and 1997?
2 Give TWO reasons why the demand for hotel rooms in London rose between 1994 and 1997.
3 Explain TWO factors which can affect room supply.
4 (a) Giving reasons, suggest what might have happened to London room prices in 1998.
(b) Do you think that Jill Baldwin will be able to increase her prices in 1998? Give reasons for your answer.

Checklist ✓

1 'British Steel is a price taker.' What does this mean?
2 (a) What is the difference between a branded and a generic product? (b) Why do makers of generic products find it much more difficult to set a market price for their products than makers of branded products?
3 What happens to the quantity demanded of a product if its price increases?
4 (a) Explain what will happen to the demand for apples if: (i) workers get a 10 per cent pay rise; (ii) the prices of oranges and pears fall; (iii) a health report is published saying that apples should be part of everyone's diet. (b) Show how the demand curve for apples shifts as a result of (i) to (iii) by drawing demand curves on a diagram.
5 (a) Explain what will happen to the supply of apples if: (i) workers on farms growing apples get a 10 per cent pay rise; (ii) a new type of tree is introduced which produces 50 per cent more apples per acre of apple orchard; (iii) the price of pears doubles and stays very high over a number of years; (iv) the apple crop is ruined by bad weather. (b) Show how the supply curve for apples shifts as a result of (i) to (iv) by drawing supply curves on a diagram.
6 For each of the situations described in questions 4 and 5, draw a demand and supply diagram showing the shift in either the demand curve (Q4) or the supply curve (Q5). On each diagram show how the price of apples has changed.

PROMOTION

the future's
bright

the future's
Orange

Making decisions

Businesses have to decide how best to promote the products they make and sell. Should they advertise, for instance, or should they use point of sale promotion? This decision involves weighing up the relative cost of each form of promotion and how best to target their potential customers. They also need to decide whether to organise the promotion themselves or use an outside organisation like an advertising agency.

Orange is a mobile telephone company. It began offering its service in 1994 and within three years had gained over 10 per cent of the mobile phone market. The company is in competition with three longer established mobile phone companies - Vodafone, Cellnet and One2One. To establish itself in the market, it has heavily promoted its services.

Communication

Businesses need to communicate with their customers. PROMOTION is about:
- making customers aware that the product is for sale;
- telling or explaining to them what the product is;
- making customers aware of how the product will serve their needs;
- persuading them to buy it for the first time or to buy it again.

Promotion is the most direct form of communication in the **marketing mix** (☞ unit 34).

There is a number of techniques of promotion: advertising; direct mailing; personal selling; public relations; sales promotion; and branding.

Media advertising

Orange, like other businesses, advertises through the **media.** This includes:
- television, radio and cinema;
- magazines;
- national and local newspapers;
- trade newspapers and journals - these are specialist publications aimed at businesses or workers in a particular industry;
- posters and transport - such as billboards on the side of the road and advertisements on buses or vans;
- directories - including *Yellow Pages*, although Orange does not use this medium.

Orange wants to reach a large number of consumers and it has a large advertising budget. It can afford to advertise on television - an expensive medium. But it also uses magazines, newspapers and billboards. Its advertising slogan, 'The future's bright, the future's Orange', is designed to encourage consumers to want to use a mobile

Each of the photographs shows a different form of advertising medium.
1 Name each of these.
2 The following want to advertise their products. Explain which of the advertising media shown in the photographs would be suitable. In your answer, consider: (i) the cost of advertising; (ii) the target audience; (iii) the impact of the advertisement on the potential customer.
 (a) Boots wants to advertise its Number 7 range of cosmetics.
 (b) Jill Hillier is a painter and decorator. She wants to advertise her business.
 (c) Redland's is a local concessionaire for Toyota cars. It wants to advertise its range of products, including servicing cars, body repairs, and the sale of new and second hand cars.

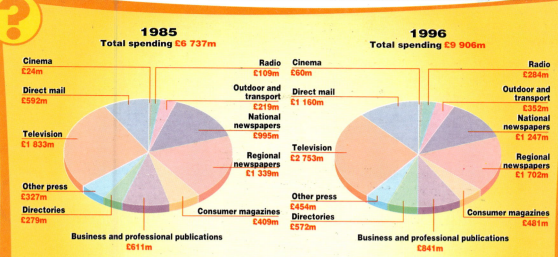

1985
Total spending £6 737m

Cinema £24m
Direct mail £592m
Television £1 833m
Other press £327m
Directories £279m
Business and professional publications £611m
Consumer magazines £409m
Regional newspapers £1 339m
National newspapers £995m
Outdoor and transport £219m
Radio £109m

1996
Total spending £9 906m

Cinema £60m
Direct mail £1 160m
Television £2 753m
Other press £454m
Directories £572m
Business and professional publications £841m
Consumer magazines £481m
Regional newspapers £1 702m
National newspapers £1 247m
Outdoor and transport £352m
Radio £284m

Figure 41.1 *Advertising expenditure (at constant 1990 prices).*
Source: adapted from The Advertising Association, *Advertising Statistics Yearbook 1997.*

1 Look at Figure 41.1. How much in 1996 was spent on advertising: (a) in national newspapers; (b) on radio; (c) through directories.

2 Between 1985 and 1996 the share of total advertising spending on cinema, radio, directories and television rose. At the same time the share of total advertising spending on national and regional newspapers and consumer magazines fell. Suggest reasons why this occurred.

3 (a) What has happened to total advertising spending 1985 and 1996? (b) Why do you think there has been this change?

phone, a technology still of the future for most people. But it also implies that Orange, rather than any of the rival mobile phone networks like Cellnet or Vodafone, is the network of the future.

If Orange wanted to recruit an accountant, however, it would be very wasteful to use television. The style of the advertisement would also be different from one selling a phone. It could use a jobs section in a quality national newspaper like the *Financial Times* or *The Sunday Times*. Alternatively, it could advertise in a more specialist trade journal like *Accountancy Age,* a journal read by accountants. A small business wouldn't be able to afford television or a national newspaper. It would want to focus its advertising, using media which was affordable and which reached its target customers.

Advertising agencies

ADVERTISING AGENCIES are businesses which specialise in organising the advertising of other businesses. Orange, for instance, uses an agency called WCRS to organise its advertising campaigns.

Within an advertising agency, an **account executive** will be appointed to run a particular campaign. As shown in Figure 41.2, three groups of people will then be involved.

- The market research department organises market research (☞ unit 36) into the product. The information collected is then used to plan the advertising campaign.
- The creative department devises the advertisement, from the words to be used (the copy) to the pictures to the sound.
- The art buying department organises the making of film advertisements, the taking of photographs, etc.
- The media buying department buys slots on television, on radio, in newspapers and magazines, etc.

An advertising agency is crucial to the success of any advertising campaign. Boring

adverts will not attract attention. 'The future's bright, the future's Orange' campaign was very successful because it captured people's imaginations. Not surprisingly, it won a number of awards, including ITV Brand of the Year in 1996.

Direct mail

DIRECT MAIL involves a business sending advertising leaflets directly to a household or business through the post. To keep costs down, the advertiser needs a list of potential customers. For instance, it may target households in a particular area, getting names and addresses from the electoral register. Or it may have a list of clients who have bought products in the past. This is often used by financial services businesses like banks and insurance companies, and mail order firms.

Orange uses direct mail. For instance, an existing Orange customer may recommend a friend to the company. It will then send promotional literature to that person hoping that they will subscribe too.

Packaging

Packaging is important for many products. It needs to be instantly recognisable so that shoppers don't buy another brand by mistake or, worse still, not recognise the product on the shelves. The colour

Figure 41.2 *An advertising agency.*

ACCOUNT EXECUTIVE

MARKET RESEARCH DEPARTMENT
CREATIVE DEPARTMENT
ART BUYING DEPARTMENT
MEDIA BUYING DEPARTMENT

of the packaging and its design need to reflect the image of the product. It also needs to give any information required by law.

Packaging is important too, though, even for Orange which provides a service. For instance, the packaging of the monthly bill is an opportunity for promotion. The envelope containing the bill has the Orange logo on it.

Personal selling

Some products are sold door-to-door. A double glazing salesman or an insurance salesman might arrange to call at a house. A sales representative (a 'sales rep') might tour local businesses trying to sell a product. These are examples of personal selling. The advantage is that the value of the product can be communicated directly to the customer. On the other hand, many people don't like feeling pressurised into buying a product and resent the time wasted by visiting sales reps. Orange, however, does not use this method of sales.

Public relations

PUBLIC RELATIONS is another way in which businesses attempt to communicate with their customers. The public relations department tries to get good news about the product into the media. For instance, it might issue a press release about the launch of a new product.

Orange has succeeded in establishing the best form of public relations: unsolicited mention in the media. For instance, in a 1996 football match between the Netherlands and Switzerland, a Netherlands player scored a goal. Barry Davies, commentator for the BBC, jokingly said: 'The future's bright, the future's Orange'. The use of Orange as a case study in this book is a form of public relations too.

Sales promotion

Sales promotion attempts to give a short term boost to sales. A number of methods can be used.

Money off Mobile phone networks like Orange use retailers to sell their

Mobile phone networks use retailers to sell their services. Retailers can give 'money off' deals to customers.

triple your monthly talk time free

45 inclusive minutes a month

for the price of **15**

Connect to Orange Talk 15 between 1 February and 30 April 1998 and enjoy Triple Talk 15 every month for 6 months giving you 30 extra free inclusive minutes for only

£17.63 per month (inc. VAT)

orange

Better value offers encourage people to subscribe.

services to customers. These retailers are paid a commission for each new customer they sign up by Orange and the other mobile phone companies. The retailers often use part of the commission to give 'money off' deals to customers. For instance, they might offer a mobile phone at a low price if the customer signs up or offer free connection on certain 'tariffs' (the length of time each month that the customer can talk at a standard charge per call).

Better value offers Orange often has offers to customers. For instance, when it first started, it offered free local telephone calls to subscribers. The offer was designed to attract large numbers of customers to the network.

Competitions A large retailer of mobile phones might offer a prize draw to new customers giving holidays or mobile telephones as prizes.

Free gifts For instance, you may get a free carrying case if you buy a mobile telephone.

Discount vouchers These usually give money off the next purchase of a product, or off another product in a manufacturer's range.

Ostrich

In September 1997, Tesco announced that it would stop selling kangaroo and ostrich meat. Sainsbury's, however, said it would continue to sell 'exotic meats' in selected stores.

The decision to stop selling was made on commercial grounds, according to Tesco. Many had thought the BSE scare would encourage some customers to switch from beef to meats such as ostrich. However, demand was disappointing. Tesco's total ostrich and kangaroo sales had been less than one tonne per week compared to 200 000 tonnes of beef, lamb and pork.

It could be argued though that Tesco's decision has been influenced by animal welfare groups. They have long campaigned against the sale of kangaroo and ostrich. For example, Dr Martin Potter, head of the RSPCA's farm animals department said: 'They are still wild animals and I question whether it's right to farm an animal that's evolved on the African plains in our climate'.

Source: adapted from the *Financial Times*, 27 September 1997.

1 Suggest why Tesco and Sainsbury's began selling exotic meats.
2 Tesco and Sainsbury's ran the risk of harming their public relations by selling these meats. Explain why.
3 A clothing manufacturer has written to all the supermarket groups offering them a new line: gloves made from genuine fox fur. Discuss whether a supermarket should take up the offer and put these gloves on sale in their stores.

PR promotions For instance, sometimes products are sold with the manufacturer promising to donate money to a charity for each item sold.

Another way to give a short term boost to sales is through the use of POINT-OF-SALE MATERIAL. This is promotion undertaken where the product is sold. Retailers selling mobile phone connections will be supplied with posters and leaflets by Orange. It may also give three dimensional cardboard displays to put, for instance, in the shop window. In a supermarket, a product like soap might be put into special **dump bins**, containers likely to be situated at the end of aisles. These attract customer attention.

Branding

The most important long term outcome of promotion for Orange is to build and maintain the Orange **brand** (☞ unit 37). Orange wants to see its name associated with value for money, quality of service and a straightforward approach to dealing with customers. Its advertising is intended to stress that Orange is the latest in mobile phone technology and that customers are buying an advanced service. Orange has already been highly successful in establishing a brand image from nothing in 1994. The reward for this successful branding is a continued growth in the number of people choosing Orange.

Source: adapted from Orange plc, *Annual Report and Accounts*, 1996.

Checklist ✓

1 What is meant by 'media advertising'?
2 (a) What is a 'directory'? (b) Give TWO examples of sales directories used by businesses.
3 How can an advertising agency help a business?
4 How can direct mail increase sales of a product?
5 What can packaging communicate to customers about a product?
6 Give ONE advantage and ONE disadvantage of personal selling for a business.
7 Why are good public relations important for a business?
8 What point of sale material might there be in a large supermarket?
9 What are the advantages to a business of owning strongly branded products?

---

key terms

Advertising agency - a business which specialises in organising the promotion for other businesses.
Direct mail - advertising leaflets sent to potential customers, usually through the post.
Point-of-sale material - promotion of a product where it is sold. Examples include special displays or distribution of leaflets in shops.
Promotion - communication between business and customer, making the customer aware that the product is for sale, telling or explaining to them what is the product, making the customers aware of how the product will serve the customer's needs and persuading them to buy it for the first time or again.
Public relations - promotion of a positive image about a product or business through giving information about the product to the general public, other businesses or to the press.

It would be easier if you did this survey as part of a group. You need to collect information about promotions currently on offer. You could do this by:

- looking through local newspapers, including free newspapers;
- noting down any promotions offered on television or radio commercials;
- checking through food, particularly tins and packets, which you have at home;
- visiting local shops, such as your nearest supermarket, and noting down products and promotions on offer.

1 Give TEN examples of different promotions you have found.
2 (a) For each one, explain why you think it could increase sales of the product.
(b) Which do you think will be the most effective promotion and why?

SUMMARY CASE STUDY

EGGS

The British Egg Industry Council represents thousands of small farmers and a fewer larger businesses which supply eggs to supermarkets and other customers. The Council wants to conduct a promotion campaign for eggs. Egg consumption has been falling over the past 50 years as consumers have switched to other foods. In 1996, people on average ate 169 eggs per year. Ten years earlier, it had been 220.

Surveys show that some consumers have been worried about the high cholesterol content of eggs. However, high cholesterol in itself is not bad in food. It is when it is associated with high levels of saturated fat that it can be a cause of heart problems and eggs are low in saturated fat.

Surveys also show that some consumers are worried about animal welfare, with 86 per cent of eggs still coming from caged hens.

Consumers are attracted to foods that they think are 'natural'. They also increasingly want fast food - food that can be eaten immediately or which takes little time to prepare.

 DTP

1 Design a promotional campaign for eggs. You need to think about all aspects including designing an advert, sketching the script for a TV commercial and suggesting ideas for promotion. Think too about how public relations could be used because the Council's promotional funds are limited. You could use a desktop publishing package to present your ideas.

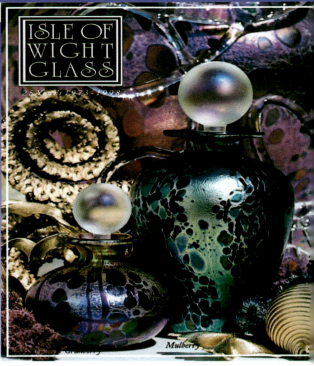

ISLE OF WIGHT GLASS

25 YEARS 1973-1998

Cranberry   Mulberry

Making decisions

A product is unlikely to be successful if customers find it difficult to purchase. So 'place' is a vital part of the marketing mix. Producers must decide how to get their product to the customer. Channels of distribution need to be efficient and effective.

Isle of Wight Glass was founded in 1973. It specialises in manufacturing fine decorative glassware, such as vases, paperweights, lamp bases, perfume atomisers and tableware. The glassware is produced using traditional methods, with most of the pieces being hand finished. Prices for single items range from £10 to £400.

Place in the marketing mix

For a product to sell, it must be in the right place at the right time for customers to buy. Gift ware, for instance, is unlikely to sell well in a bread shop because customers don't usually go into bread shops looking for presents. Gift ware needs to be in places where consumers are likely to buy a present for someone else or a treat for themselves. Shops in holiday resorts, gift shops or outlets at an airport might be good selling outlets for Isle of Wight Glass.

This is true of services as well as goods. An electrician who won't travel more than two miles to a job won't get much work in a rural area. A hairdresser on the high street is likely to get more customers than one tucked away in a back alley.

So place is very important in the **marketing mix** (☞ unit 34). If Isle of Wight Glass products are not on sale in Blackpool, then there will be no sales in Blackpool. The larger the number of outlets that stock its products, the larger the number of sales.

Channels of distribution

There is a CHANNEL OF DISTRIBUTION between the manufacturer of a product and the customer. This is the path taken to get products from producers to consumers.

Directly to retailers One third of the gift ware sold by Isle of Wight Glass is sold directly to retailers. Each year in February, the company has a stand at a gift fair at the National Exhibition Centre in Birmingham. The fair is attended by retailers who place orders for stock which they will then sell on to customers. Once the orders are placed, Isle of Wight Glass sends the stock directly to the retailers.

Through wholesalers A WHOLESALER is a type of business which specialises in selling to smaller shops and other traders. Small shops can't buy many goods directly from the manufacturer

Oysters

Christopher von Meister loves oysters, but in London, they have traditionally been very expensive compared to France. He became determined to sell oysters to the public at French prices. He researched the market and came across the phrase 'transit retailing'. It means selling to customers in train terminals and airports. The idea appealed and he approached British Rail. They negotiated with him to buy a market barrow and site it at Fenchurch Street Station in London. This is a very busy station and is used by many workers who have high powered jobs in the City of London. The barrow started trading in December 1996. Sales have been good, with the weather being the main factor in determining how many oysters are being sold each day. Von Meister plans to expand the idea by taking a mobile barrow and setting up in other busy locations like sports grounds and other railways stations.

Source: adapted from the *Financial Times*, 5 April 1997.

1 What is a 'market barrow'?

2 Von Meister gets his oysters from an oyster fishery near Belfast in Northern Ireland. Describe the channel of distribution for the oysters.

3 Why do you think Von Meister decided to locate his barrow at Fenchurch Street Station in London?

4 Suggest why the weather has an effect on sales.

5 Do you think that Von Meister will be successful in expanding his business to other locations? Explain your answer carefully.

because their orders are too small. Kellogg's, for instance, is not prepared to pay the cost of delivering a few packets of Cornflakes to a small shop. Instead, it sells large quantities to a wholesaler. The wholesaler then sells to the smaller retailer in small quantities.

The wholesaler acts then as a BREAK-OF-BULK POINT. This is a place where goods are delivered. They are then:

- either broken down into smaller quantities to be sold off as with a wholesaler;
- or they could be combined with other similar products and transported in a larger quantity elsewhere - an example of this would be grain being taken to a port in lorries and then loaded for export onto a ship.

Isle of Wight Glass does not sell through wholesalers because its products are not mass produced. It doesn't need a wholesaler to break bulk because it is prepared to sell directly to retailers in small quantities.

Through agents Isle of Wight Glass uses **agents** to sell abroad. These are people or businesses who bring buyers and sellers together. So the French agent for Isle of Wight Glass arranges sales to retailers in France. Isle of Wight Glass then sends the products directly to the French retailer. The

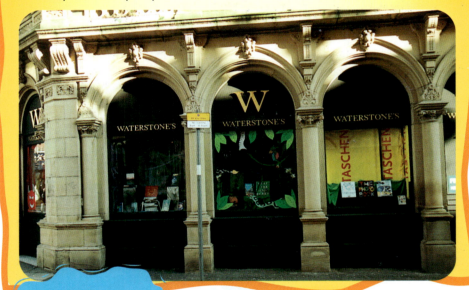

Book distribution

How did this book get to you? Publishers use two main channels of distribution. One method is through bookshops. Schools and colleges place orders for textbooks with a bookshop. It then orders the books from the publisher. Some bookshops give a discount to schools and colleges on orders for textbooks to encourage them to buy from them.

Bookshops may also choose to have a few copies of the most successful textbooks on their shelves. Customers will come into the bookshop to buy a single copy.

Alternatively, schools and colleges may also place orders directly with the publisher. This cuts out the bookshop. Publishers sometimes give a discount on textbooks ordered directly from them.

1 What channels of distribution are used by publishers?
2 A book publisher could sell a single copy of a book either to a bookshop or to a school or college directly. Why do you think it much prefers to sell class sets of books?
3 Supermarkets sell some books and magazines. Do you think that a supermarket would be a good channel of distribution for this book, *GCSE Business Studies,* from the point of view of the publisher? Explain your answer.

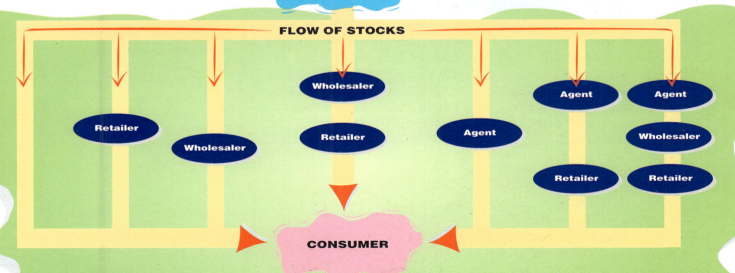

Figure 42.1 *Channels of distribution.*

agent will take a commission on each deal, usually a percentage of the value of the sale. Agents are important for Isle of Wight Glass because they sell one third of the company's output. Agents can also be used to sell goods directly to consumers. In the UK, Avon selling cosmetics and Betterware selling household goods employ agents. They go from house to house collecting orders. The agents receive a percentage of the value of every sale they make.

Directly to the consumer The last third of the output of Isle of Wight Glass is sold directly to the consumer. The company has a shop at its headquarters in St Lawrence on the Isle of Wight. It also has a shop in Shanklin, one of the main towns on the island. Both shops are well visited by tourists to the island. Other types of business sell directly to the consumer. An insurance company might send sales representatives to visit people

in their own homes to sell them financial products. A manufacturer may sell by **mail order.** A drinks manufacturer like Coca Cola may sell through vending machines.

Choosing the channel of distribution

Why does Isle of Wight Glass choose to distribute its products through certain channels of distribution and not others?

The product Gift ware is not a perishable product like a lettuce. Perishable products need to be taken to the consumer quickly and so their channels of distribution need to be quick and efficient. Neither is gift ware a complex product like central heating or double glazing. Complex products are often sold directly because the manufacturer needs to be able to deal with any installation and running problems. Nor is gift ware

a difficult product to transport. Products which are very heavy or are odd sizes are often sold directly to customers because producers provide specialist transport for delivery. Low price, high volume products, like baked beans or soft drinks, will be supplied in bulk either to large retailers like the major supermarkets or to wholesalers. Both of these can take large volumes and then perform the service of breaking bulk. Gift ware is a low volume, relatively high price product and so is likely to be delivered through specialised channels, in this case through a combination of directly to the retailer, directly to the consumer and through agents.

The market Mass market products tend to be sold either to wholesalers or to large retailers. Gift ware is a smaller market where there is a large number of different products being sold. Channels of distribution suitable for mass market products are therefore unlikely to be suitable. Hence, gift ware is sold through a variety of routes.

Effectiveness Many businesses have little choice about the channels of distribution they use. Existing patterns of selling and buying determine what distribution channel is used. Isle of Wight Glass is using three different channels of distribution. It could potentially use others. Mail order might be successful under certain conditions. Its decisions to use agents, retailers and its two own shops on the Isle of Wight are partly determined by history and also by the effectiveness of these channels. Opening new channels would carry a risk of failure. On the other hand, they might expand the business.

Source: adapted from information provided by The Isle of Wight Studio Glass Ltd.

The advertisements shown here were displayed in *TV Times* and *Yours-for the young at heart.*

1 What channel of distribution are the businesses selling these products using?

2 Why do you think they are using this channel of distribution?

3 Do you think that a shop would be a suitable channel of distribution for the products sold in the advertisements?

Ruffles

Ruffles is a mini-company whose business idea is to make and sell soft toys. It makes three designs - a rabbit, a teddy bear and a frog. It will sell the rabbit for £7, the teddy bear for £5 and the frog for £3. EITHER write a report about the channels of distribution for your mini-enterprise OR answer the following questions.

1 State THREE different channels of distribution it could attempt to use to get its products to the consumer.
2 (a) What are the advantages and disadvantages of each of these channels of distribution for the mini-company?
   (b) Which is the best channel of distribution for it to use and why?

Key terms

Break-of-bulk point - place, such as a warehouse or a port, where goods are unloaded. They are usually then reloaded, often in smaller or larger quantities, and transported elsewhere for sale.

Channel of distribution - the path taken to get products from the manufacturer or service provider to the customer.

Wholesaler - a business which buys in bulk from a manufacturer and then sells the stock on in smaller quantities to retailers.

Checklist ✓

1 What is meant by 'place' in the marketing mix?
2 What is the difference between a wholesaler and a retailer?
3 'A retailer acts as a break-of-bulk point.' What does this mean?
4 How can agents help distribute products?
5 Why are new ships and aircraft sold directly to customers rather than through other channels of distribution?
6 Why do businesses like Kellogg's choose to distribute their products through wholesalers and retailers rather than direct to the customer?
7 When might a small business use an agent to distribute its products?

SUMMARY CASE STUDY

INSURANCE

- Traditionally, insurance companies have sold insurance policies directly to the consumer through sales representatives. A potential customer rings the insurance company to enquire about insurance products. The sales representatives then visit these customers, often at home, explain the policies available and then make a sale.
- Another traditional method of selling is through brokers. These are businesses which deal directly with customers offering advice and support. They organise the buying of insurance by customers from insurance companies. The broker is paid a commission by the insurance company for every policy sold.
- More recently, a growing number of insurance policies have been sold over the telephone. Customers ring up and a telesales worker explains the policy and gives a quote (a price) for taking out the insurance. Motor insurance in particular is now dominated by direct telephone selling. Potential customers are attracted by advertising in newspapers, magazines and *Yellow Pages*.
- Another way of selling insurance directly is through mail shots. Insurance companies have lists of existing customers. They may also buy in lists from other companies. Advertising leaflets are sent out to everyone on the list inviting people to buy the insurance on offer.

Insurance companies use a variety of different channels to sell insurance.

1 (a) List FOUR ways in which insurance companies sell insurance.
   (b) What do you think might be the advantages and disadvantages to an insurance company of each of these ways?
2 Supermarkets are now offering some banking services. Do you think it would be a good idea for them to sell insurance too? In your answer, discuss whether it is likely to be profitable for them to sell insurance and whether it would have any effect on sales of existing products.

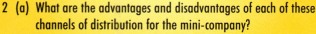

RETAILING

The Boots Company sold £4.5 billion worth of products in 1996-7. Boots The Chemists lies at the heart of the company. In March 1997 there were 1 242 stores in the UK and Eire, selling products such as medicines, health care goods and gifts. The Boots Company also owns Halfords, the car part retailer, Do It All, the do-it-yourself chain and Boots Opticians. Further back in the chain of production, The Boots Group owns Boots Contract Manufacturing which manufactures cosmetics, toiletries and medicines. The company also owns a global health and medication business, Boots Healthcare International, which markets over-the-counter medicines in 150 countries.

? The three shops shown in the photographs offer a variety of different services.
1 Which services are the same for all three shops?
2 How do the services differ between each of them?

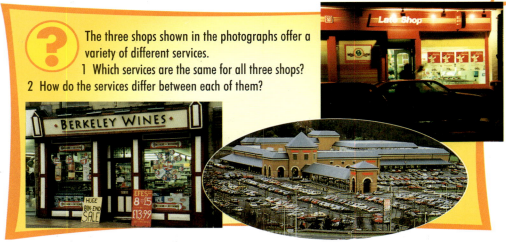

The function of retailers

A RETAILER is a business which specialises in selling goods in small quantities to the consumer. Why don't consumers simply buy these goods directly from manufacturers?

Breaking-of-bulk When you buy a packet of Strepsils, you don't want to buy another 199 at the same time. Boots Healthcare International (BHI) only sells Strepsils in bulk. Retailers, like Boots The Chemists, buy large quantities from BHI and then sell much smaller quantities to the customer. This **breaking-of-bulk** (☞ unit 42) is a very important service offered by retailers.

Convenience BHI produces Strepsils at its plant in Nottingham. Every time you want a packet of Strepsils, you don't want to have to travel to Nottingham to buy them. Boots The Chemists sells these packets in your local area. Convenience is therefore another very important service offered by retailers.

Other services The level of service in a shop or store can be very important to customers. For instance, staff at Boots The Chemists will collect repeat prescriptions from local doctors and have the medicines ready for customers who visit the pharmacy. In stores with developing machines, they offer a range of photographic services, including a one hour development service.

Types of retailers

The most common type of shop is the INDEPENDENT. The shop will be run by the owner. It will almost certainly be a small shop, perhaps in a small local parade of shops. The owner is likely to own just that one shop.

One hundred years ago, nearly all shops were independents. Boots, for instance, was founded by Jesse Boot in 1877 when he took over a shop in Goosegate, Nottingham. However, this century there has been an enormous growth in MULTIPLES. These are **chains** of shops owned by a single company like Boots. Today, the multiples sell far more than the independents. Multiples can be split up into various types.

- **Supermarket chains** sell mainly groceries.
- **Specialist multiples** are chains which sell limited ranges of products. Examples are Comet, which sells electrical equipment, and Miss Selfridge, which sells clothes. Boots The Chemists started off as a specialist multiple, being a chain of chemist shops. Smaller branches of Boots today still fit into this category. They stock a limited range of products typically found in any chemist.
- **Variety chain stores** are chains which sell a wide variety of products. Larger branches of Boots today sell not just pharmaceutical products but also kitchen equipment, gifts, CDs and food, amongst other products. So Boots The Chemists could be classified as a variety chain store.

Many large towns and cities have a **department store.** Such a store may be an independent, owned perhaps by a family. Most department stores, however, are multiples. House of Fraser is a chain of department stores. Like variety chain stores, Department Stores sell a wide variety of goods from clothes to washing machines. They offer one-stop shopping in up-market surroundings.

To try to remain competitive with large supermarket chains, some independent grocery stores have joined **voluntary chains,** like Spar or Mace. The chain is able to buy in bulk and provides support services like advertising. Voluntary chains share some of the same characteristics as **franchise operations** (☞ unit 14).

Large **mail order companies**, like Littlewoods or Great Universal Stores, act as retailers. Next, the specialist multiple, has its own successful mail order business, Next Directory.

The largest single retailer in the UK is the combined Co-operative societies. They are discussed in detail in unit 13.

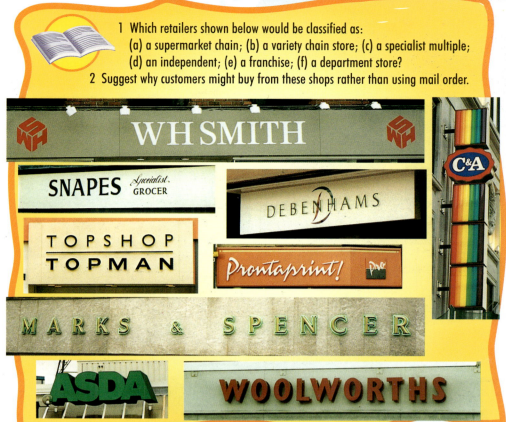

1 Which retailers shown below would be classified as:
(a) a supermarket chain; (b) a variety chain store; (c) a specialist multiple;
(d) an independent; (e) a franchise; (f) a department store?
2 Suggest why customers might buy from these shops rather than using mail order.

Changes in retailing

Retailing, like all industries, has changed enormously over the past 50 years.

Choice Rising income has altered the face of retailing. 50 years ago, most of the week's wages for a family went on basics - rent, heating and food. People had little equipment in their houses. Large increases in spending power mean that consumers can buy a much wider range of goods. Just as they want choice in what they buy, consumers want choice in where they buy.

Sometimes customers want shops which offer the lowest prices. Sometimes, they are looking for other factors, such as convenience, quality of service or after sales care.

Costs One result of increases in spending power is that multiple retailers can take advantage of **economies of scale** (☞ unit 18). Boots The Chemists, for instance, can buy photographic films in far greater bulk than a local

independent shop. This means that it can negotiate lower prices from, say, Kodak or Fuji than an independent. Survival has been difficult for independents in many areas of retailing because the big multiple retailers have such low costs.

Branding Successful multiples have another important advantage over independents. Shops like Boots The Chemists guarantee a certain **quality of service.** Shoppers know what they can expect to find in a Boots store. They know, for instance, that goods will be exchanged without any fuss if they prove unsuitable. They know that they can get advice at the pharmaceutical counter. Multiples have in fact managed to establish a **brand** identity (☞ unit 37) for the service they give. Independents don't have this national brand image. Over the past 50 years, consumers have more and more shopped at branded multiple stores, driving the independents out of business.

Investment Linked to this quality of service has been investment by the

Look at the photographs. The photograph in the centre shows retailing in Preston in 1929. The others show modern retailing.
1 (a) What changes in retailing are shown over time in the photographs?
  (b) Explain THREE factors which might have caused these changes.
2 Shopping on the Internet is a new trend in UK retailing. Do you think that shopping using your computer linked to the Internet will eventually lead to the closing down of most shops in the high street? In your answer, you need to write about the advantages and disadvantages of shopping from home or the office compared to shopping in your local high street.

successful multiples. They have continually changed their ways of operating to cut costs and meet consumer needs. The Boots Company, for instance, often spends money to update its stores. It invests in people by training staff. It also invests in the research and development of new products.

Location The location of shops has changed too. 50 years ago, shoppers either went to the local shop or went into town to the high street. Today, the local shops and the high street are still busy, but a lot of business has also gone to new out-of-town shopping developments. These are designed for people with cars. A few are shopping malls which have a wide range of shops. Examples are the Merry Hill Centre in Dudley, the Brent Cross shopping centre in London or the MetroCentre in Newcastle. Others are more specialised **retail parks** where there might be a few large stores. For

instance, amongst them there might be a Comet store (electrical retailing), an MFI store (furniture) and a Halfords store (bicycles, car parts and accessories). The great advantage to the retailer of out-of-town developments is that the cost of land is much cheaper than in the high street. Shoppers can also park their cars more easily than in the high street to wheel out their trolleys full of goods.

Some local high streets have found it impossible to compete with larger shopping centres. Large chain stores have moved out and independents have closed down. The high street then becomes filled with a mix of empty premises, charity shops, financial outlets like building societies, newsagents and food shops. To prevent this in future, the government has made it more difficult to get planning permission to build out-of-town shopping centres.

Market niches Many high streets are likely to carry on being important shopping centres. The high street can offer a large variety of shops from which customers can buy. Independents are having to offer services which the multiples don't give. Independent grocery stores, for instance, frequently open long hours. They will increasingly have to become niche retailers, providing a unique service and taking a small share of the market.

Use of technology Technology is slowly changing buying habits. Mail order is over one hundred years old, using transport services, the post and the telephone to get goods to people's doorstep. Today, though, mail order doesn't just mean replying to adverts in newspapers or buying from a paper catalogue. QVC, a shopping channel, appears on satellite and cable television. Goods are viewed on television and bought by telephone. More importantly, the Internet is providing shopping opportunities. Using the computer to order products which can be viewed on the Internet is unlikely ever to replace shopping in the high street. But it will become another medium for mail order shopping.

Source: adapted from information supplied by The Boots Company.

Boots' Internet page. Many businesses now have sites on the internet.

In this survey, you want to find out why shoppers use a local parade of shops rather than going elsewhere to do their shopping.

1 Select a local shopping parade. It could be one near school where perhaps the whole class will conduct a survey. Or it could be one near where you live.

2 Construct a questionnaire to use with local shoppers. From your questionnaire, you want to find out why people use the local parade of shops rather than going to a town centre or to a local large supermarket, and the opposite, why people use the town centre rather than the local parade of shops.

3 Conduct the survey. You may go out as a class or you may conduct the survey on your own by asking people in your local parade of shops. You may prefer to ask friends and relatives to complete the questionnaire. Your teacher or lecturer will advise you on the best course of action.

Database/Wordprocessing

4 Analyse your findings. You may want to record the results on a database. What have people said about why they shop locally rather than going to a larger shopping centre?

5 Produce a report, preferably wordprocessed. (a) Explain the purpose of the survey. (b) Describe how you conducted the survey and the nature of your sample. (c) Describe your findings. (d) Evaluate, using your findings, whether the local parade of shops has a future or whether it will disappear as competition from larger shopping centres increases.

Key terms

Independent - a retail store which is run by its owner. This owner is likely to own just one store.
Multiple - a chain of shops owned by a single business.
Retailer - a business which specialises in selling goods in small quantities to the consumer.

Checklist ✓

1 What are the THREE important functions of a retailer?
2 How can a retailer add value to a product?
3 What is the difference between (a) an independent and a multiple retailer and (b) a specialist multiple and a variety chain store?
4 What type of products might a department store sell?
5 Why are there more shops today than 50 years ago?
6 'Successful multiples are those which sell at lowest prices.' Explain whether you think this is true.
7 Why do successful retailers have to invest in their businesses if they are to survive?
8 How has the location of shops changed over the past 50 years?

THE DEPARTMENT STORE

SUMMARY CASE STUDY

In the first half of this century, department stores thrived. They offered a wide range of goods all under one roof. They were the equivalent of today's shopping mall. Then along came the multiples. They offered more choice and many offered lower prices. Department stores also didn't move with the times, catering more and more for middle aged and older customers. By the 1970s, department stores were in crisis.

Since then, though, the most successful have turned themselves around. Department store groups have tended to close their smaller unprofitable stores. They have invested money in refurbishment, changing their layouts and fittings. They have attracted in more young customers by changing their product mix. Often this has been achieved by letting out floor space to well known retailers like Oasis, Miss Selfridge, Wallis or Benetton. They have also concentrated on their strengths. Harrods in London, for instance, has exploited its drawing power as one of London's main tourist attractions. Liberty's in London, famous for its prints, has concentrated investment on its London store after a disastrous attempt to set up regional branches.

Source: adapted from the *Sunday Times*, 22 September 1996.

1 What is a department store?
2 Compare the services offered by a department store to those of a multiple retailer.
3 Explain TWO ways in which a department store benefits if it leases floor space to another retailer.
4 Suggest TWO reasons why smaller department stores tend to be less profitable per foot of selling space than larger department stores.
5 A department store is investigating whether or not to open a food hall, where it would sell upmarket produce. Do you think this would be profitable? Explain your answer carefully.

Making decisions

Businesses receive raw materials and other supplies and send out goods. They need to decide how those goods should be sent: whether by road, rail, sea or air. Their decision about which type of transport to use will depend upon a variety of factors including cost, speed, reliability and suitability.

Shell is most famous for its oil and petrol products. It is also, though, a major producer of natural gas, coal and chemicals. A subsidiary company, Shell International Trading and Shipping Company, is responsible for trading and shipping crude oil products round the world. The company operates a fleet of 36 crude oil and product carriers and is involved with 20 liquid natural gas and liquid petroleum gas carriers for gas products.

? 1 Look at Figure 44.1. What type of transport might be used to get each of the items or people shown in the diagram to and from the school?

Figure 44.1

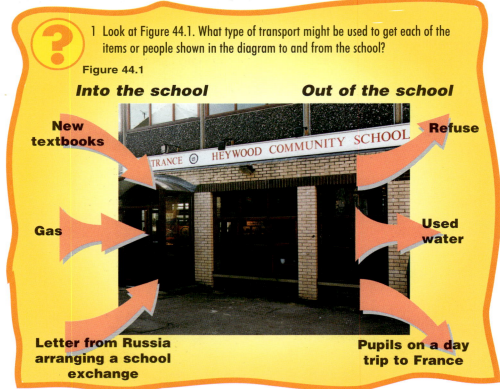

Into the school — New textbooks, Gas, Letter from Russia arranging a school exchange

Out of the school — Refuse, Used water, Pupils on a day trip to France

HEYWOOD COMMUNITY SCHOOL

Different types of transport

Shell transports many different goods, not just in Britain but worldwide. It could use a variety of different types of transport to do this.

Road Road transport is the most important type of transport within the UK today. Shell, for instance, uses oil tankers to distribute petrol and diesel to its 1 850 service stations and large business customers. It employs a transport company, Hays plc, to distribute non-petrol goods like food and motor spares to its service stations. These would be carried in closed high sided lorries. If new equipment were added to a Shell oil refinery, waste might be carried away from the site using open trucks.

Shell also uses container transport. This involves large boxes which can be fitted onto a trailer lorry. The great advantage of containers is that they can easily be lifted off the trailer and put onto a ship or onto a rail wagon.

Rail One hundred years ago, rail was an important transporter of goods. Today, only a few per cent of all goods transported within the UK are carried by rail. However, goods which are carried in bulk for long distances are most suited to rail transport.

Canals Two hundred years ago, canals were vital to inland transport. Today, almost no freight is carried on most canals in the UK, but certain canals and rivers in Europe are still very busy with barges.

Ship Shell uses oil tankers to transport oil around the world. Some oil is sent around the UK, from an oil refinery to a port in coastal tankers, rather than being sent by road or rail.

Air Air freight is growing in importance for goods which require fast delivery. Shell might need a vital component manufactured in Japan for a UK oil refinery. The part could be sent by air to minimise journey times.

Pipelines Shell uses pipelines to transport natural gas, chemicals, oil and oil products. Water is also transported via pipelines.

Choosing a mode of transport

When choosing which type of transport to use, Shell needs to take a number of important factors into consideration.

Cost Shell, like any business, wants to minimise its costs. In Britain, it uses road tankers to transport petrol where it is the cheapest form of transport. It also uses rail. For Shell, the decision about whether to use road or rail depends upon the relative cost of the two forms of transport. In 1992, for instance, when the railways put up their charges to Shell by between 50 and 100 per cent, Shell decided to switch 13 per cent of its rail freight to the roads.

For many businesses, loading and unloading costs are very important. Taking goods by lorry to a rail freight depot, loading it onto a train and then unloading it at the other end of the journey for delivery to its final destination again by road is very expensive. So, although rail transport per mile is cheaper on average than road transport, assuming full loads, the loading costs make rail journeys in the UK

Seismic trucks are used to travel in the Oman desert where Shell and the Korean Gas Company are building a liquid natural gas plant.

uneconomic for most businesses.

However, rail may be more important in the future. Rail becomes typically cost efficient on long journeys over 400 miles. The opening of the Channel Tunnel has given new opportunities for rail to take freight from the UK to European destinations. Many hope that **privatisation** (☞ unit 16) of the railways will lead to lower costs and a more flexible operating environment. Increasing congestion on roads may increase the cost of road deliveries compared to rail. Finally, the government could well tilt the balance between road and rail because it wants to see less congestion and a cleaner environment. It could do this, for instance, by increasing taxes on lorries.

Shell uses tankers to ship oil round the world. Much of the world's general cargo shipping traffic uses containers. These are boxes which can easily be stacked, loaded and unloaded from ship, lorry and rail. This saves the expense of loading and unloading individual items several times during a journey.

Using aeroplanes would be completely unsuitable for transporting petrol. Air transport tends to be used for high value, low bulk, low weight products.

Speed Getting flowers from a distribution point in the UK to a Shell service station forecourt can take hours using road. Taking them by road and sea from the Netherlands where they are grown to the distribution point in the UK

Dairy distribution

In 1972, Jarnail Singh Johal set up a milk round in Wolverhampton. Since then, his business has grown. By 1997, Johal Dairies had a fleet of 25 refrigerated vehicles and was delivering dairy products across the West Midlands region. Milk is still important with 100 000 pints a day delivered. However, today the milk is delivered to shops, cafes, restaurants, hotels, factories and retirement homes as well as to ordinary homes. The business is also building up a substantial non-milk business, delivering all other types of dairy products including cheese and yogurts.

Source: adapted from the *Express and Star*, 29 September 1997.

1 Explain THREE reasons why Johal Dairies uses roads to transport its products rather than rail, canal or air.

Wordprocessing

2 Environmentalists have suggested that far too many road journeys are made each day. If goods need to be transported, they should be transported the least possible distance. Write a letter to an environmental group explaining why it is in the interests of the consumer to have daily deliveries of dairy products across the West Midlands by Johal Dairies.

Figure 44.2 *Area covered by Johal Dairies.*

may take too long for the flowers to arrive in peak condition. So air transport may be used. Different types of transport give different times of delivery depending on the distance to be travelled and the quality of the infrastructure, such as road and rail links.

Reliability To operate efficiently, a Shell service station needs to know when supplies will be delivered. If goods aren't in the shop, Shell will lose sales. Reliability of delivery is therefore vital. In 1997, to help improve reliability, Shell signed a contract with Hays, a transport company, to deliver most goods to Shell shops. Before, a Shell service station could get up to 40 deliveries a week from 15 different distributors.

Safety Shell is always conscious of safety issues because oil and petrol can be dangerous products.

Air

Train

TYPES OF TRANSPORT

Canal

Road

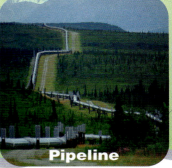
Pipeline

Ship

Whether to send its products by sea or land may be affected by safety considerations.

Location and infrastructure

Because the UK is an island, Shell may use coastal ship tankers, as well as pipelines and road tankers, to transport oil and petrol around the country. On the continent of Europe, waterways (ie canals and rivers), pipelines or road transport might be the only option for similar distances. Where a business is located and what transport links are available will, to some extent, determine the choice of transport. One reason why road transport has grown so much over the past 40 years in the UK has been the growth of the motorway network. With very few new motorway projects now going ahead over the next ten years, road transport could become more difficult and less attractive if journey times increase. On the other hand, more night time deliveries, when roads are less busy, could allow companies to continue using road transport.

Type of good Flowers delivered to a Shell service station can easily be delivered by lorry. Taking oil long distances over land is often better achieved using a fixed system like a pipeline. In general:
- the bulkier the product;
- the greater the quantities that have to be transported on a regular basis;
- the longer the distance that has to be travelled;

the more mass transit systems like railways, ships or pipelines gain a cost advantage. Road is most useful for relatively small loads taken over relatively short distances.

Source: adapted from information provided by Shell.

Colombian coal

Coal is Colombia's third most important export, after oil and coffee. In 1996, export earnings reached $871 million and the industry is still growing fast. New mines are being opened whilst existing mines are increasing their production.

Colombian coal is highly competitive internationally. It is mined in low cost open cast mines. Companies only have to remove six tonnes of material to produce one tonne of coal, compared to a world average of between 12 and 15 tonnes. Colombian coal is also clean burning, with a less than 1 per cent sulphur content. This cuts down on the need for power stations to install expensive anti-pollution equipment. Finally, most of the country's reserves are only 200 miles from their export terminals, compared to 1 200 miles in the case of South Africa and 500 miles for Australia.

However, coal is relatively expensive to transport because it is a low cost, high bulk product. The main markets for Colombian coal lie in North America, Europe and the Far East. Transport costs therefore have to be kept to a minimum. Coal is taken from Colombian ports where facilities have been built specifically to deal with the loading of coal onto ships. Some mines are connected to ports by railway lines. Others have to use higher cost road transport.

Source: adapted from the *Financial Times*, 12 December 1997.

1 (a) Why is Colombian coal cheaper to mine than the world average? (b) What other competitive advantages does it have?

2 Suggest why Colombian coal would be transported: (a) by ship rather than by air; (b) by rail from the mine to the port rather than by lorry if possible.

Wordprocessing

3 The La Loma coal mine, where production is expanding and where 5.5 million tonnes of coal were mined in 1997, is not connected to the rail system. As the manager of the coal mine, write a letter to the Colombian government explaining why it should build a 50 mile branch line to the mine.

Air transport

Transporting goods by air is expensive. Traditionally, only documents and small packages have been sent air freight because of this. However, increasing use is now being made of air freight to transport larger packages. This reflects changes in the global business environment. Businesses are demanding shorter lead times for orders. If they have a machine which is out of order, they want the part immediately, not in 15 days time. If the part is high cost, then it is cheaper to pay for air transport rather than have stocks in transit. Some customers insist that stocks be delivered within 24 hours of order. This may only be possible using air freight.

For instance, Volvo uses air freight to get some parts for its Swedish factories from its UK suppliers. Parts can be collected as late as 9 o'clock at night from UK factories and be on the production line at Volvo in Sweden by 6.30 the following morning.

Source: adapted from the *Financial Times*, 13 June 1997.

1 What is the main: (a) advantage; and (b) disadvantage; of using airfreight compared to, say, sea transport?
2 Explain TWO reasons why the demand for air freight has been increasing over time.
3 An airfreight company wants to increase its share of the market. Suggest THREE points it should emphasise to potential customers about the quality of its service and explain why they are important to the customer.

Checklist ✓

1 List SIX different types of transport.
2 Give ONE type of transport which would be suitable for transporting the following and ONE reason why it would be suitable: (a) water; (b) parcels; (c) car components from a factory in Birmingham to one in Coventry; (d) finished cars from a factory in Birmingham to a dealer in Rome; (e) flowers from a grower in Holland to a wholesale market in London; (f) iron ore from Norway to the UK.
3 Why it is expensive to use several different types of transport to carry a product on one journey?
4 Why would bulky, low value products like bricks not be transported by aeroplane?
5 Explain what sort of products might be transported by air.
6 How might the building of: (a) a new motorway; and (b) a new high speed rail link affect how businesses transport their products?
7 Why is reliability of transport important for a business?

EWS

SUMMARY CASE STUDY

EWS (English Welsh & Scottish Railway) is the company which now runs much of railfreight business in the UK. It is owned by a US company which has been successful in making a profit out of running freight in America. In contrast, the freight division of the old British Rail was loss making.

EWS needs to concentrate on two areas if it is to attract business. It must develop services which allow relatively small amounts of freight to be carried at a profit. The old British Rail had increasingly concentrated on handling only bulk cargoes. The result was that the business failed to grow. Second, EWS needs to develop services to Europe. The Channel Tunnel provides a significant opportunity to attract long distance freight away from the roads.

EWS has already been heavily marketing its services to companies which would only send relatively small shipments with some success. It has cut costs to make these services profitable. One obstacle it faces in long distance travel is the high charge being made by Eurotunnel for putting trains through the Channel Tunnel. They are charging 2½ times the amount per tonne of freight to EWS than they charge to road hauliers which send lorries through the Tunnel. The British government, which wants to see more freight carried by rail, is negotiating with Eurotunnel to cut the freight charges to make them comparable to lorry charges.

Source: adapted from the *Financial Times*, 6 and 7 October 1997.

1 What is meant by: (a) 'bulk cargo'; (b) 'long distance freight'; (c) 'road hauliers'?
2 EWS needs to increase the amount of freight it carries. Explain TWO ways in which it might achieve this.
3 A dairy company is looking at its transport arrangements. It is wondering if it could use rail: (a) to supply its Scottish customers in Edinburgh and Glasgow from its factory in Devon; (b) to buy milk in bulk from France. At the moment, it uses lorries to deliver to Scotland but has not found a profitable way of importing milk from the Continent. It should be remembered that dairy products are perishable. Discuss THREE factors which the company needs to consider in deciding whether or not to use rail in these two cases.

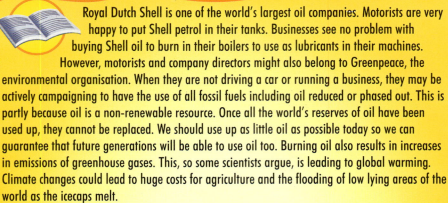

Making decisions

Marketing is about selling products to buyers. However, what if there are problems with the product? Perhaps it is unsafe, or could damage the environment. Should a business carry on selling the product? Also, what if sales can be increased if the business makes claims about the product which are difficult to prove false? Should a business make claims which it cannot back up with evidence? Finally, what if the product sold is defective or doesn't meet the description applied to it? What should the business do in these cases?

Nike is a multinational sports goods company. Perhaps most well known in the UK for its trainers, it manufactures a wide range of sports clothing and other goods. It promotes its products heavily through advertising and sponsorship. Professional sport is a major gainer from this sponsorship.

Royal Dutch Shell is one of the world's largest oil companies. Motorists are very happy to put Shell petrol in their tanks. Businesses see no problem with buying Shell oil to burn in their boilers to use as lubricants in their machines. However, motorists and company directors might also belong to Greenpeace, the environmental organisation. When they are not driving a car or running a business, they may be actively campaigning to have the use of all fossil fuels including oil reduced or phased out. This is partly because oil is a non-renewable resource. Once all the world's reserves of oil have been used up, they cannot be replaced. We should use up as little oil as possible today so we can guarantee that future generations will be able to use oil too. Burning oil also results in increases in emissions of greenhouse gases. This, so some scientists argue, is leading to global warming. Climate changes could lead to huge costs for agriculture and the flooding of low lying areas of the world as the icecaps melt.

In 1997, Shell responded to these concerns by announcing a £300 million investment programme in research and development in renewable energies spread over five years. It will focus mainly on solar power and biomass, generating electricity from burning plants and trees. It will also spend some money on wind power.

Critics point out that £300 million spread over five years is only a fraction of what Shell will continue to spend on finding and development new oil fields.

Source: adapted from the *Financial Times*, 17 October 1997.

1 Why do environmental groups want to see less oil being burnt?
2 Oil companies like Shell won't stop selling oil. (a) Why do you think they don't want to stop production? (b) Suggest TWO reasons which the oil companies might give as to why abandoning oil as a fuel would be bad for businesses.
3 Suggest TWO reasons why Shell is investing £300 million in alternative energy research.

DTP
4 Produce two posters. You could use a DTP package.
   (a) One poster should give the views of environmentalists about the issue of burning oil.
   (b) The other should give the possible views of oil companies like Shell.

Ethical considerations

Nike is a leading brand in the sports goods market. It manufactures high quality products which sell at premium prices around the world. However, in the mid 1990s it faced a marketing problem. It was criticised in the press for its factories in Third World countries. Its goods were made in the Far East because labour and materials were cheap. Many multinationals have manufacturing plants in poorer countries around the world to take advantage of lower costs of production. Nike, though, was accused of buying goods from factories where working conditions were poor and even dangerous for the workers. The press compared the high prices that Nike goods were selling for in the shops with the low wages paid to workers and the low costs of production.

Nike responded by setting up a system of inspection for the factories that it used. Where it found that working conditions were unsatisfactory, it either stopped using the factory or it improved the working conditions. However, in the meantime, it had received a lot of bad publicity which could have discouraged customers from buying its products.

Nike faced up to an ethical problem. Was it doing right or wrong? All businesses face ethical problems. With some companies, the ethical problem is obvious. Should a manufacturer of rifles be making arms which will kill people? Should asbestos companies around the world stop making asbestos because it has been shown to be such a dangerous material?

Other businesses face less obvious ethical problems. For instance, when advertising a product, should they use images which are known to offend some groups in society? Should they use images of beautiful women to sell products which are bought mainly by men? Should they use violent images in an advertisement when there is so much crime in society?

Another ethical issue concerns information. For instance, does a drugs company which has evidence that one of its drugs has side effects stop selling the drug? Should a washing powder manufacturer claim in a advert that its washing powder 'washes whiter' than other powders on the market when there is no scientific proof

1 Anti-smoking pressure groups believe that the activities of tobacco companies should be restricted. They have proposed three different measures which they believe would reduce smoking: (i) a substantial rise in the tax on cigarettes, pushing the price of a packet of cigarettes up to, say, £5 for a packet of 20; (ii) a ban on smoking in any public place, like in the street, at work or in a pub; (iii) a complete ban on the sale of cigarettes.

You work for the marketing department of a tobacco company. Write three short reports, one for each proposal, aimed at the general public and newspapers. Explain the disadvantages of the three proposed measures for the public.

2 Do you think that smoking should be curbed or banned by the government or do you think that people should be allowed to choose what to buy in a free market?

that it does? What should a tobacco company tell its customers?

Ethics and the market

Many businesses would argue that **the market** makes sure that they act correctly. If people really are shocked by an advertisement by a company then they will stop buying that company's products. If a drug company knows that one of its drugs is causing harmful side effects, but carries on selling the drug, then it could lose its reputation, its future customers and face being sued for damages.

Critics argue that, in some cases, businesses only think about the short term. A new business might advertise 'high quality double glazing at incredibly low prices'. What is installed might be very poor quality windows. Having made a short term profit, the business might stop

trading leaving plenty of dissatisfied customers.

Even more serious is when businesses are able to persuade customers over a long period of time that their products work when in fact they don't. In the past, for instance, adverts for drugs have claimed that they could cure everything from baldness to blindness, when they could not. For decades the world's tobacco companies denied that there was any link between smoking and cancer.

The law

Because the market can't always prevent businesses from misleading their customers or supplying inadequate goods, governments have stepped in to pass consumer protection laws. If a business breaks the following laws, it can be prosecuted and fined under **criminal law.**

The Trade Descriptions Act 1968
This states that it is illegal for products to be incorrectly described. If a sweater says that it is machine washable at 40 degrees, then the colours in the sweater mustn't run at that temperature.

Should these advertisements from 1945 and 1949 be used today? Could they be used?

The Weights and Measures Acts

These acts make it illegal for a business to sell goods which are underweight or short measured.

The Food and Drugs Act 1955

This makes it illegal to sell food which is unfit for human consumption. It also lays down minimum standards for what must be contained in a food. For instance, a meat sausage must contain at least 30 per cent meat.

Consumer Credit Act 1974

This gives consumers rights when taking out credit to buy products, such as the fact that a consumer must be given a copy of any credit agreement signed.

Fining the business doesn't help the consumer get his or her money back. To do this, consumers have to use **civil law** to sue businesses. The two main Acts under civil law are the **Sale of Goods Act 1979** and the **Supply of Goods and Services Act 1982.** These acts allow consumers to sue a business if it sells them a product which is not of merchantable quality, isn't fit for the purpose or doesn't meet the description applied. For instance, a sweater sold with a hole in it is not of merchantable quality. A glue sold for glass which doesn't glue glass together is not fit for the purpose. Trousers labelled yellow in a presentation pack but which turn out to be blue do not meet the description applied.

Codes of practice

The government has encouraged businesses to adopt codes of practice as an alternative to passing laws. Codes of practice are rules which businesses voluntarily agree to keep, but have no legal status. One important agency which enforces codes of practice is the **Advertising Standards Authority** (ASA). The British codes of advertising and sales promotion practice state that advertising must be legal, decent, honest and truthful and must not cause grave or widespread

offence.

The ASA monitors all advertising except on television or radio. It is concerned with such things as the portrayal of women and children, and alcohol advertisements. Large companies will often ask the ASA to check that their advertising campaign complies with the BCAP.

Consumers and businesses have a right to complain to the ASA about any advertisement. The ASA receives about 10 000 complaints each year. Many complaints do not merit formal investigation. Around one-third are investigated. If the complaint is upheld, the ASA will ask the business to stop the advertisement. This was the case in 1991 when the ASA received

UNITED COLORS OF BENETTON.

800 written complaints about a Benetton advertisement of a new born baby. The company withdrew the advertisement at the ASA's request.

The ASA can't force businesses to withdraw advertisements. However, it can make it uncomfortable for businesses to ignore its requests. It can also discourage misleading advertisements appearing in the

The Great Film Company is run by Abnash, Steve, Gary and Suk Lin. They got 100 people to their first Thursday lunchtime showing in a run-down lecture theatre. But they had problems.

Gary was supposed to bring in his parents' Nicam video recorder, amplifier and hi-fi speakers, but he didn't ask his parents whether he could borrow them till the night before. They refused, saying they were afraid that they might get stolen or damaged. Suk Lin was supposed to have asked the teacher in charge of audio-visual equipment if they could borrow the large screen TV set but she forgot. In the end, they had to show the film on a small screen school TV and a school video with mono sound.

Steve was in charge of buying the chocolate bars. He bought 30, so 70 people didn't get a chocolate bar. Abnash, who was in charge of hiring the copyright film, didn't book the film in advance. When she got to the video shop on the Thursday, someone had already borrowed Death Squads 3. So she borrowed Death Squads 2 (an 18 certificate) instead.

They forgot that registration was at 2.00 and the film lasted 90 minutes. So they said they would show the rest of the film the next day, Friday. Abnash suddenly realised that they would have to pay for two days' rental. So she shouted out as everybody was leaving that there would be an extra 20p charge to see the rest of the film.

The good thing was that, after they had paid 20p each for the chocolate bars and £4 to rent the film, they made a profit. 50 people came back to see the rest of the film on Friday.

1 Calculate how much profit the Great Film Company made on the showing of the film.
2 Explain FIVE ways in which you think the mini-company acted in an 'unfair' way.
3 Suggest TWO ways in which the mini-company broke the law.
4 Abnash is very excited by the profit the company made in its first week. She is thinking of booking Horror City for showing next Thursday. What do you think might be the customer response if the showing went ahead and why?
5 The Great film company has had organisational, legal and ethical problems in its first week. What do you think the company should do now? In your answer discuss whether or not the company can get around these problems or whether the problems are so great that it should change its business idea.

first place. The ASA does have the legal sanction of referring a business to the Office of Fair Trading, which may take out an injunction to prevent certain claims in future advertisements.

Pressure groups

PRESSURE GROUPS are a further check on the activities of businesses. The Consumers' Association, for instance, is an organisation which defends consumers' rights by investigating and publishing reports on particular products. It also lobbies industry and government to promote consumers' interests.

There are also **trade organisations.** These are organisations of businesses which defend their rights. They might take action, for instance, to curb the power of large, powerful suppliers or customers.

Source: adapted from the Observer, 10 November 1997; The Advertising Standards Authority Limited; the *Financial Times*, various.

Checklist ✔

1 List FIVE examples of areas which might give offence in advertising. For each one, give an example of an advertisement which you think might give offence to someone in this area.
2 Do you think that a manufacturer of weapons should continue to make and sell these products? Give arguments for and against.
3 How might a business be less than truthful when it deals with its customers?
4 Explain how the market can encourage businesses to act ethically when marketing their products.
5 How does the Trade Descriptions Act 1968 help protect consumers?
6 Describe the work of the Advertising Standards Authority.
7 How does the Consumer's Association work to protect consumer rights?

Key terms

Pressure group - a group which attempts to influence business, government and individuals.

'Holiday hell' couple win cash payment

A Wolverhampton couple who endured a fortnight's holiday hell in Turkey have been awarded £750 by a court. Julie and Erich Friedl now call tour operators First Choice their last choice, and claim they caught gastroenteritis in a hotel complex that they say 'had everything wrong with it'.

They arrived at the Sun Club Gunes Holiday Village last July to find more than double the number of apartments promised in the brochure. The supposedly quiet location was actually extremely noisy, said the couple, and was more than two miles from the Friedl's chosen resort of Incekum. 'We caught gastroenteritis because the complex was so dirty. We weren't the only ones, the holiday rep actually ran out of complaint forms.'

A judge at the Wolverhampton Small Claims Court awarded them a total of £750 compensation for the two week holiday which cost £1 100 after First Choice admitted failing to indicate adequate information about the complex. Earlier this year, a Yorkshire family won £1 000 compensation after experiencing similar troubles at the same holiday complex.

Source: adapted from the *Express & Star*, 30 September 1997.

1 What complaints did the Friedl's make against the holiday company?
2 The Friedl's sued the company under the Supply of Goods and Services Act. (a) How does this Act protect consumers? (b) Why did they win their case under this Act?

SUMMARY CASE STUDY

ADVERTISING

Look at the article on advertising.
1 How does: (a) the law; and (b) a voluntary association help protect the consumer from misleading claims made by the makers of medicines?

Graphics
2 Design an advertisement for a medical/health product which would be both illegal and offend against the code of practice of the Proprietary Association of Great Britain. You will need to choose a name for your product and then make claims about what it can do.
3 Explain why your advertisement is illegal and offends against the code of practice.

Source: the *Financial Times*, 19 March, 1994.

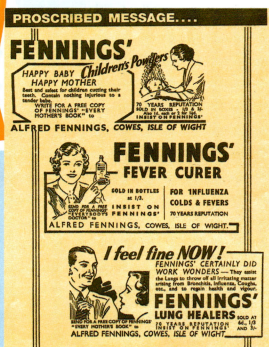

PROSCRIBED MESSAGE....

This 1940s advertisement from the archives of the Proprietary Association of Great Britain would now be illegal because of a ban on absolute statements such as "best and safest" or suggestions that any remedy could restore "health and vigour".

The association today launches its revised rules on how members are allowed to advertise products. A ban on the use of celebrities to endorse medicines is one of the changes. Advertisements will also have to carry the words "always read the label" and the name of the medicine's active ingredient.

The association scrutinises 4,000 advertisements a year to ensure they comply with the product licence, the Medicines Act and advertising codes of practice.

Making decisions

Every business has to decide how it will organise the production of the good or service it will sell. It has to plan:
- what inputs it needs to use and where it will purchase its supplies;
- how to organise production;
- what stocks it needs to keep;
- how it will sell the finished product to its customers.

Unilever is an international company, manufacturing and selling products throughout five continents. Sales turnover in 1996 was £33.5 billion. It has a number of main product areas. Foods include brands such as Magnum ice creams, Blue Band margarine and Lipton teas. Detergents include Persil soap powder and Jif cleaner. Personal products include Organics shampoo, Pond's cream and Vaseline. Unilever's plantations, plant science and trading operations include tea and palm oil plantations.

Planning

Any new product, whether it is a good or a service, goes through a planning stage before it can be produced and then sold. In the planning stage, someone has to decide:
- what is to be produced;
- how the product is to be made;
- where production is to take place;
- who will be the likely buyers of the product;
- how the product will be sold.

A manufacturer may have to carry out scientific or technological **research**. Persil washing powder was the result of research in the early part of the twentieth century. In Stuttgard, Prof. Giessler and Dr. Bauer combined a soap with a bleaching agent. This mixture was produced as a powder, named 'Persil', which dissolved in water. It was then sold by a German chemical business to Crosfields, a UK company. Crosfields joined with Lever Brothers, now part of Unilever, in 1919.

Any new product has to go through a process of **development**, where the original research idea is turned into a product which can be

sold to the customer. How can washing powder be manufactured in large quantities? In what sized packets should it be sold? What packaging will be needed to keep the washing powder in perfect condition? How long can it be stored and in what conditions?

RESEARCH AND DEVELOPMENT (R&D) is potentially risky. Unilever is constantly coming up with ideas for new products or ways of improving existing products. Nearly all are rejected before they get to the stage where they are sold to customers. However, a few survive the rigorous process of development to become successful products like Persil.

EITHER Your mini-company may be involved in the production of a good - such as book marks, photographs of your school or college, or clothes.
(a) What research and development did you undertake?
(b) How many ideas did you reject before you came to your final design?
(c) Did you still have to modify your product even after the first few were sold?
OR Assume that your mini-company is going to manufacture and sell boxer shorts.
(a) Make a list of all the things that you have got to find out about before you even make a prototype pair of boxer shorts.
(b) Discuss THREE choices that you have made from your list in (a). For instance, you would have to decide what colour your boxer shorts would be. What factors would make you choose one colour rather than another?

Purchasing

In a large business, the **buying department** is in charge of buying in goods and services needed for production. At Unilever, the buying department is responsible for buying minerals such as phosphates to soften water, enzymes to produce bio-chemical reactions, surfactants to remove dirt, and other ingredients which go into manufacturing Persil. It is also responsible for buying the packaging - the cardboard boxes - in which Persil is sold.

The buying department will look at a number of factors when deciding what to buy from the SUPPLIER.

Price The buying department will be looking for the best possible price given the quality required.

Quality The buyers will know the minimum quality standard. This may be laid down in a **product specification**, a written document which describes exactly what is required. Only suppliers able to supply to specification will be considered.

Sportpress is a small publisher. It is currently preparing for the launch of a new coffee table book called 'Golf Courses of the UK'. It plans to launch the book in August in preparation for the very important Christmas season when most of its predicted first year 2 000 sales will take place. It hopes over the 6 year lifetime of the book to sell a total of 5 000 copies and make a profit of £1 000.

The book will be in full colour using high quality glossy paper. It has invited three paper suppliers to quote for the paper which will be used for the 5 000 copies.

- Richardson and Gillick have put in the lowest quote at £12 000. One problem with its tender is that it can only supply slightly inferior quality paper compared to the paper specified by Sportpress. The book would then not have quite as luxurious a look as planned. The company has not always been totally reliable in terms of delivery dates in the past.
- John Waterson has put in the next lowest quote of £12 500. It can only deliver the paper two months later than the date on the specification. This would mean that the book would not be published till October, risking the loss of part of the first season's sales.
- HB Papers has put in the highest quote of £13 000. It is able to deliver on time and has always been reliable in the past.

1 Which paper supplier do you think Sportpress should use? Explain your reasons carefully.

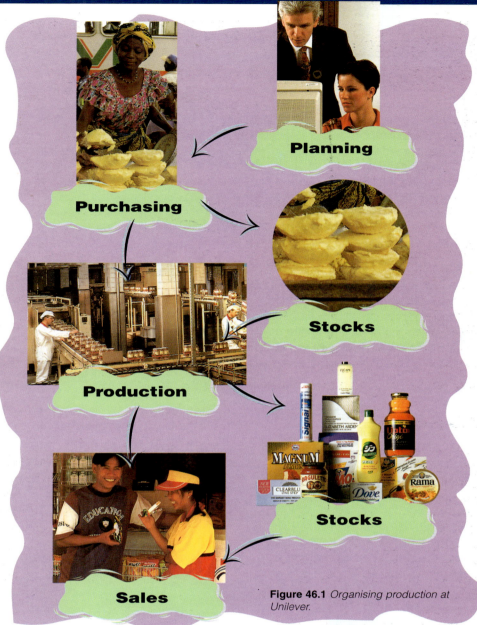

Figure 46.1 *Organising production at Unilever.*

Service The buyer will be looking for suppliers which supply on time and can be flexible, accepting lower orders or higher orders if necessary. They want to make sure that the supplier is financially stable and will not go out of business before completing an order.

Production

In a large manufacturing business, the **production manager** is responsible for deciding how goods should be produced. At Unilever, the production manager in charge of producing Persil aims to:
- produce cost effectively;

- ensure that the product meets the strict quality specifications, such as composition, colour and flow properties.

Stocks

Any business is likely to have STOCKS. Unilever has stocks of minerals and enzymes waiting to be used for the manufacture of Persil. It also has stocks of finished boxes of Persil waiting for delivery to customers. Supermarkets which sell washing powders will have stocks of Persil on their shelves and perhaps also in their store rooms. **Stock management** is very important to a business.

Office furniture

President is an office furniture manufacturer based in Hertfordshire. In 1995, it launched a new range of office furniture called Kyo, Japanese for 'today'. It was carefully designed to be stylish as well as meeting the needs of modern office workers. President identified flexibility as one key need. Increasingly, offices are being reorganised on a regular basis to keep pace with changing work patterns. Kyo is designed to be as flexible as possible with 35 items in a modular range which can be fitted together.

The company worked closely with suppliers when developing the range. For instance, discussions with Taylor Engineering and Plastics, which makes most of the plastic parts for the cupboards and other storage parts of the range, prevented President making some basic mistakes in the design.

£7 million was spent on new production equipment, including computer controlled machines. Production processes were rethought. The extra speed with which machines could be changed to do different jobs means that products can be made far more quickly. Stocks of finished products are less, despite the fact that orders can now be made within two weeks instead of four months in 1990.

Source: adapted from the *Financial Times*, 9 October 1995.

1 How did research and development affect the design of the Kyo range?
2 Why were suppliers important for President?
3 Explain why new production methods meant that less stock needed to be kept.
4 President finds that one of its suppliers is sending an unacceptably high number of faulty parts for the Kyo range. Suggest TWO ways in which it could deal with this problem. Give the advantages and disadvantages of each of your suggestions.

Cost Stocks cost money to hold. For instance, assume that Unilever holds £1 million of enzymes and it has to borrow the money from its bankers to pay for that stock. Then, at a yearly rate of interest of 10 per cent, it is costing the company £100 000 per year or nearly £300 per day to keep that stock. What's more, the stock has to be kept in a warehouse and that costs money to build or rent, insure and run. Stock can also perish. Enzymes deteriorate over time. For all these reasons, Unilever keeps its stock of enzymes to a minimum to prevent **overstocking.**

Production needs Holding too little stock, **understocking**, could lead to loss of production and sales. If Unilever does not hold enough enzyme stocks, then its production lines could be stopped because it doesn't have the raw materials. Equally, Unilever wants to hold enough stocks of finished Persil to be able to supply customers immediately when orders come in.

Price Buying raw materials and components in large quantities may mean that Unilever can buy at competitive prices. Hence, holding more stock could reduce costs.

Sometimes, levels of stock are shown on a chart as in Figure 46.2. When stocks are received by the business, stock levels rise, shown by a vertical rise in the stock line. The maximum stock level on the chart shows the maximum amount of stock the business has decided to keep at any one time. The re-order level shows the level of stock at which the business orders new stock. Because there is delay between ordering new stock and it arriving, stock levels carry on falling before suddenly rising when the stock is delivered. If stock levels go below the minimum shown on the chart, the the business may have difficulty carrying on production.

Many businesses now try to keep stocks to a minimum. They organise production so that stocks are delivered only when

they are needed. This is called 'Just-in-time' (JIT) production (☞ unit 48).

Sale

There is no point in producing if what is produced can't be sold. In the past, many businesses were **product orientated**. This meant that they made a product and hoped that it would sell. Today, an increasing number of businesses are **market orientated**. This means that they try to find out what their customers want to buy and then they make a product designed around the needs of the customer.

Production is important in sales. The product has to be of the right quality for the price to be charged. Costs of production have to be low enough for the business to set a price which will attract customers. Products must be available for sale when the customer wants to buy.

How a business sets about selling its products has already been discussed in units 34 to 45.

Source: adapted in part from Unilever, *Annual Review*, 1996 and information provided by Lever Brothers Ltd.

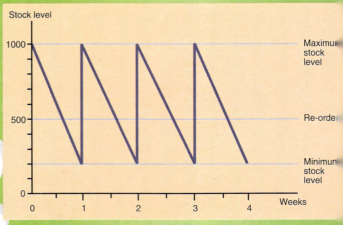

- 800 goods are used each week;
- Stock levels are not allowed to rise above 1 000 goods or fall below 200 goods;
- Stocks are re-ordered when they reach 500 goods;
- 800 goods are re-ordered and take around 3 days to arrive.

Figure 46.2

Jim is the stock manager of a small company which makes products from metal sheets. The metal sheets are purchased monthly from a steel wholesaler. Demand fluctuates during the year, and is greater in the winter months than in the summer months. The pattern of stock holding is shown in Figure 46.3.

1 Identify the: (a) maximum stock level; (b) minimum stock level; (c) re-order level; (d) re-order quantity.
2 On 1 June, Jim had 2 000 sheets of metal in stock. By the 31 July, this had fallen to 400 sheets. How many did he have in stock on: (a) 1st August; (b) 31 August; (c) 1st November?
3 (a) What happened to stock levels in June and July compared to September?
   (b) What does this indicate about sales in those months?
4 In late November, there was a sudden unexpected rush of orders. How can you tell this from the stock graph?

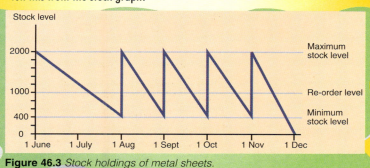

Figure 46.3 *Stock holdings of metal sheets.*

key terms

Research and development (R&D) - the process of scientific and technological research and then development of the findings of that research before a product is launched.
Stocks - materials that a business holds, either waiting to be used in the production process, or finished stock waiting to be delivered to its customers.
Supplier - a business which sells to or supplies products to another business.

Checklist ✓

1 What is the difference between research and development?
2 'R&D is a very risky activity for a business.' Why is this true?
3 What does a purchasing manager do in a business?
4 Why is a product specification important for a purchasing manager?
5 What does a production manager do in a business?
6 What is the difference between an input and an output of a business?
7 List FIVE raw materials or products which are needed by a car manufacturer to make a car.
8 What is the difference between overstocking and understocking?
9 Why is it important for a business not to carry excess stocks?
10 'Management stated that the company needed to be far more market orientated.' What does this mean?

SUMMARY CASE STUDY

NISSAN UK

Nissan UK manufactures cars from a plant in Sunderland in the North East of England. When it was built in the mid-1980s, it set standards for the rest of the British car industry. Production was modelled on Japanese work practices. Since then, it has continued to improve its standards.
    Enormous attention is paid to the purchasing of components from suppliers. Figures 46.4 and 46.5 show, for instance, how delivery times and the number of defective parts supplied have improved by working closely with suppliers. Sometimes Nissan cuts the prices it will pay for components. But it is prepared to send its experts into a supplier to work out how the supplier can cut its costs and so afford to take a price cut.
    On the production line, the time taken to assemble a car has gradually fallen. For instance, between 1992 and 1996, Nissan cut assembly time by an average 10 per cent each year. In part, this has been achieved by looking at every small part of the production process and asking whether a slightly different way of doing the job would achieve savings in time. Quality has improved too. Nissan has now achieved 'no touch' manufacturing. This means that cars coming off the production line are free of faults and don't need any work on them to put faults right. Stocks are kept to a minimum through a policy of just-in-time delivery. Wherever possible, stocks are delivered and immediately used. So hardly any stocks are kept on the site.

Sources: adapted from *The Sunday Times*, 6 April 1996.

1 What is (a) a car 'component' and (b) a 'supplier'?
2 (a) What factors do you think influence Nissan when deciding which suppliers to place orders with?
   (b) Using the charts, explain how suppliers have improved their products and the service they supply.
3 How has production been improved at Nissan?
4 There is a strike at a components supplier for Nissan. It is the only supplier of the part to the factory. Without the part, cars cannot be completed.
   (a) What might be the effect on production at Nissan?
   (b) Discuss the advantages and disadvantages of just-in-time delivery for Nissan.

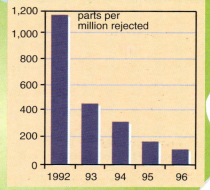

Figure 46.4 *Supplier delivery performance.*
Source: adapted from Nissan UK.

Figure 46.5 *Quality of supplied components.*

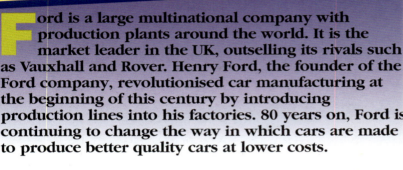

Making decisions

A business must decide how to organise production. There are three main choices:
- should each item be produced separately?
- should the product be made in batches?
- should the product be made continuously?

The decision is likely to be influenced by:
- cost - which is the cheapest method of production?
- quality - which method will ensure the right quality of product?
- quantity - how much needs to be made?

Ford is a large multinational company with production plants around the world. It is the market leader in the UK, outselling its rivals such as Vauxhall and Rover. Henry Ford, the founder of the Ford company, revolutionised car manufacturing at the beginning of this century by introducing production lines into his factories. 80 years on, Ford is continuing to change the way in which cars are made to produce better quality cars at lower costs.

Job production

Ford's car assembly plants in the UK are based at Dagenham, Halewood and Southampton. Ford is continually investing in its car production facilities. In 1998, for instance, the company announced a £36 million paint shop improvement at its Transit plant in Southampton. The method of production used to put up or improve a building, for example, is called JOB PRODUCTION. This is where a single item is produced from start to finish. Each item produced is likely to be unique. Other examples of job production include bridges, new motorways, taxi rides, a high quality restaurant meal and a work of art.

Batch production

When Ford manufactures a car, it buys in (or **sources**) many of the parts from other manufacturers. For example, it buys light components from Lucas and tyres from Goodyear. The parts have

Beaudesert

Andrew Ginger is a partner in a firm which sells four poster beds. They don't come cheap. However, for a price of between £6 000 and £15 000, you get a unique creation. Based mainly on 18th century originals, customers choose the size, the design and the hangings.

The only stock the business keeps is a display bed in the show room and samples of fabric. Each bed is made to order. Andrew Ginger designs the bed with the customer. He then has the woodwork joinery for the bed done by a business in the Cotswolds whilst the carving of the wood is done in London. The 65 metres of fabrics typically needed are made up by a firm in Kent.

The business sells 15-20 beds a year. Andrew Ginger sees clients, does the designing and also assembles the bed on the client's premises.

Source: adapted from the *Financial Times*, 12 April 1997.

1 What type of production is used to make a Beaudesert four poster bed?
2 Why do you think this might be the best way for production to be organised?
3 Suggest why customers are prepared to pay between £6 000 and £15 000 for a bed when they could get a mass produced four poster bed for as little as £500.

Job production

Advantages The quality of work done is usually high. Employing skilled workers leads to higher quality. Also, workers tend to be relatively well motivated because the work they do is never quite the same, which again leads to higher quality work. Job production allows customers to order exactly what they want, rather than having to accept something which is mass produced.

Disadvantages Job production is a relatively expensive way of producing a good or service. High quality, high wage labour is usually needed to cope with producing a one-off product. British Aerospace workers in the aerospace division tend to be **skilled workers**. The work may also be **labour intensive**, with fewer opportunities for automating large parts of the process.

A paint shop improvement at the Ford transit plant in Southampton is an example of job production.

often been made using BATCH PRODUCTION techniques. This is where a business makes a number of products (a **batch**) and then changes production to make a batch of another component or product. It will remake the original product when it is needed again. For instance, a ball bearing manufacturer might produce a million ball bearings of one size over three days and then change its machines to start making ball bearings of another size.

Flow production

Car assembly at Ford Dagenham is completed on an **assembly line**. This is an example of FLOW PRODUCTION. Partly finished products flow past workers who complete one operation, before the car passes on to another operation. On Ford assembly lines, doors, engines, bonnets and wheels and many other components are fitted to the basic chassis on the assembly line.

Production is continuous, with the assembly line making the same product month after month. Flow production is often used when producing large numbers of standardised items, such as cars. The fabric used in Ford employee overalls is also likely to be made in this way. Fabric passes through a series of processes, such as preparing, (eg cut, cleaned), dyeing and finishing (eg preshrunk) before it is ready to make overalls. Mass produced products are often made using

Batch production

Advantages Compared to job production, batch production allows workers to **specialise** (☞ unit 4) and use specialist machinery more. Costs per unit produced should therefore be lower. It also means that different batches of slightly different products can be made, such as different sizes of ball bearings.

Disadvantages Batch production leads to goods having to be stored and this costs money. Body panels, for instance, or headlamp fittings have to be held in **stock** (☞ unit 46) before final assembly on the car. Specialist machinery may have to be cleaned or reset to produce a different batch of products. This can take time. Specialisation of workers may result in some workers doing the same repetitive job all day which can be demotivating. The factory is also likely to be laid out in sections (called **layout by process**), with each section producing a particular batch of goods. In a car plant, one section might make the body panels for instance. This means that the parts have to be moved from one section to another, which takes time and therefore leads to higher costs.

Magnet, the kitchen manufacturer, makes doors for kitchen cabinets in batches.

Cadbury's chocolates

chocolate manufacturer like Cadbury is constantly making decisions out what to make in its plants. Take, for instance, a plant which akes three different 'lines' - Cadbury's Dairy Milk, Cadbury's hole Nut and Cadbury's Fruit and Nut, each in different sizes. oduction is planned on a 12 week schedule. Cadbury's don't ant to keep stocks for too long because stocks cost money to eep. On the other hand, changing production from one bar to another and from one size to another takes time.

Changing production from one type of bar to another pe of bar of the same size loses Cadbury 8 hours of roduction time as ingredients are changed. For the next 8 ours, production averages only half full capacity as the achines settle in and any problems are sorted out.

Changing production from one size of bar to another size of bar of he same type is more costly. It takes 16 hours to change the moulds and he wrapping machines to cope with the new size. In addition, for the next 16 hours the production only averages alf full capacity due to settling-in time.

If both size and recipe are changed, then it takes 24 hours to change the machines and another 24 hours settling-in time.

In a perfect world, Cadbury decides how to organise what to produce by comparing the cost of holding stock with the cost of changing the machines. In the real world, it also has to cope with what happens if:
- customers buy different quantities than forecast;
- there is a major breakdown at the plant;
- there is a delivery of faulty materials.

Source: adapted from Cadbury, 'Fact Card: Production'.

1 'Cadbury's Dairy Milk is manufactured using batch production techniques.' Explain why this is so.

2 Explain ONE advantage of batch production for Cadbury.

3 What are the disadvantages of batch production for Cadbury?

4 What should be produced is planned 12 weeks in advance. How, if at all, should Cadbury react if:
(a) an advertising campaign for 100g bars of Cadbury's Whole Nut is far more successful than Cadbury expected;
(b) a long spell of hot weather in the summer reduces demand for all chocolate bars by 20 per cent and leads to a build up of stocks in the warehouse;
(c) a major breakdown in the plants leads to two days lost production of 54g Cadbury's Whole Nut bars;
(d) raisins delivered to Cadbury are found to be faulty and can't be used as anticipated in the production of Cadbury Fruit and Nut bars, and the suppliers have promised new deliveries 12 days after the next planned production date for the bars?

Flow production at Ford.

Flow production

Advantages The great advantage of flow production is that large numbers of products can roll off assembly lines at very low cost. This is mainly because so much capital machinery is used and so little time is lost in the assembly process. The cost of producing a new car on an assembly line, for instance, is a fraction of the cost of a garage putting a whole car together from a pile of components as a one off job. Also, what is produced can be extremely complex because it is the result of the work of so many different types of worker and machine.

Disadvantages Assembly lines require a large amount of capital equipment to start with. Once built, it is difficult, if not impossible, to adapt the assembly line to make other products. Much of the equipment is designed to be used by workers with few skills, cutting down the cost of labour. However, jobs on the assembly line tend to be very monotonous. A worker might perform the same operation several hundred times a day. This can demotivate workers and might result in poor workmanship. The product being assembled must be fairly standard because both workers and machinery have been trained or designed to cope with only one type of operation. There are likely to be stocks of products waiting to be used on the assembly line and stocks cost money to hold. A breakdown of the assembly line at any point can also lead to a complete shut down. For instance, a strike by workers on one part of the assembly line can bring the whole line to a halt.

Flow production in the manufacture of material.

Forging ahead

Mark Thorpe runs a business which makes up-market architectural ironmongery for designers, manufacturers and distributors throughout the world. For instance, it manufactures door fixings such as knobs and handles as well as fixings for furniture.

Growing sales has meant that the company's forge has been kept very busy in recent years. In fact, one of the key problems that has faced the company has been running out of stock of products. The forge might make 2 000 of a particular door handle in January, expecting the stock to last till June. But a large order can wipe out the stock and leave other customers frustrated. They have to wait for delivery until the forge has enough time to make more handles. With 500 different products being made, it is difficult to juggle the exact timing of when more of one item will be produced.

As recently as two years ago, the company also made one-off items. These were sold mainly to design clients who wanted a unique product to put into their latest house or office project. However, the company's designer and most skilled worker retired. The profit on these jobs was often almost zero. So the company decided not to replace him.

1 (a) Describe the method of production used by the company to make door fixings. (b) How does this method of production differ from that used to make one-off items?
2 Suggest why the profit made on the sale of one-off items was 'often almost zero'.
3 The company is thinking of increasing sales to retailers. It would buy in components for door and furniture fixings from other manufacturers. It would then package the fixings so that they could be displayed and sold in shops. Discuss what might be the best method of production for this.

repetitive flow production techniques. This is where large quantities of the same product are manufactured. Complicated machinery is needed to carry out the precise repetitive work. This machinery can sometimes run continuously for 24 hours. Plastic containers to hold milk or oil and chemical containers may be manufactured in this way.

Petrol to power Ford cars is made through PROCESS PRODUCTION methods, a form of flow production. At an oil refinery, crude oil is refined into petrol. An oil refinery is like a single huge machine (and hence is called a **plant** rather than a factory) with the oil flowing through pipes and tanks as it is chemically changed to turn it into petrol. Process production occurs where products like chemicals or liquids are fed through a plant on a continuous basis.

Source: adapted in part from information provided by Ford Motor Company Limited.

Mail order film processing

Nashua is one of the UK's largest mail order film processing companies. It has two main processing centres, one at Telford, the other in Newton Abbot in Devon. In the mid-1990s, both plants moved over to a cell system of production.

Processing involves about 12 steps, including films being removed from envelopes, stripping the films from cases, negative production, printing and final dispatch to the customer. Before, this had been done on a production line. A group of operators would remove films from envelopes. Then the films would be sent on to another group of operatives who would 'string' the films from the cases and so on. Now, operators are organised in cells, with the production 'line' taking the form of a circle. Operators can switch jobs within the cell if they so wish.

There is a number of advantages from cellular production. The new layout means that workers can learn from each other. One operator commented that: 'if my (negative) splicing isn't right, someone can come over and tell me'. Another said: 'You can do a greater range of jobs, it's more interesting so you're less likely to make mistakes'. Workers are encouraged to comment on the work of the team. This has led to a series of improvements, such as a new system of transporter rollers to help speed film development.

Production is now more reliable. In 1995, the first year cell production was introduced, the plant saw a reduction in prints having to be reprocessed because of errors of 15-20 per cent. Customer complaints have fallen too from over 1 per cent to under 1 per cent, a significant fall given the importance of repeat business.

Source: adapted from the *Financial Times*, 21 February 1996.

1 Explain what method of production was used previously at Nashua in its mail order film business before the introduction of cell production.
2 What is the difference between the old and the new production systems?
3 Suggest TWO reasons why film processing might be more reliable now than before.
4 Discuss why reliability is so important for a mail order company.

SUMMARY CASE STUDY

RENOLD

Renold is one of the world's leading makers of engineering chains. Its chains power a wide range of machines from ships' engines to conveyor belts in food processing plants and come in thousands of different variations. Some of Renold's automated machines churn out chains of the same specification constantly.

However, the profit margins on high volume, mass production chain are less than on low volume, customer driven orders. Renold, as a market leader in chain manufacture, wants to sell on quality and customer service. Trying to compete with lower quality, lower price, less flexible Far Eastern producers would drive down profits.

So Renold is increasingly moving to 'mass customisation'. It is gearing its factories to producing small batches of chains as orders come in from customers, rather than making chain, putting it into stock and hoping that customers will order. At its Bredbury plant in Manchester, large, heavy chain is made to customer specification as a one off. For instance, chain on a ship's engine may have broken. Renold will manufacture and deliver the chain within a few days. An £8 million investment programme in new machines between 1990 and 1993 has been used to give the Bredbury plant the flexibility to deal with mass customisation.

Source: adapted from the *Financial Times*, 12 June 1996.

1 'At the Bredbury factory, Renold uses job production, batch production and flow production methods.' Explain the differences between the three methods of production, giving examples from Renold.
2 Explain why Renold uses the three different methods of production.
3 Suggest why a shipping company might be prepared to pay more to replace a broken ship's engine chain by buying from Renold rather than from a South Korean manufacturer.
4 Discuss TWO ways in which Renold might market its products to its customers.

Key terms

Batch production - method of production where a product is made in stages, with a particular operation being carried out on all products in a group or batch.

Flow production - method of production where a product is made continuously, often through the use of an assembly line. Mass produced goods are most suitable for this type of production.

Job production - method of production where a product is made individually from start to finish like a bridge or an aeroplane. Each product is likely to be different and unique.

Process production - method of production where a product is made continuously by being passed through a production plant rather than on an assembly line.

Checklist ✓

1 What is meant by job production?
2 Explain why: (a) building a bridge across a motorway; and (b) painting a house may be examples of job production.
3 What are: (a) the advantages; and (b) the disadvantages of job production?
4 What is the difference between job production and batch production?
5 What are: (a) the advantages and (b) the disadvantages of batch production?
6 What is the difference between batch production and flow production?
7 How are cars produced using a flow production method?
8 What are: (a) the advantages; and (b) the disadvantages of flow production?

Stainless steel chains are used in the food industry.

Making decisions

Businesses must decide how they will produce goods and services. Their choices will change over time because the business environment is changing. They need to consider:
- whether they can use techniques of mass production;
- how to minimise inputs to the production process in order to achieve lean production;
- if they are manufacturers, whether production should be organised in cells;
- how they can minimise holdings of stocks;
- how best they can involve the workforce in achieving their goals;
- whether they can check how competitive they are through benchmarking.

Hardy Spicer is a subsidiary of GKN, the multinational engineering company. Hardy Spicer makes components for cars at its factory in Birmingham. In the 1960s and 1970s it was a highly successful component plant. It manufactured the constant velocity joint, which enabled front wheel drive on cars. However, in the 1980s Hardy Spicer faced problems. Nissan's new car manufacturing plant in Sunderland demanded higher quality and lower prices from British car component manufacturers. Radical changes to traditional production techniques were needed as the company began making losses.

Mass production

Henry Ford founded the Ford motor car company in the USA in 1903. He revolutionised production with his Model T Ford motor car. This was the first complex product to be MASS PRODUCED. Before, cars were built individually. Workers came to each car in the factory and worked on the car. Ford built the first **production line** (☞ unit 47). On the production line the workers and machines stayed fixed. Cars were brought to the workers. Workers and machines could then **specialise** (☞ unit 4). Each worker only did one small operation. The tools used were specifically designed to help with that one operation. Workers had limited skills. They just needed to know how to complete one operation.

Mass production reduced costs because the same product was being made many times. 15 million Model T Fords were made in the USA in just one colour - black. But mass production techniques had their problems.
- Production lines meant that the product was travelling long distances. This took time and meant that factory buildings had to be large.
- Large volumes of **stocks** (☞ unit 46) were kept. If stocks of a particular part ran out, the production line could come to a halt.
- **Communication** between workers was poor. They were scattered along the production line. There were no systems to get workers to talk to each other about their work. They were seen more as robots than as people who could help improve production through their ideas.
- Workers had no responsibility for the **quality** (☞ unit 51) of their work. It was someone else's responsibility to make sure that products were of the right standard. This often led to large numbers of faulty products that had to be rejected.
- Production was inflexible. With poorly skilled workers and a rigid production line, it was difficult to change to produce different products quickly. Japanese industry found

solutions to these problems. Toyota, the car manufacturer, helped bring about a second revolution in how products are manufactured. This system is called LEAN PRODUCTION. It is a system which reduces to a minimum all inputs to the production process - everything from workers to raw materials to factory space.

Hardy Spicer moved from traditional mass production techniques to lean production methods in the 1990s. It revolutionised its production.

Cell production

Up to the end of the 1980s, there were traditional straight production lines at Hardy Spicer's Birmingham plant. This was changed in the early 1990s to a system of CELL PRODUCTION. This is where production is broken down into a number of 'cells'. Each cell has similar tasks or processes which, together, complete a process or make a product. Cells may be 'U' shaped or horse shoe shaped similar to Figure 48.1. Materials are

Toyota

In February 1997, there was a fire at Aisin Seiki. The company made brake parts for Toyota in Japan. The consequences of the fire were serious. The company was the sole supplier of these brake parts to Toyota. Because of the just-in-time system of deliveries, Toyota only held half a day's stock of the parts at its factories. So, Toyota's production lines ground to a halt. It took Toyota a week to locate alternative supplies. During this time, Toyota's other suppliers, from seats to headlights, had also stopped production because they too were supplying on a just-in-time basis.

The incident has not shaken Toyota's faith in its production system. A week's production was lost. But the alternatives are even worse. Going back to holding large amounts of stock at Toyota factories would be enormously costly. Moreover, Toyota works closely with its suppliers. They are expected to design and develop parts for new cars as well as change their production systems to bring about reductions in costs. This very close working with individual suppliers is one reason why Toyota has reduced its cost base by $820 million each year for the past three years.

Source: adapted from the *Financial Times*, 7 February 1997.

1 What is meant by just-in-time manufacturing?
2 Explain how a fire at a component supplier lead to the production lines at Toyota stopping for a week.
3 Suggest why 'holding large amounts of stock ... would be enormously costly'.
4 What might be: (a) the advantages; and (b) the disadvantages to a component company of being the sole supplier of a part to Toyota?

brought to a point at the start of the cell. They are then worked on at different machines around the cell. The finished product ends up near to where it started.

Cell production at Hardy Spicer brought many benefits.

- Machines in cells were placed much closer together than on traditional production lines. Cell production took up less space on the factory floor as a result.
- Working more closely together, workers in the cell co-operated and sorted out problems together. Cells were given production targets. This helped increase **productivity**.
- Quality improved because of

better co-operation between workers. It was also easier to see where faults in production were coming from.

Just-in-time (JIT) production

JUST-IN-TIME (JIT) production is where stocks (☞ unit 46) are delivered only when they are needed by the production system. This means that stocks are kept to a minimum. In a large factory, stocks will be delivered by the supplier straight to the right point on the production line. Hardy Spicer was forced by its customers such as Nissan to offer just-in-time deliveries. This means that Nissan can order parts from Hardy Spicer and take delivery within, say, 24 hours. But Hardy Spicer has also moved to JIT production in its own Birmingham factory. There are many advantages to JIT production.

- Holding stocks is costly. Money is tied up in stocks which could be used elsewhere. Stocks have to be held somewhere, like in a warehouse. This space costs Hardy Spicer money.
- Moving stock is costly. Stocks may be delivered to a

warehouse and then taken out to go on the production line. This costs more than if the stock is delivered straight to the production line.

- Holding stock can lead to poor quality. If workers know that there are large stocks, they won't be worried if some of their work is poor. Good components can always be taken out of stock and the poor work thrown away. If there are no stocks, work must be accurate because faulty materials can stop production.

The workforce

Key to the changes at Hardy Spicer have been changes to the workforce. Lean production is associated with KAIZEN. This is Japanese for 'continuous improvement'. Kaizen implies that production can always be improved. Quality can be better, production times can be reduced and costs can be lowered. In a traditional system, workers have no control over their work. It arrives on the production line which has been designed by someone else. With Kaizen, workers have to be involved. In each cell, workers are typically part of a team. Problems faced by one worker in the cell become problems for all the workers in the cell. The cell cannot produce anything if there is a problem with one part of it.

At Hardy Spicer, there is a commitment to ongoing training of the workforce. If workers are to be able to work flexibly, then there has

At Hardy Spicer, there is commitment to ongoing training of the workforce.

Figure 48.1 *Cell production.*

MACHINING CENTRE

MATERIAL STOCK

MACHINING CENTRE

WORK STATION

MACHINING CENTRE

WORK STATION

ASSEMBLY

FINISHED STOCK

Leyland Trucks

There has been an enormous change at Leyland Trucks since its management bought the company from Daf, the former owners, in 1993. The company had to change to survive in the fiercely competitive world of truck manufacturing. A key element of that change has been changes in the workplace culture.

A survey found that, under the old ownership, employees thought they were not being given sufficient responsibility for their work. They were told what to do and were not trusted to make decisions. Now, contributions from workers are encouraged.

One example of this change occurred when Leyland Trucks began assembling Izuzu N series trucks. Before, a team of engineers would have sorted out how the trucks were to be assembled on the factory floor. What in fact happened was that employees were asked to look at the problem and shopfloor teams devised their own plans for the production. Just one of the benefits that came out of this was that a reduction of stocks in the form of work in progress of between £180 000 and £200 000 was achieved. Another example is the company suggestion scheme. Workers are given a £1 shopping voucher for every suggestion for improvement they make. On average, each worker makes 20 suggestions per year. The vast majority are not pursued but occasionally a really good idea is generated which can have a significant impact on production.

Communication is also now better. For instance, the production line is stopped for two hours every month to allow teams of workers to discuss ideas.

Source: adapted from the *Financial Times*, 9 July 1997.

1. What were the results of the survey of workers conducted after the company was taken over by its management?
2. Explain TWO ways in which workers at Leyland Trucks are now involved in the process of decision making.
3. Quality has improved considerably. In 1986, there were between 27 and 28 defects per vehicle on average. By 1996, this was between 4 and 5. Suggest why defects should have fallen.
4. A vehicle manufacturer has a problem. Orders are not regularly spaced out during the year. So during peak demand periods, employees are having to work overtime. In other slack periods, there isn't enough work for all the workers to do. How would you suggest it solves this problem?

to be MULTI-SKILLING. This is where workers are trained to be able to do a variety of jobs because they have more than one skill.

Workers are also far more involved in problem solving. At Hardy Spicer, for instance, there is a 'concern management room' on the shop floor. Any worker can go to the room to raise concerns about their work or the work of others. Any problem has to be brought under control within 24 hours and solved within five days.

Another way of involving workers in problem solving is to run company **suggestion schemes**. Workers are invited to suggest ways in which the business could be improved. Most ideas are

impractical. But a few can lead to important changes.

Quality circles are another method which became very popular in the 1980s. Workers are encouraged to meet to discuss ways of improving work. Not only do good ideas come from the discussions. But also workers become more aware of what is going on in the rest of the business and how their performance affects others.

These changes tend to lead to increases in **productivity** - output per worker. At Hardy Spicer, the improvements were so large that the company was able to cut the workforce from 2 000 to 1 000 in five years. This **downsizing** of the business meant that Hardy Spicer

was able to stay competitive against other businesses which were also changing rapidly. It also means, though, that some workers had to find work elsewhere.

Benchmarking

Another technique used to achieve lean production is BENCHMARKING. This is where one business compares its performance with another. Hardy Spicer, for instance, knew that its performance had greatly improved in the 1990s.

- In 1992 faults per million on components produced for the Nissan Micra were measured in thousands per million parts. This was very high. In 1993, it fell to 815 per million and by 1995 it was just 75 per million.
- Between 1993 and 1995, output per worker doubled.
- Stock turnover is the number of times per year an item of stock on average is moved in the production process. Stock turnover increased from 11 times to 20 times between 1993 and 1995. This showed much better stock control and the move toward just-in-time production.

However, when Hardy Spicer compared itself to other businesses, it could see that there was still room for improvement. For instance, output per worker at the Birmingham factory in 1996 was still 20-30 per cent below the best factories in GKN's international network. In terms of quality, it was equal to the average Japanese plant, but below the best Japanese plants. It also knew that other businesses were continually improving their production methods. Standing still would mean losing competitiveness. Only by improving at a faster rate than its competitors could it become a **world class** manufacturing facility - one which matched the best in the world.

Source: adapted from the *Financial Times*, March 25 1996 and information provided by GKN.

Lake Centre Industries (LCI)

In 1989, Lake Centre Industries (LCI), a US company, was taken over by Lucas, a British company. LCI manufactures automotive controls, such as heating and ventilation control panels, whilst Lucas produces a wide range of components for the world's car manufacturers.

Although well run, LCI did not match world manufacturing standards. Lucas asked it to adopt a competitive action plan (CAP). This is a tool used by Lucas to benchmark its operations against those of its main rivals. For instance, LCI became aware that it had to improve its stock control. It was also able to tap into Lucas's huge buying power which enabled it to reduce the cost of its supplies. These and other measures helped the company to lift its profit margins after the takeover.

Source: adapted from the *Financial Times*, 7 March 1996.

1 What does LCI manufacture?
2 Explain what is meant by 'benchmarking'.
3 How has benchmarking enabled LCI to increase its profit margins?
4 Ford is looking for a new supplier of automotive controls. Why would LCI being a world class manufacturer help it win a contract with Ford?

Checklist ✓

1 Give THREE features of mass production.
2 Explain FOUR problems with mass production.
3 How is production organised in a cell?
4 What is meant by just-in-time production techniques?
5 How does JIT help reduce costs for a business?
6 New production techniques often require fewer but better trained workers. Why is this?
7 Why might greater efficiency in production lead to downsizing?
8 Why would a business want to benchmark its activities against world class companies?

Key terms

Benchmarking - comparing the performance of one business or one factory with another and, in particular, with the best in the world.
Cell production - a production system where a number of machines are grouped together, sometimes in a horse shoe shape, to perform a series of related operations.
Just-in-time - a production system where stocks are only delivered when they are needed by the production system. This minimises stock levels in a business.
Kaizen - a production system which is operated to generate continuous improvement in performance over a period of time.
Lean production - a system which attempts to reduce to a minimum all inputs from workers to raw materials to factory space to the production process.
Mass production - the production of large quantities of identical products often on assembly lines.
Multi-skilling - where workers have more than one skill and are able to perform several tasks or jobs.

GENERATING ELECTRICITY

Summary Case Study

Applying the lessons of lean production is not just limited to factories. PowerGen, Britain's second biggest electricity generator, has transformed its production of electricity by benchmarking the 17 best performing coal fired power stations in the USA. Before it started the exercise in 1994-95, it thought that it was doing fairly well. For instance, at Fiddler's Ferry, a 2 000MW coal-fired power station in Cheshire, PowerGen had improved productivity by halving the workforce between 1989 and 1994. The benchmarking exercise, though, showed that PowerGen was still very inefficient compared to the best US plants.

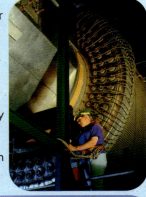

Two examples show up these differences. PowerGen used to have permanent scaffolding at its power stations to help maintenance. Scaffolding is expensive. In the USA, they often used harnesses for work rather than scaffolding. When scaffolding was essential, they hired it by the day. PowerGen has not fully adopted US practices, but it has looked hard at whether it needs all the scaffolding it has. The result has been a halving of the amount of scaffolding at power plants.

Another example concerns cleaning. At Fiddler's Ferry, they used to employ 30-40 cleaners. In the best USA plants, no cleaners were employed. This was because workers cleaned up after themselves. Seeing this, PowerGen decided to redesign jobs. Workers were retrained to become multi-skilled. They were organised into 'multi-disciplined process teams'. Each team contains workers with all the skills to do a job, including cleaning up.

The result has been an enormous increase in productivity. Fiddler's Ferry employed 1 100 workers in 1990. By 1997, there were only 226 workers at the power station.

Source: adapted from the *Financial Times*, 2 July 1997.

1 What does PowerGen make?
2 How did PowerGen know that it was inefficient?
3 Explain how PowerGen made cost savings on its scaffolding.
4 John is an electrician at Fiddler's Ferry. He has been at the power station since 1985.
   (a) How do you think his job might have changed since 1985? (b) Explain TWO ways in which you think the changes might have motivated John to do his job better.

NEW TECHNOLOGIES

Making decisions

Businesses must decide how they will produce goods and services. New technology has transformed the range of choices open to them. In manufacturing, businesses need to decide whether to invest in machines controlled by computers in the design and manufacturing processes. They also need to decide to what extent they wish to integrate different processes in a factory. In service industries, today's key technological decision is the extent to which IT applications can be used to make production more efficient.

MGA Developments Limited is a design and engineering company based in Coventry. It specialises in designing motor vehicle bodies and aerospace structures. It also produces models and prototypes from designs. Another service it provides is the design and production of manufacturing tools for components. In 1997 it employed over 200 designers, engineers and craftspeople.

Automation

Technology is constantly changing. However, the rate of change of technology has been particularly fast over the past 200 years and is still increasing.

- **Mechanisation**. There was widespread mechanisation during the UK Industrial Revolution in the late 18th century and 19th century. Machines driven by steam or water power replaced workers, but the workers still operated the machines.

- **Automation**. This century, the process of automation has meant that some workers no longer have to operate machines. Now they just supervise them as the machines work automatically. Automation has largely come about through the use of computers in the production process.

New technology in manufacturing

Prior to the 1980s most design work would have been done by hand. Designers would sketch ideas on paper. These would be developed into more detailed drawings. Then the drawings could be used to build prototypes or models. Prototypes could then be tested for strength and durability before the final product is made. The designer would have to work out, using mathematical equations, whether the proposed materials would be strong enough to do the job. Although some of this is still done today, increasingly computers are being used in designing and manufacturing. MGA uses new technology extensively.

Computer aided design (CAD)

MGA designs structures on computer using a COMPUTER AIDED DESIGN (CAD) package. CAD packages allow an MGA designer to:
- produce drawings so that the end product looks good and is aesthetically pleasing to the customer;

Design fabrics

Carrington Career & Workwear specialises in making high performance fabrics for both the 'workwear' and 'careerwear' market. For instance, it makes fabrics which are fire resistant. Clothes made from these fabrics are used in general heavy industry, including the oil industry in the North Sea where danger is ever present. It also makes careerwear or uniforms for companies, designed to express the ethos and tradition of the business.

Key to its success in the careerwear market is an in-house design facility utilising state-of-the-art CAD equipment. This allows new print or colour-woven designs to be made or existing designs recoloured to meet customers' precise requirements.

Source: adapted from IPT Group.

1 What is the difference between 'workwear' and 'careerwear'?
2 Explain in your own words how CAD technology helps the company.

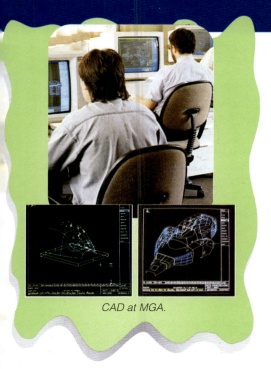

CAD at MGA.

- put in details of the structure of a body, like stress bars;
- make sure that the structure and the materials used are physically strong enough to do the job for which they are designed; the computer program does the mathematics involved in working this out;
- produce two and three dimensional images of the structure, as well as drawings of individual parts of the design. These can be rotated so that all aspects of the design can be seen.

CAD speeds up the design process considerably. It allows designs to be more sophisticated. Possibilities for alternative designs can be explored. Changes can be made easily, at little cost. The computer program will, in many parts of the design process, be able to show where there is a 'best' or optimal solution to a design problem. It also cuts out much of the need to build many physical models or prototypes because the computer pictures of the product are so good and because the programs can work out strengths of materials.

Computer Numerical Control (CNC) machines
When MGA wants to built a model or prototype

of a vehicle, for example, it uses COMPUTER NUMERICAL CONTROLLED (CNC) machines. There is a number of different machines traditionally used in manufacturing. Some examples might be:

- **milling machines** to cut grooves, rebates and slits into materials;
- **lathes** to cut materials as they turn, to make cylinder shapes;
- **routers** to shape materials;
- **spinning, cutting, sewing, knitting** and **printing** machines used in the textile industry.

A modern CNC machine is one which can be programmed to do a particular task. Instructions are inputted into the CNC machine by the operator. The machine then carries out the task automatically, controlled by the computer.

MGA benefits from using CNC machines. They are fast. This is because patterns or shapes can be cut quickly from stored and controlled information, compared with traditional machines that are controlled by hand. They are also highly accurate, cutting out human error in traditional manufacturing.

Some businesses also make use of **probes** and **coordinate measuring machines** (CMM). These check measurements accurately. MGA uses surface measuring software to ensure that measurements of models are correct. Computer controlled temperature is used at McCain foods when making pizza.

Computer aided manufacturing (CAM)
Using computers in design and production means that the two processes can be linked. The computer data generated in design can then be fed into the programs of CNC machines. This linkage of design and production is called COMPUTER AIDED MANUFACTURING (CAM) or CAD/CAM ENGINEERING. MGA offers a CAM service to its customers. A car manufacturer, for

Robots cut costs

W&G Sissons, based in Chesterfield, is a manufacturer of stainless steel sinks for the catering and bathroom industry. In 1997, it took delivery of a £25 000 cutting robot. It won't just cut stainless-steel. The company expects it to cut £30 000 of costs each year as well. Three years previously it had bought a welding robot for £65 000. It welded three times faster than using skilled workers.

Source: adapted from the *Financial Times*, 6 March 1997.

1 What does W&G Sissons manufacture?
2 How has the company used robots in production?
3 Why has the company decided to buy robots?

instance, can take away computer software from a design commission with MGA and feed it into its CNC machines on its factory floor. Large businesses link up many computer operated machines to carry out identical processes, such as injection moulding at Lego. Large businesses also make use of computerised assembly lines.

Robots
All large motor manufacturing companies like Ford or Rover now use robots on their production line. A ROBOT, like a CNC machine, is controlled by a computer. The difference is that a robot has some form of arm which moves materials. For instance, a robot might take a component from a rack and install it into a car engine. Like CNC machines, robots can be programmed as part of a CAM package, linking CAD design with the manufacturing process.

Automatically Guided Vehicles (AGVs)
Many motor manufacturing companies also use AUTOMATICALLY GUIDED VEHICLES (AGVs). These are carriages on which components or parts can be put. They are then taken to another part of the factory. The AGV is guided by inductive

CAM at MGA.

maintenance work. Parts can be ordered by computer for the production line as and when they are needed. An AGV may collect the parts from a store room. Or an outside supplier may be expected to deliver to the door of the factory from where it will be taken by an AGV to the production line. A robot may take the parts from the AGV and place them into components on the production line. Larger CIM systems can be complex, relatively expensive and difficult to set up. They might also be inflexible if, say, a production line needs to be used to manufacture a different product.

New technology in service industries

Many service industries have seen radical changes in the way they work due to INFORMATION TECHNOLOGY. Banking and financial services have been transformed by the ability of **computers** to **store information.**

Instead of holding paper records about a client, details are now held on computer. This has made it possible vastly to increase the amount of information held. It has also speeded up the **handling of information,** like a withdrawal of money from the the bank. This speed makes it possible, for instance, to use 'hole-in-the-wall' banking machines, which has reduced the need to have so many bank branches.

Communication (☞ units 58 and 59) has also been transformed. Computers have considerably increased the amount of information available to a worker. **E-mail** allows workers to communicate in written form to each other through their computers. The **Internet** has given businesses access to a wider range of information. It also allows a business to advertise and sell its products on its **website.**

In retailing, computer links between what is sold and what is

wires which are put into the floor or on the ceiling along the route that the AGV will travel. The AGV has sensors which prevent it from crashing into objects if there is something in its path. The sensors are linked to the **programmable logic controller (plc).** This is the microprocessor on board the AGV which has been programmed to control its movements in a particular way.

Computer integrated manufacturing (CIM)
Some manufacturing plants have COMPUTER INTEGRATED MANUFACTURING (CIM) systems in place. CIM is where the whole of the production process is controlled by computer technology. Workers are in the factory to supervise and check that the systems are operating properly. They also do

Electronic cheque scanners

Whenever a cheque is paid into a bank, a member of the bank staff keys in the value of the cheque in computer-readable magnetic ink onto the cheque. The details of the bank account number and with which bank the customer has an account is already on the cheque in printed numbers. The value of the cheque, though, has been handwritten by the account holder. Up till now, a computer scanner has been able to read the printed numbers on the cheque but not what is handwritten. Hence, there has been a need to key in that information separately.

The Midland Bank is about to introduce a new electronic image processing system where scanners will be able to read handwritten figures. The scanners are not perfect and at the moment only read about 50 per cent of the cheques presented. However, more advanced software will hopefully soon be available which will be able to read the amount written in letters on a cheque. This could raise recognition rates to 70 or 80 per cent.

Keying in the value of cheques manually might seem unimportant. But it accounts for no less than 60 per cent of the cost of processing a cheque to a bank. With a 50 per cent recognition rate, that would mean a 30 per cent cost saving on the 3.2bn cheques written in 1996. With a recognition rate of 80 per cent, it would cut costs nearly in half.

Source: adapted from the *Financial Times*, 7 October 1996.

1 What new technology is the Midland Bank planning to introduce?
2 Why is it planning to introduce it?
3 Other banks are interested in the idea of copying the Midland Bank. Discuss what factors they would want to consider before doing this.

in **stock** help to decide what needs to be re-ordered (☞ unit 46). Bar codes are used which can be scanned to give information about the product and its price. Some supermarkets allow customers to scan in the cost of products as they pick them up in the store. This saves queuing time.

IT is increasingly being used in administration. **Databases** are basically lists, for instance of customers or of stocks, which can be manipulated in certain ways. For instance, the database might be used to send a circular to every customer which has purchased a product over the past 12 months. Spreadsheets allow data to be manipulated. **Spreadsheets** are often used in

accounts, for instance to help calculate cash flow or costs. **Desk top publishing (DTP)** packages allow graphics and text to be manipulated on screen. They can be used to produce promotional leaflets, internal memos or reports for instance.

Source: adapted in part from information provided by MGA Developments.

Computers are used by businesses to store product and customer information.

Radio controlled scanners and terminals control stock at Marks & Spencer's warehouse in Neasden.

WORKING ONLINE

SUMMARY S CASE STUDY

The internet is set to change the way manufacturers do business. At Purchase Engineering, for instance, a small components company, they are using their web site to inform customers when their order is made. CNC machines are linked to the internet. When the machine has finished a batch of production for a customer, its computer program automatically puts this onto the web site. John Purchase, the joint managing director, also predicts that businesses will be able to download machine programmes being worked on anywhere in the world.

The internet is already being used for ordering parts and components. Many distribution companies have put their catalogues online. RS Components, for instance, with 150 000 customers buying electronic and mechanical parts, has spent £1 million setting up a web site which allows its customers to buy parts online and consult technical data.

The internet is also allowing engineering companies to share information. PressTech Controls, a medium sized company in Hemel Hempstead which makes electronic controls for printing presses, has seven offices around the world. 'We share confidential information on the intranet such as technical manuals.' The intranet is in effect a private internet where only those with the right passwords and programs can access information.

Source: adapted from the *Financial Times*, 20 March 1998.

1 (a) What is a CNC machine and (b) how can it be linked to the internet?
2 What advantage might there be in linking a CNC machine to the internet?
3 How can the internet help an engineering company in ordering parts for a CNC machine?
4 An engineering company based in Bristol is thinking of establishing a small factory in Scotland. Discuss FOUR ways in which it could use the internet to help it run the factory.

Checklist ✓

1 What is the difference between mechanisation and automation?
2 A manufacturer wants to design a new bicycle. How could CAD help it to do so?
3 What are the advantages of a CNC lathe over a traditional manual lathe operating by a worker?
4 How might a manufacturer of train carriage components use CAM to speed up production of a new design?
5 What is the difference between a robot and a CNC machine?
6 (a) How does an AGV know where to move and (b) what prevents it from bumping into an object in its path?
7 Why is CIM more complex than CAM?
8 Give TWO examples of the use of information technology in service industries.

key terms

Automatically guided vehicle (AGV) - carriages on which materials can be carried round a factory guided by inductive wires and sensors.
Computer aided design (CAD) - the use of computers to design products.
Computer aided manufacturing (CAM) or CAD/CAM engineering - the use of computers to control production processes, for instance from design using CAD technology through to manufacture on CNC machines.
Computer integrated manufacturing (CIM) - the use of a computer or computer network to control production of a whole factory or part of a factory.
Computer numerical controlled (CNC) machines - machines in factories which receive instructions about what to do from a computer rather than directly from a worker.
Information technology - the use of computers to store, handle, produce and retrieve information.
Robot - a machine controlled by a computer which is able to move materials to achieve set tasks.

Making decisions

Businesses must decide how they will produce goods and services efficiently. Their choices will change over time because the business environment is changing. When considering whether to introduce new technology into the workplace, businesses must decide whether it will make them more competitive. Will it:

- reduce their costs of production;
- improve quality;
- improve working conditions and, in particular, health and safety;
- allow greater variety of products to be manufactured;
- lead to the manufacture of new products?

The LEGO Group is a Danish based manufacturer of toys and educational materials. Its name is taken from the words *leg godt*, meaning play well. The business was founded in 1932 and is a family owned limited company. It has development departments in Denmark, USA and Japan, mould factories in Germany and Switzerland, and toy factories in Denmark and Switzerland. Today it has around 9 000 employees.

Competitiveness

LEGO operates in **competitive markets** (☞ unit 2). It has become one of world's 'top ten' toy manufacturers through a business strategy which involves:

- designing toys which stimulate children's imagination and play;
- manufacturing toys to a high technical standard which are safe, long lasting and aesthetically pleasing;
- distributing its products through a wide range of retailers - around 60 000 worldwide.

Technology plays a key role in making LEGO a competitive company. Why is technology so important to LEGO?

Lowering costs

Whenever LEGO buys new machines or invests in new systems, it carefully calculates the costs and benefits of the investment. Introducing new technology often leads to lower costs of production. This could be for a number of reasons.

- New technology could reduce the amount of labour needed in the production process. Installing

robots in LEGO's automated moulding factories to collect finished products, for instance, has reduced the number of workers needed per unit of production.

- Waste might be reduced. Using CAD (Computer-Aided-Design) rather than designing a component without the aid of

Robots at work

Perlos is a Finnish plastic component moulder and toolmaker with two factories in the UK. At its factories near Newcastle it uses 20 robots to take finished pieces of plastic out of injection moulding machines and do basic assembly jobs.

The company uses robots partly to stay competitive with factories in cheap labour countries. It also wants to provide more consistent quality than it could achieve using manual labour.

However, robots are not common in UK manufacturing. There are 16 times as many robots per worker in Japan than there are in the UK. Teemi Saloranta, UK managing director of Perlos, pointed out that : 'The golden rule in robotics is you need input from the design process to simplify the parts; it must be a whole manufacturing philosophy. If not, then human labour is actually more flexible because people can bend and manipulate components to fit together.' With Britain near the bottom of the wage cost league in the industrialised world and with laws which make it easy to hire and fire workers, robots are not as attractive financially as in, say, Japan or Germany.

Source: adapted from the *Financial Times*, 6 March 1997.

1 Which four countries shown in the data have: (a) the highest use; and (b) the lowest use of robots per worker?

2 What advantages did Perlos see in using robots?

3 Explain why UK businesses might be reluctant to invest in robots.

4 A business uses CAD/CAM technology. Why is it more likely to use robots than a competitor which doesn't use CAM techniques?

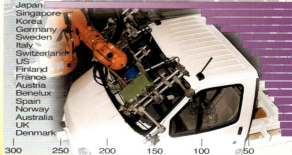

Figure 50.1 *Robots per 10 000 people employed in manufacturing industry.*
Source: adapted from International Federation of Robotics; British Robot Association.

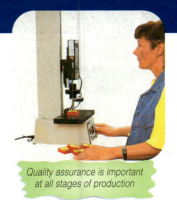

Quality assurance is important at all stages of production

computers often brings about designs which reduce the amount of waste in manufacturing.

- The rate or speed of production may increase. Compared to the existing technology, new technology may increase output using the same amount of workers and factory space.

Quality

Quality is vital to any business. It is vital to LEGO because one of the reasons why people buy LEGO products is the certainty that they are buying a product which is safe, will last and will be fun to play with.

Technology allows businesses to produce to the necessary specifications. The introduction of CNC (Computer Numerical Controlled) machines, for instance, has allowed businesses to reduce the variance on work. Variance is the difference in size or weight between each component made. A 10mm bolt is unlikely to be exactly 10mm. It will be slightly longer or slightly shorter. CNC machines can reduce the differences between each bolt to, say, plus or minus 10/million mm.

At LEGO, the plastic moulds used to manufacture bricks have to be accurate to a tolerance of 0.005mm. The colour, temperature and moisture content of plastic granules have to be absolutely accurate before they are sent to injection moulding machines which make the coloured bricks. Technology allows LEGO to check the quality of its output far more easily and accurately than before. This is essential in a business environment where customers expect toys to have no defects (**zero defects** ☞ unit 51).

Health and safety

Working conditions today in factories are much better than even 30 years ago. New technology is a major reason for this. Many dangerous and unpleasant jobs which used to be done by workers are now done by machines.

LEGO makes use of AGVs (automatically guided vehicles) at its factories. These can take finished components from the factory to the warehouse. They also take components from the warehouse to be assembled and packed into finished products. These driverless trucks make it unnecessary for workers to handle work in progress round the factory. This might prevent back injuries and injuries associated with dropping objects.

Painting and spraying of products like cars is another area where technology has transformed the workplace. Many coatings contain dangerous chemicals which, if breathed in or touched, can harm the worker. Use of fully automated spraying machines in sealed conditions means that workers do not need to be exposed to these dangers.

New technology also allows products themselves to be much safer for consumers. LEGO, for instance, tests the physical, mechanical, chemical and electrical properties of its toys, as well as flammability. Technology allows checks to be made, for instance, on the raw materials used in plastics and the ability of toys to resist being pulled apart. LEGO's products meet international safety and production standards (☞ unit 51).

New products

Computers and information technology have been at the heart of the technological revolution of the past 30 years. They have created new machines and new ways of working. They have also created new products, including the personal computer, the internet and digital television.

However, technological change is nothing new. The original LEGO brick was only made possible because of the development of plastic and its commercial production in the 1940s and 1950s. Injection moulding machines were created, which allowed plastic granules to be put into a machine and transformed into finished

Camcorders

Camcorders first came onto the market in 1983. Before, cameras and recording equipment were separate, bulky items. Camcorders have come a long way since then. Autoexposure controls were introduced to remove the need to set the camcorder for light and distance. Image stabilisers take the wobble out of recordings caused by filming on the move. Edit controllers make it easy to edit the film. Weight and size have been reduced by miniaturising components.

The race is now on to produce a machine which will act both as an ordinary camera and a camcorder. The way forward is through digital technology. There are already digital cameras on the market which don't use conventional film. Expanding the size of the memory card on the camera will enable moving pictures to be taken alongside stills.

Source: adapted from the *Financial Times*, 6 March 1998.

1 'Camcorders are one of the products which have come out of new technologies.' Explain what this means.

2 Sony and other Japanese electronics manufacturers are significant users of new technologies such as robots in production. How might the use of robots give an electronics manufacturer a competitive advantage over other businesses?

3 Sony licences its technology to other companies. Suggest why it does this.

4 An electronics manufacturer is about to launch a combined still camera and moving picture camera. Discuss THREE factors which will determine whether it sells well.

Moulding machines manufacture plastic bricks.

products like LEGO bricks. New technology, including computerised manufacturing systems, has enabled LEGO to produce more complicated designs and improve the quality of its products.

LEGO needs to stay at the forefront of change in order to survive. For this reason, it spends money on **research and development** (☞ unit 46). About 100 new LEGO sets reach the production stage each year. These are only a small fraction of the ideas which have been worked on by the design teams at LEGO.

Whenever LEGO creates new processes of production or new products it will try to PATENT these. The design of the original brick, with its unique stud-and-tube coupling system, was patented in 1958. DUPLO, the LEGO range for children aged 6 months to 6 years, was patented in 1967. A patent prevents other businesses or individuals from copying the process or product. The LEGO name or trademark is protected by COPYRIGHT. This prevents other businesses selling toys under the LEGO name.

Some companies LICENCE their trademark to other businesses, allowing them to use the trademark on products in return for a fee.

Mass customisation

One of the problems with **mass production** (☞ unit 48) is that customers are forced to accept a standard product. Ford's Model T Ford, for instance, was only available in one colour, black. However, buyers often want mass produced products which are

customised to their own needs. New technologies reduce the cost of doing this. For instance, car manufacturers are now able to make each car on a production line to a different specification from each customer. This process of manufacturing a standard product in a large number of different variations to cater for the individual needs of customers is called MASS CUSTOMISATION. So Leyland trucks, for example, can now produce many different variations of a basic truck on one production line.

Service industries

LEGO is a manufacturing company. **Secondary** or **manufacturing industry** (☞ unit 4) has possibly been more affected by changes in technology than **service industries**. Not only has technology created new products but it has also transformed the way in which those products are made.

However, many service industries have been changed too. Information technology has transformed banking and insurance. IT has allowed huge quantities of information about customers to be

stored and accessed. Retailing too has been changed. Systems like **EPOS** (☞ unit 60) have changed the way in which goods are ordered and money is handled. Even, say, the restaurant trade has been affected. Much better refrigeration systems have allowed pubs and cafes to offer affordable meals to a mass market. Freezer food together with microwaves, another new invention of the past 30 years, have cut costs.

On the other hand, service industries like education or tourism remain highly LABOUR INTENSIVE. This means that the number of workers relative to the amount produced is very high. It is the opposite of CAPITAL INTENSIVE, where the amount of capital, such as machines, factories and other buildings, is high relative to the amount produced. LEGO is a capital intensive producer. In labour intensive industries, relatively little capital is used. So the scope for changing producing methods through technology is limited.

Source: adapted in part from *An Introduction to the LEGO Group, Developing a Product, Facts and Figures, Toy Safety, A Product - An Idea,* The LEGO Group.

The drive to mass customisation

Stoves is a manufacturer of cookers based on Merseyside. It has moved more than most businesses towards mass customisation. In 1996, it launched a range of electric cookers initially aimed at the German market. Customers placing their orders at a retail outlet can specify what they want from a large menu of variations. This includes the number of hobs, the appliance's shape, size and colour, whether it uses normal radiant heat or a fan, the type of controls, handles and knobs and whether the door is glass or metal. In theory, there are 50 million different combinations possible.

The order will be sent electronically to the factory on Merseyside where it will be completed within two weeks and dispatched to the retailer. To achieve this at a reasonable cost, suppliers to Stoves are required to deliver parts on a just-in-time basis. Workers in the factory are also organised into small teams concentrating on making small batches of appliances.

Stoves is charging about 10 per cent more for a custom made cooker compared to an equivalent mass produced cooker. However, its market research has shown that customers are prepared to pay more to get exactly what they want.

Source: adapted from the *Financial Times,* 27 December 1996.

1 What is meant by 'mass customisation'?
2 How is Stoves customising the range of cookers described in the article?
3 Explain TWO ways in which Stoves has kept the costs of customisation to a minimum.
4 You can pick up leaflets about different cooker ranges from different manufacturers in shops.
 (a) Give THREE key points you think Stoves should include in its leaflets about the range described in the article. (b) Explain why you think these key points will help to sell the range.

A clothes retailing revolution?

Too many people wear ill-fitting clothes. Too small, too tall, arms too long or waist too large. Buying clothes could be a nightmare for you. Even if you are a fairly standard size, some clothes will fit you better than others.

This could all be a thing of the past if clothes retailers adopt a revolutionary new way of serving customers. A number of manufacturers including Telmat Industrie, a French company, has produced automated machines which measure your size. The machine combines a camera and computer. The customer is photographed and an image is produced on computer with accurate size measurements. These can be sent instantly to a clothing manufacturer. It will produce a unique garment based on a model in the shop using CAD/CAM technology. For instance, a customer might want a pair of jeans or a dress that they have seen displayed in the shop.

The cost of making unique size products would not be that much greater to a clothing manufacturer if it had an automated system of production. As for the retailer, there are great possibilities of cutting costs. At the moment, retailers have to buy in stock of all differing sizes, hold the stock for up to three or four months whilst it waits to be sold and then hold sales to get rid of what remains. With the new system, they would only have one or two samples of a garment, no stock and no need for sales.

Source: adapted from the *Financial Times*, 13 February 1998.

1 What technologies are involved in the distribution of the made to measure garments described in the passage?
2 Explain how profit margins of retailers might increase if they could sell made to measure garments through this new system.
3 'I don't believe that automated measuring systems will have much impact on clothes shops.' Think of THREE reasons why this might be true, explaining each carefully.

key terms

Capital and labour intensive production - in capital intensive industries, large amounts of capital are used relative to the amount produced; in labour intensive industries relatively large amounts of labour are used.
Copyrights and patents - legal protection to prevent inventions or new products being copied by other businesses for their own use.
Licence - the legal right to use the copyright or patent of another business, usually in return for a fee or a royalty.
Mass customisation - the process of manufacturing a standard product in a large number of different variations to cater for the individual needs of customers.

SUMMARY CASE STUDY

THE TITANIC

The Titanic was a technological marvel of its day. Fast, unsinkable and luxurious, it summed up a hundred years of technological progress. But even the best of technologies can sometimes fail and the Titanic was especially unlucky. 85 years on, the film Titanic was a technological marvel too. Until thirty years ago, no one could have filmed the real Titanic on the sea bed. The makers of the film in 1997 used a Russian ship equipped with submersibles to achieve those shots. Thirty years ago, the film company would have had to hire thousands of extras to shoot all the crowd scenes. In the actual film, there were plenty of extras used. But computer technology allowed some of the extras to be recreated from footage taken for other scenes. Computer technology also allowed backdrops to be created using software rather than real sets. The blending of shots from real sets and those created by computer was so good that the film goer was totally unaware of what was real and what was not.

At $200 million, the film was not cheap to make. But the latest in technology does not come cheaply and it was money well spent to create the highest revenue earner in the history of cinema.

Source: adapted from the *Financial Times*, 24 March 1998.

1 Explain TWO ways in which the film Titanic was made using the latest in technologies.
2 How did the use of these technologies help make the film a success?
3 A film company is evaluating a proposal for a $300 million film which would use all the latest in film technology in its production. Should the film company go ahead with the film? In your answer, assess what is likely to make a film a box office success and whether using expensive technology is likely to increase a film's chance of success.

Making decisions

Every business needs to ensure quality. Poor quality products are likely to lead to low sales and possible insolvency. A business must decide:
- what is the minimum acceptable quality level to customers;
- who in the business is responsible for making sure that quality is maintained;
- how the business can be organised to ensure quality at least cost.

Street Crane is a manufacturer of industrial cranes. These are used, for instance, in factories to lift and transport materials from one part of the factory floor to another. It is a private limited company based in Derbyshire. Much of its profits is ploughed back into investment to make the company more successful. Investment alone, though, is not enough. Street Crane is committed to ensuring that all its products meet quality standards all of the time.

What is quality?

Some products have different specifications to others. A Rolls Royce may have different parts to a Vauxhall Corsa. One hi-fi may have more features than another. One crane may lift a greater weight than another. However, these products might all be seen as having quality. A poor quality product is likely to be one that has faults or does not work correctly. QUALITY is about achieving a standard for a product or service which meets the needs of customers. For Street Crane, quality is about producing a product which lifts a certain maximum weight. It is about making sure that cranes work safely and reliably. It is about

Lifetime testing of the load carrying ability of cranes.

providing an efficient after sales service, where cranes are tested and maintained and where parts are delivered on time. Quality may also be about the **production process.** Street Crane aims to achieve a high standard in the processes used to manufacture industrial cranes.

Traditional quality control

Twenty years ago, like the rest of British industry, Street Crane saw quality control as part of the chain of production. A crane would be designed and the materials to be used would be chosen. The design would be handed over to the production department. It would decide how the crane should be made and set about making it. The crane would be tested for quality at the end of the production process by quality controllers or inspectors, whose responsibility it was to check for quality. If the crane didn't meet the quality standard, it would

New fries from Burger King

Burger King and McDonald's are locked in a worldwide battle in the fast food market. In December 1997, Burger King announced its latest weapon to help win the war - improved fries. The widely accepted view in the US burger industry was that Burger King had better tasting burgers than McDonald's, but that McDonald's was better on its fries.

The new Burger King fries have a coating. The company claims that this makes them crispier and tastier, and keeps them hotter for longer. The last point is very important when 75 per cent of Burger King's customers in the US take food away.

Jim Watkins, vice-president of marketing for Burger King North America said: 'Until now, our fries were not up to our standards of superior, better-tasting food. Now we can honestly say that Burger King is the best place for burgers and fries.'

Source: adapted from the *Financial Times*, 11 December 1997.

1 What is Burger King claiming about the quality of its fries?
2 Suggest TWO ways in which Burger King might make sure that the quality of its fries is the same in every one of its outlets worldwide.
3 How might McDonald's react to Burger King's launch of its new fries?

have to be altered or made again. In other factories, goods which didn't meet quality standards might be thrown away or sold as 'seconds'. Quality inspectors would also test materials bought in from suppliers. There was no guarantee that they would be of the right standard.

Total quality management (TQM)

At the end of the 1980s, Street Crane moved over to a TOTAL QUALITY MANAGEMENT (TQM) system. This brought about a complete change in the way in which quality was dealt with.

Quality as part of every process

TQM makes quality part of every process. So quality is not tested just at certain stages of the production process. It is built into production. For instance, quality is an important issue in the paintshop. How can the paintshop work so that a crane is painted without any defects?

Quality is everyone's job

Before, quality was the responsibility of the quality inspector. With TQM, every worker is responsible for quality. This may mean that a worker or group of workers does the job that a quality inspector did before. It may mean that quality is being tested at a stage of the production process where it wasn't being tested before. If products are not of the right quality, then it is important that the problem can be identified quickly so that it can be put right.

Customers and suppliers

To help build quality into the production process, workers need to recognise the needs of customers. Suppliers must take into account the requirements of businesses, their customers. Workers in sales must take into account the needs of the public or other businesses buying their products or services. By recognising that their work affects customers, workers become more responsible for what they do. They see their importance in the overall work of the business.

Just-in-time manufacturing

Street Crane uses just-in-time manufacturing (JIT ☞ unit 48) techniques. This means that stocks are kept to minimum levels. When Street Crane takes delivery of stocks, it wants to use them as soon as possible in the production process because stock is expensive to keep. So the stocks coming in must be of the right quality. If they aren't, production could come to a halt. Equally, Street Crane builds to order. It fixes a delivery date with the customer and the crane is built for this date.

Street Crane can't then afford to have problems with quality which involve reworking if it is to meet strict delivery deadlines.

Zero defects

The ultimate aim of a business using TQM techniques like Street Crane is to have zero defects. This means that all its work meets the required quality standards at every stage of the production process. To reach this, the business may set itself intermediate targets where it aims to reduce defects to a certain level within, say, the next year.

The role of management

Although every worker is responsible for quality, it is the responsibility of management to set up systems which will ensure this quality. For instance, if a

---

Quality control in textile manufacturing

Textile manufacturing has come a long way over the past three hundred years, from handlooms to fully automated computer controlled machines. However, checking for flaws in fabric as it emerges at high speed from weaving or knitting machines is still done by humans. The problem is that the fabric emerges at too high a speed from the machine for an electronic scanner to cope.

In future, though, even checking might be automated. Zellweger Luwa, a leading Swiss manufacturer of electronic instrumentation for textiles, is now testing a scanner which will cope with cloth up to 2 metres wide coming out of a machine at a speed of 120 metres a minutes. The scanner uses a configuration of microprocessors which works at 1 000 times the speed of a conventional Pentium microprocessor found in a desk-top computer.

The system is not cheap at about £200 000 per machine. However, at the moment, human workers can only cope with checking fabric at 10-20 metres per minute. This can reduce the speed at which weaving and knitting machines can work. Humans are also not perfect. Quality defects can get through because the job is so monotonous.

Source: adapted from the *Financial Times*, 19 March 1998.

Checking for flaws in fabrics is often still carried out by workers.

1 Explain: (a) the disadvantages; and (b) the advantages of using workers rather than the new scanners to check for quality.
2 Why is it important for a textile manufacturer to build quality checks into the production process?
3 Do you think a company with a factory in Germany is more or less likely to buy the new scanner than one with a factory in India? Explain your answer carefully.

worker or group of workers is producing faulty goods, then there must be a system for identifying the nature of the problem. It could be they are working with inadequate machinery. It could be that they haven't been trained sufficiently to do the job. It could be that there is inadequate lighting where they work or that machines are poorly spaced out on the factory floor. Then the system must put the problem right.

Quality assurance When products or services are sold to customers a business gives its assurance that certain standards have been met. It will guarantee that legal requirements have been observed and that quality has been maintained in the production process, for example. It is impossible for every customer to check this, so codes of practice tell a customer that standards of quality have been achieved. Examples are ISO, an international standard, and EN, a European standard.

Quality standards

Many products are made to standards which are laid down by quality assurance bodies. The **British Standards Institution** (BSI), for example, is an organisation which draws up standards for a wide range of products from beds to nails. Some consumer products like kettles are sold with **kite marks** on them. This shows that they have been made to a standard drawn up by the British Standards Institution. Other examples are the British Electrotechnical Approvals board, which tests and approves electrical products, and The British Toy and Hobby Association which grants a Lion Mark for approved toys.

Product standards are very helpful in measuring quality. However, they don't say anything about how that quality was achieved. A business might, for

ISO 9001 requirements

Procedures are required for the following
- Management responsibility, eg for creating a quality policy and quality systems, and appointing quality representatives.
- To review incoming orders.
- To control design planning, inputs, outputs, changes etc.
- To control documents and data, eg drawings, specifications.
- To control purchasing, eg lists and performance of suppliers.
- To control customer-supplied products, eg verify, store, handle.
- To identify and trace products.
- Controlling and planning of production, eg use of equipment, work instructions, monitoring and control of processes.
- Inspection and testing of a product at all stages of production.
- The control of inspection, measuring and test equipment.
- To check a product has or has not been tested.
- To identify products that do not meet standards.
- To take corrective or preventative action.
- Handling, storage, packaging, preservation and delivery.
- Control of quality records.
- Internal quality audits.
- Training.
- Servicing, eg site regulations.
- The use of statistical techniques, eg for sampling or testing.

instance, have a defect rate of 50 per cent on what it produces. So there are also standards for the quality of **production systems**. One standard is ISO 9000. Street

Crane has gained ISO 9001 accreditation. ISO 9001 is the quality system standard for manufacturing and service businesses with design. ISO 9002

Mortgage Express

In 1992, Mortgage Express adopted Total Quality Management. Mortgage Express sold mortgages - loans to buy houses. At the time, it was in difficulties. It was losing money. The economy and the housing market were in deep depression, meaning that new business was hard to come by and one third of borrowers were late in making repayments. For these reasons, its owner, the TSB (Trustee Savings Bank now owned by Lloyds Bank) had decided to close it down.

TQM helped turn the company round. The company doubled the amount spent on staff training. Workers were retrained away from selling new mortgages to dealing with customers repaying existing mortgages. Staff became more involved in decision making. The company encouraged them to make suggestions about how work could be more efficiently done. Quality at every stage was stressed.

The results were that productivity increased by 26 per cent between 1992 and 1995. The same number of workers could now process one quarter more mortgages. One key reason for this was a reduction in the number of mistakes being made in dealing with mortgages.

Source: adapted from the *Financial Times*, 4 December 1996.

1 Explain TWO ways in which the management of Mortgage Express implemented their policy of Total Quality Control.
2 Mortgage Express was criticised in the first half of the 1990s for putting pressure on customers who were behind with their mortgage repayments to keep up with their payments. (a) Why might this have seemed unfair to a worker with a mortgage who has been made unemployed? (b) Why might it have led to a better performance for Mortgage Express as a company?

is for manufacturing and service businesses, without design, and ISO 9003 is for suppliers only.

To get ISO 9000, Street Crane registered with the British Standards Institution. It had to show the BSI, through its documentation and through factory visits, that its operating processes met the required standard. Where they didn't, it had to modify its processes to comply with the standard.

There are two main advantages in meeting ISO 9000 standards. First, Street Crane was forced to review its quality procedures and make improvements to them. Second, because ISO 9000 is an international standard, it is widely recognised by Street Crane's potential customers. By buying from Street Crane, they know that the company is committed to and able to deliver quality products. This helps Street Crane to sell its products.

Source: adapted from information provided by Street Crane.

Volvo

Volvo Cars UK has worked with ISO 9000 since 1992. The company imports Volvo cars from Sweden and sells them to customers in the UK. So it is essentially a marketing and retailing operation and not a manufacturing business. Customer satisfaction is a key measure of success for Volvo Cars.

To gain the standard, businesses have to write down everything they do in a manual, define the role of each employee and put in place mechanisms for spotting errors, learning from them and preventing them recurring. To start with, Volvo Cars gained accreditation for 50 dealerships. They found it worthwhile. All reported improved efficiency and better ability to keep promises to customers. Mistakes were down, whilst the understanding of employee roles was up. Two thirds reported improved care. The experience was good enough for Volvo Cars to gain ISO 9000 accreditation across its whole dealer network.

Source: adapted from *The Times*, 16 January 1997.

1 (a) What is ISO 9000? (b) How did it help Volvo Cars UK?
2 Why might gaining ISO 9000 give a business a competitive advantage over its rivals?

Checklist ✓

1 What is meant by 'quality' of a product?
2 How is quality maintained in a traditional business?
3 Why does everyone need to be involved in quality control issues in a business?
4 Who are a worker's customers?
5 What is meant by 'zero defect' production?
6 Explain the role of management in TQM.
7 What does the British Standards Institution do?
8 How can ISO 9000 help a business achieve quality?

key terms

Quality - achieving a standard for a product or service, or a production process, which meets customers' needs.

Total quality management (TQM) - a method for a business to focus on quality by making it an important aim of every department and worker.

SUMMARY CASE STUDY

BERTRAND FAURE SEATING

Bertrand Faure Seating is a manufacturer of car seats. Sited in Oxfordshire, it supplies Honda's Swindon factory 17 miles away and Rover's Cowley plant 22 miles away.

Quality is all important for the company. One aspect of quality is delivery times. Honda and Rover expect just-in-time deliveries. For Honda, a truck leaves the Bertrand Faure factory every 34 minutes with 54 cars' worth of front and rear seats. The cars they are to be fitted into are already going down the production line at the Honda factory. It costs Honda £10 000 per minute to stop the production line should the seats not arrive on time.

The finish on the seats is another aspect of quality. Rover operates a quality scoring system. Bertrand Faure scores 28 demerits on the system for every wrinkle in the cloth on a seat delivered for instance. Rover expects any ongoing quality problems to be sorted out.

Source: adapted from *Management Today*, November 1997.

1 Why is quality important: (a) to Honda and Rover; and (b) to Bertrand Faure?
2 Suggest and explain FOUR ways in which Bertrand Faure might achieve high quality standards in the production of car seats.

LG Group (formerly Lucky Goldstar) is a South Korean company. Its products have long been exported from South Korea. However, in the 1990s the company has expanded by establishing manufacturing plants overseas. In 1996 it announced that it was going to build an electronics complex in South Wales near to Newport. The complex would manufacture television monitors for computers, colour picture tubes and semiconductors.

Making decisions

Every business has to be located somewhere. A sole trader who works as a freelance cartoonist may operate from home. A multinational chemical company will have sites in several countries and probably several continents. So where is the best place to locate a business? The choice is likely to be affected by:
- cost - where is the cheapest place to locate?
- the market - which location will enable the business to exploit its market best?
- labour - where is labour available?
- government - what opportunities will government offer and what restrictions will it place on location?

Cost of land and premises

The UK has become a popular choice for overseas companies wanting to set up in Europe. LG chose to locate on a GREENFIELD site in South Wales. One of the reasons for choosing the location was that the cost of the land was very low. A greenfield site is an area of rural land where businesses have not previously built. Buying land in a town or city which has already been built on is likely to be far more expensive. It was also much cheaper to build an electronics complex from scratch than to buy an existing factory and try to convert it.

Retailers selling computers need to consider the cost of their sites as well. Most computer retailers are sited on the high street. But some, like PC World, have gone for cheaper locations out of the town centre. They can build larger stores and offer free parking for less cost than if they were in the high street.

Cost of transport

Electronics manufacturers like LG need to consider costs of transport when deciding where to locate.

Costs of transporting raw materials and other inputs In some industries, like the steel industry, costs of transporting raw materials are high. Large quantities of bulky raw materials, such as coal and iron ore, are needed to make steel. So steel producers need to be sited where the cost of transport of raw materials is lowest.

In the past in the UK, this has meant that steel works have been

The cost of moving

Hiring office space in central London is expensive. A typical office in the City area, for instance, might cost £425 per sq. metre per annum. Move to Hull or Middlesbrough and the same space would cost only a fraction of that price. Yet Hull, at £80 per sq metre or Middlesbrough at £75 per sq metre are not being besieged by bargain hunters. This is because moving offices is a costly business. £30 000 per worker should be built into any calculation for a move. What's more, many offices are tied to a local area. Trying to run an accountancy firm serving clients mainly located in London from an office in Hull is a guaranteed route to failure. That is why most businesses only move a few miles.

An insurance company is considering moving its 2 000 sq metres office in the City area of central London with a rent of £400 per sq metre **either** to the Euston area of central London with rents of £300 per sq metre **or** to Hull with rents of £80 per sq metre. It currently has 200 employees.

1 Calculate: (a) the rent cost per year of staying in its present offices; (b) the new rent cost per year if it moved to the same sized offices in the Euston area; (c) the yearly rent cost of the same sized offices in Hull.

2 Would it be financially worthwhile to move: (a) within London; and (b) from London to Hull if moving costs of £30 000 per worker were taken into account?

3 There would be non-monetary benefits for the company if it stayed in London rather than moving to Hull. For instance, a move to Hull could mean that a lot of existing workers might resign because they were not prepared to move. This would be disruptive for the company. Suggest TWO other non-monetary benefits for the company of staying in London.

Siting a convenience store

S&R is a business which runs convenience stores throughout the UK. The exact mix of products sold varies from location to location. However, in a city centre, it would be confectionery, soft drinks, tobacco products, magazines and possibly greetings cards and/or snacks such as sandwiches and/or selected groceries.
The business is considering opening a store in the centre of Balsford.

1 Consider the five possible sites on the map (A-E). Which do you think would give the highest level of sales turnover? Explain your answer carefully.
2 Which do you think would be the most expensive and the least expensive to rent per sq ft? In your answer, rank in order the five sites in terms of likely cost and explain your reasons.
3 What other factors would you have to take into account when making a final decision about where to site the store?

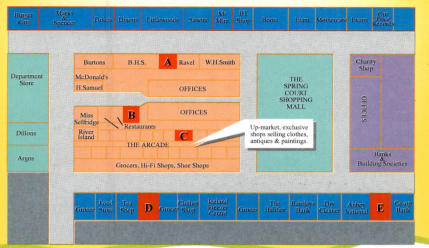

built next to coal mines and iron mines. However, the UK's iron ore deposits are now exhausted. So a steel producer like British Steel today buys its iron ore from abroad. Its plants are now sited on the coast, where the iron ore is delivered in large ships to reduce transport costs.

Transport costs of raw materials and components are not particularly high relative to final cost for electronics manufacturers. So LG is not really affected by this when it decides where to locate. Being near to the M4 motorway helps, but LG could have sited its plant in France, Thailand or Brazil without having much impact on transport costs.

Costs of transporting the finished goods
Some industries need to be sited near to their customers because the cost of transporting the finished product is very high in relation to the value of the product. Bricks, for instance, used to build the LG factory, may come from a local brick plant because the cost of transport is so high in relation to the value of a

single brick.

The transport costs of finished electronic products are not high in relation to the value. So LG doesn't need to locate near to its customers for reasons of transport.

LG then is typical of many businesses which are FOOTLOOSE. They are free to locate anywhere because transport costs are not very important,

The market

An electronics manufacturer like LG can site itself anywhere in the world and ship components and finished products in and out of the country. However, an electronic goods retailer is in a different situation. A retailer like Dixons or PC World sited on the high street or on a retail shopping park is likely to sell far more computers than a shop in a small town. Location is crucial to the success of any retailer.

There are many other industries apart from retailing where being near to the market is vital. For instance, in personal services such as hairdressing or the restaurant

trade, location is important. Banks and building societies also need convenient locations for the customer.

Many industries don't need to be near their markets. LG, for instance, can transport its product anywhere around the world to its customers. Even in retailing, many computers are now sold via mail order. So computer sellers don't need to be near their customers.

Labour

Availability of workers, their skills and the wages they need to be paid can be very important for a business in deciding where to locate itself. Labour was one of the key attractions for LG of the South Wales site.

First, the cost of employing labour in South Wales was not very high. Wages paid to workers in the UK are low in comparison with most European Union countries like Germany or France. They are also lower than in some far eastern countries like Japan. What is more, the taxes on employing labour in the UK are very low too by international standards. In Germany, for instance, employers have to pay about half as much again as the wage of the worker to the government for contributions to health care, pensions and welfare benefits. In the UK, employers' National Insurance contributions are only about 10 per cent.

Second, unemployment in Wales is higher than the national average. LG had a large number of applicants to choose from for every job it advertised.

Third, workers in Wales had basic skills such as literacy and numerary. This would not necessarily have been true if LG had located in Thailand or India for instance. The government, through Gwent TEC (the local **Training and Enterprise Council**, ☞ unit 58), trained the workers in the skills they needed.

Import restrictions

All countries impose restrictions on imports (☞ unit 7) to some extent. The European Union (EU) imposes common restrictions on all imports coming into Europe. A non-European manufacturer may find that the only way to sell into Europe is to locate a factory within the EU. For instance, one of the reasons why Nissan and Toyota set up car plants in the UK was because there were restrictions on imports of Japanese cars into the EU.

Regional aid

Businesses create jobs and prosperity in a **local economy** (☞ unit 5). Attracting a business to set up in an area can therefore be very important to a local council or a government.

In the UK, businesses may get help with locating from the local council, a regional body, the UK government or the European Union (☞ unit 8).

Local councils Many local councils in the UK have a department which tries to attract new businesses into the area. They advertise in newspapers, magazines and on television. They can help a business thinking of setting up by providing it with all the information it needs about how to get grants or other aid from the government or the EU. They can suggest where land or premises can be bought or rented locally. They can also help the business with any regulations for new buildings. Newport County Council, for

instance, worked with the Welsh Development Agency to persuade LG to come to Wales. It granted LG planning permission to build the factory.

Regional development agencies A number of regions in the UK have development agencies. They are responsible for attracting businesses to set up in their region or expand their existing operations. The Welsh Development Agency was the main body with which LG negotiated. It arranged with the government for up to £200 million worth of grants to be given to LG for siting its plant near Newport.

The government The government offers a variety of help to businesses. It may give grants to firms setting up in high unemployment areas of the country designated as **Developmant Areas**. Part of the £200 million was given under this **Regional Selective Assistance (RSA)**. Businesses willing to set up in run down urban areas may be able to get financial help from the **City Challenge** scheme. Various areas in the country have won grants from the government to help transform run down areas through a mixture of new housing, industrial development and training for the local workforce. **English Partnerships** is a government-sponsored

Source: Lancaster City Council, Economic Development Service.

agency which also helps industry to regenerate run down urban areas. It gives help and advice. It is prepared to take an equity stake (i.e. put up money to buy shares) in a business which locates in a deprived area. It also offers loans to businesses. Businesses in rural areas can get financial help from the **Rural Development Commission for England**. If a business creates new jobs, for instance, it may be able to get a grant from the commission. There are many other forms of assistance that the government offers through a variety of other schemes. Most businesses seeking help might approach their local **Training and Enterprise Council (TEC)** or **Business Link**. These give help and advice to businesses. This

Toyota

In 1997, Toyota announced that it was looking for a location to build a plant which had the capacity to build up to 200 000 cars per year. It already had a very successful plant at Burnaston near Derby. One possibility was that this plant would be expanded. Toyota was also considering a site in Northern France.

Source: adapted from the *Financial Times*, 17 March 1997 and 10 December 1997.

DTP

1 Write an article about the Toyota decision to build a new plant.
   (a) Explain the alternatives available to Toyota.
   (b) Put forward the advantages and disadvantages of each site.
   (c) Argue which site you think ought to be chosen. If possible, use a DTP to lay out the article as it might appear in a newspaper.

Burnaston, UK

Government aid : little or none because Derby is not a high unemployment area.

Labour: established workforce which could be expanded for needs of the new factory. Pay rates lower than in France.

Taxes: taxes on workers and social security contributions add about 10 per cent to the cost of employing a worker.

Factory: plenty of room on the Burnaston site to add another facility.

Market: Toyota is unlikely to lift its market share of cars sold in the UK significantly. It sells far more cars into the UK as a percentage of the market than in the rest of the EU.

Valenciennes, Northern France

Government aid: up to 10 per cent of the cost of the factory is being offered in various forms of government aid, including reduced taxes and training grants for workers.

Labour: pay rates above UK pay rates. Valenciennes is a high unemployment area and therefore recruiting workers should not be a problem.

Taxes: taxes on workers and social security contributions add about 45 per cent to the cost of employing a worker. However as part of the aid package, the government is waiving some of these taxes for a fixed period.

Factory: a greenfield site has been made available. Valenciennes has good motorway and rail links to the rest of France and to the Channel ports and the Channel Tunnel. Links to the UK are important because engines for any new production would come from Burnaston in Derby.

Market: Toyota only has 1.1 per cent of the French car market. In the long term it wants to raise this to 5 per cent.

means that they inform the business of the assistance it might be able to get and then help it to apply for the grant.

The European Union The EU gives a wide variety of loans and grants, mostly linked to high unemployment and factory closures. Certain areas of the UK have been particularly targeted because their income is below the EU average. The EU is a major supporter of agriculture, through the Common Agricultural Policy (CAP). Businesses also benefit from the funding that the EU gives to local authorities on **infrastructure** (☞ unit 5) schemes, such as the building of new roads.

Source: adapted from *The Times*, 11 July 1996; Business Link.

Key terms

Footloose industries - industries where costs of transport of raw materials and finished goods are relatively low, so that they can be situated in a wide variety of locations.

Greenfield site - location available for industrial building which is currently agricultural land.

PODMORE'S

The business - Podmore's is a fast expanding company which makes electrical components. Its customers are mainly in the south of England. However, it has a growing trade with Europe, particularly Holland, Germany and Scandinavia. It is currently based in Newham in London. Its factory is now too small and the company is looking for new premises. It could stay in Newham. There is a suitable site just 1/4 of a mile away. It could also move elsewhere in the country. A variety of costs, including the cost of transporting goods to buyers and the cost of employing staff, would be different depending upon the location. These are shown in Table 50.1.

Marketing - The marketing department is concerned about rumours that the company is thinking of moving away from the London area. It feels that being near its customers is essential if sales are to continue to grow and current customers kept satisfied. If the company did move from the south of England, the marketing department feels that it may be necessary to open a new office in the south. This would add considerable cost to the marketing effort and lead to communication problems with a factory based hundreds of miles away.

Staff - Staff are concerned by reports that the company might move out of London. Very few shop floor workers would be prepared to go with the company to a new location hundreds of miles away. Some senior staff have also expressed reservations about moving. It would take time to build up an effective new team of workers if key workers failed to relocate with the company.

1 As a director of the company, study the information provided about the four sites. Write a short report explaining which of the four sites the board should choose.

Checklist ✓

1 Why might a business choose to locate on a greenfield site?

2 Why might a shoe manufacturer choose not to locate in a city centre site whilst a shoe retailer would be attracted to the area?

3 It costs more to transport clay to make bricks than do the bricks themselves. Where should a plant making bricks be located?

4 'Computer manufacturers are footloose.' What does this mean?

5 Give FIVE examples of businesses which need to be located near to their markets and explain why this is the case.

6 A business wants to employ workers who are as highly skilled and motivated as possible. It also wants to keep costs to a minimum. Wages are higher and unemployment lower in East Anglia than in Scotland. Which region should prove the most attractive to businesses and why?

7 Why does government offer incentives to businesses coming to a particular area of the country?

Hull An existing factory near the port, with good motorway connections to the A1 south and the west coast via the M62. The factory is ideally suited to present capacity needs.

Edinburgh New factory shell premises on an industrial estate with good road access to Glasgow and the south. Land included on the site could allow up to 30 per cent expansion of the building.

Liverpool Renovated 19th century building of great historical interest near to the city centre. The inside has been completely gutted to make it suitable for 21st century manufacturing. The building is about 20 per cent larger than is currently needed for production.

Table 50.1 *Estimated costs (+) and savings (−) of the move.*				
	£ million estimated			
	Edinburgh	Liverpool	Hull	Newham
Annual change in labour costs	− 2.0	− 2.5	− 1.7	0
Annual change in transport costs	+ 1.2	+ 1.0	0	0
Annual change in other costs	− 0.3	− 0.3	− 0.3	0
Cost of new factory with equipment (including any regional aid)	+ 9.0	+ 7.0	+ 7.5	+ 11.5
Cost of moving	+ 2.0	+ 2.0	+ 2.0	+ 0.5

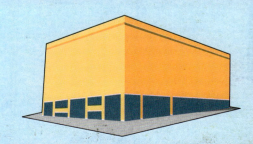

Newham An existing factory with about 10 per cent more space than is currently needed. Office accommodation is cramped and poor quality.

Making decisions

Businesses need to recruit the best possible workers. To achieve this, they have to decide what procedures to adopt for recruitment and selection. For instance, how will they attract workers to apply for the job? How will they choose which applicants to appoint? Will they use interviews? Will they use other methods of selection? What use will they make of references?

Powell & Heilbron (Paper) Ltd is a limited company. It is a wholly owned subsidiary of an international company, Bunzl plc. Based in Liverpool, the company is a paper merchant supplying the printing and stationery trade throughout Merseyside and the North West. It operates from a purpose-built warehouse covering 15 000 square feet and containing paper stocks worth over £0.5 million. 25 people are employed by the company.

Why recruit and select?

Businesses need workers. How many workers they employ depends upon what tasks need to be done, the cost of the workers and how much they can afford to pay. A business might carry out

SALES ASSISTANT

Due to internal promotion we are looking for an experienced sales assistant in our busy Liverpool Sales Office.

You will be respnsible for dealing with customers' orders and enquiries received by phone and fax within the guidelines of our 'customer care' policy. You should possess a good telephone personality, negotiating and sales skills, with a knowledge of data input and computer-based stock control systems. Some experience of printing would be an advantage.

We are able to offer planned product and skills training development and the right person will be rewarded financially by means of an excellent salary and commission.

Please apply in writing with your C.V. to:-

The Sales Director
Powell + Heilbron (Paper) Ltd
Bevington House
6 Gardners Row
Liverpool L3 6HX

Figure 53.1 *Powell & Heilbron's advertisement for a Sales Assistant.*

human resource planning to find out how many workers and what types of worker are needed. Recruiting workers with the right skills and at a wage or salary the business can afford to pay is very important.

Recruitment

In 1996, Powell & Heilbron (Paper) needed to fill a vacancy which arose in its Sales Office. A Sales Assistant (who took orders from telephone and fax requests to Powell & Heilbron) had been promoted to become a Sales Representative (who visits companies to gain orders). Businesses wanting to recruit workers have a variety of ways in which they can seek applicants.

INTERNAL RECRUITMENT occurs when the business appoints someone to a post who is already working for the organisation. For instance, the promotion of the Sales Assistant to the post of Sales Representative was an example of internal recruitment.

Powell & Heilbron (Paper) has a policy of recruiting internally wherever possible. However, there was no one suitable within the company to fill the vacant post of Sales Assistant. So it had to RECRUIT EXTERNALLY, looking outside the company for a worker.

Jobcentres One way to do this is to notify the local Jobcentre of the vacancy. Jobcentres are paid for by the government. They are responsible for helping workers, including the unemployed, to find jobs or to get training. They also provide a service to businesses which want to recruit workers. The services they provide are mostly free both to workers and businesses. However, most of the jobs notified to Jobcentres tend to be manual jobs rather than white collar jobs in manufacturing or lower level work in service industries. Because of this, Powell & Heilbron (Paper) did not consider it worthwhile to advertise its vacancy at the local Jobcentre.

Private employment agencies There is a large number of private employment agencies which, like Jobcentres, advertise jobs on

Using the web

According to a new report from recruitment consultants Robert Walters, 10 per cent of all internet traffic now relates to recruitment.

If people are talking so much about recruitment about jobs on the internet, it's not surprising that some companies are now advertising jobs on the world wide web.

Advertising on the web has its advantages. 'I can advertise on the web for £6 a pop, and it's immediate' says Peter Burden, IT manager for Direct Approach, a private recruitment agency. 'If we put an ad in even the best paper-based product, it can take two weeks for it to go in depending on the product's frequency.' What's more, a 1997 National Opinion Poll survey showed that 20 per cent of people with access to the internet don't read newspapers. Paying £30 000 for an advert in a Sunday newspaper therefore misses out a lot of people who might consider applying.

The web has its limitations though. Most jobs advertised on the web are IT related jobs. Senior management positions are also popular because senior managers are likely to have access to and use the web. However, the web 'is appalling for non-technical people' says Peter Burden. Alistair Lamont of online recruitment company, Where It's @, warns that 'there's no point going to the likes of JobServe for anything like marketing jobs, for instance'.

Source: adapted from *Management Today*, March 1998.

1 Direct Approach is an example of a private recruitment agency. How might a business like Woolworth's or Ford use private recruitment agencies?

2 Explain the advantages of advertising on the world wide web rather than advertising in, say, a national newspaper or a specialist magazine?

3 A car manufacturer wants to recruit a computer programmer, a marketing executive and a canteen worker. It is considering advertising on the web, in national newspapers and in the local newspaper.
Where do you think it should advertise?
Explain your answer carefully.

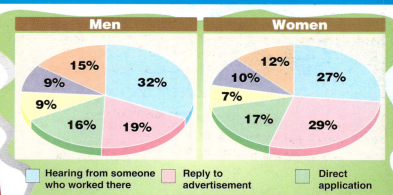

Figure 53.2 caption area:

Men	Women

- 32%, 15%, 9%, 9%, 16%, 19% (Men)
- 12%, 27%, 10%, 7%, 17%, 29% (Women)

Hearing from someone who worked there (light blue)
Reply to advertisement (pink)
Direct application (green)
Jobcentre, jobmarket etc (yellow)
Private employment agency, business (purple)
Other (orange)

Figure 53.2 *How employees obtained their current job (within last three months), GB, Summer 1996.*
Source: adapted from *Labour Market Trends*, February 1997.

behalf of businesses. Most private employment agencies specialise. For instance, there are agencies which deal mainly with temporary work, nursing jobs or executive posts. This helps businesses looking for these types of workers to find them. However, unlike Jobcentres, agencies charge for their services.

Advertising Powell & Heilbron (Paper) chose to use newspaper advertising to fill its vacancy. It placed an advert in a local Merseyside newspaper. Newspapers can reach a large readership. Different newspapers can also reach different types of reader. Powell & Heilbron (Paper) was quite happy to recruit a local person for the job. If the job had been more high-powered, it would probably have advertised nationally, in a specialist newspaper or magazine, or in a national newspaper. National advertising would be seen by a wider range of people and therefore the business would hopefully have more applicants from which to choose. The problem with advertising is that newspapers and magazines charge for the advert.

Word of mouth Agencies and advertising are important ways of attracting recruits. However, the most important way in which people find jobs is through word of mouth as Figure 53.2 shows. Somebody may know that a job is vacant and tell the person who actually applies for the job. If a vacancy can be filled by word of mouth, it can save on advertising costs. Businesses will find it easiest to fill vacancies by word of mouth when there are plenty of suitable workers looking for a job. This could be, for instance, at a time of high unemployment.

Application

Some jobs may only attract a few applicants. If the job is unskilled, the business may interview immediately anybody who rings up or calls in. For many jobs, though, there will be a more formal procedure.

Applicants will have to ring up or write for **particulars** for the job. These are likely to be a general description of the business together with details of the job itself. These details may include a JOB DESCRIPTION. This sets out what

Cut out TEN different job advertisements from one or more newspapers or magazines. They should be for a wide variety of jobs. Some should be large display advertisements, others should be small adverts.

1 Compare the advertisements. Do they all give salary levels? Do they all give an address and a telephone number? How much detail about jobs do they give? Do they state what experience and qualifications are needed?

2 Which advertisements do you think are going to get the most enquiries? Explain your reasons carefully.

the person appointed to the job will have to do. An example of the job description for the job at Powell & Heilbron (Paper) is shown in Figure 53.3.

The particulars will explain how the applicant should apply. For some jobs, the business asks for a CURRICULUM VITAE (CV) and a letter of application. A CV is simply a document, often one or two sides of A4 paper, which gives the main details about the applicant, such as name, address, age, qualifications and employment history. The letter of application is a letter in which the applicant explains why he or she wants the job and is particularly suited to that job. A comprehensive and up-to-date CV and a letter of application is what Powell & Heilbron (Paper) expected from its applicants.

Alternatively, the applicant will be sent and asked to fill in a JOB APPLICATION FORM. This asks for the information which would typically be contained in a CV. It also often includes space for the letter of application.

Selection

Having received CVs and letters of application, Powell & Heilbron

(Paper) was in a position to start the process of **selection**. The company was looking for someone with a good telephone personality. Ideally, the person should have experience in the print/stationery market. Previous sales experience would be an advantage. The successful person would have to be familiar with computers.

23 applications were received. Having looked through the CVs and letters of application, 10 people were **shortlisted** and invited for an **interview**. The interview is very important because it allows the employer and the applicant to meet. The employer is trying to find out whether the person would make a suitable employee. The applicant is trying to decide whether the job and the business is right for him or her. At the initial interviews, Powell & Heilbron (Paper) asked the candidates to complete an application form giving details of their medical history, education and previous employment as well. This helped the company get more information on paper about the candidates than was contained on the CVs and

letters of application.

After the first round of interviews, four applications were invited back for a second interview. The interviewers then prepared an Interview Report. This graded each of the four remaining applicants on important qualities such as appearance, conversational ability and knowledge of work field. Conversational ability is very important for a sales assistant for instance. If you find it difficult to

Figure 53.3 *Powell & Heilbron (Paper), job description*

Powell & Heilbron (Paper) Ltd

Job Description
Job Title: Inside Sales Assistant
Reporting to: Sales Director
Job Outline: Dealing with orders and enquiries received by phone/fax and processing same through computer based systems.

Responsibilities:
1. Taking orders from our large customer base, checking stock availability and processing orders through computer.
2. Receiving enquiries for various grades of paper and sourcing the right paper that meets the customers' requirements.
3. Costing enquiries and preparing quotation sheets.
4. Developing a positive and confident attitude to our customers' needs, in lin with our 'customer care' policy.
5. Ensuring orders are delivered on time in line with the commitments given to our customers.
6. Undertake a formal three year training program run by the Institute of Paper.
7. Attend 'in-house' training programmes as required from time to time.
8. To achieve agreed sales targets in accordance with the Company's sales and marketing strategy.
9. To maintain and develop at all times a favourable company image by always seeking to achieve a professional approach and a high level of personal presentation and appearance.

Telephone interviews

Kevin Peters was looking for a senior management job. He had climbed as far as he was going to go in his current organisation and had been combing the ads for months. Just before Christmas, he spotted a very promising job. He sent in his CV and a covering letter.

A few days later, the phone went in the middle of a very busy day for him. It was the company to which he had sent his application. At first he thought they were just ringing to make an appointment but then they started asking questions about his current job and experience. After a few minutes, he realised he was in the middle of a preliminary interview.

He didn't get on the short list to be invited to a face to face interview. This didn't surprise him. He had felt distracted on the phone and didn't sell himself very well at all. If he had had a face to face interview, he would have been prepared and psychologically ready for the questions he would have been asked. As it was, he didn't feel that he had been fairly treated.

1 Explain the importance of the following in getting a job:
(a) 'combing the ads'; (b) sending in your CV and letter of application; (c) getting onto a shortlist; (d) being interviewed.
2 Why did Kevin Peters fail to perform well in his telephone interview do you think?
3 How well do you think you would perform in a telephone interview? Give reasons for your answer.

talk to people you don't know, or have a very abrupt way of talking, then you won't make a very good sales assistant.

One person was then offered the job subject to **references**. These are reports on the potential employee from his or her current employer or someone else who knows the applicant and can say something about them. School leavers, for instance, might ask someone from their school to be a referee. The reference is a final check that the information given by the candidate at interview is correct.

The whole process from placing the advertisement in the local paper to the person being appointed took Powell & Heilbron (Paper) one month.

Source: Powell & Heilbron (Paper) Ltd.

KEY TERMS

Curriculum vitae - a brief listing of the main details about an applicant, including name, address, age, qualifications and experience.

External recruitment - when an employee is appointed from outside the organisation.

Internal recruitment - when an existing employee is appointed to a post.

Job application form - form which a business issues to applicants to complete when applying for a job, which asks for relevant details about the applicant.

Job description - document that describes the duties of a worker and his or her status in the organisation.

Thinking of becoming a hairdresser?

Grants of Newcastle

is now interviewing school leavers for its two year hairdressing and beauty training programme, leading to N.V.Q. qualifications.

Apply by letter, including a CV to Janet Williams, Grants, Heaton Road, Newcastle.

We are an equal opportunities company.

71 Addycombe Terrace
Heaton
Newcastle Upon Tyne
6 June 1998

Dear Mrs Williams

I've seen the advert you put in the newspaper and I want to apply for the job, I am very interested in hairdressing and beauty. I can come to an interview this week but next week I'm going on holliday.

Yours sincerely

Sharon White

Sharon White

CV

Name	Sharon White
Address	71 Addycombe Terrace, Heaton, Newcastle Upon Tyne
Date of birth	1 April 1982
Age	16
Qualifications:	exams taken this summer GCSE English, Maths, Science; History, Child Care, Business Studies

Checklist ✓

1. Why do businesses need to recruit workers?
2. Distinguish between internal and external recruitment.
3. Describe THREE different ways in which a business could recruit externally.
4. Look at Figure 53.2. Explain how workers get a job.
5. An applicant for a transport lorry driver's job is sent a job description. What is a 'job description'?
6. How might a business ask applicants to send in details about themselves and why they want to apply for a job?
7. Why do businesses often ask for references for an applicant?

Sharon White has sent a letter and her CV in response to the advertisement. Grants has received Sharon White's letter. Do you think it should invite her for interview? In your answer, consider: (a) who else might be applying; (b) the sort of post being offered, and (c) the training involved.

SUMMARY CASE STUDY

MANN + HUMMEL

1. Describe the job that is being offered in the advertisement.
2. What are the advantages and disadvantages to Mann + Hummel of advertising in a local newspaper like the Express & Star rather than: (a) using a Jobcentre; or (b) advertising in a national newspaper?
3. To apply, you are asked to forward your full CV. (a) What is a CV? (b) Describe THREE characteristics the company is looking for in a suitable applicant which might be found on their CV. (c) Having received CVs, how is Mann + Hummel likely to select a candidate?
4. Draw up a list of FIVE questions that might be asked of candidates who are interviewed for the job. For each one, explain why you think it is an important question.

Source: *Express & Star*, 13 November 1997.

YOU'LL NEGOTIATE THE BEST PRICES

PURCHASER

At MANN+HUMMEL, we are acknowledged global leaders in the automotive components industry, supplying virtually all the major car manufacturers from our 16 European sites. At our 11-acre UK site in Wolverhampton, opened earlier this year, we are committed to maintaining our distinctive world-wide reputation for quality and now we are seeking an experienced and disciplined individual to help sustain our cost-effectiveness and profitability.

By tough price negotiation and your determination to minimise costs for the company, you'll arrange special rates and contracts with suppliers and contractors when you purchase consumables, investments and services for all our departments. You'll also raise purchase orders on SAP R/3 client server software and maintain an up-to-date database of our current suppliers. Your broader scheduling responsibility will entail keeping close contact with our Central Purchasing Department in Germany, as well as planning all material requirements, controlling purchased items and dealing with any problems arising from goods delivered.

With several years' background in purchasing, you'll already be an articulate and tough negotiator, strongly aware of cost responsibility and knowledgeable about the local market. Your determined and professional hands-on approach, combined with a commitment to quality and accuracy, means that you cope well with pressure and work the hours needed to complete your tasks. To succeed in a role requiring initiative, you must be computer literate, educated to at least GCSE in English and Maths, and possess a current driving licence and the flexibility to travel in Europe on occasion.

MANN+HUMMEL

To apply, please write, forwarding your full CV, including current salary package, to Louise Coss, Human Resources Manager, MANN+HUMMEL (UK) LTD., Hilton Cross Business Park, Cannock Road, Featherstone, Wolverhampton WV10 7QZ.

Making decisions

Businesses want their workers to work hard and produce goods and services of a high standard. Workers are more likely to do this if they are well motivated. How can businesses motivate their employees? Should they try to motivate workers simply through pay? Or are they going to appeal to the needs of workers other than pay, such as being given responsibility or achieving their own goals? How can businesses create an environment where their workers are putting all their efforts into making a success of the business?

Richer Sounds was started by Julian Richer in 1979. He specialised in selling end of line hi-fi equipment at a low price from his single shop. Today, his business is too big to buy end of lines from the manufacturers and his shops sell standard hi-fi equipment at low prices. Richer Sounds is now an important part of the retail hi-fi market, setting standards for price and customer service. Julian Richer himself sets the pace for the company, constantly trying to come up with new ideas to improve the business.

The importance of motivation

A business like Richer Sounds needs to MOTIVATE its workers. A well motivated workforce is more likely to work hard. This will help a business improve the quality of its product, keep its costs down, make a profit and remain competitive. There is a number of different ideas about what motivates workers.

Basic needs

One idea, first put forward by Frederick Taylor in *The Principles of Scientific Management*, published in 1911, is that workers are motivated mainly by pay. **The scientific management school** argues that pay should therefore be linked to performance, for instance through

The John Lewis Partnership

The John Lewis Partnership was created in 1928 by John Lewis. He owned a chain of department stores, including George Henry Lee, and decided to give them to his workers. He created a trust which owned the shares in the business. Profits were to be given to the workers, or 'partners' as they became called. In 1997, a 'partner' earning £8 000 a year received a profit bonus of £1 538, equivalent to ten weeks' salary. The John Lewis Partnership is a very successful company on a number of measures. In 1997, a record year, profits were £217 million on sales of £3.2 billion, a net profit ratio of 7 per cent. Sales and profits have increased over time. Labour productivity is high. Staff turnover (the rate at which staff leave the company) is relatively low. As a previous company chairperson said, accountability is at the heart of the organisation. Workers, whether managers or shop floor workers, feel accountable to others for the success of the business. 'It makes people think ahead. It makes people consider the consequences of their actions.'

Source: adapted from the *Financial Times*, 19 February 1992, 7 March 1997 and 22 March 1997.

1 Who owns the John Lewis Partnership?

2 Worker motivation is high at the John Lewis Partnership. Why do you think this helps make the company successful?

3 Why do you think that the partnership structure of the business might increase worker motivation compared to a normal company, where outside shareholders own the business?

Wordprocessing

4 Each week, the company issues a magazine, the *Gazette*, to its staff. In the *Gazette*, there is always a large number of letters from partners (the employees) about how the business should be run. One partner, Mrs Wigmore, has written in on the subject of the annual bonus. She pointed out that in 1997, the company made a pre-tax profit of £217 million, but only paid £57 million to the 'partners'. She wants all the profit to be distributed to partners. You are a manager who has to write a reply to this suggestion. Write this reply (preferably wordprocessed) putting the advantages and disadvantages of the suggestion. You might find it helpful to look back at unit 25 to see what companies do with their profits. At the end, state whether you agree or disagree with the suggestion.

Figure 54.1 *Maslow's hierarchy of needs.*

the use of **piece rates** or **bonuses** linked to sales (☞ unit 56).

This view says that workers, like the staff at Richer Sounds, go to work mainly to earn money to survive. Without money, staff at Richer Sounds wouldn't be able to buy food, clothes, shelter and heating essential to satisfy their basic human needs (☞ unit 1).

Higher needs

People, however, have other needs. An American researcher called A H Maslow put these in order of importance (a HIERARCHY OF NEEDS) as can be seen in Figure 54.1.

Physiological needs Staff at Richer Sounds want to satisfy their basic human needs (called **physiological needs** by Maslow). Richer Sounds achieves this through paying its workers a wage.

Safety needs Workers want to know that they won't be made redundant and that their working environment is safe. As a slowly expanding business, staff at Richer Sounds know that they are unlikely to be made redundant because of a downturn in trade. Safety of

workers and customers is also a key priority of the business.

Love and belonging This is a higher order need. People want to feel accepted as part of a group, like a family at home or a team in a workplace. They want to be trusted and be able to support others. One of Julian Richer's great strengths is that he has created a business where staff feel that sense of belonging. He encourages them to feel part of a team. The effect of this is shown in the very low rate of absenteeism. On average, only between 1 and 2 per cent of staff are off sick on any day, less than half the national average.

Self-esteem needs People want to feel that others respect them for what they can do. They want to respect themselves too, feeling that they have achieved something and are good at a task. For instance, the Richer Sounds stores which have been judged each month to give the best service to customers are given the use of a Jaguar or Bentley. Staff are therefore rewarded for fulfilling a key management objective - customer satisfaction.

Self-actualisation This is the highest order need, according to Maslow. It is the ability to realise your full potential. One way in which Richer attempts to achieve self-actualisation for his workers is through the company suggestion scheme. Staff are encouraged to put forward ideas for ways to improve the business. Staff are even given £5 each month to go to a pub with other staff to talk about ideas.

Fulfilling needs

When businesses try to motivate their workers, they need to be aware of three things.

- If a worker is well paid, pay is no longer a motivator. A worker is motivated by achieving the next level within the hierarchy of needs. Only the highest level, self-actualisation, can in itself carry on motivating workers who have achieved this.

Electronic Data Systems (EDS)

Electronic Data Systems (EDS) is an information technology (IT) company which specialises in devising software systems for clients. An American company, it has won several important contracts in the UK, including devising the computer system which runs all the work of the Inland Revenue, the government body that collects income tax.

Sometimes, customers decide to close down their IT departments completely. They then contract out the work to a company like EDS. Workers are going to be made redundant when a customer closes down its IT department. EDS, on the other hand, if it wins the contract, will need to take on extra workers. So what often happens is that the workers are transferred from the customer to EDS.

Not surprisingly, this transfer is usually a stressful experience for workers. They are worried that they will have to move. They fear that their contracts will be changed in such a way that they get less pay and fewer benefits. They suspect that the new job will be less satisfying than the old one. They think that their promotion prospects might be damaged or that they will be demotivated. At worst, they fear that they will be made redundant.

EDS is well aware of these fears. The director of human resources in Europe, Tony Ebbutt, was himself transferred from Unilever to EDS in 1984 when Unilever sold its computer services subsidiary to EDS. The company has a blue print which it uses when drawing up new arrangements for incoming employees. It doesn't mask the fact that there may be a few redundancies. However, most will be offered either the standard EDS contract of service or a contract matching the one they had with their former employer. They are told about the potential for promotion within EDS. They are also offered retraining if that is suitable.

Source: adapted from the *Financial Times,* 9 February 1996.

1 What is EDS and what service does it provide?

2 (a) List Maslow's five needs in his hierarchy of needs. (b) Explain how these needs are NOT met when workers are told that they will lose their job with a company and be redeployed to EDS.

3 EDS is careful to try to meet workers' needs when they transfer. What do you think workers will still be fearful of despite the efforts of EDS to ease their transition into the company?

4 A worker has been told that she, together with another 100 workers in her department, are being transferred to EDS. She considers whether to resign and look for a job elsewhere. Suggest what might be: (a) the advantages; and (b) the disadvantages for her of looking for a new job rather than being transferred to EDS.

- If a need is not satisfied, then it can lead to demotivation. For instance, workers threatened with redundancy or who are worried that their boss thinks their work is poor are not going to be well motivated.

- If a lower order need is not met, then meeting higher order needs becomes irrelevant. If staff felt they were poorly paid, this would demotivate them however much their other higher order needs were being met.

Human relations

Frederick Taylor believed that pay was the main reason why people worked. They needed to be closely supervised and told what to do. This was because workers would tend to do as little as possible and would not necessarily work in the most efficient way. They also didn't want to accept responsibility, such as organising their own work.

These views were called Theory X by another American researcher, Douglas McGregor. However, he argued that a company like Richer Sounds would fail to motivate workers if they adopted Theory X views. This is because workers want their higher needs fulfilling when they go to work. He called this view Theory Y. This says that workers, like those at Richer Sounds, will be motivated to work if they are given responsibility and allowed to make decisions. This **Human Relations School** of thought says that workers work best in conditions where they are trusted, and where they are given an opportunity to fulfil themselves. These views are shown in Table 54.1.

Job satisfaction

Another American researcher, Frederick Herzberg, came to similar conclusions. He suggested that some factors about a job, shown in Table 54.2, would motivate workers and give them JOB SATISFACTION. This is the amount of enjoyment, satisfaction or pleasure that a worker gets out of doing a particular job. Julian Richer wants his staff to enjoy their work. For instance, when staff join the company, they go on a three day course at Julian Richer's home in York. They work hard but also they play hard, having a choice of tennis, badminton, snooker, swimming, cinema or a discotheque. Richer says: 'We have a lot of fun. This is a deliberately important part of it.' Employees are also able to use five holiday homes owned by the business which they can book free of charge.

Frederick Herzberg also found what he called **hygiene factors** could demotivate workers if they were not met. Workers at Richer Sounds would be demotivated if they didn't receive a reasonable wage. On the other hand, once a Richer Sounds' employee was reasonably paid, offering them higher pay would not motivate them. According to Herzberg, hygiene factors can demotivate but not motivate.

Job enlargement and job enrichment

The work of people such as Maslow and Herzberg has led to ideas that workers' jobs could be made more satisfying through:

- **job enlargement** - instead of a worker doing one small task every day, they would be able to do a variety of tasks. This would make the work less monotonous and boring;

- **job enrichment** - where workers are given some opportunities to choose how to complete a particular job of work, usually working in a team.

Source: adapted from information provided by Richer Sounds.

Table 54.1 McGregor's Theory X and Theory Y.

Theory X	Theory Y
Workers are motivated by money	Workers are motivated by many needs
Workers are lazy and dislike work	Workers can enjoy work
Workers are selfish, ignore the needs of organisations, avoid responsibility and lack ambition	Workers can organise themselves and take responsibility
Workers need to be controlled and directed by management	It is up to management to allow workers to be creative and apply their job knowledge

Table 54.2 Factors which motivate and demotivate workers.

Motivating factors	Demotivating or 'hygiene'
Sense of achievement	Pay
Chance of promotion	Working conditions
Responsibility	Company rules and policy
Nature of the job itself	Fear of redundancy
Recognition by management	Treatment at work
Personal development	Feelings of inadequacy

'Before I started this job, I used to work on an assembly line. It was like school. We sat in rows and if we wanted to go to the toilet we had to put up our hands and ask.'

'All I was doing was putting extra bits on to a product and passing it on every 7 minutes. It was too boring and we were making a lot of mistakes.'

'Every 15 minutes, I mount a magnetic head on a tape-drive, and then test it, glue it and clamp with round it. This is better than my previous job where I sat by a conveyor-belt and put screws into machine 158 times a day.'

'We experimented with workers changing jobs every hour. It was more interesting, but the number of products we produced per hour went down and there were more mistakes. We had to abandon the system.'

1 What is assembly line work?

2 What problems about assembly line work are talked about in the quotes above?

3 Discuss how the higher needs of assembly line workers might be met.

Eatmaster is a national fast food chain. It serves hamburgers, fries, milkshakes and the other familiar foods found in a fast food outlet. The workers in its outlets are nearly all young, below the age of 25. Pay is very low. Labour turnover is high; the average worker only works for three months for the company before leaving.

New workers are given one morning's training to introduce them to the company philosophy of hard work and customer care. The rest of the training is done on the job. It only takes a few minutes to teach a worker the simple routines involved in preparing food or taking orders or cleaning.

Machinery and fittings in the kitchen, serving and eating areas have been designed so that workers have to make as few decisions as possible. This enables the outlet to deliver reasonable customer service even if the work team is not particularly effective at the time.

Eatmaster runs a number of schemes to keep workers motivated. For instance, each week one worker in the outlet is designated 'worker of the week' and can wear a badge stating this. Outlets are given sales targets. If they exceed this, workers are given a small bonus and get their photograph in the company's newsletter.

1 How does Eatmaster try: (a) to motivate its workers; and (b) ensure that a higher quality of service is given to its customers?

Wordprocessing

2 Eatmaster is worried about its high rate of labour turnover. Write a report (preferably word processed) suggesting ways in which it could retain more of its staff for longer periods. In the report, point out the possible costs to Eatmaster of your recommendations.

This is to Certify
B. Sc.
(Burgers & Shakes [hoc])

WORKER OF THE WEEK

a'bmaster

Checklist ✓

1 Why is a motivated workforce important for a business?
2 What, according to Frederick Taylor, motivates workers to work?
3 What is the role of management in motivating workers according to the scientific management school?
4 Explain FOUR higher order needs according to Maslow.
5 Explain what needs you think would be met if you took on a paper round.
6 What is the difference between Theory X and Theory Y?
7 (a) What are 'hygiene factors'? (b) What, according to Herzberg, motivates workers?
8 How could an employer increase the amount of job satisfaction gained by its workers?

SUMMARY
S
CASE STUDY

WOODS

Woods is a national chain of shoe shops. It is looking for a full time shop assistant for one of its stores. It has interviewed the five candidates below. Some of the comments made at the interviews are shown next to each candidate.

Rachael Boswell - You are offering good pay and I need the money. I'm very keen on doing overtime. I'm sure the job will be OK. I've done a number of different jobs before. Some of them have been much worse than this. I've had some terrible managers in my time. I hope the one you put me with will be better.

Sean McDermott - I know my qualifications aren't very good. I messed around at school a lot. Then I had some awful work placements. But the last one in a shop was great. It really opened my eyes. I want to get on. I want to go right to the top. I want to be in charge and make big decisions. I know this sounds stupid because this is just a job at the bottom of the ladder. But you've got to start somewhere, haven't you?

Belinda Tombs - It looks as though my branch is going to go. They call it 'rationalisation'. I've been looking around because I could see this coming. There's nothing worse than turning up every day thinking that this is the day when you'll get your redundancy notice. My boss says she'll give me a good reference. I pride myself on being a good worker. I like everything to be perfect. My boss says I'm too much of a perfectionist. I don't really need the money.

Elizabeth Flowers - Being at home all day can be very depressing. I used to work in a shop before I had the children. I'm really looking forward to getting out of the house and back to work again. I really enjoyed the friendships with the rest of the staff. You always had a few awkward customers and a lot of the work was rather boring, but some customers were really nice. What are the opportunities for promotion?

Willford Pond - I've just got married. My wife says I've got to settle down and get a decent job. She works in a shop too and says its OK. It will bring in the money and that is what's most important isn't it? What are your overtime rates? I expect I'll get used to dealing with the public. Do you give free uniforms or anything like that?

1 What do you think will motivate each candidate to do the job?
2 On the evidence of the interview comments, which candidate would you choose for the job? Explain your reasons carefully.

LEADERSHIP STYLES

Making decisions

Leadership is important for a business. A business rarely does well unless it has an effective leader. There are many different styles of leadership, each of which has its own strengths and weaknesses. A larger business has to decide what sort of person it wants to lead it. In a small business, the leader may have to change his or her style to make the business run effectively.

Virgin was started by Richard Branson, one of the best known business people in Britain today. The activities of the business include air travel and holiday services, rail travel, music retailing, the production of cola drinks and pension services.

Leadership

Richard Branson is a LEADER. Leadership is difficult to define precisely but it usually involves:
- setting targets or goals for a group, like Richard Branson setting sales targets for Virgin Atlantic or a captain setting goals or points targets for a team;
- organising work - like Richard Branson appointing key personnel in the management **hierarchy** (☞ unit 20) at Virgin who will manage the various parts of the company;
- monitoring work to see whether goals are being achieved and, where necessary, motivating workers to achieve most goals.

Types of leader

What sort of leader is Richard

Branson? There are four main types of leader.

Autocratic leaders An AUTOCRATIC LEADER is one who makes all the decisions. The leader then tells the group working under him or her what to do. The role of workers lower in the

hierarchy is to carry out the orders of the leader.

Communication (☞ units 59 and 60) tends to flow from the leader to subordinates and back again. There is little need for subordinates to communicate with one another because they receive orders from

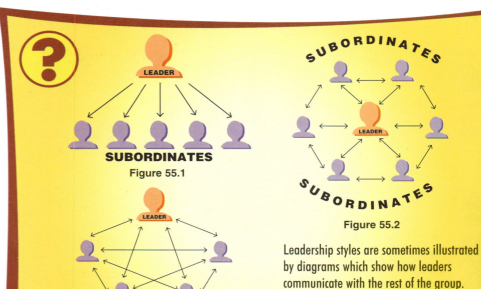

SUBORDINATES

Figure 55.1

SUBORDINATES

Figure 55.2

SUBORDINATES

Figure 55.3

Leadership styles are sometimes illustrated by diagrams which show how leaders communicate with the rest of the group. Explain which style of leadership (autocratic, democratic or laissez-faire) is shown in Figures 55.1 to 55.3.

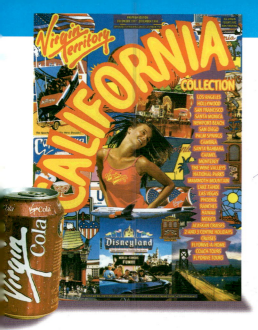

Virgin activities - holiday services and cola production.

above. If the leader is making the right decisions, there can be very effective leadership because the leader is having a powerful influence on the organisation under him or her. However, it can mean that subordinates feel frustrated and become demotivated because they can't fulfil their **higher order needs** (☞ unit 54). Richard Branson is not an autocratic leader. He leaves the day to day decision making to the people who work for him.

Persuasive and democratic A

DEMOCRATIC LEADER is one who shares some of the decision making with subordinates. Persuasive leaders, like autocratic leaders, make decisions alone. But then they 'persuade' workers under them to accept the decision through discussion and reasoning.

Workers are likely to be more motivated under this type of leadership because they feel more involved in decision making. However, decision making can take longer because the leader has to spend time persuading others. Richard Branson could be seen as this type of leader. He is well known for being willing to make hard decisions, such as when he started off his airline, or when he sold his record company. However, Richard Branson is probably the next type of leader.

Consultative and democratic This is a different type of democratic leader. Consultative leaders 'consult' or ask for other's opinions before coming to a decision. The final decision will take account of what subordinates have said. More time probably has to be spent making decisions than with a persuasive leader, but equally workers feel

even more involved and motivated with an effective consultative leader. Richard Branson listens very carefully to the views of the people who work for him. He appoints people who are happy to contribute to discussion about the future of his companies. He encourages workers throughout the organisation to listen to and contribute to debate about how work should be done.

Laissez-faire A LAISSEZ-FAIRE LEADER is one who makes very few decisions. These leaders allow workers under them to make many of their own decisions. Although it allows **subordinates** (workers under them) to be highly creative, laissez-faire leadership can also lead to a feeling by subordinates that no one knows or cares about what is going on. Another unofficial or informal leader often then emerges who gives the organisation more of a sense of direction. Richard Branson is not a laissez-faire leader. He makes decisions and there is a strong sense of purpose and direction within the Virgin companies.

Source: Virgin Management Ltd.

key terms

SUMMARY CASE STUDY

ROBERT MAXWELL

Robert Maxwell did things very much his own way. During the 1970s and 1980s he built up a multi-billion pound business empire. Some have commented that it was like a medieval court, with Maxwell as the leader. People who opposed his rules were banished, while those who flattered him stayed.

He was notorious for attempting to bully people into doing what he wanted. Few people would stand up to him, including the board of directors of the companies which he part owned and ran.

In 1992, he was found drowned. Within weeks, his empire crumbled as it emerged that it owed billions of pounds. Even worse, it was discovered that he had been illegally transferring money from one company to another company in his empire, attempting to keep them afloat. Over a billion pounds of that money belonged to the pension funds of Maxwell-owned companies. The people who were paid to protect ordinary shareholders and pensioners, the directors of these companies, and all the other financial specialists involved, had failed to spot the massive fraud taking place.

Source: adapted from the *Financial Times*, various.

1 What type of leader (autocratic, democratic or laissez-faire) was Robert Maxwell? Explain your answer.

2 Why do you think that a democratic leader would have been more likely to have been found out if they had been attempting to steal billions of pounds from the companies they ran?

Checklist ✓

1 What qualities might a leader have?
2 Explain why the head chef in a large restaurant could be described as a 'leader'.
3 What are the differences between an autocratic leader and a laissez-faire leader?
4 Compare TWO types of democratic leadership.
5 Explain what type of leadership you think might be most effective in: (a) a rock band; (b) the army; (c) a school; (d) a car manufacturer; (e) a hairdressing salon.

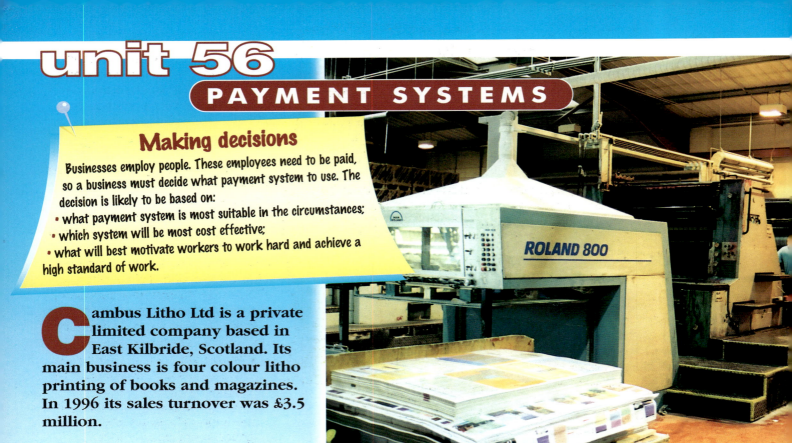

Making decisions

Businesses employ people. These employees need to be paid, so a business must decide what payment system to use. The decision is likely to be based on:
- what payment system is most suitable in the circumstances;
- which system will be most cost effective;
- what will best motivate workers to work hard and achieve a high standard of work.

ROLAND 800

Cambus Litho Ltd is a private limited company based in East Kilbride, Scotland. Its main business is four colour litho printing of books and magazines. In 1996 its sales turnover was £3.5 million.

Payment systems

Cambus Litho employs 48 workers in its printing works in East Kilbride. It also employs other workers, such as sales representatives in London and Nottingham. It uses a number of different PAYMENT SYSTEMS. These are different ways of paying workers.

Alison Pickett is a production manager at a bottling plant.

Richard Tranter is a refuse collector.

PrimeKey

Superior cover for household possessions over £25,000

COMMERCIAL UNION

Kamran Saghir is an insurance salesperson selling life and pension policies.

Anne Lobb is a casual worker. During the harvest season she works on a number of farms in her local area and is hired to pick fruit and vegetables.

1. List the THREE main types of payment system available to employers.
2. Which payment system do you think might be used by a business for each of the workers shown in the photographs? Give reasons for your choice.

Time-based systems MANUAL WORKERS or BLUE COLLAR WORKERS are workers who tend to do physical work like operating machines in the Cambus factory. They have tended to be paid WAGES on a time based system. They are paid 'so much' per hour worked. If they work longer than the agreed basic working week, such as 38 hours, they usually get OVERTIME. This is often paid at a higher hourly rate, such as **time-and-a-quarter** or **double time.** This means that they are paid $1\frac{1}{4}$ or 2 times the BASIC PAY per hour for every hour of overtime worked.

For instance, John Clive works a basic working week of 36 hours. He is paid £10 an hour. This means his basic pay is £360. Last week he worked 2 hours overtime at time-and-a-half. So he earned an extra 2 hours at £15 an hour. His GROSS EARNINGS or GROSS PAY were therefore £390.

Salaries NON-MANUAL or

Supermarket vouchers

Drabble is a small Scottish engineering company. Like a number of other businesses, it has recently started to give supermarket vouchers as a fringe benefit to staff. Although employees have to pay income tax on the vouchers, they are not as yet subject to National Insurance contributions (NICs). If a worker received an extra £10 in his pay packet, he would have to pay approximately £1 of that in NICs. What's more, Drabble as his employer would also have to pay £1 in employers NICs. Giving a £10 supermarket voucher saves the worker £1 and the company another £1.

Supermarket vouchers are not universally popular amongst the staff at Drabble. The company gives Tesco vouchers. But some of the workers either don't live near a Tesco or prefer to do their main shopping at another supermarket. The company is also waiting for the time when the Department for Social Security declares the tax avoidance scheme illegal. They will then have to look for another way of paying staff which reduces tax costs.

1 What is a fringe benefit?
2 (a) Explain what advantages supermarket vouchers give to Drabble and its workers. (b) What disadvantages do they have?
3 Drabble is considering giving additional supermarket vouchers as a bonus to workers or groups or workers who achieve production or sales targets. Do you think this would motive workers to achieve the targets? Explain your answer carefully.

WHITE COLLAR WORKERS tend to be paid SALARIES. A non-manual worker is one who does non-physical work, like an estimator at Cambus Litho or a teacher. Salaries tend to be paid monthly rather than weekly as with wages. Salaried workers are paid for doing a particular job. No overtime is usually paid because salaried workers are expected to work for as long as it takes to do their job. Salaried managers at Cambus Litho typically work 50 hours a week.

Results-based systems Some workers are paid according to how much they produce. Workers on PIECE RATES are paid for every item they produce. If they produce nothing during the day, they get paid nothing. Sales staff may be paid on COMMISSION. For every sale they achieve, they get paid a certain amount. Some sales staff are paid totally on commission, and so if they sell nothing, they get paid nothing. Others are paid commission as a BONUS. Bonuses are given as a reward for doing well. Non-sales staff may be given bonuses if, for instance, their department achieves a particular target for work. This is called a **group bonus.**

Other forms of payment

Workers can be paid in other ways than money. In the coal industry, for instance, it was traditional to give coal miners an amount of coal in addition to their wages. Cambus Litho offers a variety of FRINGE BENEFITS. The more senior the position you hold in a company, the more fringe benefits you are likely to receive. One of the most important fringe benefits for most workers is the subsidised company pension scheme. The company usually provides a proportion of payments into the scheme so that workers can get an occupational pension when they retire.

Fringe benefits are often given for tax reasons. The business pays less tax and other contributions in providing £1 000 worth of fringe benefits than it would if it paid an extra £1 000 in wages to a worker. Similarly, a worker may find there is a tax gain in receiving a fringe benefit rather than cash.

Fringe benefits are also used to motivate workers. The company car, for instance, is very important to many workers. Giving a car with a larger engine seems to motivate some people. At Cambus Litho fringe benefits include company paid private health insurance and a death in service scheme.

Gross and net pay

The gross pay or gross earnings of workers are likely to be different from their NET PAY or NET EARNINGS. Gross earnings are earnings before any tax and other **deductions** have been taken away. Net earnings are earnings after deductions. This is often called **take-home pay** because it is what the worker is left with to spend. The three most common deductions are as follows.

- **Income tax** - an employer like Cambus Litho is responsible for keeping back some of its employees' pay and sending it to the Inland Revenue, the government department responsible for collecting income tax. This system is known as the PAYE system (pay-as-you-earn).
- **National Insurance contributions** - these are another type of tax on earnings paid to the government which entitles the worker to receive state benefits, such as Jobseekers' Allowance and state retirement pension.
- **Payments to a pension scheme**, such as a private scheme, the pension scheme of the company for which the employee works, or the additional state pension scheme (called SERPS - the State Earnings Related Pension Scheme).

Other deductions which a worker at Cambus Litho might have are trade union membership payments or payments to a charity (a scheme called Gift Aid).

Details of these are found on a pay slip which by law must be given to every employee.

Which payment system?

Cambus Litho has to make decisions about which payment

Percentage of
companies providing benefits

Benefit	Percentage
Car	98%
Pension	93%
Life assurance	93%
Private medical assurance	92%
Parking	84%
Long-term disability cover	71%
Private use of petrol	66%
Subsidised cafeteria	65%
Annual health screening	63%
Share ownership	44%
Personal loans	26%
Financial planning	20%
Subsidised health club membership	19%
Self-help clinics	19%
Mortgage subsidies	19%
Luncheon vouchers	15%
Travelling expenses	15%
On-site exercise facilities	14%
Optical care	12%
School fees	5%
Dental care	4%
On-site creche	4%
Child-care vouchers	2%

Source: adapted from CBI/Towers Perrin.

Figure 56.1 *The main fringe benefits: percentage of companies providing benefits.*

Factory workers at Cambus Litho are paid wages and overtime. They would not be paid commission as they don't sell anything.

systems to use for different groups of workers. Which payment system is used depends partly on what is possible. Cambus Litho might find it very difficult to use piece rates for a manager, for instance, because it is so difficult to measure output. Equally, Cambus Litho paying its factory workers on a commission basis wouldn't be possible either because they don't sell anything. Even sales staff might not be paid commission if sales are a team effort rather than the result of the work of one individual.

Some payment systems are used because they reduce the tax bill of employers and employees. Fringe benefits are an example of this. More importantly, payment systems reflect different views about what **motivates** workers (☞ unit 54). One view (the scientific management school, or McGregor's Theory X) says that pay has an effect on workers' motivation. Linking pay directly with work done should ensure that workers work as hard as possible.

The opposite view (the human relations school or McGregor's Theory Y) says that pay is only one factor affecting workers' motivation. Cambus Litho, like many companies today, stresses how important it is for workers to feel part of the company. Even paying wages, where workers work a fixed number of hours, can lead to 'clock watching'. Workers can feel that **being at work** is more important than **what they do** in the time they are at work. Effort and the quality of what is produced can be poor. An increasing number of workers are now paid a salary. This partly reflects changing views about motivation. It also reflects the increasing number of **white collar** and **service** jobs in the economy (☞ unit 4).

Source: adapted from information provided by Cambus Litho.

? Erica James works in the accounts department at Brady's. Figure 56.2 shows her payment slip.
1 What is the gross pay of Erica James?
2 What are her deductions? In your answer, include the figure for the total level of deductions.
3 What is the new pay of Erica?
4 Erica gets a 10 per cent pay rise on basic pay. There is no change in overtime payment. Copy out the pay slip and put in the new figures for: basic pay; overtime; P.A.Y.E. tax; National Insurance; pension payments; total gross pay; net pay. When making your calculation, you need to take into account the following:
• Pension payments are 10 per cent of the basic pay;
• National Insurance is payable at 10 per cent of any increase in salary;
• income tax is 23 per cent of any increase in earnings minus deductions for pension payments (e.g. if extra earnings were £100, pension payments would then be £10, and so income tax would be charged on £100 - £10 or £90).

Company	BRADY'S			**Pay Advice**			
Payments/Adjustments				**Deductions**		**Totals**	
Description	Hours	Rate	Amount	Description	Amount	Description	Amount
BASIC PAY :			1250.00	P.A.Y.E. Tax	186.39	TOTAL GROSS PAY TD	1330.00
OVERTIME :	8.00	10.00	80.00	National Ins.	110.96		
				Pension	125.00	Tax paid TD	186.39
						National Ins. TD	110.96
						Pension TD	125.00
						TOTAL GROSS PAY	1330.00

Wk./Mth.	Date	Dept.	P/Methd.	Tax Code	Employee No.	Employee Name	Net Pay
1	30/04/1998	0	CM	419L	1	E JAMES	907.65

RE-ORDER CODE SE 32 © N.C. 06/96

TD = amounts paid so far 'to date' this year.
Figure 56.2 *Erica James' payment slip.*

Changing payment systems

The management at Routh, a small component manufacturing business, wants to change its payment system for its shop floor workers. Some workers are currently on piece rates. Others are paid weekly for a 38 hour week but receive no payments if they achieve their production targets. This causes resentment between the two sets of workers because each feels that the other is better off with their payment system. The management also wants to get round the problem caused by different amounts of work at different times of the year. Sometimes, workers are being asked to work 50 hours a week to complete orders. At other times, they are idle in the factory because there isn't enough work to keep the average worker occupied for more than 30 hours per week.

The management has proposed to the workers that all workers be put onto an annualised work system. This would mean that all workers would work 1 800 hours per year. The management could choose when those hours were worked. However, no worker would be expected to work more than 11 hours per day or 50 hours per week. 20 days holiday per year would be guaranteed. Workers would be organised into small groups who work together. Each group would be given a production target. Workers in groups meeting their targets would be paid a bonus equal to up to 10 per cent of their basic pay.

1 (a) Two workers work 50 hours this week. How would the pay of a worker on piece rates be worked out compared to a worker on a weekly wage? (b) Last week, there was only enough work for 30 hours for each worker. How would their pay differ?
2 Suggest TWO reasons why workers on piece rates and those on weekly wage rates might think they are worse off than the other group of workers.
3 What advantages would there be to the management of the proposed new pay system?
4 Do you think that the workers should accept the new pay system? In your answer, explain the possible advantages and disadvantages to workers.

BLUE CIRCLE CEMENT

In January 1997, Blue Circle Cement, the cement manufacturer, agreed a new five year pay deal with its 'core fleet' lorry drivers. The drivers will receive a pay rise on their wages of 3.5 per cent in 1997 plus a one off bonus of £200. They will get no pay increase in 1998. In the next three years, a new pay review body will set their pay in comparison with rates in other haulage companies. At the moment, the core drivers' gross pay averages £21 000.

The working week of the drivers will be cut by one hour. Blue Circle has also offered to 'maximise' job security over the five years. It has promised not to contract out the driver's jobs by inviting another company to provide the transport it needs. If there is a need for fewer drivers, then redundancies will be voluntary or drivers will be retrained to do other jobs at Blue Circle. Job security was the most important priority for drivers according to their union, the GMB (the General and Municipal Boilermakers Union).

The drivers have agreed in addition to do immediate maintenance on their lorries and to operate fork-lift trucks to load them if no one else is available. In-cab computer systems will be used to help Blue Circle improve efficiency by cutting journey times.

Source: adapted from *The Times*, 7 January 1997.

1 What was the average gross annual pay of core drivers at the time of the pay deal?
2 (a) Gross pay for the drivers is likely to be made up of basic pay and overtime. What is the difference between these? (b) Why might the drivers do more overtime after the pay deal has been agreed?
3 Explain what deductions are likely to be made out of gross pay by the drivers.
4 Suggest what benefits Blue Circle will get from the pay deal.
5 How might the pay deal motivate workers? Use theories of motivation in your answer.

FIXING PAY LEVELS

Making decisions

Businesses have to decide how much to pay their workers. Pay is determined by how much a business wants workers (the demand for workers) and how many workers want the job (the supply of workers). A business is likely to consider factors such as the qualifications and experience of workers, their contribution to the business, and what the going rate is for the type of worker in the market.

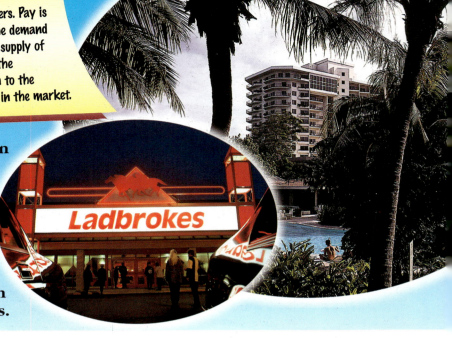

Ladbroke Group PLC operates within the worldwide hospitality and gaming industries. Its Hilton hotels are luxury hotels operating at the top end of the market. Ladbroke is the world's largest off-track betting organisation, with operations in the UK, Ireland, Belgium, Gibraltar, the USA, Argentina, Puerto Rico and Peru. In the UK it runs betting shops and casinos.

Demand and supply

Different workers at Ladbroke earn different amounts of pay. The Group Chief Executive of the company, for instance, earned a basic salary of £410 000 in 1996 with bonuses and fringe benefits raising this to £1.28 million. On the other hand, a part time waiter or waitress in a Hilton hotel might earn £2 000. There is a number of reasons why workers earn different amounts. However, they can best be summarised in terms of **demand** for and **supply** of workers (☞ unit 40).

For instance, there are very few people who have the skills needed to be a successful chief executive of Ladbroke. On the other hand, the company is prepared to pay a high price to attract the right person to the job. In 1996, the company made a profit before tax of £59.2 million. A less successful chief executive could have lost the company millions of pounds of profit through making the wrong decisions. £1.28 million is relatively small when so much money is at stake.

However, there are millions of people in the UK and the rest of the world who could be a waiter or waitress in a hotel. It is also true that Hilton Hotels needs a lot of staff for its hotels. Overall, though, the company can attract enough staff to work for it at relatively low rates of pay. In general, the greater the demand for workers and the less the supply, the higher will be the rate of pay.

Factors affecting demand and supply

Skills, training and education
Most workers could do unskilled

Bricklayers earning '£700 a week'

An industry survey shows that the wages of top bricklayers have risen to £700 a week in southern England. Construction in the South of England is booming after nearly two years of strong growth. Construction firms need bricklayers if they are to fulfil contracts. But they are finding it increasingly difficult to find workers with the right skills. The recession of the early 1990s, when bricklayers' wages fell to as low as £250 a week, drove many skilled workers out of the industry. Lack of training of new workers has meant that they have not been replaced.

The situation is different in other areas of the country though. In Scotland, where construction companies are still having to compete fiercely for any contracts, there are relatively few skill shortages. Wages for workers like bricklayers are also much lower than in the South of England.

Source: adapted from the *Financial Times*, 21 October 1997.

1 Explain carefully TWO reasons why the wages of bricklayers have risen in the South of England.
2 Gary McKendry is a bricklayer living in Glasgow. He is married with two children aged 7 and 9. He has read about the high wages being paid to construction workers in London. Suggest TWO reasons why he doesn't move to London to work there in the construction industry.
3 Suggest what might be the effect of large increases in the wages on construction workers in the South of England on: (a) a construction company based in London; (b) a brewery company which is finalising plans to build a new brewery in the South of England; (c) a pub run by its owner in the City of London which is used by construction workers on building sites nearby.

Dealers at Ladbroke gaming tables are likely to be paid less than the directors of the company.

work, like general cleaning in a Ladbroke betting shop. There are far fewer workers with skills and qualifications, for instance, to become accountants for the company. So, as there are fewer skilled workers, they tend to be paid more than unskilled workers. That is why education and training is so important for any future career.

Experience Experienced workers are likely to know more about the job than someone new to the job. This tends to make them more

productive and so more in demand by the employer. Businesses like Ladbroke often recognise this by building age and length of service into some of their payment systems. In some payment systems (☞ unit 56), workers are given **increments** (or extra amounts) for each year of service completed. Each increment is worth £X more in salary.

Motivation and retention Pay is an important **motivator** for workers (☞ unit 54). Ladbroke doesn't want its workers to feel underpaid because this will demotivate them. It may also lead to workers leaving the company to work for another employer paying higher wages. So in the long term Ladbroke has to pay the market rate - the wage which is just high enough to retain existing staff and recruit new staff.

Conditions of work The more desirable the conditions of work, the lower the pay a business tends to offer its workers. For instance, managers of Hilton hotels are offered free accommodation. Without this perk, Ladbroke would have to pay more to find people to work as managers. Coal miners and North Sea oil rig workers tend to be paid

more because their jobs are unpleasant and dangerous.

Trade unions Trade unions are organisations which exist to protect the interests of their members (☞ unit 61). They fight for high pay on behalf of their members. Strong trade unions may be able to force a higher rate of pay out of a business than if workers had to negotiate individually.

The economic environment
Workers at the Hilton Hotels in Egypt are paid less than workers at Hilton Hotels in London or Australia. This is mainly because Egyptian workers are prepared to work for lower wages. Equally, workers in Northern Ireland or Wales are prepared on average to work for lower wages than workers in London and the South East. When the economy is growing, as in the mid-1990s, wages tend to rise at a faster rate than the trend. Employers need to take on more workers to cope with increased demand. This extra demand for workers leads to higher wages. In a recession, as in the early 1990s, with orders falling and unemployment rising, wage increases tend to be lower than the trend.

Source: adapted from Ladbroke Group PLC, *Annual Report and Accounts*, 1996.

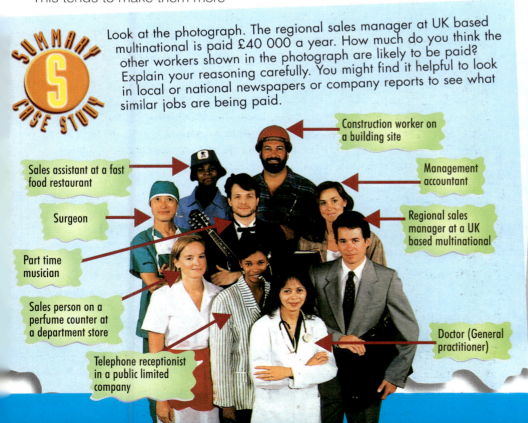

SUMMARY CASE STUDY

Look at the photograph. The regional sales manager at UK based multinational is paid £40 000 a year. How much do you think the other workers shown in the photograph are likely to be paid? Explain your reasoning carefully. You might find it helpful to look in local or national newspapers or company reports to see what similar jobs are being paid.

Construction worker on a building site

Sales assistant at a fast food restaurant

Management accountant

Surgeon

Regional sales manager at a UK based multinational

Part time musician

Sales person on a perfume counter at a department store

Doctor (General practitioner)

Telephone receptionist in a public limited company

Checklist ✓

1 'Employers demand labour. Workers supply labour.' Explain what this means.
2 Use demand and supply to explain why (a) doctors tend to be highly paid but (b) doctors' receptionists tend to be lower paid.
3 Explain TWO factors which might affect the level of pay of: (a) coal miners; (b) workers in the Third World; (c) a manager of an Allied pub; (d) a production line worker making Lyons cakes.
4 Why might age affect a worker's pay?
5 Explain how the qualifications you gain at school, college and university will affect how much you are likely to earn when you get a job.

TRAINING

Making decisions

In a modern economy, a business needs well trained workers if it is to remain competitive. Businesses therefore have to identify their training needs. They have to decide how much they can afford to invest in their workers. They also need to decide who should receive training and what sort of training is needed.

Marks & Spencer plc is an international retailing group. In 1996 it had a turnover of £7 209.2 million and operated 628 stores. This included 373 Marks & Spencer stores, selling clothing, footwear, home furnishings and food, 78 Franchise shops, 157 Brooks Brothers stores and 20 Kings Super Markets. In 1996 it recruited 1 500 extra staff to improve customer service. The training of staff is vital if Marks & Spencer wishes to meet its objectives.

Training in the tourist industry

A government report published in 1996 said that the UK tourist industry was being held back by a lack of trained workers.

Most businesses in the industry are small. 81 per cent of hotels and 94 per cent of restaurants have fewer than 25 employees. This means that businesses do not have the resources to train people. The report found that 45 per cent of full time and 74 per cent of part time staff in the tourist industry had received no job related training since leaving education.

Lack of training was part of a vicious circle in the industry. Low levels of training meant that many workers were relatively unproductive. This meant that employers could only afford to pay low wages to workers. Low wages meant that the industry had difficulties recruiting workers with the right qualifications.

Source: adapted from the *Financial Times*, 31 October 1996.

1 What did the 1996 report say about the level of training in the UK tourist industry?
2 Explain why businesses in the tourist industry need to train their workers.
3 Suggest THREE ways in which the government could encourage and help tourism businesses to train their staff.

The objectives of training

Training is a cost for a business. So it is important that businesses get 'value for money' from training programmes. There is a number of objectives of training for a business like Marks & Spencer.

Induction INDUCTION training is usually given to new workers. The objective is to familiarise them with the workings of the business and the area in which they are going to work. New workers at a store may be trained, for instance, to deal with customers, to check stock and to use cash tills.

Upgrading skills With technology and markets changing all the time, workers need to be adding to their existing skills. At Marks & Spencer, a worker may need to be trained to use a new stock control system. Or the worker may need to learn new skills to get promotion.

Retraining Over time, jobs disappear or change. Workers with

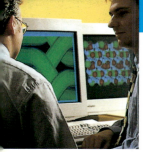

skills to do these jobs need retraining to do different jobs.

Creating flexibility

Like other businesses, Marks & Spencer wants its workers to be increasingly flexible in what they can do. Employees are more likely to be flexible if they have a number of skills. This **multi-skilling** can be achieved through training.

For workers, training should result in greater job satisfaction because they are now able to do their job more effectively. Training also opens the door to promotion and better pay.

Methods of training

There are two main methods of training. ON THE JOB training occurs when workers pick up skills by working alongside other workers. At Marks & Spencer, a new worker at a store may learn about the job by working alongside existing employees. On the job training is cheap and often effective. However, it is unlikely to provide in depth training. It is also unable to help whole groups of workers to change their skills.

To do this, OFF THE JOB training is needed. Workers are taken away from their jobs to be trained. This may be done within the company. Marks & Spencer regularly runs in-service courses for its employees. Either experts within the company lead the course or an outside trainer is brought in. Alternatively, employees may be sent on training courses provided by outside agencies. These include management colleges, further and higher education colleges and training consultancies.

Off the job training is more expensive than on the job training. Outside trainers have to be paid and workers can't produce anything on the days they are being trained. On the other hand,

a wider range of skills can be obtained and it can provide workers with qualifications needed in their job.

Types of training

Businesses use a variety of types of training.

Induction training

This has already been described above.

Apprenticeships, Youth Training and graduate training

Young people straight out of school, college or university have specific training needs. They need short term induction training. They are also likely to need longer training to bring their skills up to the level required for a particular job. Some businesses offer **modern apprenticeships.** These give young people an extended period of training leading to qualification at NVQ levels Two (GCSE level), Three (equivalent to A level) or even Four (approaching university degree standard). Certain businesses also offer **Youth Training (YT)**. This is a scheme funded by the government where young people are given training and work experience. Marks & Spencer offers youth training under a scheme called the Young Employees Scheme (YES). 16-18

year olds are employed in stores and placed on a one year's training programme. This equips them with the core skills needed as a sales assistant and enables them to work towards an NVQ in retailing. In 1996 over 3 000 employees had completed level Two, with a further 3 000 expected the following year. The business has also introduced an NVQ in Health & Safety.

Young people coming from university also need training. Many companies offer **graduate training** schemes to cater for their needs.

Staff training

Groups of workers may need to be trained together. Perhaps, as at Marks & Spencer, they need to learn the skills associated with new technology (skill training). They might need to learn about new health and safety procedures. The buying team might need to learn about new products available from suppliers.

Staff development

Individual workers have training needs too. Marks & Spencer has a policy of supporting staff who wish to gain promotion through training. Staff are involved in their own development through a personal development programme and review. They collect evidence of their strengths and weaknesses

---

Preece plc

Preece is a manufacturer of transport equipment, including parking meters and emissions testing equipment.

John has just joined the company and will be working on the factory floor making parking meters.

Laura has been with the company for five years as a personal assistant to one of the managers. In a company reorganisation, this manager is changing jobs. Laura has been given a new job description which not only includes being her personal assistant but also being responsible for other office workers reporting to the manager.

Pete has been a skilled machinist. However, the introduction of new technology means that his skills are no longer needed. He has been offered a new job in logistics, getting the product to the company's customers.

Swati is an ambitious junior manager in the accounts department. She wants to gain promotion within the company.

1 Explain why each of the four workers has training needs.

2 The company has a limited budget for training. It can only afford to spend money on formal training for two of these workers. Which two do you think it should be? Explain your answer carefully.

which provides an ongoing record of achievement. Staff can also spend 100 hours completing a project at a charitable organisation. This gives them with a chance to make a contribution to the local community and develop their skills.

Government and training

Marks & Spencer has a good training record. However, many middle sized and small businesses spend little or nothing on training. They rely on schools, colleges and other businesses to do the training. They then recruit (some businesses would say 'poach' or 'headhunt') workers with the right skills and qualifications.

Businesses therefore do not spend enough on training when left to themselves. So the government has to intervene, either to provide money directly for industry training or to encourage businesses to take training seriously.

The Department for Education and Employment is the government department directly responsible for training. At a national level, it is responsible for the Training, Enterprise and Education Directorate (TEED) to promote training. At a local level, it provides the funding for and monitors the work of **Training and Enterprise Councils** (TECS). These have full time staff. They are responsible to a board made up of local business people together with government representatives.

TECs manage and promote all the training needs in a local area. This includes Youth Training (YT). It also includes **New Deal.** This is designed to provide jobs for unemployed 18-24 year olds. After assessment, unemployed young people will be given help to find a job. This may include offering employers a subsidy to take them on. If they don't succeed then they will be

offered two options. They may be given up to 52 weeks of full time education and training to raise their level of skills and make them more employable. Or they may gain work experience on schemes designed to benefit the local community and the environment. The local TECs are particularly interested in schemes which promote training for existing workers. The TECs work with local colleges or training consultancies to fund and provide courses.

The government has set itself and industry an ambitious target. By December 2000, it wants 60 per cent of the employed workforce to have been trained to NVQ level Three or equivalent. NVQ stands for National Vocational Qualification. NVQ level Three is the equivalent of 2 'A' levels.

NVQs are qualifications which can be gained by people in work. GNVQs, General National Vocational Qualifications, are pre-vocational qualifications which can be gained by people before they

start work. This means that GNVQs are qualifications offered by schools and colleges as an alternative to qualifications such as GCSEs and 'A' levels.

To achieve its target, the government wants 70 per cent of organisations with 200 or more staff and 35 per cent of organisations with between 50 and 199 staff to be taking part in its **'Investors in People'** programme by December 2000. This commits businesses to put training as a priority.

Government has a key role to play in training. Some argue that it needs to put more money into local TECs to fund training. Others argue that businesses will always train workers if there is a need for training whether or not they get help from government. Even if this is true, government can help provide the training framework which the economy needs if it is to be successful.

Source: adapted from *Marks & Spencer Fact File*, *Annual Report and Financial Statements*, Marks & Spencer; *Labour Market Trends*, ONS.

UK restaurant trade

Jennie Foulkes is responsible for recruiting chefs for a chain of pub-restaurants. With the restaurant trade booming, she is finding it very difficult, so difficult that she regularly recruits from as far away as Australia. However, foreign nationals rarely stay. They want to come to England for a year, practise their language skills, see the country and then go home. She would far prefer to recruit British chefs who on average will stay four years in a post.

The problem is that there is an acute shortage of British chefs. Plenty of young people complete full time catering courses at college or go to a culinary school but only a fraction of these go on to take up a career in the catering industry. They are put off by the unsocial hours and the relatively low pay.

Jennie is considering whether a solution might be to offer an apprenticeship scheme within the company. Apprentices could be trained to NVQ level 2 or 3 and the company would get funding for the scheme through local TECs. The company might use local colleges for part of the training. Otherwise, selected chefs in some of the pub-restaurants would give on the job training.

1 Explain what is meant by: (a) an apprenticeship; and (b) on the job training.
2 Why might a 19 year old be attracted to an apprenticeship offered by Jennie's company?
3 What training needs might existing chefs have who become responsible for apprentices?
4 Do you think that such a training scheme would reduce problems of recruitment for the company? Explain your answer carefully.

Checklist ✔

1 What are the objectives of training for a business?
2 What might a worker gain from being trained?
3 What is the difference between on the job training and off the job training?
4 Where might a worker be trained off the job?
5 What types of training exist?
6 What might be the advantage to a business of taking in students on a Youth Training scheme?
7 What is a TEC?
8 What targets does the government have for training?

key terms

Induction - period of training for workers new to a business when they find out about the business and the job they have to do.
Off the job training - training undertaken away from the job, either at the business or outside the business, for instance, at a college of further education.
On the job training - training in the workplace undertaken whilst doing a job.

SUMMARY CASE STUDY

TRAINING AND DEVELOPMENT

The development needs of our employees are primarily delivered at operating company level as an intrinsic part of each company's strategy. These activities are supported from the centre, either where the issue is strategically important, as in Health and Safety training, or where there is a benefit in doing so. A prime example of this is our work on delivering employee development through structured evaluation of the competencies required to meet future business needs.

Recognising the importance of increased manufacturing efficiency, the competencies approach is currently being used by a group of operation directors to increase skills and knowledge throughout their function. At a local level the same approach has been successfully applied in Dale Farm and Express Dairy to aid depot staff in slowing the doorstep decline. Also an increasing number of businesses, including Pork Farm Bowyers, Fox's Biscuits and Premium Savoury Products, have used NVQ frameworks to raise the skill levels of large numbers of their employees.

The importance placed on training and developing employees by Walter Hollands was formally recognised this year by its achievement of the Investors in People standard, making it the second Northern Foods company to obtain such recognition.

Our Riverside and Evesham Foods business is currently implementing a major change programme involving the whole workforce in creating the appropriate culture and environment to meet the business challenges of the future.

In parallel with increased local activity, the focus on Food Safety and Health and Safety issues continues to be a high priority this year for all our businesses. Over 500 managers have now successfully completed the Northern Foods Certificate in Advanced Food Safety and participation in the recently developed Health and Safety Programme continues to grow.

Source: Northern Foods PLC, *Annual Report and Accounts*, 1997.

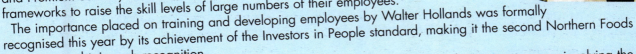

Northern Foods plc is a food manufacturer. It is the UK's largest supplier of milk. It sells to supermarkets as well as providing a door step delivery service under the Express Dairy and Dale Farm brands. Other dairy products are sold under brands such as Eden Vale and Ski. It has a large non-dairy business too, making products which sell as own brands, including Marks & Spencer, Sainsbury's and Tesco. It also manufactures food under its own brand labels at Fox's Biscuits and Goodfella's pizzas. Northern Foods is made up of eight main subsidiary companies.

1 Give TWO examples of training at Northern Foods.
2 Suggest why Northern Foods has given training in: (a) Food Safety; (b) Health and Safety.
3 Explain TWO ways in which Northern Foods has delivered training to its employees.
4 Northern Foods has to decide how much to spend on training. Discuss the advantages and disadvantages to the company of spending more on training its workers.

COMMUNICATION

Making decisions

Communication is vital to a business. How best can employees in a business communicate with each other and with outsiders? What makes communication effective? What are the best channels of communication?

Commercial Union is one of the largest insurance companies in Europe. With headquarters in the UK, it is an international group with operations in over 50 countries and 25 600 employees around the world. The Group manages worldwide assets of £65 billion and collects £9 billion each year in revenues from premiums. Effective communication is vital for the success of the company.

This letter of complaint has been sent to a rail company.

1 Who is the sender of the communication?
2 What is the sender trying to communicate in the letter?
3 Do you think that the company should reply to the letter? Put arguments for and against.

Wordprocessing

4 Assume it decides to reply. (a) Write the letter of reply using a wordprocessing package if possible. (b) Do you think that Mr Nichols will respond? Explain why or why not.

> 6 Greenacres Road
> Milton Keynes
> 15.5.98
>
> I want to complain about your ticket collector. I was on the train back from London last Friday after a nice day's shopping when he asked to see my rail ticket. He said it wasn't valid because it was five o'clock and it was a cheap day ticket and demanded that I pay more money. I bought a return ticket. He really showed me up in front of the passengers. You would have thought I was a thief the way he was talking.
>
> Yours disgustedly
> P. Nichols (Mr)

Senders and receivers

There are always two parties to any COMMUNICATION.

- The **sender**. An example would be Commercial Union sending out information in its Annual Report and Accounts. It might be an employee in the sales department giving details about a policy to a customer. It might be the head of the personnel department giving instructions to other heads of department about how to deal with a staff problem.
- The **receiver**. This may be the shareholder getting a copy of the Annual Report through the post. It may be the customer finding out about a policy. It may be heads of department receiving instructions from the head of personnel.

The receiver may give FEEDBACK. The shareholder getting a copy of the Annual Report may, for instance, write a letter to the company commenting on its performance. Figure 59.1 shows feedback that may take place in an insurance business.

Internal and external communication

Some communications are INTERNAL to the business. Examples of internal communication would be:

- one salesperson talking to another salesperson;
- the finance director sending a memo to sales staff;
- the head of the claims department sending a message by E-mail (electronic mail) to be read by others on their computer

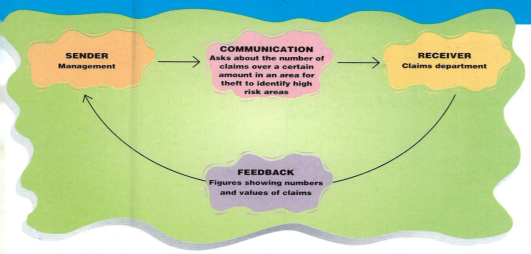

```
SENDER              COMMUNICATION              RECEIVER
Management        Asks about the number of   Claims department
                  claims over a certain
                  amount in an area for
                  theft to identify high
                  risk areas

                       FEEDBACK
                  Figures showing numbers
                   and values of claims
```

Figure 59.1 *Sending and receiving a message.*

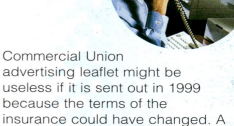

In 1996 the Vietnamese government gave permission for Commercial Union to form a joint venture with Vietnam International Insurance Company - an example of external communication.

Good communication is essential. Electronic data links allow brokers to print out or quote Commercial Union policies on the spot.

mailboxes;
- a copy of an invoice being faxed from the Wolverhampton branch of the Commercial Union to the Birmingham branch;
- a broker in a Commercial Union business abroad obtaining a quote from a central data system.

Other communications are EXTERNAL, where Commercial Union communicates with people or organisations outside the business. Examples would be:
- a salesperson talking to a customer;
- a customer finding out about the premiums on a policy;
- a building company faxing Commercial Union to confirm a specification to repairs on a building.

The importance of good communication

Good communication is essential to any business. For instance, at Commercial Union:
- accurate advertising brochures avoid disappointed customers;
- a clear instruction by a manager makes sure that a task gets done;
- an accurate memo from the accounts department might help clear up a misunderstanding.

Poor external communication can lead to dissatisfied customers, a poor business image and problems with suppliers. Poor internal communications can lead to workers not understanding what

they have to do, poor motivation of the workforce and duplication of effort. Overall, poor communication can lead to a loss of sales as customers are not satisfied. It also increases costs because work is not completed in the most efficient way. Mistakes are made and things get overlooked. All this may lead to lower profits.

Communication skills

There is a number of key factors which make a communication effective.

Information What is communicated must be accurate. It must be **complete**, giving all the information necessary. It must also be **simple** and **clear**, so that the receiver can understand the information as quickly and easily as possible.

Sender and receiver The message must be sent from the right people to the right people. A memo sent to all employees dealing with motor insurance which is received only by those working in the Birmingham Commercial Union branch may be an example of poor communication.

Time and place
Communication must take place at the right time and right place. A 1998

Commercial Union advertising leaflet might be useless if it is sent out in 1999 because the terms of the insurance could have changed. A notice about fire safety which

D J Quine, Accountants

D J Quine is an accounting business which employs assistant accountants who work together in offices in Ormskirk, Lancs. The business provides accounting services for other small businesses. Its keeps the books of local shopkeepers, garages, doctors and electricians, for instance. These businesses are more likely to use D J Quine than larger accountancy firms because its services are more suitable for their needs.

1 What service does D J Quine offer its customers?
2 Give FIVE examples each of: (a) external communications; and (b) internal communications which D J Quine might have.
3 Make a list of points which D J Quine might use when trying to win new custom for the business. In your list, include some ideas about why communication might be better in a small business than in a larger accountancy practice.

nobody can read because it is pinned too high up is in the wrong place. An urgent memo from London head office mustn't arrive at branches three weeks later.

Method The **method** of communication (☞ unit 60), must be right. Methods include face to face communication, memos, telephone calls and the use of information technology.

Barriers to communication

Not all communication is effective. There is a number of reasons why communication breaks down. The person sending the communication might not explain themselves very well. The receivers might not be capable of understanding the message because they lack understanding of technical **jargon**. The receiver might not hear the message because he or she is not paying attention or chooses to focus in on part of the message, but not all of it. Messages can get distorted if they go through too many people like in a game of Chinese whispers. Equipment might break down or not be working very well. A fax machine may have a fault or a telephone may have a

fault or a telephone line might be very noisy.

Channels of communication

Information passes along CHANNELS OF COMMUNICATION. These are channels which are recognised and approved by the business and by employee representatives such as **trade unions** (☞ unit 59). There are two main types of formal communication.

- **Vertical communication** is communication up and down the hierarchy (☞ unit 20) of the business. For instance, a clerical assistant might seek authorisation to pay a claim from a supervisor. Or the chief executive of Commercial Union might send a note to a personnel secretary asking a venue to be booked for the next meeting of the board of directors.
- **Horizontal communication** occurs when workers at the same level in a business communicate formally with each other. One tele-sales assistant

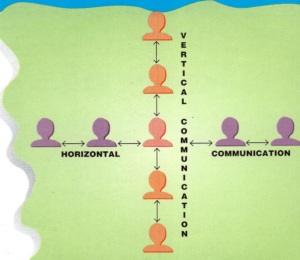

Figure 59.2 *Horizontal and vertical communication.*

might leave a note for another tele-sales assistant about problems with the equipment she is using for example. Often, communication doesn't get passed along official channels in the organisation. INFORMAL COMMUNICATION is called communication through the GRAPEVINE. For instance, a manager in the claims department may have a friend who works in sales. When they chat and exchange gossip about what is going on in the company, they are passing on information through the grapevine.

Channels of communication should be clearly laid down by a business. If they are not, then vital information can get sent to the wrong people, or get lost. Communication through the grapevine can sometimes be a problem because messages may get distorted the more people they go through. On the other hand, the grapevine can be very useful. A manager may know that to do his job properly, he needs as much information as possible. This might mean getting more information than he 'officially' receives.

In general, the fewer the number of stages through which a communication passes (i.e the shorter the **chain of communication**), the less likely it is that a message will be

1 What makes the front cover of a travel brochure an effective piece of communication?

2 Write a short report suggesting how and where brochures might be distributed. For instance, should a travel business post a copy to every house in the country? Should it be distributed to all travel agents in Europe? When writing your answer, bear in mind that distribution costs should be kept as low as possible and that the brochures should reach those people most likely to use the service.

misinterpreted. One of the possible advantages of a small company compared to Commercial Union is that, with very few people employed, it may be easier to communicate effectively. This is why Commercial Union has to work hard to maintain the effectiveness of its communication systems.

Source: adapted from Commercial Union, Annual Report and Accounts.

Your school or college is likely to be a business organisation. It has formal channels of communication. Find out the formal channel(s) of communication for the following situations.

1 A pupil or student is persistently late for business studies lessons.
2 A pupil or student needs a bus pass.
3 A teacher or lecturer wants to order some business studies textbooks.
4 A teacher or lecturer wants a white board installed in the teaching room.
5 A pupil or student needs afternoon release to be able to appear in a show running for two weeks at the local theatre.

key terms

Channel of communication - the path taken by a message, such as horizontal communication, vertical communication or grapevine communication.
Communication - messages passed between a sender and a receiver, through a medium such as a letter or a fax.
External communication - communication between the business and an outside individual or organisation like a customer, a supplier or a tax inspector.
Feedback - response to a message by its receiver to the sender.
Formal channels of communication - channels which are recognised and approved by the business and by employee representatives such as trade unions.
Informal communication or communication through the grapevine - communication through channels which are not formally recognised by the business.
Internal communication - communication within the business organisation.

Checklist ✓

1 In communication, what is the difference between a sender and a receiver?
2 A company sends out a brochure to a customer. What feedback might it expect to receive?
3 What is the difference between internal and external communication?
4 List FOUR external communications which a local newsagent might send or receive.
5 Why is good communication important for a business?
6 What makes communication effective?
7 What is the difference between vertical and horizontal communication?
8 Why is communication through a grapevine both useful and a possible problem for a business organisation?

SUMMARY CASE STUDY

THE POT PLANT COMPANY

This exercise could EITHER be completed using a meeting of your own mini-company OR using the Pot Plant Company below.

Five friends have formed The Pot Plant Company. Their business idea is to buy potted plants in bulk from a local garden centre and sell them at a higher price individually to customers. One member of the company works at the garden centre and the manager has said that the plants can be bought for cost price plus 10 per cent. The typical plant has a cost price of 50p and is sold at the garden centre for 99p.

A meeting of the company has been called to discuss marketing strategies – what price will be charged for the plants, how sales will be promoted, whether the company should attempt to add any value to the plants to be sold and where and when the plants should be sold.

Divide into groups of seven.

Five are to be the members of the Pot Plant Company.
• Assume that the Pot Plant Company is operating in your own school or college environment.
• Your task is to make decisions about price, promotion, product and place.
• At the start, you must appoint a chairperson and a secretary. The chairperson will chair the meeting. The secretary will keep minutes of the meeting.

Two are to be observers. You need to take note of the quality of communication in the meeting. For instance, was what was being said accurate, complete, simple and clear? To what extent did people communicate through the formal channel of communication - through the chair of the meeting? Did anyone communicate informally, perhaps talking to their neighbour instead of addressing the group as a whole?

After 20-30 minutes, the meeting should be closed.
(a) The observers can then feed back their observations to the whole group.
(b) Do the five members of the company agree that these are accurate observations?
(c) Look through the minutes kept by the secretary. Were they an accurate reflection of the meeting? Explain why or why not.

BURP!!

METHODS OF COMMUNICATION

Making decisions

Every business needs to communicate. People within the business need to communicate between themselves. The business needs to communicate with outsiders such as customers, suppliers and government. So businesses have to decide what is the most effective means of communication. Is it a letter, a fax, a set of minutes or a telephone call, for instance?

Allied Carpets is Britain's largest carpet retailer. At the start of 1997 it operated 207 stores. A further 24 Allied Carpet stores and 12 more Carpetland stores were opened during the year. Successful communication within the company and with customers and suppliers is essential if the company is to continue to be successful and boost the £255.7 million of sales it made in the 1996/7 financial year.

Body language

When two or more people meet, many messages are passed by the way they act and react physically. For instance, an Allied Carpets manager in a job interview might laugh. This could be interpreted in different ways. It might relax the interviewees. Equally, it might signal to them that they have given a wrong answer.

The way we laugh, frown, walk and dress are all examples of **non-verbal** communication.

Verbal communication

Verbal or **oral** communication is when two or more people talk together. They may meet together informally. For instance, an Allied Carpets store manager might talk about a problem which has just come up with an assistant, an example of **face-to-face** communication. The store may also wish to find out about an order it has placed with a carpet manufacturer. Ringing up the manufacturer would be an example of **telephone** communication.

Examples of more formal types of verbal communication include:

- a store manager attending a **meeting** with other store managers;
- a manager **interviewing** people for a job;
- a store manager attending a **conference** to discuss forthcoming promotional events;
- a group of managers **teleconferencing**, where more than two people can join in and listen to a conversation over the telephone;
- a group of directors **videoconferencing**, where they can see and hear each other through the use of

Look at the photographs.
1 What does each of the photographs show, do you think, about how each person is feeling?
2 A manager is to deliver a verbal warning to a worker. The worker has been persistently late to work for no good reason. The verbal warning will be given in the presence of the worker's union representative.
(a) What information might be given to the worker in the verbal warning? (b) What non-verbal messages might the manager give to the worker during the interview? You might carry this out as a role play exercise.

1 Describe in words the visual communication used in this poster for beds.
2 Why do you think visual images were used as well as words on the poster?

DTP

3 Design a poster to be displayed in an office or factory building, explaining the dangers of running down stairs or pushing other people on crowded staircases. You could use a desktop publishing package for this.

THE ONLY WAY THEY'LL ROLL TOGETHER

VISIT THE SILENTNIGHT BEDS SLEEP CENTRE AT
T J HUGHES, LONDON ROAD, LIVERPOOL

Silentnight Beds
No Roll Together

video cameras, telephone lines and monitors.

Videoconferencing is likely to grow rapidly in future as technology develops and businesses need to communicate with people far away.

The store manager can use the telephone and contact someone immediately. Compare this to a letter which may only get through 24 hours later. The conversation can be confidential. The two parties can exchange views. So, receivers of the message can question anything not understood or can give instant feedback.

The larger the number of people involved, though, the less likely it is that there will be feedback. In an Allied Carpets staff meeting with 20 people involved, the chances are that some people will not give any feedback at all.

Visual communication

Allied Carpets uses visual communication a great deal. In its stores, it carries thousands of samples of carpets which show both the look and the feel of the carpet. It uses **posters** which carry **photographs** of carpets in rooms to help customers visualise the carpet in their own homes.

Information technology is used too. Allied Carpets has a HomeVision system which allows customers to see, on a computer screen, how any flooring will look once a carpet is fitted.

Visual communication can take place within and outside the organisation. A manager, for example, may be sent a **bar chart** or **graph** by head office showing trends in sales or costs, taken off the company's computer system. A manager may read a **newspaper article** which shows the market share of Allied Carpets by means of a **pie chart**. The manager may access some information on Allied Carpets' **computer network**. The manager may also watch a BBC *Money Programme* **video** about competition in the carpet market. In its marketing, Allied Carpets uses **advertisements** in newspapers and magazines communicating with potential

customers.

Visual images can improve communication for a business. Photographs, for example, may affect people's feelings and perceptions about something in a way that a letter or a written article cannot. A consumer should get a far clearer idea of a carpet being bought if they can see it on computer using the HomeVision system.

Written communication

Written words are a useful means of communication. Because they can be stored, on paper or on a computer system for instance, they can give a permanent record of the communication. In contrast, there is unlikely to be a permanent record if an Allied Carpets store manager has an informal talk with his **line manager** (☞ unit 20). Written communication can also reach large numbers of people. A company newsletter, for instance, can be sent to all employees. Written communication can be very detailed. A contract between Allied Carpets and one of its suppliers can be drawn up so that there can be no misunderstanding later on.

Written communication can often be used to explain product details or to pass information to

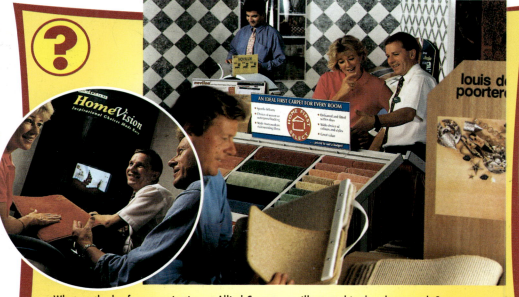

HomeVision
Inspirational Choices Made Easy

AN IDEAL FIRST CARPET FOR EVERY ROOM

louis de poortere

What methods of communication at Allied Carpets are illustrated in the photographs?

customers. A brochure can explain the fitting service offered by Allied Carpets. Or it can give details of credit terms on purchases.

Written communication rarely gives an opportunity for instant feedback. This means that it can be ignored. A notice on a notice board, for instance, might not be seen by an employee.

There are many types of written communication.

Letters A letter is versatile and can convey plans, instruction, comment and analysis for instance. A **personal letter** is one which is sent with the understanding that it will only be read by the named receiver of the letter. An **open letter** is one where the sender wants anybody who is interested to read the letter. The letter might be **faxed** to the receiver rather than being sent by mail. This is when the letter is sent, via a fax (facsimile) machine, down the telephone wire to be printed out by a fax machine in the receiver's office.

Memorandum or memo A memorandum (or 'memo') is a short letter, usually giving instructions such as a request for information. Memos are sometimes written on standard forms.

Circular or newsletter A circular is a communication which is sent to a number of people. The head office of Allied Carpets might send out a circular to all store managers with information about a new range of carpets. Allied Carpets has a weekly communication from departments within head office to stores. Information can be passed from store to store if, for example, help is needed to supply a product in limited distribution.

Forms Forms are designed to make sure that all the information required is included in a communication. For instance, an application form for a job at Allied Carpets asks applicants to give their name, address and age as well as details of their past work experience.

Minutes These are a written record of a meeting. Someone at the meeting makes a note of what was discussed and then writes this up. Minutes are important because they might be referred to. If there is a dispute about what was said at a meeting, the minutes might be able to clarify what really did happen. Because minutes are referred to, it is usual for the people attending the meeting to confirm the minutes. This means that they agree that the written minutes do accurately reflect what

Kept in the picture

Telephone and video conferencing are not for amateurs. When IBM, one of the world's largest computer companies, wants to hold a conference, it uses an outside company to organise it. That company is Geoconference, which employs just 40 people.

George Mackintosh, the managing director of Geoconference, explains that it is not difficult for three or four people to make a conference call by telephone. But staging a conference for more than that 'requires something more than your telephone normally gives you. It requires an operator and a whizzy box'.

The operator connects all the people participating in the conference, keeps them on hold and puts them through to the chair of the conference at the scheduled time. The operator then monitors the conference to make sure that the participants remain connected. He then ends the connections when the session is over. For video conferencing, Geoconference uses its own equipment including a computer to set up the links.

Naturally, telecom companies like BT provide teleconference and videoconference management facilities. But Geoconference believes that it can supply both a better service and a keener price than the major telecom companies.

Source: adapted from the *Financial Times*, 2 September 1997.

INTERNAL MEMO

From	Bill Kale	Date	4/5/98
To	Stephen Deane	Ref	
Subject	FT article on conferencing		

What do you think? Following our recent discussion, do you think we ought to get in touch with Geoconference to talk about a contract?

Bill Kale is a director of a medium sized household and personal products company. It manufactures a range of goods including shampoo, soap, deodorant and perfume as well as household cleaning products and washing powders. The company has six factories, four scattered round the UK, one in Ireland and one in Hungary, as well as a head office in London. At the moment, management from the factories and at head office only talk on a one to one basis over the telephone. Twice a year, the senior managers from each factory hold a one day conference in London to discuss issues. On top of that, managers from each factory spend an average ten days scattered through the year at head office on company matters.

1 Write a short report for Bill Kale, outlining the benefits of teleconferencing and videoconferencing compared to what happens now. Explain how you would decide whether it was financially worthwhile to change to more tele and videoconferencing.

was said at the meeting.

Reports A report is an extended piece of writing on a particular topic. Public limited companies like Allied Carpets have to produce an Annual Report for their shareholders. This gives details about how the company has performed over the past 12 months. There are many other types of report. The Director in charge of stores operations might, for instance, have to present a report to the board about future staffing levels in stores. A report may contain graphs, charts and photographs as well as words and is likely to be word processed on a computer.

Databases Allied Carpets keeps a variety of databases, mostly on computer. These are files of information kept, for instance, on customer orders or on products. A salesperson could look at a database to find details of a customer's order if there was a query.

Other information technology applications Computers can now store and retrieve information in a whole variety of formats. For instance, Allied Carpets has a sophisticated **Electronic Point of Sale** (EPOS) system. This stores information about sales as the customer pays for products at the till. Retailers like Allied Carpets can use the system to give them written information about stock levels, sales and new orders.

Word processing packages enable files to be handled and stored on computer rather than on paper. Allied Carpets' computer customer ordering system enables an order to be made out with the customer in a store and sent by telephone via a **modem** to a computer at the Allied Carpet warehouse in Bolton. Allied Carpets also uses **E-Mail** (Electronic Mail) as a means of communication. E-Mail allows messages to be sent from one computer to another, both within the Allied Carpets group and to those outside. **Computer networks** allow computers to be linked together to provide information. Many businesses have a **web site** on the **Internet** to give information about the business and the products it sells.

Allied Carpets did not have a site in 1997 but was considering it in future.

Information technology is often quicker and easier to use than paper communications. It is also more powerful, enabling far more information to be handled than would be possible using pen and ink.

Source: adapted from Allied Carpets, *Annual Report and Accounts*; Pgc.

Checklist ✓

1 Why might a manager use verbal communication to pass a message to another manager rather than write them a memo?
2 What are the disadvantages of verbal communication?
3 List and then describe in words THREE pieces of visual communication you can find in this book.
4 Why might a manager present sales figures over the past five years in the form of a graph rather than in words?
5 What is the difference between a letter and a memo?
6 When might a business use a circular?
7 What are forms used for?
8 What is a report?
9 What makes an instruction manual effective?

SUMMARY CASE STUDY

ANN RAWLINGS

Ann Rawlings is head of marketing in a medium sized limited company manufacturing ceramics, based in Stoke-on-Trent. Below is an entry in her diary for Tuesday 5 June.

1 For each entry in her diary, describe the types of communication she is likely to have used.

A potential new customer has approached the company. Ann has to decide whether to:
go and meet the customer in London;
ask the customer to come and meet her in Stoke-on-Trent;
set up a teleconferencing or videoconferencing discussion (where people can talk to each other or see each other on screen if they have the correct equipment);
send promotional material about her company and its products.

Which of these four ways of communicating with the potential customer do you think she should choose? Give reasons for your answer, thinking about cost, time spent and effectiveness of the communication.

5 June
Tuesday 1998

8.30 Briefing meeting with Claire about the day
8.45 Respond to incoming mail
9.15 Contact John Tyler in London
9.30 New product committee meeting
12.00 Lunch meeting with representatives from Sealware plc
14.00 Interviews for deputy assistant marketing
16.00 Preparation for board meeting in 7 days time
18.00 Home

INDUSTRIAL RELATIONS

Making decisions

Management and workers need to decide how they should relate to each other. They both have common interests, such as ensuring the survival of the business. However, they also have conflicting objectives, such as the size of pay increases or the quality of working conditions. Workers need to decide whether to join a trade union to protect their interests. Management needs to decide whether it will work with trade unions and how to communicate with workers. Both management and trade unions are responsible for relations between workers and managers in business.

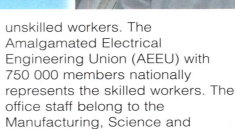

Kennaby is an engineering company in Tipton in the West Midlands. It was founded in 1955 when the engineering industry was strong. Today, it employs only one third of the workers it did just 20 years before.

Unions at Kennaby

The 326 workers at Kennaby are still represented by the same unions that were recognised by the business 20 years ago. The Transport and General Workers Union (TGWU) with 900 000 members nationally represents the unskilled workers. The Amalgamated Electrical Engineering Union (AEEU) with 750 000 members nationally represents the skilled workers. The office staff belong to the Manufacturing, Science and Finance Union (MSF). It has 450 000 members nationally.

Communication

The management at Kennaby communicates with its workforce over a whole range of issues, such as pay, holidays, working conditions and contracts of employment, redundancies and staffing levels. INDUSTRIAL RELATIONS is the term used to describe the relationship between the two groups.

Since the company was founded, the workers have always been members of TRADE UNIONS. They exist to protect the interests of their members. At Kennaby, trade union representatives negotiate on behalf of members with the management. This negotiation is called **collective bargaining**. It is 'collective' because many shareholders are represented by just a few managers. Equally, many workers are represented by just a few trade union representatives. Collective bargaining provides a **channel of communication** (☞ unit 59) between workers and management.

Trade unions

Workers at Kennaby belong to trade unions because they provide

1 Hannatu Abubakar is an administrative assistant for a cable TV company. Explain what benefits she might gain by joining the CWU.
2 How might the CWU help the communications industry?

Source: The Communication Workers Union.

Women under-unionised

Nearly half of all workers are women but only a third of them (3.1 million) belong to a trade union. However, the proportion of female union members is higher than men in professional occupations such as teachers, lawyers and engineers. 63 per cent of female professional workers belong to a trade union compared to only 43 per cent for men. Women are also more represented among associate professional and technical jobs such as nursing and social work. 57 per cent of these female workers are in unions compared to only 37 per cent for men.

The fall in union membership since 1979 still continues. The fall has been higher for men than for women, however. For instance, between 1989 and 1994, male union membership has dropped from 5.2 million to 3.9 million while the number of women in unions has fallen only from 3.3 million to 3.1 million.

Source: adapted from the *Financial Times*, 13 March 1997.

1 What is a 'professional worker'?

2 (a) What has happened to: (i) total trade union membership; and (ii) male trade union membership recently according to the data? (b) Suggest TWO reasons why there has been this change.

3 A union representing professional workers wants to increase its membership. (a) Explain whether you think it should target men or women. (b) What benefits could the union offer which might attract new members?

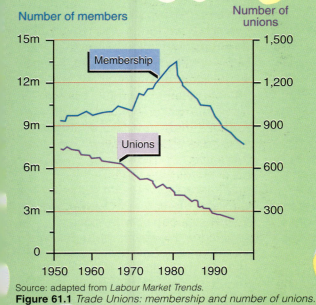

Number of members

Figure 61.1 *Trade Unions: membership and number of unions.*

Source: adapted from *Labour Market Trends.*

a range of services.

- They negotiate with employers and employers' associations over conditions of work including pay, hours, holidays and safety.
- They give legal protection to workers, offering advice about issues such as unfair dismissal and dismissal. If matters are serious enough, they will employ legal experts to defend members in court.
- They provide monetary benefits. These vary from union to union. They can include strike pay, death insurance, mortgages and personal loans.
- They act as a **pressure group** (☞ unit 45). They try to pressure employers, their associations and government to bring further benefits to workers. They also resist changes which are likely to harm workers' interests.

At Kennaby, like other businesses, the union members elect SHOP STEWARDS to represent their interests. A shop steward is an unpaid volunteer. He or she deals with problems of members either directly or by passing the problem on to someone better able to sort it out. Shop stewards therefore act as a channel of communication between workers and management.

The shop stewards elect one of their number to be the senior shop steward. He or she acts as CONVENOR. The convenor sits on the

JOINT CONSULTATIVE COMMITTEE with the other shop stewards. This is a committee made up of:

- the shop stewards;
- representatives from management, which include the personnel manager.

It meets regularly to discuss whatever issues either unions or management want to have discussed. Issues which can be raised include:

- pay - including pay rises, overtime pay and bonuses;
- conditions of work - such as hours, holidays and shift working;
- health and safety at work;
- redundancies;
- equal opportunities.

Alongside the voluntary workers of the union, there are full time officials. These are paid by the union to give advice and help to members, shop stewards and branches.

Each year, a union holds an **annual conference**. This is the AGM of the union. Representatives are elected by members to go to the conference. The **motions** of the conference which are passed become policy for the union. The full time officials of the union then have to follow that policy.

Trade associations

Kennaby belongs to a TRADE ASSOCIATION. Trade associations represent the interests of businesses. There are 114 trade associations in the UK.

Like trade unions, they act as pressure groups, representing their members' interests to government and other organisations. They give advice to member businesses. They can also be involved in research and development for the benefit of members. Some trade associations, negotiate industry wide pay agreements with trade unions. Minimum pay levels at Kennaby are set by these yearly negotiations at industry-wide level. However, Kennaby is free to pay its workers more if it so wishes. For instance, in the past it has paid more when there have been **skill shortages** and it has found it difficult to recruit workers with the right skills.

At a national level, many trade associations and large businesses belong to the **Confederation of British Industry (CBI)**. Like trade associations, it is a pressure group representing the interests of British business to the government and to the European Union.

Industrial action

Nearly all worker-management problems are sorted out peacefully. However, very occasionally an issue arises which sets workers against management without any agreement. Various forms of **industrial action** can then be taken to try and force the other side to back down. Workers, for instance, can :

- go on strike - perhaps a one day strike, or a strike where only key workers don't come in to work, or, most serious, an all out strike by all workers;
- ban overtime work;
- boycott work, such as refusing to work with new machinery.

Management too can take action against workers. In particular, it can lock out its workers, either sacking them all and employing new workers, or stating that only workers who are prepared to accept management terms will be allowed to resume work.

If management and workers are in dispute, they can bring in ACAS to help them resolve their disagreement. ACAS is the Advisory, Conciliation and Arbitration Service. It is an independent body, financed by government, which is responsible for giving advice to both businesses and employees about industrial relations matters. It also provides a CONCILIATION service. This means that it is prepared to help management and workers to come to an agreement when they are in dispute. Finally, it provides an ARBITRATION service. This is where management and workers agree to allow an outside person, an

arbitrator, to make a decision about something in dispute.

The new unionism

Industrial relations at Kennaby in the 1950s, 1960s and 1970s were not always good. The unions didn't always get on together. In the 1970s, for instance, skilled workers belonging to the AEUW (the union that became the AEEU) went on strike twice because they felt that the unskilled workers had received too high pay increases. This eroded the pay differential between skilled and unskilled workers. Many strikes were **unofficial** - not given the official support of the trade union. They were often **wildcat** strikes - very short strikes that flared up over an issue and were quickly resolved.

However, the climate of industrial relations changed in the 1980s for a number of reasons.

- The government introduced new laws which made it much more difficult for workers to take industrial action. For instance, unions now have to call a secret ballot and win at least 50 per cent of the vote in favour before they can call a strike.
- Between 1979 and 1997, there was a 2.7 million fall in the number of jobs in manufacturing, the sector of the economy where trade unions were strongest. This was a

cause of the 6.1 million drop in the number of trade union members over the same period. Fewer members weakened the power of trade unions.

- With so much unemployment in the economy, workers became afraid to take tough industrial action in case their job went next.
- Employers became tougher. In a number of key strikes, such as the miners' strike in 1984-85, the employers won the dispute. This discouraged trade unions from taking industrial action.

Union recognition

In the late 1990s, the management of Kennaby discussed two proposals. One manager wanted to **de-recognise** unions altogether. Many employers have done this since 1979. Workers can still join a trade union, but management won't allow a trade union to represent any worker in negotiations (i.e. it no longer **recognises** a union for bargaining purposes).

The advantage from a management viewpoint is that it weakens the power of workers to gain better pay or working conditions. However, the personnel manager pointed out that he would then have to communicate and negotiate with every individual worker which would be time consuming. He preferred to deal

Threat of strike action

Firefighters in Greater Manchester were being balloted on strike action following plans to reduce the staffing establishment by 24 full-time and 12 part-time posts, which would involve seven redundancies. The fire authority also plans to reduce the number of fire engines by three. The ballot result will be known on 8 September and could result in a number of stoppages.

Source: adapted from *Labour Research*, September 1997.

1 Explain what is meant by: (a) a ballot; and (b) a strike.
2 The firefighters are employed by a local authority. Suggest TWO possible reasons why it might have wanted to make firefighters redundant.
3 What other types of industrial action could the firefighters take apart from going on all out strike?
4 Discuss whether firefighters, who provide an essential emergency service, should ever go on strike.

Marshall's

Marshall's is a chain of department stores. The workers, represented mainly by USDAW (the Union of Shop, Distributive and Allied Workers) want an annual pay rise. With inflation at 3 per cent, they have put in a claim for a 5 per cent rise. The company is suffering financial difficulties. Last year it made a large loss and this year it hopes at best to break even. It says it cannot offer any pay rises this year and has hinted that it may even have to make some workers redundant. After a great deal of bargaining, the two sides have agreed to bring in ACAS and go to arbitration.

1 How would the information provided help the arbitrator make a decision?
2 What other information do you think the arbitrator would need?
3 As the arbitrator, do you think the final pay settlement you will give will be nearer the 5 per cent demanded by workers or the 0 per cent offered by management? Explain your answer.

with a few trade union representatives who could then act as management-worker go between. He also suggested that a change in the law was possible, giving trade unions a right to recognition.

Single union agreements

The other proposal discussed at Kennaby was forcing through a **single union agreement**. The management would only recognise one union. This would simplify negotiations and mean that the company wouldn't be drawn into disputes which were more disputes between unions than union-management disputes.

Single union agreements are still fairly rare in the UK. They have often been introduced alongside other industrial relations measures such as **no-strike deals**, where workers agree never to strike in return for compulsory arbitration when management and workers can't agree.

key terms

Arbitration - a method of settling a dispute which involves both parties agreeing to put their case to an independent outside arbitrator and accept his or her judgement as to how the dispute should be settled.
Conciliation - process of helping two parties to a dispute to discuss and settle their dispute.
Convenor - the senior shop steward in a place of work.
Industrial relations - the relationship between businesses and their workers.
Joint consultative committee - committee of trade union and management representatives which meets regularly to discuss issues of concern.
Shop steward - a trade union member elected by workers in a place of work to represent their interests to management.
Trade Association - an organisation which represents the interests of the businesses which are its members.
Trade union - an organisation which represents the interests of the workers who are its members.

SUMMARY CASE STUDY

A QUESTION OF RECOGNITION

Dixons is a high street electrical retailer. It also owns the Curry's chain of stores. Dixons has traditionally had a policy of not recognising unions. There is almost no collective bargaining within the company.

When it took over Curry's, it inherited two collective bargaining agreements covering engineers and clerical workers in the Curry's Mastercare service centres. These workers formed only a small part of the Curry's workforce. In the mid-1990s, Dixons decided to put some engineers into its superstores to provide quick in-store repairs for customers. However, it refused to allow these in-store engineers to be covered by collective bargaining. This was despite the fact that they did the same work as the engineers at Curry's.

After talks with the AEEU (the Amalgamated Electrical Engineering Union), Dixons agreed to hold a ballot of the 380 in-store engineers asking whether they wanted a union to represent them. The ballot, held in 1996, was conducted by ACAS. Nearly 60 per cent of the workers backed recognition for the AEEU.

Despite the ballot, Dixons has still not granted collective bargaining rights to the union on behalf of the in-store engineers. The union representative said that: 'My strong suspicion is that Dixons are talking about some sort of council with union and non-union representation'.

Source: adapted from *Labour Research*, December 1997.

1 What is meant by 'collective bargaining'?
2 Which groups of workers at Dixons and Curry's were covered by collective bargaining agreements in 1996?
3 You are an in-store engineer at Dixons who voted for trade union recognition. Suggest TWO advantages to you of being covered by a collective bargaining agreement.
4 Why do you think Dixons is reluctant to give recognition to trade unions?
5 As an in-store engineer, you have got fed up with the failure of Dixons to give collective bargaining rights to the AEEU. You want the union to call a strike to force Dixons to grant recognition. What would be: (a) the advantages; and (b) the disadvantages to in-store engineers of taking industrial action?

Checklist ✓

1 'Collective bargaining provides a channel of communication.' What does this mean?
2 What is the purpose of a trade union?
3 Describe FOUR different types of trade union.
4 Explain the difference between a trade union member, a shop steward, a convenor and a full time union official.
5 Describe THREE types of industrial action that a trade union might take.
6 What is the difference between conciliation and arbitration?
7 Why might a business want to de-recognise a trade union?
8 What are the advantages to a business of working with trade unions?
9 What are the advantages to a business of signing a single union agreement?

EMPLOYMENT AND THE LAW

Making decisions

There is a number of laws which relate to employing workers. Some affect how a business recruits workers. Others protect workers when they are employed. Businesses must have policies and procedures to make sure they stay within the law.

Navdeep Ghosal is employed by Matthew Watters, a small business offering a skip service to local businesses and individuals in Ipswich. She was appointed as an administrative assistant and does most of the clerical work in the company. This includes answering telephone calls and acting as receptionist for clients who call into the office.

The law

Businesses have to obey the law. If they fail to obey, they risk two things:

- they can be prosecuted by a number of government departments and agencies, such as the Health and Safety Inspectorate, and possibly fined;
- they can be sued by people or other businesses which have lost out as a result of their actions.

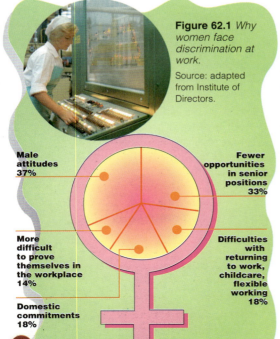

Figure 62.1 *Why women face discrimination at work.*
Source: adapted from Institute of Directors.

Male attitudes 37%

Fewer opportunities in senior positions 33%

More difficult to prove themselves in the workplace 14%

Difficulties with returning to work, childcare, flexible working 18%

Domestic commitments 18%

Damages might then have to be paid.

Getting a job

Navdeep was one of ten applicants for the job. In law, applicants for a job have certain rights. These rights try to give all applicants EQUAL OPPORTUNITIES when seeking work. In particular, employers are not allowed to DISCRIMINATE because of gender or racial origin. Matthew Watters, for instance, could not have advertised for a 'female secretary' because this would have been against the Sex Discrimination Act 1975. Equally, it could not have advertised for a 'secretary of European origin' because this would have been against the Race Relations Act 1976.

The Disability Discrimination Act 1995 says that employers with 20 or more workers are not allowed to discriminate against disabled people when recruiting or promoting. Disabled applicants must be given the job when they are clearly the best applicant.

The only exception to this is if there are 'substantial reasons' for not doing so. These reasons might include having to make hugely costly alterations to a building so that one disabled person can do a job there. Employers, however, must be prepared to make 'reasonable adjustments' for disabled staff. For instance, Navdeep suffers from arthritis which prevents her from driving. However, she is an excellent computer operator and receptionist. Asking for a driving

Discrimination

Tahir Hussain was unemployed. Despite good qualifications, he found that he was not getting job interviews when he applied for jobs. So he decided that he would test the system. For every application he made in his own name, he put in an application in the name of a fictitious white woman. He found that this white woman was more successful at getting job interviews.

Since the end of 1994, he has launched 12 claims of race discrimination at industrial tribunals. He has won four of them and five have been settled out of court in his favour. Among the employers who had discriminated were a number of car dealers.

Source: adapted from *Labour Research*, December 1997.

1 'The businesses to which Tahir Hussain applied failed to give applicants equal opportunities.' What does this mean?
2 (a) What immediate penalty did the businesses involved in discrimination suffer? (b) Suggest why else businesses which discriminate against better qualified candidates lose out in the longer term.

licence when the job requires no driving at all would be discrimination. Her arthritis also means that her typing can be a little slow and she has problems holding the phone. She suggested that her keyboard and the telephone handle be adapted to help her. This might be a reasonable adjustment.

Starting work

Navdeep signed a CONTRACT OF EMPLOYMENT with Matthew Watters before she started work. This is an agreement between the employer and employee. It includes conditions such as rates of pay, hours of work, holidays, pension contributions and the amount of notice that must be given if the worker wants to leave or the employer wants to make the worker redundant, for example. Employees taken on for a month or more must be given a written statement of the conditions within two months of the date the job starts.

Under the Equal Pay Act 1970, Navdeep must be paid the same rate of pay as a male doing the same job, a similar job or a job with equal demands. Navdeep was the only administrative assistant working at Matthew Watters. This meant there was nobody who was directly comparable to her. However, Matthew Watters could be acting illegally if it could be shown that other jobs at the business which were equally demanding in terms of effort, skills, tasks or responsibility were better paid.

Protection at work

Matthew Watters, like any business, needs to conform to the Health and Safety at Work Act 1974. This lays down standards of **health and safety** that must be met. The premises are regularly visited by inspectors from the Health and Safety Executive, the body responsible for checking that the 1974 act is being followed. The

POSITIVE *ACTION*

Equality Pays

EMPLOYMENT LEGISLATION

UNFAIRLY DISMISSED?

business must also conform to a number of EU regulations introduced in 1992. For instance, drivers at Matthew Watters take skips to and from sites. They have to be able to operate the lifting equipment on their lorries safely, without endangering themselves or the people on the site. Matthew Watters must also ensure the health and safety of Navdeep. This could include providing a suitable chair and giving her regular breaks.

Matthew Watters must also be aware of **equal opportunities**. If Navdeep applied for a more senior post in the company, the law says that she must have the same chance as any other employee. It would be illegal for Matthew Watters to discriminate against her because she was a woman, disabled or from an ethnic minority.

Some of the drivers belong to a **trade union** (☞ unit 61). Navdeep is not in a union. The law says that any worker has a right to join or not to join a trade union. A business doesn't have to **recognise** or negotiate with a trade union. It can choose to deal with workers individually rather than trade union

---

John Whitley has just been appointed at Nelson-James Ltd, an aluminium recycling company. He has been sent a written statement showing conditions of his contract of employment to sign.

1 Give THREE conditions of employment mentioned in the contract.

2 What would happen if John Whitley wanted to leave the company, according to the contract?

3 After six months at work, John Whitley was reprimanded by his line manager on safety grounds for carrying out a minor repair on a machine. John disagreed. Where might John have found out whether he was allowed to carry out the repair?

Statement of main terms and conditions of employment

Nelson-James
Unit 57
Calleva Park
Industrial Estate
Reading

Mr J Whitley
3 Fairfield Drive
Aldermaston
Reading

Dear Mr Whitley

I have pleasure in confirming your appointment as a machine operator with effect from 15 May 1998.

Pay and hours of work Your wages will be at the rate of £5.20 per hour. Your basic pay per week will be £192.40. Overtime will be paid at time and quarter up to six o'clock in the evening Monday to Friday and time and a half at other times. Your hours of work will be 37 hours. The company reserves the right to choose when you work those hours between 8 a.m. and 6 p.m. Monday to Friday.

Annual Leave Your annual leave entitlement is 20 working days plus statutory bank holidays.

Notice Your appointment is terminable by 4 weeks notice on either side.

Continuous employment For the purpose of the Employment Protection (Consolidation) Act, the start of your period of continuous service is 15 May 1998.

Disciplinary As an employee of Nelson-James, you are protected by its Disciplinary Policy, a copy of which may be obtained from the Personnel Department.

Health and Safety at Work Your attention is drawn to the Company's 'Statement of General Policy', a copy of which may be obtained from the Personnel Department.

Yours sincerely

Mr M Murphy
Personnel Manager

Form of Acceptance

I hereby accept the appointment mentioned in the foregoing Contract on the terms and conditions referred to in it and return one copy signed.

Date .... Signature ....

representatives. However, it can't prevent workers taking **industrial action**, such as striking.

Leaving work

The law affects workers when they leave their job.

Finding a new job Workers who have found new jobs have to resign from their posts. They then have to 'work out their notice'. Their contract of employment will state how much notice a worker needs to give his or her employers when leaving. In Navdeep's case, her contract says that she must give a month's notice before leaving.

Retirement Most workers pay into a pension scheme so that they can receive a pension when they retire. The law doesn't force a business to have its own scheme, but Matthew Watters does have one. Both Navdeep and Matthew Watters pay regular amounts into a scheme with the Standard Life Insurance Company.

Redundancy
During the recession (☞ unit 6) of 1990-92, the construction industry suffered badly. Orders for the hire of skips fell sharply. Matthew Watters made nearly half its workforce redundant because there wasn't enough work for them to do. In law, a business can make workers redundant if their job 'no longer exists'. Nearly all the workers made redundant became entitled to redundancy payments. If the company makes any workers redundant in future they will be entitled to redundancy payments if they had worked for the business continuously for more than 2 years.

Dismissal In law, workers can be dismissed (i.e. sacked) if they are either unable to do the job or there is misconduct involved. In 1998, a new worker at Matthew Watters was

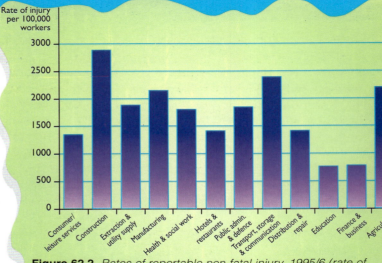

Figure 62.2 *Rates of reportable non-fatal injury, 1995/6 (rate of injury expressed per 100,000 employees).*
Source: adapted from Health and Safety Executive.

Deaths in farming

On average, someone working in farming dies every six days from an accident. In 1996/7, 63 people died including eight children. The cost to an individual family or farming business of a fatal accident averages £500 000. The total cost to the industry is more than £30 million per year.

The Health and Safety Executive is responsible for inspecting farms. Mike Walters, an agricultural inspector, was inspecting farms in the Sussex area in October 1997. On one farm, he found a hay turning machine which had no protective cover on the revolving shaft that attached it the tractor. Shafts rotate at up to 1 000 revolutions a minute. A few years ago, he had been involved in a case where a young farmhand was killed when his coat caught in a partly exposed revolving shaft and he was sucked into the blades. On this occasion, he put a prohibition order on the hay machine, stopping it from being used until the farmer replaced the guard.

On the same day, Mike Walters visits another farm and puts three prohibition orders on insufficiently protected machines. He also orders the farmer to move a stack of hay bales further away from power lines in case the telescopic arm of a lifting machine hits them, electrocuting the operator.

The next farm he visits has dangerous chemicals in a pesticide store which have long been banned. He writes out an enforcement notice giving the farmer four months to remove them via a waste disposal contractor.

Source: adapted from the *Financial Times*, 27 October 1997.

1 Why do you think that workers need to be protected by health and safety legislation on farms?

2 What are the costs to farmers of accidents to their workers?

3 You are a farmer who has been forced to pay £1 500 in repairs to comply with health and safety legislation. Write a letter to your local newspaper explaining how: (a) prices of food in the shops would be cheaper if there wasn't so much legislation that farmers had to comply with; (b) health and safety legislation is unfair to British farmers because food is being imported from many Third World countries like Argentina.

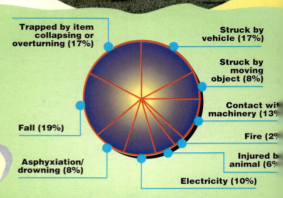

Trapped by item collapsing or overturning (17%)
Struck by vehicle (17%)
Struck by moving object (8%)
Contact with machinery (13%)
Fire (2%)
Injured by animal (6%)
Electricity (10%)
Asphyxiation/drowning (8%)
Fall (19%)

Figure 62.3 *Deaths in farming: fatal injuries in farming, forestry and horticulture, 1996/7*
Source: adapted from Health and Safety Executive.

found to be regularly taking lunch breaks far in excess of what he was entitled to. The business issued a formal verbal warning to the worker. He carried on exceeding his lunch break time and so Matthew Watters issued a written warning. With still no improvement in the situation, Matthew Watters finally sacked him.

In a more serious case, a worker can be sacked immediately in cases of gross misconduct, such as failure to observe safety regulations, theft or fighting. A driver a few years ago at Matthew Watters was sacked after being involved in a minor accident with his lorry. The police breathalised the driver and he had been found to be over the limit.

If Matthew Watters had not gone though the correct procedures of verbal and written warnings, the worker taking too long over lunch breaks could have taken the company to an INDUSTRIAL TRIBUNAL on grounds of unfair dismissal. An industrial tribunal is a court of law which deals with issues such as **unfair dismissal**, discrimination at work and sexual harassment. Unlike in most courts, lawyers don't have to be used. People can argue their own case in front of the tribunal. The tribunal is also informal, with members listening to presentations and asking questions to find out the truth about what happened. The idea is that the law is then accessible to every worker. The tribunal has the power to fine a business if it is breaking the law and can pay damages to workers.

Source: adapted from DTI, *Employment Legislation* (various); DFEE, *The Disability Discrimination Act 1995 - What Employers Need To Know, Equality Pays*; HSE, *Guidance on Regulations* (various); Equal Opportunities Commission, *Code of Practice On Equal Pay*.

Job-sharing

Janet Schofield took maternity leave from her full time job with the Zurich insurance company. When she returned to work, she applied to share a job with another manager. The two would do the job normally done by one person. Zurich had a job-sharing scheme for workers at non-managerial levels. However, they refused Janet Schofield's request stating that it was not possible to do a manager's job under a job-share.

Janet wrote to the company saying that she had been constructively dismissed and claimed sex discrimination. The Equal Opportunities Commission, responsible for promoting equal opportunities in the UK, gave legal support to Janet Schofield. The outcome was that Zurich agreed to settle out of court. It paid Janet Schofield £20 000 in compensation and agreed to review its job-share policy in relation to managers.

Source: adapted from *Labour Research*, October 1997.

CODE OF PRACTICE ON EQUAL PAY

1 What is a 'job-share'?
2 Suggest why it might be more difficult for two workers to job-share compared to one person doing the job.
3 Do you think that Zurich was right to refuse Janet a job-share? Give reasons both for and against.
4 Industrial tribunals can force a business to give compensation to a worker but they can't force it to give workers back their job if they have been sacked. Do you think workers should be able to get their old jobs back if they have been unfairly dismissed? Give reasons both for and against.

Key terms

Contract of employment - an agreement between the employer and employee, about the conditions under which the employee will work, including rates of pay and holiday entitlements.

Discrimination - favouring one person rather than another. In the UK, it is illegal to discriminate in most jobs on grounds of gender or race.

Equal opportunities - where everyone has the same chance.

Industrial tribunal - court which deals with the law relating to employment.

CATERING STAFF

SUMMARY CASE STUDY

Hundreds of dinner ladies are claiming sex discrimination in a pay battle with Walsall Council. Nearly 130 council catering staff in Walsall have already lodged industrial tribunal claims for equal pay. Unison branch secretary Paul Macmanomy said the town's 500 dinner ladies, who get £4 an hour, want parity with the £5.30 an hour paid to workers like roadsweepers. He also said that catering services was the only direct services organisation which did not have a bonus system. Walsall education committee on Tuesday will be told that the council could have to fork out up to £3 million if the industrial tribunal claims succeed.

Mr Macmanomy said: 'We are adamant that we won't be reaching any agreement which puts our members on the dole. There is no point succeeding in getting extra money for our members if the consequences are that they are out of a job'. He said that they hoped to reach a settlement by negotiation, before the cases got to an industrial tribunal.

Source: adapted from *Express & Star*, 4 October 1997.

1 Explain why dinner ladies in Walsall might be able to claim higher pay in law from their employers.
2 Their trade union branch secretary, Paul Macmanomy, was worried that the pay rise might cause redundancies. Explain why Walsall Council might sack some dinner ladies if their wages went up to £5.30 an hour.

Checklist ✓

1 'Businesses are not allowed to discriminate on grounds of gender or race.' Explain what this means.
2 What help does the law give to disabled people wanting to work?
3 What information does a contract of employment contain?
4 A man and a woman are paid different rates of pay for doing exactly the same job in a company. Is this legal? Explain your answer.
5 What help does the law give to workers on health and safety issues?
6 What does the law say about trade unions in a workplace?
7 On what grounds can a business dismiss a worker?
8 Describe the work of an industrial tribunal.

STARTING UP A BUSINESS

Making decisions

Starting up a business is difficult and risky. Anyone setting up needs to consider:

- whether they have the right experience and skills to make the business a success;
- how they are going to produce and market their product or service;
- where they are going to get finance for the business;
- how they can get help and advice that is available to them from outside the business;
- what will happen if the business is not a success.

Tree House Collection.

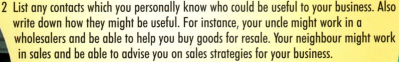

Ben-Go-Tig is a private limited company which designs and sells girlswear aged from 0-13 years. It was started up by Kiren Darashah in 1993. Initially, she sold her clothes through organised parties in people's homes. Today, she sells through retailers and in 1997 won her first export order to Spain.

Identifying the opportunity

John is a plumber working for a building company. He decides to set up his own business. Gemma works as a manager in a plastics factory. She decides to set up her own business making chairs from recycled plastic. Tom is 16 and has just left school. He wants to set up his own business but doesn't know what he could do. John and Gemma both have a lot of experience working for others. They know a lot already about their business. Tom has no experience. He is going to find it very difficult to make a success of any business he sets up. This is the reason why most people who set up their own business have already had experience of working in that industry.

Kiren Darashah is no exception. She gained a BA Honours in fashion and went on to get an MA in fashion knitwear. While a student, she worked with designers like Vivienne

Westwood. She also worked with a children's wear company. It was this experience which enabled her to set up her own business designing children's clothes.

Identifying a business opportunity is the first thing a person

Identifying the opportunity

 You need to find a business opportunity for your mini-company.

1 Start off by listing any experiences you may have had which could be useful in a business. For instance, have you had or do you have a part-time job? Have you any hobbies which could be turned into a business idea? Have you helped do to anything at home, like sewing or gardening which could be seen as a job? Have you helped anyone with their job or business? Have you done anything at school or college which could be turned into something which could be sold, like helping in the school tuck shop or making a product in a Technology lesson?

2 List any contacts which you personally know who could be useful to your business. Also write down how they might be useful. For instance, your uncle might work in a wholesalers and be able to help you buy goods for resale. Your neighbour might work in sales and be able to advise you on sales strategies for your business.

3 List any resources which you would easily be able to use for your business. For instance, if you need transport, could you get hold of a car and a driver? If you need a room to store materials, could you arrange that?

4 Pool your answers to questions 1-3 amongst all the members of your mini-enterprise. Are there any similarities? Does one person have a skill or talent which the rest of the members could support? Do the results show that you want to make/manufacture a good rather than sell a service?

5 Most mini-enterprises find it very difficult to come up with a business idea. Why does lack of experience partly explain why this is so?

SuperSkyTrips

SuperSkyTrips is a company which provides tethered balloon rides in the world's largest helium filled balloon. The founder of the company, Robert Ollier, was a ballooning enthusiast long before he set up his business. Having worked for himself in the construction business, he spent 10 years piloting hot-air balloons across Europe, carrying sponsored advertisements for companies such as British Airways and American Airlines.

He then began investigating setting up a tethered passenger balloon ride. The helium balloon is fixed to a hydraulic winch which is powered by electric motors hidden underground. The winch controls how quickly the balloon goes up and then brings the balloon down again. Passengers pay to have a 15 minute ride up and down.

Robert Ollier had to do a lot of research into the project. He had to make sure that the design of the balloon and its fittings conformed to standards laid down by the Health and Safety Executive (HSE). Seams of the balloon, for instance, have been welded rather than sewn together to give added strength. The passenger platform beneath the balloon is made of aircraft standard stainless steel. The balloon had to be tested rigorously before receiving a fairground ride certificate from the HSE.

He also had to find somewhere to locate the balloon. Many cities with a strong tourist base turned him down. In the end, he set up his first balloon at Milton Keynes. This was then moved to Spring Gardens, Vauxhall, London, next to the Thames. It is only 1 000 meters from The Houses of Parliament, giving spectacular views of London.

Source: adapted from information provided by SkySuperTrips. (www.londonballoon.co.uk)

1 What were the experience and skills of Robert Ollier which helped him start his SuperSkyTrips business?
2 What did he have to find out before he could start the business?
3 Suggest TWO ways in which the company could attract customers to use SuperSkyTrips. Explain why you think that these would be successful in drawing in customers.

SuperSkyTrips™ presents

THE LONDON BALLOON
The World's Largest Tethered Balloon Ride

AT
**SPRING GARDENS
VAUXHALL BRIDGE
LONDON SE11 5HF**

Only 100 metres from Vauxhall Tube Station opposite The Tate Gallery

LONDON

FANTASTIC VIEWS of **LONDON**

Darashah started her business by making up a range of designs for boys and girls. She then went round shops, schools and playgroups giving parents questionnaires and finding out whether there was a market for the clothes she had designed.

Researching the product

Some people who set up their own business know exactly what they are going to sell and how they are going to sell it. Most people, though, have to research their product. Kiren Darashah, had to decide on which fabrics to use for her range. In 1995, with the help of a business adviser, she changed her suppliers - the companies from which she bought fabric - to improve quality and prices. Businesses also have to decide how the product is to be made. Kiren Darashah made all the clothes herself to start with. But in 1994 she decided to take on two machinists to cope with the expanding business.

Finance

No business can be set up without finance. Kiren Darashah started her business with a £250 grant from the Prince's Youth Business Trust. This is a Trust which helps young people to set up their own business. The grant paid for the initial market research. The Trust was impressed enough with the market research to then give her a loan of £2 500. This paid for her to make up the initial stock to sell.

Kiren Darashah has been very careful with finance. Most people who start their own business underestimate the amount of money they will need to set up. They are often UNDERCAPITALISED and this

---

wanting to set up their own business must do. The business opportunity is most likely to come from what they are already doing in work and the contacts they have. They then have to find out whether the idea will work.

Researching the market

Businesses only survive if they can attract customers and at least make enough money to cover their costs. So it is important to find out

whether there are likely to be enough customers. There are two main ways of **researching the market** (☞ unit 36).

- **Desk research** involves finding existing information about the market. For instance, a person wanting to set up a hairdressing salon might look in Yellow Pages to find out the location of all the salons in a local area in order to assess the likely competition.
- **Field research** involves finding information which is not available in books etc. Kiren

causes problems as the business expands. Some businesses have the potential to be highly profitable but fail because they run out of cash at a crucial early stage in the life of the business (☞ unit 28). So it very important to work out how much money is needed to start the business and identify where the money will come from.

Kiren Darashah has financed her **expansion** by putting back the profits made into the business. In 1994, she won £2 500 by getting to the finals of the national Shell LiveWIRE Young Entrepreneur competition. In 1997 she took out a **bank loan** (☞ unit 31) of £5 000 and another £5 000 loan from the Prince's Trust to expand the business further.

Identifying sources of help

Most new businesses don't survive for more than three years of trading. However, their chance of success is much greater if those setting up the business have received help from experts before the launch.

Kiren Darashah received help from the Prince's Youth Business Trust to set up the business. Two years later, with the business expanding, the Trust put her in contact with a business adviser, Dianne Smith. She was a 'whiz in the rag trade', who had the experience Kiren Darashah was lacking.

Many new small businesses turn to **Business Link** or to their local **TEC** (☞unit 52). They can identify any grants, loans or benefits that are available from government or from bodies such as the Prince's Trust. They can also organise training in setting up small businesses that is so often vital to the survival of the business.

The business plan

Drawing up a **business plan** (☞ unit 22) is very important. The

business plan sets out how the business is to be set up and run. It contains projections of future sales, revenues and costs. It will include how the product is to be made or bought and how it is to be marketed.

Drawing up the business plan makes sure that all aspects of the new business have been researched and considered. It helps people to be more realistic about the problems they are likely to face when the business starts trading. What is more, any applications for loans or grants will usually need to be supported by a business plan. So a business plan is crucial for financing the business.

Operating the business

Ben-Go-Tig started small. In her first year, Kiren Darashah made all the 500 dresses she sold at clothes parties. In the second year, she expanded, taking on the two machinists and an agent to help organise party sales.

Then came her lucky break when she was a finalist in the national LiveWIRE Young Entrepreneur Competition. She won £2 500 and

three free invitations to show her designs at the biannual Premier Collections trade exhibition at the NEC (National Exhibition Centre) in Birmingham. This allowed her to start selling to the retail trade (i.e. to shops).

All the time, she was having to think about designing new ranges, making the clothes, financing the business and marketing her ranges.

The environment in which businesses work is constantly changing. Businesses like Ben-Go-Tig Ltd need to adapt by changing themselves. For Kiren Darashah, for instance, this has meant stopping sales through the party plan system and concentrating on sales to retailers. It has meant changing from being a sole proprietor to becoming a limited company. It has meant coping with disappointments, like the loss of a £10 000 order in August 1996. Unless businesses change, they die. If, like Ben-Go-Tig, they are constantly adapting to changing conditions, then they are likely to survive and prosper.

Source: adapted from the *Financial Times*, 13 July 1996 and information provided by Ben-Go-Tig.

Micro-brewing

Toby Mynott, a marketing whiz-kid, picked up a business idea when on a business trip to Toronto. He visited a do-it-yourself micro-brewery. Canadians could come in, receive advice and brew their own brand of beer.

He decided to set up a similar operation in Canterbury. In February 1996, having put £55 000 of his own money into the business, the Great Stour Brewery was opened. The initial response was excellent with thousands of inquiries in the first few weeks. But few of these turned into customers. Within three months, he decided to wind down the business and within twelve months the business closed.

Looking back on the experience, Toby identified a number of key problems. The overheads of the business, such as rent and rates, were too high. Arguably, beer drinkers in Kent are less committed to drinking and cost saving than beer drinkers in the North of England. What's more, Canterbury was too near Calais, the source of cheap beer.

Source: adapted from *The Times*, 18 November 1997.

1 What was Toby Mynott's business idea?
2 What skills did he have to open the business?
3 Toby Mynott decided very quickly to close the business. Why do you think he saw little chance of the business surviving?
4 Discuss whether he would have been more successful if he had opened in Manchester instead of Canterbury.

Mike Dixon Cycles

In the 1970s, Mike Dixon was a teacher in Liverpool. In his spare time he was a cyclist, often taking part in races in foreign countries such as Belgium. He and a friend noticed that cycle clothing and parts were cheaper in Belgium. Friends would often ask him to bring back cycle accessories from his trips.

Mike thought that there was a possible business opportunity here. Using £1 000 of his own money he imported a small amount of cycle clothing and parts from Belgium. Driving to Essex to pick them up from the ferry, he returned to Liverpool and began selling the accessories to local contacts in cycle clubs. He also advertised in cycle magazines, setting up a mail order business.

From 1980 to 1989 Mike continued to sell imported cycle accessories. The business grew, financed by sales of clothing and parts, and also from Mike's salary as a teacher. An overdraft facility was available, but only used in emergencies. By 1989 Mike's business was doing so well that he was able to leave his teaching job. The business was so well established that it was now able to get accessories on 30 days credit from suppliers.

Cycle shops had also seen his advertisements in magazines. They wanted parts and clothing at the competitive prices at which Mike was selling. He had so many requests that he started to buy in bulk and operate as a wholesaler to cycle shops and run down the mail order side of the business. By 1998 Mike Dixon cycles employed 4 staff, including his son Martin, and had an annual turnover of over £1 million.

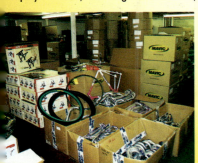

Source: adapted from information provided by Mike Dixon.

1 What service does Mike Dixon offer to customers?
2 What type of research did Mike carry out before starting the business?
3 Suggest THREE ways in which Mike financed the business.
4 Suggest TWO possible problems that the business faced as it grew.
5 Do you think that Mike was right to change how the business operated? Explain your answer.

Checklist ✓

1 'Businesses are most likely to succeed when they are started by people who have experience and training in the business area already.' Why is this true?
2 How can someone research a market?
3 Suggest and explain TWO ways in which someone wanting to set up a health and fitness club might research the market?
4 How might a new business research the product it is going to sell?
5 Give TWO ways in which a business might find the money to set itself up in business.
6 What help is available to businesses setting up?
7 (a) What is a business plan? (b) How does a business plan help a business setting up?

Key terms

Undercapitalised - lacking the necessary financial resources to allow a business to trade without getting into constant financial difficulties.

SUMMARY CASE STUDY

PHONING HOME

Juanne Driscoll had been a salesperson for 10 years in London. She had worked for a number of magazines, often selling advertising space to large companies. She was a keen coin collector and would often visit coin fairs, particularly in her home town of Dublin. In 1994 she visited a coin fare in Dublin. There she saw a stand selling phone cards with pictures on which seemed to interest a number of collectors. The value of the card was not the number of units of telephone calls that it could pay for, but what a collector would be interested enough to pay.

Juanne thought that she could use her experience to produce phone cards and sell them at fairs in the UK and The Irish Republic. She would get a sponsor to put up money for the card. There might be a card for a special event such as The Republic of Ireland's football matches in the World Cup, a company's product or a tourist board's services. Her advertising skills and contacts would help her to find sponsors who would see the cards as advertising. She would then manufacture a limited number using her print contacts, to sell at a fairly high price. She would also buy cards new from telephone companies and dealers and sell them at a higher price. Cards could also be bought from foreign telephone companies and sold in the UK and The Irish Republic.

Over the next few years sales of telephone cards boomed, with people often buying cards with themes, such as trains or cars. Juanne sold her cards at coin fairs and by advertising in coin magazines. The second hand value of rare cards soared.

By 1996, however, the market had become flooded. Juanne would often find many stalls at coin fairs undercutting her prices. By the end of the year the business had ceased to operate.

1 What was Juanne's business idea?
2 What experience did she have which she could use in her telephone card business?
3 (a) Why did the business fail? (b) Suggest TWO ways in which she might have changed her business to make it more successful.

unit 64

BUSINESS AND CHANGE

Making decisions

Businesses face constant pressures both internally and externally. To survive and prosper, they have to adapt to changing conditions. They have to decide how to change their business strategy in order to cope with changes such as new laws, new technology, increased competition or different foreign exchange rates.

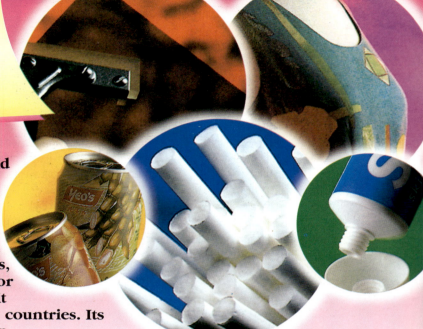

I n 1998 Courtaulds was an international chemicals group. It supplied coatings and sealants, polymer products (packaging and films), and chemicals and fibres to a wide range of markets from shipbuilding, aerospace, automotive and construction to pharmaceuticals, electronics, food and textiles. It was a major employer worldwide. In 1997 it employed 17 000 workers in 45 countries. Its 1997 sales turnover was £2 billion.

Internal pressures

In 1998 Courtaulds, like many businesses, faced **internal pressures**. An internal pressure is one which comes from within the business. For instance, Courtaulds is likely to have faced demands for pay rises from its workers. Directors of Courtaulds had to make decisions about which investment projects it should 'back' with the funds it had available. Managers at the company's Grimsby plant which makes Tencel, a synthetic fibre, had to find ways of cutting costs so that efficiency could be improved.

External pressures

External pressures, though, were perhaps more important for Courtaulds in 1998 than internal pressures.

Competition Courtaulds is a major manufacturer of acrylic and viscose, two synthetic fibres used in clothing. These two fibres make up nearly one quarter of the total sales of the company. But there are many other manufacturers of acrylic and viscose round the world. Manufacturers in the past have overinvested in plant to make these fibres. The result was oversupply. The prices of acrylic and viscose were so low in 1998 that Courtaulds made no profit on their sales. Companies can't keep on making products which generate no profit. So there was intense pressure for change.

New technology Courtaulds is an innovative company. For instance, it is the market leader internationally in marine paint. It also has a strong business in industrial coatings, especially for the aerospace industry. It is constantly improving products in this coatings and sealants parts of its business. In its fibres business, Courtaulds took the decision to back a new 'wonder' fibre called Tencel. It is exceptionally strong but very soft. By 1998, Tencel had cost Courtaulds £350 million in research and development, new plant and marketing. Yet, 1997 was the first year in which it earned a profit on its investment in Tencel, and that was only a profit of £10 million. How could Courtaulds change to make Tencel more successful?

Booms and slumps In 1997 and 1998 Courtaulds was benefiting from increased economic growth in Europe and North America. It had

Whirlpool

Whirlpool is one of the world's two largest manufacturers of white goods - cookers, washing machines, refrigerators, etc. It is constantly facing pressures to cut costs in order to stay competitive and earn profit for its shareholders. In the late 1990s, it began to design and build 'world' platforms for its models. In the past, a washing machine built for the UK market would have few common parts to one built for the US market. The new strategy was to cut costs by building models using as many common parts as possible. For a refrigerator, this would include the casing, the compressor, the evaporator and the sealant system for instance.

Source: adapted from the *Financial Times*, 24 March 1998.

1 What internal pressures for change did Whirlpool face?
2 'Building common platforms will cut costs through greater economies of scale.' Explain, using examples, what this means.

also hoped to increase significantly its sales to the Far East. It had set itself a target of 10 per cent growth in sales. But at the end of 1997 many Far East countries entered a crisis period. Their economic growth slumped. So too did the hopes of Courtaulds that it would see large increases in sales to the region. How would it respond to this?

Exchange rates The crisis in the Far East didn't just lead to a fall in the economic growth rates of countries in the region. Many countries also saw a very large fall in the value of their currencies. This meant that imports became very much more expensive to them. It also meant that their exports became much cheaper to buyers in countries like the UK or Germany. This affected Courtaulds. It became much more difficult to sell to countries like South Korea because prices were higher. It also meant that Far East manufacturers of products like viscose could offer lower prices to European and North American buyers, putting Courtaulds at a competitive disadvantage.

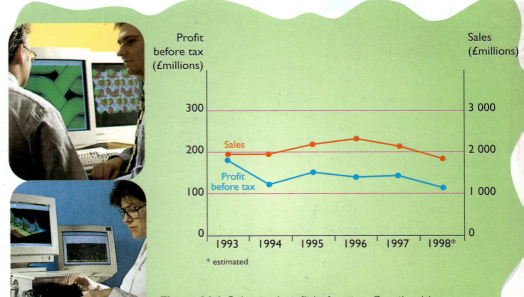

Figure 64.1 graph:

Figure 64.1 *Sales and profit before tax: Courthaulds.*
Source: adapted from Courtaulds, *Annual Report and Accounts*, 1996-7; Datastream/ICV.

Stakeholders

Courtaulds, like any large company, has a number of **stakeholders** - groups who have an interest in the business. There are the managers, under pressure to increase sales and cut costs. Workers want to see their working conditions improved. They might be worried that the difficulties in their company could put their job at risk. Governments of the countries where Courtaulds has plants will want the company to grow, creating prosperity for its citizens and contributing taxes. Governments, along with environmental groups, will also monitor pollution levels. Many of the technologies used by Courtaulds are potentially environmentally dangerous if there was an accident. So Courtaulds has to make pollution control a high priority. Customers want high quality products at competitive prices. Suppliers are reliant on Courtaulds for orders.

The owners of the company, the shareholders, are also very

Steel vs aluminium

The world's steel and aluminium producers are locked in a battle which will decide billions of pounds of business per year for the foreseeable future. At the moment, the bodies of the 40 million cars manufactured worldwide each year are made out of steel. However, aluminium has a number of important advantages over steel. It is one third lighter. With demands from governments, environmental groups and motorists for better fuel consumption, this gives aluminium a distinct advantage. It also doesn't corrode like steel. What's more, aluminium bodies don't need as much expensive machinery to manufacture as steel bodies. Volkswagen is already producing its Audi A8 in aluminium and has said that it can't see why it won't move to aluminium for mass produced cars like the Golf in the future.

The steel industry is afraid that other major car manufacturers will follow Volkswagen's lead. So, the major steel producers have clubbed together to finance research into producing lighter steel car bodies. In 1998, they were displaying a steel car body which was 25 per cent lighter than traditional car bodies. Made out of a mix of high tensile steels, the car body would cost no more to produce than a traditional body.

Source: adapted from the *Financial Times*, 5 March 1998.

1 Why could steel companies lose the sales they make to car manufacturers in the future?
2 How have steel producers responded to this threat?
3 Car manufacturers are reluctant to change to aluminium because they have traditionally worked with steel and they have made large investments in steel related machinery. Suggest TWO ways in which aluminium producers could make it more attractive for them to change to using aluminium.

important. The directors of Courtaulds are answerable to the shareholders to protect their interests. The company's recent record had been poor. Figure 64.1 shows that growth of sales between 1993 and 1998 had been weak whilst pre-tax profits had fallen. This meant that profit margins - profits on each £1 of sales - had fallen too. Not surprisingly, the price of shares in the business had fallen. So there was pressure on the directors to come up with a strategy which would improve the returns to shareholders.

Restructuring the company

The directors of Courtaulds could have adopted a number of strategies to deal with these problems. They could have hoped that the setbacks were temporary and that the company would **grow** in the future. They could have cut costs by **rationalising** the business. This means closing down or selling off parts of the company. They could have **diversified**, buying other businesses or investing in new products as they did with Tencel. However, it was not clear that increasing sales or cutting costs would be possible.

Instead, in February 1998, the directors of Courtaulds announced that the company would be split up into three parts, based on the existing product divisions of the company. Courtaulds would continue as a fibres and chemicals company. Coatings and sealants, which include the successful paints business, would be set up as a separate company. The polymer products part of the business would be sold off to the highest bidder. Shareholders would benefit from this sale. They would also hold shares in two companies rather than one. The directors hoped that stock market investors would value the two companies at a higher price than

the existing Courtaulds.

Then, in April 1998, Akzo Nobel, a Dutch chemicals group, announced that it was interested in **taking over** Courtaulds. It is a major manufacturer of paints and wanted to buy the profitable paints business of Courtaulds. Akzo Nobel also had a fibre business. It would **merge** this with the unprofitable fibre business of Courtaulds and then hope to sell the combined business. The fact that the UK and the Netherlands are part of the European Union makes this sort of takeover increasingly common. Large businesses need to span a number of countries to remain

competitive.

The shareholders of Courtaulds would gain from this. Akzo Nobel was willing to pay twice the price that Courtaulds shares were selling at in December 1997 before the changes were announced. The different parts of Courtaulds' business would probably be more competitive as part of a larger group. However, almost certainly some plants would be closed and some workers would lose their jobs. Change would have costs as well as benefits.

Source: adapted from the *Financial Times*, 25 February 1998, 26 February 1998, 3 April 1998, 7 April 1998; Courtaulds, *Annual Report and Accounts*, 1996-7; *The Times*, 3 April 1998.

The UK record industry

1997 was a very successful year for the UK record industry. British acts like The Verve, Radiohead, Oasis, Texas, The Spice Girls and Prodigy had high sales both in the UK and the USA. However, the industry is under pressure.

The high value of the pound poses one problem. Record companies fix the price of CDs in a country according to what other competitors are charging. When exchange rates change, the local currency price of a CD is kept the same. In 1997, the value of the pound increased by 20-30 per cent against currencies like the German deutschmark. It then became highly profitable to buy CDs in, say, Germany and sell them in the UK at prices below the official CD price set in the UK. The music industry estimates that these 'parallel imports' account for about 1 in 5 copies of popular CDs sold in the UK. The UK record companies lose out because they would have got more money selling a CD officially in the UK than selling it in Germany at a lower price and seeing it imported back to the UK. The artists lose out too because their royalty is based on the price received by the record company.

Another problem facing small independent companies in the industry is a lack of capital. The cost of signing and promoting acts is rising. Independents are under even greater pressure to sell out to the major record companies. For instance, in 1998, Skint and Loaded, two dance labels, sold a substantial shareholding to Sony.

Source: adapted from the *Financial Times*, 9 February 1998.

1 Who are the stakeholders in a record company?
2 Explain which stakeholders: (a) gain; and (b) lose because of parallel imports.
3 Dan Cox owns an independent record label. What would be the advantages to him of selling part of this company to a large multinational record company?

The pressures of recycling

More and more material is being recycled. Pressure to do this is coming from environmental groups like Greenpeace. The government too is convinced that this is the right course of action. It is encouraging companies to recycle materials in a number of ways. One is the tax on material dumped into landfill sites.

The construction industry has traditionally been a major source of waste. Even with the landfill tax, only about half of construction waste is recycled, the rest being dumped. Companies which specialise in waste disposal for the construction industry win either way. For instance, Pinden Plant and Processing, a small company with a £4 million turnover in Kent, both recycles materials and dumps into the ground what is not profitable to recycle.

Environmental law, though, is becoming more demanding. Small companies like Pinden Plant and Processing are finding it difficult to raise the money to comply with ever tougher legislation. For that reason, many are selling out to larger companies. Pinden Plant and Processing itself was sold to Hanson plc, a large multinational construction materials business, in February 1998.

Source: adapted from the *Financial Times*, 5 March 1998.

1 What external pressures are being put on construction companies to recycle more waste?
2 Why do these pressures provide a business opportunity for companies in the waste disposal business?
3 A small waste disposal business has calculated that it would need to invest £500 000 over the next two years to comply with new legal requirements and stay competitive with other companies. It only has £200 000 in retained profit to finance this internally. To borrow £300 000 - £400 000 would push borrowing levels to dangerously high levels. (a) Explain why it might be tempted to sell out to a larger company. (b) What might be the benefits to the two owners of the company to sell just part of the company?

Paper recycling.

SUMMARY CASE STUDY

THE ABOLITION OF DUTY FREE

In 1999, duty free sales for those travelling between countries of the European Union will be abolished. A report published in 1998 forecast that:

- 19 000 jobs in the UK travel, tourism and drinks industry would disappear;
- 5 000 of those jobs would disappear in Kent around the Channel ports, whilst the Scottish whisky industry would see 1 000 job losses;
- the cost of travelling to the continent from the UK would rise by an average £14 per traveller;
- investment at sea and airports would fall.

Source: adapted from the *Financial Times*, 27 February 1998.

Ferry companies offer sea transport services for passengers between Dover and Calais. In the past, they have set the prices of tickets below the full cost of travelling. They covered the rest of the cost and made their profit from sales of duty free goods on board ship.

1 Explain FIVE ways in which you think ferry companies might be affected by the abolition of duty free goods.
2 (a) How should ferry companies change in order to survive in business? (b) How might these changes affect other businesses, like Scottish Distillers or Dover Port?

Index

Page references which appear in colour are defined in the Key Terms sections in each unit.
Page references to subjects in the case study sections appear in italics.